British Social Attitudes

Attitudes The 21st REPORT

The **National Centre for Social Research** (NatCen) is an independent, non-profit social research organisation. It has a large professional staff together with its own interviewing and coding resources. Some of NatCen's work – such as the survey reported in this book – is initiated by NatCen itself and grant-funded by research councils or charitable foundations. Other work is initiated by government departments or quasi-government organisations to provide information on aspects of social or economic policy. NatCen also works frequently with other institutes and academics. Founded in 1969 and now Britain's largest social research organisation, NatCen has a high reputation for the standard of its work in both qualitative and quantitative research. NatCen has a Survey Methods Unit and, with the Department of Sociology, University of Oxford, houses the Centre for Research into Elections and Social Trends (CREST).

The contributors

Catherine Bromley
Senior Researcher at the *Scottish Centre for Social Research*, part of NatCen, and Co-Director of the *British Social Attitudes* survey series

John Curtice
Research Consultant at the *Scottish Centre for Social Research*, part of NatCen, Deputy Director of CREST and Professor of Politics at Strathclyde University

Helen Cooper
Research Fellow in Psychology at the University of Surrey

Sonia Exley
Research Assistant in the Department of Sociology and a member of Nuffield College, Oxford

Chris Fife-Schaw
Senior Lecturer in Psychology at the University of Surrey

Anthony Heath
Professor of Sociology at the University of Oxford

Mark Johnson
Researcher at NatCen and Co-Director of the *British Social Attitudes* survey series

Lauren McLaren
Lecturer in Comparative Politics at the University of Nottingham

Pippa Norris
McGuire Lecturer in Comparative Politics at the John F. Kennedy School of Government, Harvard University

Alison Park
Research Director at NatCen and Co-Director of the *British Social Attitudes* survey series

Miranda Phillips
Senior Researcher at NatCen and Co-Director of the *British Social Attitudes* survey series

Mark Sandford
Research Fellow in the Constitution Unit at University College, London

Richard Shepherd
Professor of Psychology at the University of Surrey

Patrick Sturgis
Lecturer in Sociology at the University of Surrey

Peter Taylor-Gooby
Professor of Social Policy at the School of Social Policy, Sociology and Social Research, University of Kent

Katarina Thomson
Research Director at NatCen and Co-Director of the *British Social Attitudes* survey series

James Tilley
Lecturer in Quantitative Political Science and Fellow of Jesus College, Oxford

British Social Attitudes

Attitudes The 21ST REPORT

EDITORS

Alison Park
John Curtice
Katarina Thomson
Catherine Bromley
Miranda Phillips

SAGE Publications
London · Thousand Oaks · New Delhi

NatCen
National Centre *for* Social Research

SAGE Publications Ltd
1 Oliver's Yard, 55 City Road
London EC2A 4PU

SAGE Publications Inc.
2455 Teller Road
Thousand Oaks, California 91320

SAGE Publications India Pvt Ltd
B-42, Panchsheel Enclave
Post Box 4109
New Delhi 110 017

British Library Cataloguing in Publication data

A catalogue record for this book is available from the British Library

ISSN 0267 6869
ISBN 0-7619-4278-5

Library of Congress Control Number availalbe

Printed in Great Britain by The Cromwell Press Ltd, Trowbridge, Wiltshire

Contents

List of tables and figures

Chapter 1

Chapter 2

Chapter 3

Chapter 7

Chapter 8

Chapter 9

Appendix I

Introduction

This volume, like each of its annual predecessors, presents the results and interpretations of the latest *British Social Attitudes* survey – the 21st in the series of reports on the studies designed and carried out by the National Centre for Social Research (NatCen).

The series has a widely acknowledged reputation as painting an authoritative and impartial picture of contemporary British values. Its reputation owes a great deal to its many generous funders. We are particularly grateful to our core funder – the Gatsby Charitable Foundation (one of the Sainsbury Family Charitable Trusts) – whose continuous support for the series from the start has given it security and independence. Other funders have made long-term commitments to the study and we are ever grateful to them as well. In 2003, these included the Departments for Education and Skills, Health, Transport, Trade and Industry, and Work and Pensions, and the Office of the Deputy Prime Minister. Our thanks are also due to the Leverhulme Foundation, the Nuffield Foundation, the Institute of Philanthropy and the Hera Trust. Indeed, so many funders came forward in 2003 that the survey was run with a larger than usual sample to allow the inclusion of ever more modules of questions.

We are particularly grateful to the Economic and Social Research Council (ESRC) who provided funding for three sets of questions in the 2003 survey. These covered: the impact of internet use on social and political engagement (funded as part of the ESRC's 'e-society' Programme); devolution and national identity (funded as part of the ESRC's Devolution and Constitutional Change Programme); and attitudes towards genetic technologies. The ESRC also supported NatCen's participation in the *International Social Survey Programme*, which now comprises over 40 nations, each of whom help to design and then field a set of equivalent questions every year on a rotating set of issues. The topic in 2003 was national identity and these questions can be seen at the start of version B of the self-completion questionnaire in Appendix III.

As always, the *British Social Attitudes* survey is developed in co-operation with its sister survey, *Scottish Social Attitudes*. This year two groups of questions, those on devolution and national identity and those on attitudes to immigration, were asked on both surveys in order to enable Scottish/English comparisons.

We were delighted to be able to repeat in 2003 the *Young People's Social Attitudes* survey, a survey of 12 to 19 year olds living in the same households as adult *British Social Attitudes* respondents. This followed similar exercises in 1994 and 1998. Our thanks are due to the Children, Young People and Families Directorate in the Department for Education and Skills for the funding which enabled us to do this.

For those of you who want more information than is available in this Report, we draw your attention to a useful internet resource. Developed by the Centre for Comparative European Survey Data at the London Metropolitan University, the web site allows contents based or free text search of all *British Social Attitudes* questionnaires since 1983 and will produce tables and charts for the questions you are interested in. We would like to thank Professor Richard Topf for all his hard work in bringing this to fruition. This facility can be accessed at http://www.britsocat.com/. The full datasets also continue to be deposited at the UK Data Archive (http://www.data-archive.ac.uk/).

The *British Social Attitudes* series is a team effort. This year, the group bids farewell to Lindsey Jarvis, our valuable colleague who has been an editor and/or author for the last four Reports. At the same time, we are pleased to welcome two new team members, Miranda Phillips and Mark Johnson.

The researchers who design, direct and report on the study are supported by complementary teams who implement the sampling strategy and carry out data processing. They in turn depend on fieldwork controllers, area managers and field interviewers who are responsible for getting all the interviewing done, and on administrative staff to compile, organise and distribute the survey's extensive documentation. In this respect, particular thanks are due to Pauline Burge and her colleagues in NatCen's administrative office in Brentwood. Other thanks are due to Sue Corbett and Sandra Beeson in our computing department who expertly translate our questions into a computer-assisted questionnaire. Meanwhile, the raw data have to be transformed into a workable SPSS system file – a task that has for many years been performed with great care and efficiency by Ann Mair at the Social Statistics Laboratory at the University of Strathclyde. Many thanks are also due to Lucy Robinson and Fabienne Pedroletti at Sage, our publishers.

As always, we must praise above all the anonymous respondents across Britain who gave their time to take part in our 2003 survey. Like the 53,000 or so people who participated before them, they are the cornerstone of this enterprise. We hope that some of them will one day come across this volume and read about themselves with interest.

The Editors

1 The work-centred welfare state

Peter Taylor-Gooby[*]

Whatever else historians of the future say about the New Labour governments elected in 1997 and 2001, they will be judged as having implemented one of the most active, radical and thoroughgoing reform programmes in public policy of any UK government. The reforms range from a policy of shifting from 60 per cent public to 60 per cent private provision in the largest single area of state spending – pensions – to the biggest expansion of education from pre-schooling to further and higher education ever undertaken, affecting more people than the post-1944 expansion. To bolster the incomes of those in work they introduced Britain's first ever minimum wage as well as a system of negative income tax (administered via Tax Credits) available in the first instance to families with children, and from 2003 to all working people, subject to eligibility. As well as raising the incomes of those in work, the last few years have also seen a radical expansion of government activity in relation to childcare for working parents and work–life balance policies.

This chapter focuses on the cornerstone of this 'new welfare settlement' – the emphasis on mobilising as many people as possible into paid work. It offers an approach to the way in which government discharges its welfare responsibilities that is in tune with social and economic change, fits with the direction of the EU European Employment strategy and represents a significant new departure in Labour Party welfare state policy.

The Prime Minister has summarised the guiding principles of this new settlement in a series of Fabian Society pamphlets, speeches and lectures (1994, 1998, 2001, 2003). These identify four underlying themes: the equal worth of individuals, equality of opportunity rather than equality of outcome, the claim that rights entail responsibilities, and the view that the state should be enabling rather than providing (1998, 2003). Such themes form the bedrock of the kind of thinking encapsulated by the 'Third Way', a philosophy which has heralded a

---

[*] Peter Taylor-Gooby is Professor of Social Policy at the School of Social Policy, Sociology and Social Research, University of Kent.

shift in centre-left assumptions about the role of government (Giddens, 1998; Driver and Martell, 2002). Rather than providing extensive passive benefits to meet the needs of its citizens as a whole, government should seek to empower people and equip them to take the opportunities available in a flexible modern economy, and this includes maximising engagement in paid work. The responsibility to seize such opportunities ultimately lies with the citizens; as the guiding mantra of this approach states: "Work for those who can, security for those who can't" (DSS, 2000: v). This vision was set out in Tony Blair's 2003 Fabian Society annual lecture as:

> a modern welfare state with people at work not on benefits; and where rights were matched by responsibilities [in a] something for something rather than something for nothing social contract (Blair, 2003: 2).

This approach seeks to achieve economic goals through the mobilisation of all citizens who can enter paid work, and social goals by ensuring that they are in a position to pursue jobs and receive a fair return. It enables the government to follow up the 1994 Commission on Social Justice report, which argued that "Britain needs to change if it is to find its place in a changing world" (1994:91), and that a central part of that process must be a redirection of the social policy effort to support economic competitiveness. The first paragraph of Labour's 1997 manifesto set out the programme of "building a modern welfare state, of equipping ourselves for a new world economy" (Labour Party, 1997:1). The argument goes that the 'New Welfare State', directed at supporting citizens into paid work, contributes to individual income and opportunity at the same time as it enhances economic competitiveness through the provision of a flexible, available labourforce, assisting economic success in a more globalised and competitive world.

There is a further aspect to the new policies. These are not simply directed at changes in provision, but are also concerned to alter fundamentally the way people think about entitlement and the role of government. The Prime Minister states:

> the challenge for us now is to make our progressive changes across the board irreversible ... we have to make the cultural changes necessary as well as the policy changes (Blair, 2003: 12).

There are a host of questions in *British Social Attitudes* which lend themselves to examining public views on these issues, and the developing story of changing opinions has been charted from a number of perspectives in previous *British Social Attitudes Reports* (for example, Hills, 2001; Taylor-Gooby and Hastie, 2002; Sefton, 2003). In the most recent survey, there are three areas which enable us to examine how far people endorse and support the New Labour approaches. The first of these is concerned with the government's efforts to move people off benefits and into paid work. The second area addresses the issue of state *versus* personal responsibility for welfare. Finally, we consider how far it might be appropriate to talk of 'a new culture of welfare' in the terms advanced by the Prime Minister.

Throughout this chapter we examine the extent to which government policies accord with public thinking. We do this first by looking simply at overall patterns of support for various aspects of welfare policy. We then go on to consider the pattern of attitudes across different social groups. New Labour succeeded in elections in 1997 and 2001 partly because groups who had not supported the party in the past were attracted by its new policies (though we must not discount the added advantage afforded to them by disarray among the opposition parties). One central question addressed in this chapter, therefore, is the extent to which New Labour policies of the kind discussed above attract support from all social groups. Is it the case that such policies appeal to voters across the political spectrum, including those beyond Labour's more traditional electoral heartlands, namely those who hold left-wing political views, working-class people, and those living in northern England, Scotland and Wales? Or are some groups decidedly more lukewarm than others about the prospect of renegotiating Labour's traditional approach to social welfare? The important issue for the party is, of course, to attract new groups in the centre, the middle classes, and the south of England, while not alienating traditional supporters.

To explore this we split the population in three ways. The first is by its political views from left to right. The *British Social Attitudes* survey includes a number of questions designed to measure people's views on government intervention in the economy, the role of income redistribution, and relations between management and workers. These questions cover issues different to those about welfare that we are analysing in this chapter. Taken together, the responses people give to these questions can be used to form a scale which spans a spectrum ranging from very left-wing (where those most likely to favour a strong role for government and to express concerns about the balance of power between society's haves and have-nots would be located) to very right-wing (where those most likely to support individualism and the role of the market would be located). More details of the left–right scale are given in Appendix I of this report. We use this scale to see whether New Labour's welfare policies might attract new groups in the centre, without antagonising voters on the left.

Secondly, we split the population by social class. As discussed in *The 20th Report*, social class continues to be an important dividing factor in political attitudes in Britain today (Park and Surridge, 2003). Thirdly, we analyse by region. Here we distinguish between the Labour heartlands of Scotland, Wales[1] and the north of England on the one hand, and the South East and South West on the other.[2] As with the left–right scale, we are looking for evidence that support for New Labour welfare policies extends beyond its traditional powerbase and into the middle classes and the south of England.

We start by looking at the issue of encouraging all those who can work to do so.

Work for those who can?

There are two main aspects to the government's policies in this area: first, a range of policies designed to 'make work pay', drawing mainly on American rather than European experience (Walker and Wiseman, 2003). These policies include holding down the rates of benefits for those out of work, so that Income Support fell from 22 per cent of median earnings in 1997 to 19.5 per cent by 2001 and continues to do so (NPI/Rowntree, 2003) and introducing a minimum wage and various top-up benefits, mainly through an innovative Tax Credit system to ensure that those on low wages can command an adequate income. The second aspect of work policies concerns new measures to ensure that all claimants actively pursue paid work and particularly to expand the range of those to whom the expectation of work is brought home. Thus groups sometimes considered marginal to the labour force such as lone parents, carers, or sick and disabled people are now often included among those for whom paid work is seen as appropriate. To put it crudely, these policies include both carrots and sticks. The survey includes questions relevant to both these aspects and we begin by looking at the former.

'Carrots'

One significant way of making paid work attractive for those on the margins of the labour market is the system of tax credits now paid to low-income families and individuals. The concept of supplementing the incomes of low-paid families is not new to Britain: 1971 saw the introduction of the Family Income Supplement which was later replaced by Family Credit, an in-work benefit. In 1999, Family Credit was replaced by the Working Families Tax Credit and the Children's Tax Credit, paid via employers to the main carer of each family's child or children. At the same time other tax credits, such as the Disabled Persons Tax Credit, were introduced with the intention of targeting specific groups experiencing disadvantage within the labour market. In April 2003 the system was simplified somewhat and these various credits were replaced with just two, the Working Tax Credit and the Child Tax Credit, which for the first time extended eligibility to some adults without children.[3]

To examine attitudes to this policy we asked whether the government should top-up the wages of three types of low-income families. The example below shows the question we asked about couples with children; this was followed by similar questions about couples without children and lone parents.

Some working couples with children find it hard to make ends meet on low wages. In these circumstances, do you think ...
... the government should top-up their wages,
... or, is it up to the couple to look after themselves and their children as best they can?

Table 1.1 presents the responses people gave to these questions. The most striking thing to note is the strong (though not overwhelming) support for government topping up the wages of parents with children, slightly more marked in the case of lone parents, and the comparatively low support for such a policy for people without children. In each case a noticeable proportion (of just over one in ten) were unable to choose between the options offered, indicating some uncertainty in judgements on this issue – possibly because respondents found the distinction between government top-ups and "looking after themselves" too stark. However, there is a clear indication that, when it comes to people in work, the majority view is that state help should be limited to cases where vulnerable groups, such as children, are involved. While this fits with the main thrust of current government policy, as noted above, the Working Tax Credit is now available to certain low-paid workers without children.

Table 1.1 Should the government top up the incomes of families on low wages?

		Government should top-up	Individuals should look after themselves	Can't choose
Lone parent	%	66	22	12
Couple with children	%	59	29	12
Couple with no children	%	26	63	10
Base: 2649				

As discussed earlier, in order for New Labour to maintain its broad electoral appeal its policies need to garner the support of people who are not naturally inclined to vote Labour while at the same time keeping its traditional supporters happy. As Table 1.2 illustrates, it would seem that income top-ups – for people with children at least – fulfil both these criteria. Although people on the left and centre of the political spectrum are more likely to support such a system than are people on the right, majorities of *all* groups across the political spectrum are in favour of income top-ups for families with children.

Table 1.2 Should the government top up the incomes of families on low wages, by position on the left–right scale

% who say the government should top up the wages of:	Left	Centre	Right
Lone parent	71	68	61
Couple with children	67	60	53
Couple with no children	33	24	22
Base	*813*	*808*	*956*

Quite why low-paid workers without children are seen as less deserving remains unanswered. It is possibly a reflection of the fact that the case for such a policy has not been made as forcibly as it has been for low-paid working parents, or it could be that people have particular concerns about the impact on children of low pay.

Having established that policies to make work pay attract support across the political spectrum, we now look in greater detail at the views of those who have traditionally been regarded as Labour's core supporters – working-class people and those living in Scotland, Wales and the north of England.

Table 1.3 looks at support for income top-ups across the social classes. While there is a hint that people in jobs which have been traditionally classified as working class are slightly keener on such policies, the differences are not significant.

Table 1.3 Should the government top up the incomes of families on low wages, by social class

% who say the government should top up the wages of:	Managerial / profes-sional	Inter-mediate	Self-employed	Lower super-visory and technical	Semi-routine and routine
Lone parent	66	66	62	67	69
Couple with children	59	57	55	61	63
Couple with no children	26	24	24	28	28
Base	928	323	195	345	791

The geography of people's attitudes on this matter is more varied. Looking at Table 1.4, we find that it is indeed the case that people in the south of England are less likely to support these policies than are those in the more traditionally Labour-oriented parts of the UK. However, as we saw before in relation to the left–right scale, a majority of those living in the south are also in favour of income top-ups for working parents.

Table 1.4 Should the government top up the incomes of families on low wages, by region

% who say the government should top up the wages of:	Scotland and Wales	North West, North East, Yorkshire and the Humber	South West and South East
Lone parent	71	68	61
Couple with children	66	61	54
Couple with no children	33	28	22
Base	435	632	572

Policies which offer the potential to increase the rewards of work for certain groups are clearly widely popular. Whether there is the same kind of support for the 'stick' side of the equation is explored next.

'Sticks'

A second set of questions reflect a more punitive direction in policy and ask what sanctions, if any, should be used to punish benefit claimants who fail to attend an employment-focused interview. Such interviews play a central role for the government's New Deal policies and are effectively being introduced for all claimants of working age through the new Jobcentre Plus and Single Gateway benefit application system. An adviser encourages the claimant to move into paid work and discusses the support, training and in-work benefits available. For young people aged 18–24 and those unemployed for long periods (the length varies according to the claimant's age), participation in New Deal is a condition of receiving benefits. The interviews are now compulsory for lone parents and those on incapacity benefit. As the minister responsible for developing the approach put it:

> Why are we setting up Jobcentre Plus? The main reason is so we can provide everyone with the help they need to get into work, or if they lose their job – to get back as quickly as possible. It is a work first approach (Darling, 2002).

To test the extent to which the public supports the general direction of this approach we presented respondents with three examples of potential benefit recipients: a lone parent, someone on long-term sickness or disability benefits, and a carer on benefits. Taking the example of the lone parent, the question asked:

> *Suppose a lone parent on benefits was asked to visit the job centre every year or so to talk about ways in which they might find work. Which of the statements on this card comes closest to what you think should happen to their benefits if they did not go?*
>
> *Their benefits should not be affected*
> *Their benefits should be reduced a little*
> *Their benefits should be reduced a lot*
> *Their benefits should be stopped*

The idea that benefits should be cut for those who don't attend the interview carries the implication that members of the group should be making every effort to pursue work opportunities. At present, such sanctions are being implemented for lone parents and for some groups of sick and disabled people, but are not anticipated for carers.

As Table 1.5 outlines, there is a fairly distinct split between attitudes towards lone parents on the one hand, and sick or disabled people and carers on the other. Only one in six say that lone parents' benefit should *not* be affected if they fail to attend an interview at the job centre and just over a quarter favour the most severe sanction on offer – the withdrawal of state benefits. In contrast, four in ten say that sick or disabled people should avoid any sanctions, and half say this of carers, while only around one in eight would stop the benefits of these groups altogether if they failed to make this effort to pursue work.

We have already seen that public support for income top-ups for working lone parents is pretty widespread, we now see that a majority also agree that they should be actively seeking work.

Table 1.5 Benefit sanctions for those failing to visit the job centre to talk about ways of finding work

		Benefits for people failing to attend job centre interviews should be...			
		... not affected	... reduced a little	... reduced a lot	... stopped
Lone parent	%	17	38	14	27
Sick or disabled person	%	41	32	9	13
Carer on benefits	%	48	28	7	13
Base: 3272					

Tables 1.6, 1.7 and 1.8 look at attitudes to compulsory New Deal interviews across our social groups. First, we look at these views by people's left–right position.

Table 1.6 Support for cutting or stopping benefits for those failing to visit the job centre to talk about ways of finding work, by position on the left–right scale

% who say benefits should be cut a lot or stopped	Left	Centre	Right
Lone parent	42	42	45
Sick or disabled person	22	21	24
Carer on benefits	19	19	21
Base	*813*	*808*	*956*

We saw before that, although there was majority support for income top-ups for lone parents, this policy is more popular amongst those at the centre and left of our scale. When looking at the more punitive side of welfare policy it would not be unreasonable to suggest that here the reverse might be true – that those on the right of the scale would be most likely to support significant benefit sanctions for those not taking advantages of opportunities to help them find work. As Table 1.6 reveals, however, this is not the case. People at the left, centre and right of the scale have very similar views about benefit sanctions, and this is true for all three examples of claimants.

We find the same when it comes to social class and region in Tables 1.7 and 1.8. People in managerial professions and those in routine occupations have very similar views on this matter. Those in the traditional Labour heartlands of Scotland, Wales and northern England are as likely to support – or oppose – severe benefit sanctions as are those in southern England.

Table 1.7 Support for cutting or stopping benefits for those failing to visit the job centre to talk about ways of finding work, by social class

% who say benefits should be cut a lot or stopped	Managerial / profes-sional	Inter-mediate	Self-employed	Lower super-visory and technical	Semi-routine and routine
Lone parent	42	44	47	43	40
Sick or disabled person	26	21	27	23	19
Carer on benefits	22	18	23	20	18
Base	1093	389	247	426	1012

Table 1.8 Support for cutting or stopping benefits for those failing to visit the job centre to talk about ways of finding work, by region

% who say benefits should be cut a lot or stopped	Scotland and Wales	North West, North East, Yorkshire and the Humber	South West and South East
Lone parent	39	41	44
Sick or disabled person	24	23	23
Carer on benefits	19	20	20
Base	537	758	700

One of the underlying principles of New Labour's welfare policies is that those in work, even at the lower end of the pay scale, should be better off than those out of work and that people should not be caught in what is commonly termed the 'benefit trap' whereby potential earnings don't cover what a claimant loses in benefit by going back to work. The following question, asked as part of the survey series since it began, can help us gauge the extent to which people think this is indeed the case. It is also a useful barometer of people's general level of sympathy for unemployed people.

*Opinions differ about the level of benefits for unemployed people.
Which of these two statements comes closest to your own view ...*

*... benefits for unemployed people are **too low** and cause hardship,
or, benefits for unemployed people are **too high** and discourage them
from finding jobs?*

One-third (34 per cent) believe that benefits are too low, while slightly more,
four in ten (40 per cent) say they are too high. A substantial minority (17 per
cent) opted to say neither answer is correct. The largest single group in the
population thinks that unemployed people are discouraged from finding work
by overly generous benefits and, by implication, that benefit rates should
perhaps be reduced even further. This has not always been the case. As seen in
Figure 1.1, the proportion of respondents who think that benefits are too low
outnumbered those who thought they were too high throughout the period
1983–1997. As discussed in last year's Report, attitudes towards benefit
claimants tend to harden during periods of economic growth and soften during a
recession, and this can be seen in the shape of the curve in Figure 1.1. It is
hardly surprising to see an upturn in the proportion saying that benefits are too
high after 1997. Nevertheless, the position in 2003 is very different to that of
the late 1980s, which were also years of economic growth, so there appears to
be a real shift in attitudes over and beyond that which can be explained by the
economic cycle (Sefton, 2003).

We shall return to these changes in attitude towards benefit claimants in the
last section of the chapter where we look at whether there has been a shift to a
new culture of welfare.

Figure 1.1 Benefits for the unemployed are too high or too low, 1983–2003

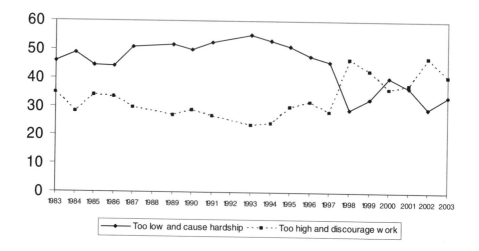

The question here is whether policies that make sure work pays attract support across the political and social spectrum. The answer is fairly complex. It is certainly the case that those on the left, working-class people, and people living in traditionally Labour parts of the UK are the most likely to take the view that benefits are too low and cause hardship. For example, four in ten (40 per cent) on the left of the left–right scale say this compared with one in four (26 per cent) of those on the right. However, it is *not* true that those in managerial professions, and those in southern England are more likely than their respective counterparts to say that benefits are too high and discourage unemployed people from finding work. Here, the differences between our key groups are not significant. While there is a quite predictable social pattern surrounding views about hardship, it is not clear that any one group particularly supports cutting benefits to counter disincentives. Given that traditional Labour supporters are concerned about the hardship benefit recipients suffer, any attempt to cut them further could potentially face significant opposition.

Whose rights, whose responsibilities?

We turn now to the second of the three elements of New Labour's welfare agenda we set out to explore in this chapter. This centres on the issue of where responsibility lies for various aspects of public policy. We start by looking at another of our long-standing questions which concerns itself with the issue of taxation and public spending. Arguably one of the biggest responsibilities placed on citizens by all governments is the requirement to pay taxes to fund public spending. Since the start of the survey series, we have been asking this question:

> *Suppose the government had to choose between the three options on this card. Which do you think it should choose?*
>
> *Reduce taxes and spend less on health, education and social benefits*
> *Keep taxes and spending on these services at the same level as now*
> *Increase taxes and spend more on health, education and social benefits*

Figure 1.2 shows how views on this have changed over time. Every year since 1987 those wanting to increase taxes and spending have been in the majority, while the proportion who actively support tax and spending *cuts* has always been a small minority, standing now at six per cent. Two years stand out however. In 2000 and, most recently, in 2003 the proportion in favour of increases drops to half (51 per cent in 2003), while those opting for the status quo rises to around four in ten.

Figure 1.2 Attitudes to taxation and spending, 1983-2003

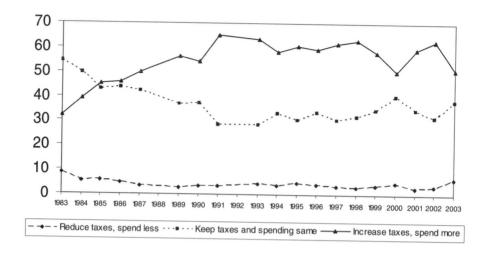

The decline in support for further taxes in 2003 may reflect awareness of the particularly well-publicised increase in National Insurance contributions to finance higher NHS spending which was implemented three months before the 2003 survey began. However, this does not explain the drop in support seen in 2000. In general, answers to this question indicate a continued acceptance of a major role for a tax and spend welfare state and the concomitant responsibilities for taxpayers that go with that. The very low support for real cuts is most striking, but the fact that support for increased spending does on occasion waver suggests that Labour cannot take for granted that it has the public with them on this matter at every instance.

Having looked at an area where responsibility lies most heavily with citizens, we turn now to look specifically at state *versus* private responsibility for a range of social needs. Table 1.9 outlines various scenarios we presented to our respondents. The suggested options in terms of who should be responsible for providing each need were: the government, as in the traditional welfare state; employers (which might reflect a shift towards a more corporatist European model, as advocated in Frank Field's unsuccessful proposals for pension reform in 1998, see Economist, 1998), or the individuals themselves and their families, as in the liberal market approach advocated by right-wing Conservatives.

There appears to be a fairly consistent pattern of answers. In all cases, the government is seen as bearing the major responsibility – in fact, only when it comes to provision in retirement does support for government responsibility fall below four-fifths. It is interesting to note that most of those who advocate non-state responsibility in this area suggest that individuals or families should shoulder this burden, and just one in ten advocate employer responsibility (presumably through occupational pensions although it is difficult to know exactly how respondents interpreted this answer option).

Table 1.9 State *versus* personal responsibility

Who should be responsible for ...		The government	Employers	Individuals and their families
... paying for the care needs of elderly people in residential homes*	%	84	–[1]	13
... paying the cost of health care when someone is ill	%	83	7	8
... ensuring that people have enough to live on if they become sick or disabled	%	83	8	7
... ensuring that people have enough to live on if they become unemployed	%	81	3	14
... ensuring that people have enough to live on in retirement*	%	58	11	29

Base: 3272
*Base: 4432

Note:
1. The employer option was not offered for this scenario

Table 1.10 looks at the views of those who believe the government should be responsible by their left–right position. The most striking feature of this table is that, with the exception of retirement provision, attitudes are fairly similar across the political spectrum. Even though those on the left are slightly more likely to endorse the state's role than the centre and the right, there is overwhelming support for the role of government amongst all three groups. As was the case with the population as a whole, support for the state taking the lead role in providing a decent standing of living in retirement is rather weaker overall, and just under half of those on the right of the scale support this.

As responsibility for care of the elderly, sick and unemployed is so overwhelmingly seen as lying with the government, there is little value in extending this analysis much further. However, it is interesting to note that for retirement provision we find that support for government responsibility is strongest amongst traditional Labour supporters (those in routine occupations, and people living in Scotland, Wales and northern England). As already discussed, New Labour has presided over a major shift towards employer and individual responsibility for pensions, and while it appears to have the backing of less traditional supporters for this kind of approach, the policy doesn't sit comfortably with its heartland voters.

Table 1.10 Support for government responsibility for welfare, by position on the left–right scale

% who say the government should be responsible for ...	Left	Centre	Right
... paying for the care needs of elderly people in residential homes*	89	86	80
... paying the cost of health care when someone is ill	87	86	81
... ensuring that people have enough to live on if they become sick or disabled	85	83	80
... ensuring that people have enough to live on if they become unemployed	86	80	79
... ensuring that people have enough to live on in retirement*	68	60	47
Base	*813*	*808*	*956*
*Base	*1101*	*1128*	*1302*

Having looked at the role of work within the welfare system, and the role of government writ large, we turn now to our third line of enquiry, that is whether New Labour has managed to engineer a broad shift in thinking about welfare.

A new culture of welfare?

As pointed out in the introduction, New Labour has been actively pursuing a shift in the way Britain thinks about its welfare state and the nature of the duties the state has towards its citizens, and *vice versa*. The Attlee ideal was for cradle-to-the-grave care supported by a large network of universal entitlements. The new approach stresses the idea that the state has a duty to provide support when needed, but also encourages people to support themselves whenever possible. We have already seen that New Labour-style welfare policies, such as the limiting of benefits for those not actively seeking work and the topping up of wages for parents on low incomes, attract support from across the political spectrum. Can we go on to show that there has been a wholesale shift in people's thinking about the welfare state of the kind that Blair has been seeking to advance?

To investigate this, Table 1.11 looks at some broad attitudinal statements designed to measure people's attitudes to the welfare system in general, rather than specific policies, and compares them with what people thought in the past. The first three rows cover issues such as the desirability of increased benefits, whether welfare recipients are genuinely deserving, and the question of whether the welfare state acts as a disincentive to people looking after themselves. The bottom two rows include the question on whether benefits are too low which we have already examined, and also a measure of perceptions of welfare fraud. If people have indeed come round to Blair's way of thinking then we should see a hardening of attitudes towards welfare recipients.

This certainly appears to be the case: for example, almost six in ten supported the idea of having higher welfare benefits in the early 1990s, whereas since 1998 the figure has consistently been just over four in ten. A similar pattern is evident when it comes to the question of whether the welfare system prevents people from fending for themselves. In the early to mid-1990s, just over one in four agreed with this proposition, whereas since 1998 it has been as high as four in ten.

The bottom two rows of the table are also very interesting. As already seen in Figure 1.1, the proportion who say that unemployment benefits are too low has tended to decline over time. In this table we can contrast that with the proportion who think that "many people falsely claim benefits" which has tended to increase, rising from two-thirds in 1987 to over three-quarters in 2003. People's views of welfare, and of welfare recipients in particular, have certainly hardened in the past few years.

It is possible that some of this tougher stance on benefit recipients is due to the better economic circumstances in recent times and, if so, attitudes may soften again if there were to be another recession. Unfortunately, most of the questions in Table 1.11 were not asked before 1987 but, as we saw earlier in relation to Figure 1.1, there does seem to have been a more fundamental shift in attitudes, over and above what can be explained by the economic cycle.

Table 1.11 Attitudes towards welfare, 1987-2004

% agree	1987	1991	1994	1998	2001	2003
Government should spend more money on welfare benefits for the poor, even if it leads to higher taxes	55	58	50	43	43	43
Many people who get social security don't really deserve any help	31	26	26	32	32	39
If welfare benefits weren't so generous, people would learn to stand on their own two feet	33	26	27	40	39	42
Base	1281	2481	2929	2531	2795	873
Many people falsely claim benefits	67	69[†]	72	83	80	78
Unemployment benefit is too low and causes hardship	51	50[†]	53	29	37	34
Base	2847	2797	3469	3146	3287	3272

[†]Figures for 1990

However, in order to be sure that this represents a widespread shift in values, we also need to demonstrate that they are now held by all social groups. After all, it could simply be the case that some groups have become a lot more critical in their thinking while the views of others have remained the same. For Labour to gain any electoral advantage from such a shift in thinking, it needs to have occurred amongst both traditional and non-traditional Labour supporters. We pursue this analysis by looking once more at the left–right-scale, social class and region.

Table 1.12 looks at the views of those on the left, centre and right of our scale in 1987 and 2003 respectively. Some interesting trends stand out. The most obvious is in relation to the issue of increased spending on "benefits for the poor" and the level of unemployment benefits (the first and last rows in the table). Although the proportion in favour of welfare recipients has declined amongst all groups, it is the case in both years that a majority of those on the left support this. However, the size of the gap between those at the far ends of our spectrum is smaller in 2003 than was the case previously.

The second and third rows in the table show a quite different pattern. On the question of whether or not social security recipients genuinely deserve help, there was no significant difference of views across the political spectrum in 1987, but in 2003 we can see that those on the *left* are now the most likely to believe that recipients don't really deserve help. On the question of whether the generosity of benefits inhibit people from "standing on their own two feet" there has been a reverse in opinion: in 1987 those on the right were the most likely to take this view; by 2003 it switched to being those on the left.

Table 1.12 Attitudes towards welfare by position on the left–right scale, 1987 and 2003

	1987			2003		
% agree	Left	Centre	Right	Left	Centre	Right
Government should spend more money on welfare benefits for the poor, even if it leads to higher taxes	76	57	35	63	44	29
Many people who get social security don't really deserve any help	32	28	33	47	38	33
If welfare benefits weren't so generous, people would learn to stand on their own two feet	28	27	42	48	43	37
Base	*419*	*361*	*493*	*265*	*272*	*320*
Many people falsely claim benefits	66	65	71	77	79	77
Unemployment benefit is too low and causes hardship	64	56	34	40	37	26
Base	*868*	*677*	*914*	*813*	*808*	*956*

Turning to look at social class, Table 1.13 also shows that unsympathetic views about welfare have become more common across the board. For example, whereas in 1987 a majority of both middle- and working- class people[4] favoured increased spending on welfare benefits, by 2003 support had fallen to around two-fifths in both groups.

Closer inspection of the figures reveals some interesting patterns, many of which echo what we saw above. Take the issue of whether welfare benefits prevent people from "standing on their own two feet", in 1987 around a third of both classes agreed with this statement, by 2003, however, we find that not only has a gap opened up between middle- and working-class people's views (of 12 percentage points) but it is the views of working-class people that stand out as being particularly strident. On the issue of whether welfare recipients are genuinely deserving we find that working-class people have actually always tended to be the most doubtful and have become more so. This echoes the finding in *The 20th Report* that Labour supporters have moved to the right on a variety of issues under Tony Blair's leadership, whereas Conservative supporters have not necessarily changed their views (Curtice and Fisher, 2003).

On the other hand, however, in both 1987 and 2003, working-class people were more likely than middle-class people to say that unemployment benefit is too low and causes hardship.

Table 1.13 Attitudes towards welfare by social class, 1987 and 2003

% agree	1987		2003	
	Middle class	Working class	Middle class	Working class
Government should spend more money on welfare benefits for the poor, even if it leads to higher taxes	55	61	40	43
Many people who get social security don't really deserve any help	27	36	32	44
If welfare benefits weren't so generous, people would learn to stand on their own two feet	31	33	39	51
Base	*320*	*443*	*223*	*197*
Many people falsely claim benefits	62	66	73	80
Unemployment benefit is too low and causes hardship	48	55	31	40
Base	*675*	*1026*	*768*	*813*

As Table 1.14 illustrates, there is an equally complex pattern when we look at views across the regions. On the issue of welfare spending there has been a quite marked decline in support for an increase amongst those living in Scotland, Wales and the north of England, whereas for those living in the south, views are pretty much unchanged since 1987. A similar pattern is evident for the question about whether welfare recipients are genuinely deserving.

When it comes to the question of people standing on their own two feet we see a slightly different trend. There was a small increase between 1987 and 2003 in the proportion of those in Scotland, Wales and the south of England agreeing with the proposition, but in the north of England the change is much more marked – in 1987 just three in ten said this, compared with over four in ten in 2003. The biggest shift in attitudes is for the question about levels of unemployment benefit. In this period the proportion of those in Scotland and Wales who say they are too low halved (from almost two-thirds to a third), and there was a similar, though not quite so sharp, decline amongst those living in the north of England.

Table 1.14 Attitudes towards welfare by region, 1987 and 2003

	1987			2003		
% agree	Scot-land / Wales	North	South	Scot-land / Wales	North	South
Government should spend more money on welfare benefits for the poor, even if it leads to higher taxes	62	58	45	51	40	43
Many people who get social security don't really deserve any help	28	31	36	39	37	39
If welfare benefits weren't so generous, people would learn to stand on their own two feet	29	30	40	33	44	43
Base	194	366	341	153	212	183
Many people falsely claim benefits	66	66	70	82	77	77
Unemployment benefit is too low and causes hardship	62	60	38	32	39	28
Base	445	797	753	537	758	700

On most of these measures, the views of those in the more traditional Labour heartlands have changed so much that the difference between them and their southern English counterparts has narrowed or even disappeared. The biggest change overall has been on whether unemployment benefit is too low. This could possibly reflect changes in the economy across Britain rather than a change in people's cultural values about welfare *per se*, but, on balance, the analysis here does seem to suggest that the kind of welfare system New Labour has been keen to promote has gained broad support.

It is not possible to draw simple conclusions from these analyses. While the new culture of welfare promoted by Blair has attracted criticism on the left, certain elements of it strike a chord with Labour's traditional support base. Given the increased perception that Britain's welfare system is subject to abuse, recent increased efforts to clamp down on fraud will probably have been much welcomed by both traditional Labour supporters and those beyond its normal reach. The views of those on the political left and right can no longer be assumed to follow traditional patterns on a number of issues. For example, those on the left still favour a tax and spend approach to welfare, but are now a lot more circumspect when it comes to the desirability of overly generous provision, largely due to concerns about fraud.

Conclusions

We have discovered that when it comes to New Labour welfare policies such as tax credits and the promotion of work as an alternative to welfare, the public largely support the new approach. True, they are keener on 'carrots' such as income top-ups than 'sticks' such as benefit sanctions for those not co-operating with efforts to enhance people's employability, but views on both issues are similar across all the social groups examined. However, the recent extension of the tax credit system to adults without children has low levels of support, and this will be worth monitoring in future.

We also find that Britain is still very much wedded to the idea of government responsibility for a broad range of policy areas, such as health care, support for those out of work through sickness or disability, and the care needs of older people in nursing homes (something which is not current policy in England and Wales, though it is in Scotland). Only when it comes to pensions do we find any appetite for an increased role for individuals or employers, though Labour's more traditional support base is far from happy with this prospect.

The issue of whether New Labour has succeeded in bringing about a radical shift in the way we think about welfare overall is harder to interpret and there is certainly more analysis to be done before a definitive answer can be reached. However, on the evidence presented here, it seems that the more guarded approach to welfare that Labour has recently pursued, coupled with a shift in emphasis towards personal responsibilities as well as rights, has been broadly popular. Not only has it brought the party platform closer to the views of many on the centre and right of the political spectrum, but in some cases there has also been a sea change in the views held by those on the left. Labour has succeeded in realigning its policy stance so that it now fits more closely the views of a wider section of the electorate, in keeping with its new status as a centrist rather than a left political party.

Notes

1. Despite the presence of nationalist parties in Scotland and Wales, Labour remains the dominant party in Westminster elections. Labour has won every UK general election in Scotland since 1959 (Bromley, 2005 forthcoming), as it has done in Wales throughout the post-war era. In fact, since 1945 the Welsh Labour Party has only once secured less than 40 per cent of the vote (in 1983) (Wyn Jones and Scully, 2005 forthcoming).
2. London and Eastern England are difficult to classify in these terms: while there is a strong Labour vote in these areas, it is less strongly associated with the legacy of an industrial powerbase than is the case in Scotland, Wales or northern England, and these areas are therefore excluded from the analysis.
3. The Working Tax Credit provides support for families with children, and disabled adults provided they work more than 16 hours per week. There is a further incentive built-in to encourage these groups to work for 30 hours a week or more. Adults over 25 who are not disabled and do not have children are also eligible for the Working Tax Credit providing they work more than 30 hours a week. The Child Tax Credit brings together elements of all four previous tax credits, plus Income Support and Job Seekers Allowance, and is payable to all families regardless of whether they are in work, subject to eligibility (for greater detail see HM Treasury, 2002).
4. In the earlier tables in the chapter, social class was shown in terms of the National Statistics Socio-Economic Classification, which is the most recent social class definition. However, this is not available for the older datasets, so in the tables investigating change since 1987, we revert to a classification based on the Goldthorpe schema. Appendix I to this Report contains further information about these classifications.

References

Blair, A. (1994), *Socialism*, Fabian Society Pamphlet 565, London: Fabian Society

Blair, A. (1998), *The Third Way*, Fabian Society Pamphlet 588, London: Fabian Society

Blair, A. (2001) 'Power of community can change the world', Labour Party Conference, Brighton, 2001

Blair, A. (2003), 'Progress and Justice in the 21st Century', Fabian Society Annual Lecture, 2003

Bromley, C. (2005 forthcoming), 'Devolution and Electoral Politics in Scotland', in Jeffery, C. and Hough, D. (eds.), *Devolution in Comparative Context*, Manchester: Manchester University Press

Commission on Social Justice (1994), *Social Justice: Strategies for National Renewal*, London: Vintage

Curtice, J. and Fisher, S. (2003), 'The power to persuade: a tale of two Prime Ministers', in Park, A., Curtice, J., Thomson, K., Jarvis, L. and Bromley, C. (eds.), *British Social Attitudes: the 20th Report – continuity and change over two decades*, London: Sage

Darling, A. (2002), 'The New Deal – Interview', *Pioneer*, **7**, January.

Department of Social Security (2000), *The Changing Welfare State: Social Security Spending*, London: HMSO

Driver. S. and Martell, L. (2002), 'New Labour, Work and the Family', *Social Policy and Administration*, **36(1)**: 46–61

The Economist (1998), 'Field of Dreams', 28th March: 39–41

Giddens, A. (1998), *The Third Way*, Polity Press, Cambridge

HM Treasury (2002), *The Child and Working Tax Credits*, London: HM Treasury

Hills, J. (2001), 'Poverty and social security: What rights? Whose responsibilities?', in Park, A., Curtice, J., Thomson, K., Jarvis, L. and Bromley, C. (eds), *British Social Attitudes: the 18th Report – Public policy, social ties*, London: Sage

Labour Party (1997), *New Labour Because Britain Deserves Better*, Election Manifesto

NPI/Rowntree (2003), *Monitoring Poverty and Social Exclusion*, London: New Policy Institute

Park, A. and Surridge, P. (2003), 'Charting change in British values', in Park, A., Curtice, J., Thomson, K., Jarvis, L. and Bromley, C. (eds.), *British Social Attitudes: the 20th Report – Continuity and change over two decades*, London: Sage

Sefton, T. (2003), 'What we want from the welfare state', in Park, A., Curtice, J., Thomson, K., Jarvis, L. and Bromley, C. (eds.), *British Social Attitudes: the 20th Report – Continuity and change over two decades*, London: Sage

Taylor-Gooby, P. and Hastie, C. (2002), 'Support for state spending: has New Labour got it right?', in Park, A., Curtice, J., Thomson, K., Jarvis, L. and Bromley, C. (eds), *British Social Attitudes: the 19th Report*, London: Sage

Walker, R. and Wiseman, M (2003), 'Reforming US welfare again and again', *Social Policy and Society*, **2(2)**: 109–112

Wyn Jones, R. and Scully, R. (2005 forthcoming), 'Devolution and Electoral Politics in Wales', in Jeffery, C. and Hough, D. (eds.), *Devolution in Comparative Context*, Manchester: Manchester University Press

Acknowledgements

The *National Centre for Social Research* is grateful to the Department for Work and Pensions, and its predecessors, for their financial support which enabled us to ask most of the questions reported in this chapter over the years, although the views expressed in the chapter are those of the author alone.

2 Has modern politics disenchanted the young?

Alison Park [*]

Considerable concern has been expressed over the last decade about the extent to which young people appear to be becoming increasingly disengaged from conventional politics (see, for example, Bentley and Oakley, 1999). Fear about youth disinterest and apathy increased further still after the 2001 general election, in which it emerged that turnout among young people had fallen even more sharply than it had among older groups (Bromley and Curtice, 2002; Clarke *et al.*, 2004). A range of initiatives have been promoted as ways of increasing young people's political awareness and engagement, most notably Citizenship teaching, introduced in 2002 as a compulsory element within the National Curriculum in English secondary schools, following recommendations from the Advisory Group on Citizenship (1998). Experiments with new voting methods have also taken place, although their impact upon young people's willingness to vote has been mixed (Electoral Commission, 2002).

This chapter examines the political engagement of young people, and traces how this has changed over the last decade. It largely does so by focusing upon the *Young People's Social Attitudes* surveys that took place in 1994, 1998 and 2003. Each survey involved interviews with young people aged between 12 and 19 who lived in the same households as adult *British Social Attitudes* respondents, allowing us to examine not only young people's views about politics but also how they relate to those of their parents. The chapter begins by assessing the extent to which young people *really* have become increasingly disinterested in, and disillusioned with, contemporary politics. In so doing, it examines the significance of age differences in political engagement in order to see whether young people now, as in the past, simply tend to become more interested in politics as they get older. Finally, it focuses upon those young people who are *least* engaged in an attempt to examine what our findings imply for the future.

[*] Alison Park is a Research Director at the *National Centre for Social Research* and is Co-Director of the *British Social Attitudes* survey series.

Parties and politics

We begin by examining how interested young people are in politics, and the extent to which they identify with Britain's political parties. In particular, we consider how their levels of engagement differ from those found among older groups, and whether they have changed over time. We then examine the views young people have about politics and their attitudes towards voting.

Political engagement

It is certainly true that young people are less interested in politics than adults. As Table 2.1 shows, while 30 per cent of adults express "a great deal" or "quite a lot" of interest in politics, the same is true of only eight per cent of young people. Moreover, young people's interest has declined over the last decade. In 1994, when we carried out our first survey of 12 to 19 year olds, 38 per cent had at least some interest in politics; now only 31 per cent do so. And, while in 1994, just over a quarter said they had *no* interest in politics at all, this now applies to over a third of young people.

Table 2.1 Political interest, 12–19 year olds (1994-2003) and adults (2003)

	12–19 year olds			Age 18+
	1994	1998	2003	2003
	%	%	%	%
A great deal/ quite a lot of interest	12	10	8	30
Some interest	26	24	23	33
Not very much interest	32	32	32	25
None at all	27	34	36	13
Base	*580*	*474*	*663*	*4432*

Questions about political interest have been asked on the *British Social Attitudes* survey of adults since the mid-1980s, allowing us to set these findings in a wider context. As Table 2.2 shows, there has been no equivalent decline in political interest among adults over this period. True, the proportion of adults expressing at least "some" interest in politics has fluctuated over the years but, at 63 per cent now, it differs little to the level found in 1986. However, it is clear that political interest *has* fallen among the youngest adults in our sample, those aged between 18 and 24. Among this group, the proportion expressing at least some interest in politics has declined by over ten percentage points, an even sharper fall than that which has occurred among 12–19 year olds. The table also suggests that political interest was at something of a high point in the mid-1990s, at 67 per cent among adults as a whole and 58 per cent among young adults. So, while it is clear that political interest among young people has fallen since 1994, this might at least partly reflect particularly high levels of interest that year.

Table 2.2 Political interest, 1986-2003

% a great deal/ quite a lot/ some interest in politics	1986	1991	1994	1998	2003
12–19 year olds	n/a	n/a	38	34	31
All adults	60	63	67	65	63
Adults aged 18–24	52	52	58	50	41
Base (12–19 year olds)	–	–	*580*	*474*	*663*
Base (all adults)	*1548*	*1445*	*2302*	*3146*	*4432*
Base (adults aged 18–24)	*239*	*166*	*199*	*321*	*348*

n/a = not asked

There have been more dramatic changes in the extent to which young people 'identify' with political parties – that is, in the extent to which they feel an emotional attachment to one party rather than another. Such attachment is thought to develop at a young age and then be consolidated during early adulthood, particularly once an individual reaches voting age (Butler and Stokes, 1969). Others, however, dispute the extent to which party loyalties remain fixed over a person's lifetime, arguing that, although people might well feel a loyalty to one party over another, this can change in response to current political reality (Clarke *et al.*, 2004). Here, however, our interest is largely in whether young people feel an attachment to *any* political party (rather than in which party), and the extent to which this has changed over time.

To establish party attachment, we asked young people whether they think of themselves as a *supporter* of any one political party (and, if so, which). We then asked those who did not whether they think of themselves as *a little closer* to one party than another (and, if so, which). Finally, those who neither support nor feel close to a particular party were asked who they would hope to win a general election if there was one held the next day (and, if so, which). Combining responses to these three questions gives us a measure of party attachment. Similar questions were also asked of adults, allowing us to compare their responses to those of young people.[1]

Table 2.3 shows the proportion of young people who support or feel close to a particular party, as well as the proportion who would *not* hope that any party would win a general election, or who 'don't know' who they would hope to win. It also shows, for 2003, adult responses to these questions. Two key points emerge. Firstly, as in 1994 and 1998, far fewer young people than adults support or feel close to a political party. In 2003, only eight per cent of young people supported a party (compared with over a third of adults), while a further

13 per cent felt closer to one party than another (compared with over a quarter of adults). As a result, over three-quarters of young people neither support nor feel close to a party, double the rate found among older groups. This is not, in itself, surprising, given that theories of party identification stress its development from childhood into early adulthood. Secondly, young people are much less likely than adults to be able to say *who* they would support if there was a general election the next day. As Table 2.3 shows, they are four times more likely than adults not to *know* who they would support in a general election, and are twice as likely to say that they would not support *any* political party. Moreover, the proportion of young people in these two categories has increased significantly since 1994, the most notable change being the considerable rise in the numbers of young people who say they would not hope *any* party would win an election, up nearly fivefold from six per cent in 1994 to 29 per cent in 2003.

Table 2.3 Party attachment, 12–19 year olds (1994–2003) and adults (2003)

	12-19 year olds			Age 18+
	1994	1998	2003	2003
	%	%	%	%
Supports a particular party	21	15	8	35
Not a supporter, but feels closer to one party than another	22	20	13	26
Would not hope any particular party to win a general election	6	9	29	16
Don't know who would hope to win a general election/other answer	26	30	32	7
Base	*580*	*474*	*663*	*4432*

When it comes to *which* party young people support, feel closer to, or would hope to win a general election, the Labour Party is by far the most popular, supported by one in five 12–19 year olds. One in eleven support the Conservative Party, and one in sixteen the Liberal Democrats. Only one in a hundred young people opt for the Green Party, suggesting the view that the young find green politics more engaging than the mainstream agenda is misplaced. Given the substantial decrease we have seen in the proportion of young people who identify with *any* political party, it is not surprising that there has been a decline in the popularity of each of these parties since 1994. The Labour Party has suffered most; down from 35 per cent in 1994 to 21 per cent now, although Conservative and Liberal Democrat identification has also fallen. These changes are notably more pronounced than those found among adults over the same period. In 1994, for instance, 40 per cent of adults identified with the Labour Party, compared with 37 per cent in 2003.

The increase in the proportion of people who feel no attachment to any political party is not a recent phenomenon (Crewe and Thomson, 1999); nor has it by any means been confined to the young, although its increase has been slightly less dramatic among adults (Bromley *et al.*, 2001). This is demonstrated in the next table, which shows that one in ten adults in 1983 had no party attachment (this measure combines those who say they do not know *who* they would support in an election and those who say they would not support *any* party). By 2003, this had doubled, and now stands at one in five adults, with a particularly marked jump taking place between 1998 and 2003. This falling off in party attachment has been more marked still among young adults, aged between 18–24. In 2003, 41 per cent of 18–24 year olds fell into this category, nearly three times the proportion who did so in 1983. And, as we have already seen, a similarly stark change has taken place among young people aged between 12–19.

Table 2.4 No party attachment, 1983–2003

% with no party attachment	1983	1986	1991	1994	1998	2003
12–19 year olds	n/a	n/a	n/a	32	39	61
All adults	10	11	10	12	14	21
Adults aged 18–24	15	18	13	18	25	41
Base (12–19 year olds)	–	–	–	*580*	*474*	*663*
Base (all adults)	*1761*	*3100*	*2918*	*3469*	*3146*	*4432*
Base (adults aged 18–24)	*211*	*436*	*318*	*289*	*241*	*348*

n/a = not asked

"There's no point to politics"

So far we have seen that young people are less interested in politics than before, and that they are less likely to identify with any of Britain's political parties. What, then, is their view of politics and voting? Might, for instance, the rapid decline in party identification reflect an increasing disillusionment with British party politics? And is it likely to affect young people's willingness to turn out and vote in future elections?

None of the young people interviewed in 2003 would have been old enough to vote in 2001, but all will be entitled to cast a vote at one or both of the next two general elections. And, as we explored earlier, considerable concern exists about the extent to which they will make use of this vote. To examine their views, we asked young people to choose one of the three following views about voting in a general election: "it's not really worth voting"; "people should vote only if they care who wins"; and "it is everyone's duty to vote". As seen in

Table 2.5, in 2003, as in 1998, we found the instrumental view to be the most popular – that people should vote only if they care about the outcome. The view that it is an individual's 'civic duty' to vote is less common now than in 1998, having fallen from 36 to 31 per cent, though this change is not quite statistically significant. However, less than one in ten young people think there is no point to voting at all.[2]

Table 2.5 Views about voting in general elections, 1998 and 2003

	1998	2003
	%	%
It's not really worth voting	7	9
People should vote only if they care who wins	55	59
It is everyone's duty to vote	36	31
Base	*474*	*663*

In order to examine views about politics more generally we also asked young people whether they "agree", "disagree" or "neither agree nor disagree" with three negative assertions about British politics. Table 2.6 shows the proportion who *disagree* with these statements – that is, who take the *least* disenchanted view. Nearly half disagree with the notion that politics has "no point", over six in ten disagree that voting is "a waste of time", and just under a third disagree with the assertion that there is no "real difference" between Britain's main political parties.[3] In all cases, fewer young people disagree than did so in 1998. The relatively small sample size means that changes of this magnitude are not statistically significant – with the exception of the fall in the proportion who disagree that voting is a waste of time – but they all point in the same direction: towards increasing disenchantment about politics and voting.

Table 2.6 Views about politics, 1998 and 2003

% who disagree	1998	2003
There's no point to politics – in the end, everything goes on just the same	52	47
Voting in elections is a waste of time	68	62
There isn't any real difference between the main political parties in Britain	37	32
Base	*474*	*663*

So far we have seen evidence of a significant decline in young people's interest in politics since 1994 (although it is reasonable to think that 1994 might have been a year in which levels of political interest were particularly high), and a sharp fall in the extent to which this age group identify with Britain's political parties. Moreover, there are tentative hints of an increased disenchantment in their overall views about politics and voting.

Differences in political engagement: lifecycle or generation?

We have seen that levels of political engagement among young people, as measured by their interest in politics and their party identification, are substantially lower than those found among adults. Of course, this might simply reflect the fact that interest and identification increase as a person gets older (Heath and Park, 1997). Alternatively, they might be the product of deep-rooted differences between particular generations; differences which, if they remain constant, could have profound implications for future levels of political engagement in Britain.

Political interest

We begin by considering political interest. Earlier, in Table 2.1 we saw that levels of interest were markedly lower among young people than they were among adults, and that they had declined over time. But this is not necessarily surprising; after all, none of the young people we interviewed will have yet had the chance to vote in a general election, and we might expect that concerns about issues such as interest and mortgage rates, Council Tax, or the state of local hospitals might loom less large for them than they do for older groups. For some, the older members of our group of young people, these issues will increasingly matter soon; for those aged 12–15 they will no doubt appear somewhat more remote.

As our surveys of young people did not involve interviewing the same groups of people in 1994, 1998 and 2003, we cannot use them to track how an individual's interest might change as they get older. However, by combining information from the *Young People's Social Attitudes* surveys with that from the adult *British Social Attitudes* surveys carried out in the same years we *can* track levels of political interest among particular *cohorts* of young people (that is, people born during the same period). For example, we can track how political interest has developed over time among those young people aged 12–15 in 1994 by looking at 16–19 year olds in 1998 and 21–24 year olds in 2003.

This analysis is shown in Table 2.7. Each cohort's years of birth are described in the first column of the table. Each row then traces the level of interest found among a particular cohort in 1994, 1998 and 2003, in order to see whether, as they get older, their political interest increases. Take the cohort born between 1979 and 1982 (who are highlighted in bold in the table). In 1994, when they were 12–15, just over a third (34 per cent) were interested in politics. Four years later, in 1998, their interest had grown only slightly. But between the ages of

16–19 and 21–24, their interest increased markedly, from 38 to 46 per cent. Exactly the same shift, at the same age, occurred among the preceding cohort (born between 1975 and 1978), whose interest increased from 45 per cent in 1994 (when they were 16–19) to 56 per cent in 1998 (when they were 20–23). Certainly, therefore, young people's interest in politics increases as they get older, with the most marked increase taking place between their late teens and early twenties.

Table 2.7 Political interest among young people, cohort analysis, 1994-2003[4]

% with at least some interest in politics	1994	1998	2003
All 12–19 year olds	38	34	31
Cohort	(age in brackets)	(age in brackets)	(age in brackets)
1975–1978	45 (16–19)	56 (20–23)	57 (25–28)
1979–1982	**34 (12–15)**	**38 (16–19)**	**46 (21–24)**
1983–1986[5]	–	30 (12–15)	39 (17–19)
1988–1991	–	–	29 (12–15)

However, we should not just focus upon the fact that political interest increases with age – we also need to consider the level of interest young people show at a particular age. After all, even if interest does develop at a steady pace as a person gets older, if their initial interest at 12–15 is lower than that found among previous cohorts, each generation of young people will be successively less interested in politics than their predecessors (unless their interest increases sufficiently to allow them to 'catch up'). When we focus on this comparison, we see that, while 12–15 year olds in 1998 were significantly less interested in politics than the same age group in 1994, there is no significant difference between the levels of interest displayed by this age group in 1998 and 2003. In 1998, for instance, 30 per cent of 12–15 year olds had some interest in politics; in 2003, this applied to 29 per cent of this age group. As we have already suggested that our 1994 readings might represent something of a high point in political interest, this appears to provide little evidence of marked generational differences in political interest among young people over the last decade.

So it seems clear that young people's political interest does indeed increase as they get older. Moreover, there is little here to suggest that over this period successive generations of young people are becoming less interested in politics. There is, however, an important caveat to this conclusion. If we look at the 1979–82 cohort in 2003 (when they were aged 21–24), we can see that the proportion who were interested in politics, 46 per cent, is markedly lower than the 56 per cent found among the previous cohort in 1998 when they were at a similar age (20–23). This suggests that, before we rule out any evidence of generational change, we also need to examine levels of political interest among young adults, and how these have changed over time. Is there any evidence here that successive generations of young adults are becoming less interested in politics? We can do this by carrying out similar analyses using the adult *British Social Attitudes* survey, which gives us the additional advantage of being able to look back over a longer time period.

Table 2.8 is based upon a similar analysis of different cohorts of people and focuses on their political interest in 1986, 1996 and 2003. It shows that an upsurge in political interest takes place when people move from their twenties to their early thirties. The clearest example of this phenomenon can be found in the cohort born between 1959 and 1968 (highlighted in bold in the table). In 1986, when this group were in their late teens and twenties, 53 per cent had at least some interest in politics. Four years later, as they moved into their late twenties and early thirties, 61 per cent were interested, increasing further still to 66 per cent as the cohort entered their late thirties and early forties in 2003. Shifts of a similar magnitude, at the same sort of age, are evident among the previous and subsequent cohorts. By contrast, political interest does not appear to increase as substantially after a cohort reaches its mid-forties.

This does not, however, mean that we can automatically expect interest among young adults to remain at the levels it has been in the past. For, as the more eagle-eyed reader will have already spotted, the youngest cohort in our table, born between 1979 and 1985, have a lower level of interest than any cohort before them (41 per cent). Consequently, the 'generation gap' between the levels of interest shown by the oldest and youngest age groups in each year has grown markedly since 1986. Then, the difference between the interest shown by these two groups stood at just nine percentage points; now, it is three times larger, at 28 points.

Table 2.8 Political interest among adults, cohort analysis, 1986-2003 [6]

% with at least some interest in politics	1986	1996	2003
All	60	63	63
Cohort	(age in brackets)	(age in brackets)	(age in brackets)
1979–1985	*	*	41 (18–24)
1969–1976	*	49 (18–27)	56 (25–34)
1959–1968	**53 (18–27)**	**61 (28–37)**	**66 (35–44)**
1949–1958	63 (28–37)	69 (38–47)	68 (45–54)
1939–1948	65 (38–47)	69 (48–57)	69 (55–64)
1929–1938	65 (48–57)	71 (58–67)	69 (65–74)
1919–1928	57 (58–67)	61 (68–77)	*
1909–1918	62 (68–77)	*	*
'Generation gap'	9 points	12 points	28 points

These analyses clearly show that political interest does indeed develop as a person gets older, particularly during their twenties and thirties. However, there is evidence that the levels of interest now found among some younger generations are so low that they will need to increase substantially over the next decade or so if these groups are to 'catch up' with previous generations.

Party attachment

Earlier, in Table 2.3, we saw that far fewer young people than adults are able to say which political party they favour, something that should not surprise us unduly, as the attachment that people might feel to one party over another is likely to develop during early adulthood as people vote for the first time and begin to take more of an interest in politics. However, we also saw a very sharp increase between 1998 and 2003 in the proportions of young people who do not feel attached to any political party.

Cohort analysis along the same lines to that conducted earlier for political interest does provide some evidence that attachment to a particular political party increases as young people get older. If we focus upon the cohort born between 1975 and 1978 (highlighted in bold in Table 2.9), we can see that the proportions who felt no party attachment fell from 29 per cent during their late teens to 23 per cent during their early twenties. However, this cohort was clearly affected by the dramatic upsurge since 1998 in the proportions of young people with no party attachment; by their late twenties, this applied to a third of this group. The same pattern is evident among the two subsequent cohorts, although it is worth noting that levels of non-attachment were already very high in 1998 among the cohort born between 1984 and 1987.

The table also clearly shows that the level of non-attachment among the youngest age groups in our surveys has increased markedly, from just under a third in 1994 to two-thirds in 2003.

Table 2.9 No party attachment among young people, cohort analysis, 1994-2003[7]

% no party attachment	1994	1998	2003
All 12-19 year olds	32	39	61
Cohort	(age in brackets)	(age in brackets)	(age in brackets)
1975–1978	**29 (16–19)**	**23 (20–23)**	**32 (25–28)**
1979–1982	32 (12–15)	29 (16–19)	41 (21–24)
1983–1986[5]	–	44 (12–15)	46 (17–19)
1988–1991	–	–	66 (12–15)

When we replicate this analysis using data from the *British Social Attitudes* survey over a longer time period, the same pattern emerges. Among younger cohorts, the period between 1986 and 1994 is marked by a decline in the proportion who felt no attachment to a particular party, compared with considerable stability among older groups, exactly what we would expect if party attachment develops during young adulthood. Between 1994 and 2003, however, there is an increase among all cohorts in the proportions who display no party attachment. Moreover, the age gradient in non-attachment has become more pronounced, as measured by the gap between the measures for our oldest and youngest groups in any single year, from nine points in 1986 to 26 points in 2003.

Table 2.10 No party identification among adults, cohort analysis, 1986-2003 [8]

% no party identification	1986	1994	2003
All	11	12	21
Cohort	(age in brackets)	(age in brackets)	(age in brackets)
1977–1985	*	*	39 (18–26)
1969–1976	*	19 (18–25)	25 (27–34)
1959–1968	**17 (18–27)**	**13 (26–35)**	**23 (35–44)**
1949–1958	11 (28–37)	12 (36–45)	18 (45–54)
1939–1948	10 (38–47)	7 (46–55)	15 (55–64)
1929–1938	8 (48–57)	8 (56–65)	13 (65–74)
1919–1928	9 (58–67)	8 (66–75)	*
1909–1918	8 (68–77)	*	*
'Generation gap'	9 points	11 points	26 points

In summary, it is clear that both political interest and favouring a particular party, rather than none at all, increases as a person gets older. This process is very clear in relation to political interest, although there are some signs that it has not been of a sufficient magnitude to allow younger generations to 'catch up' with previous generations. As a result, there is now a more marked age gradient to political interest than ever before. Unless this gradient diminishes, overall levels of political interest in Britain do seem likely to fall over the next few decades, as older, more engaged generations die out and are replaced by ones with lower levels of interest in politics. Added to this, the last few years have seen a more rapid fall in party attachment among the young than among older age groups, meaning that younger groups now lag substantially behind their older counterparts. Again, if this gap between older and younger generations fails to close, the extent to which people feel attached to any party, rather than none at all, is likely to decline over time.

Why are young people turned off politics?

The fact that levels of party attachment among both younger *and* older groups have changed so rapidly over the last decade leaves open the question as to whether this is as much a response to short-term political reality as a stable long-term trend. It is to this question that we now turn. To shed some light on the changes we have found, we need to identify the factors most strongly associated with these forms of political engagement, allowing us to gain a better understanding of those who are most and least engaged. In so doing, we also need to establish whether levels of engagement have fallen most sharply among particular groups of young people. Is it, for instance, the case that interest and attachment have fallen the most among those young people traditionally *most* likely to be politically engaged? Or is the decline most marked among those groups who in the past have proved particularly disinterested in politics?

We do this by using multivariate analysis techniques (logistic regression) which allow us to assess the relative importance of a range of factors in predicting a young person's interest in politics or their likelihood of identifying with a political party. The advantage of this method over simple cross-tabular comparisons of different groups is that it allows us to assess the importance of a range of different characteristics while taking account of their relationship with each other (an important advantage, as many of the characteristics we are interested in are themselves interrelated). Further details of this form of analysis can be found in Appendix I of this Report.

We included seven characteristics in each of our analyses and compared their importance with those found in 1994. Some of the characteristics relate to the young person (their age, sex, and own interest in politics or party identification), while others relate to the parent who we interviewed as part of the *British Social Attitudes* survey that year (their educational attainment, political interest and party identification) or to the household within which they both live (household income).[9] Age, sex, parental education and household income were selected as they have previously been found to be related to political interest and party identification among young people (Park, 1995, 1999; Egerton, 2002). And adult political interest and party identification were included so as to explore the relationship between the political engagement of parents and their children.

Figure 2.1 describes the factors that emerged as significantly associated with political interest in 1994 and 2003, with the group who were *most* likely to be interested in politics or to identify with a party shown in brackets. The top half of the table focuses upon characteristics associated with young people themselves; the bottom lists characteristics associated with their parents. In 1994, three characteristics were significantly associated with a young person's political interest: party attachment, age and parental educational background. The young people *most* likely to be interested in politics were those who already had an attachment to a party, 16–19 year olds, and those whose parent was a graduate (or had another higher education qualification). Meanwhile, those young people most likely to have formed an *attachment* to a party were those who were politically interested and whose parent identified with a political party themselves.

The picture in 2003 is, however, slightly different. Now, just two characteristics are significantly associated with a young person's political interest: whether he or she already has an attachment to a political party, and their parent's interest in politics. The young people *most* likely to have at least some interest in politics are those who had an attachment to a particular party, and whose parent has a great deal or quite a lot of interest in politics. Once these two factors are taken into account, none of the other characteristics we included in our analysis proved to be significantly associated with whether a young person was interested in politics (including age and parental education, both of which were important in 1994). Parental political interest is also significantly associated with whether a young person had formed an attachment to a political party, as is the young person's own interest in politics. Age, sex and the educational background of their parent are also associated with party attachment. The young people *most* likely to have an attachment to a particular party were those with a parent who has a great deal or quite a lot of interest in politics, who themselves have at least some interest in politics, are aged 16–19, male and whose parent has a higher education qualification. Details of the analyses described in Figure 2.1 can be found in the appendix to this chapter.

The most noteworthy finding to emerge here is the important role that parental political interest (which we can see as a reflection of the likely political stimulation that young people receive at home) now appears to play in shaping their engagement with politics. Those whose parents are interested in politics are both more likely to be interested in it themselves, and to have formed an attachment to a particular political party. In 1994, whether or not a young person's parent was interested in politics was not related to their own engagement once other factors were taken into account; now, this relationship is a very important one.

Figure 2.1 Groups most likely to be interested in politics or identify with a party, 1994 and 2003

	Political interest		Party identification	
	1994	**2003**	**1994**	**2003**
Young person:	Party identification (identifier)	Party identification (identifier)	Political interest (some)	Political interest (some)
	Age (16–19)			Age (16–19)
				Sex (male)
Parental:	Education (higher education)	Political Interest (great deal/quite a lot)	Party identification (identifier)	Political Interest (great deal/quite a lot)
				Education (higher education)

If we look at young people's attitudes towards voting, a similar pattern emerges. In 1998, when we first asked this question, only two characteristics were significantly related to a young person holding the view that "it is everyone's duty to vote": their own level of political interest and whether they had an attachment to a political party or not. Young people who *were* interested in politics, and who had an attachment to a party, were the most likely to believe that it is everyone's civic duty to vote. Beyond these two factors, none of the other characteristics of the young person or their parent was associated with variations in their views. In 2003, however, while young people's own political interest and attachment remain associated with their views about voting, so too is their parent's level of interest in politics. Most notably, those whose parent has *no* interest in politics are significantly less likely to think everyone has a duty to vote (further details of this analysis can be found in the appendix to this chapter).

Table 2.11 sheds some light as to how the changes described in Figure 2.1 might have come about. The first column shows levels of political interest among young people with a parent who *is* themselves interested in politics. Of this group, nearly half express at least some interest in politics, while only a fifth say they have no interest. The third column shows levels of interest among young people whose parent has *little or no* interest in politics; under a quarter of this group have some interest in politics, and nearly half have no interest at all. This, of course, confirms the findings of our multivariate analysis. However, the more interesting observation relates to the changing levels of interest among these two groups since 1994. Political interest among young people with politically interested parents has changed little since then. But it has fallen dramatically among those whose parents are not interested, with a 15 percentage point rise in the proportion expressing no interest in politics whatsoever (from 32 to 47 per cent). (Very similar findings apply when we examine the relationship between parental political interest and whether or not a young person favours a political party, rather than no party at all.)

Table 2.11 Political interest (12–19 year olds) by adult political interest, 2003 and change since 1994

	Parental political interest			
	Great deal, quite a lot	Change 1994–2003	Not much, none	Change 1994–2003
Young person's political interest	%		%	
Great deal/ quite a lot/ some	48	+2	23	-6
Not very much	32	-2	31	-6
None	20	-1	47	+15
Base	*147*		*212*	

Note: Based on all young people for whom parental data is available.

Why might interest and party attachment have fallen most among those who receive the least political stimulation at home? A strong possibility is that this group, more than any other, are simply not being engaged by current political reality. This assertion is given weight by Table 2.12 which shows that, while views about politics among those with politically interested parents have barely changed since 1998, they have changed significantly among those whose parents are not interested. For example, only a fifth of those with disinterested parents *disagree* with the view that there "isn't any real difference between Britain's main parties", down 11 points since 1998, when a third disagreed. They are also markedly less likely than they were in 1998 to disagree with the view that there is "no point" to politics or that voting is a simply a "waste of time".

Table 2.12 Views about politics, by parental political interest, 2003 and change since 1998

	Parental political interest			
	Great deal, quite a lot	Change 1998-2003	Not much, none	Change 1998-2003
% who disagree				
No point to politics – all goes on the same	66	+3	30	-10
Voting is a waste of time	77	-2	46	-9
No real difference between main political parties	45	-3	22	-11
Base	*147*		*212*	

Note: Based upon all young people for whom parental data is available

Parental political interest has, it seems, helped 'protect' some young people from an increasing disillusionment with politics. However, as Table 2.13 shows, while young people with politically interested parents are more likely than those with disinterested parents to think that everyone has a duty to vote, even they are less likely to think this than they were five years ago. In 1998, 45 per cent of young people with politically interested parents thought people had a civic duty to vote; now, only 38 per cent do, a fall of seven percentage points.

Table 2.13 Attitudes to voting (12-19 year olds) by adult political interest, 2003 and change since 1998

	Parental political interest			
	Great deal, quite a lot	Change 1998-2003	Not much, none	Change 1998-2003
	%		%	
It's not really worth voting	3	+ 2	16	+ 4
People should vote only if they care who wins	57	+ 6	62	+ 4
It is everyone's duty to vote	38	- 7	22	- 3
Base	*147*		*212*	

Note: based on all young people for whom parental data is available

The important role that parental political interest appears to play in shaping young people's attitudes towards politics (and, to a lesser degree, their views about voting) provides some clues as to how opinions might change in the future. Previous research among the *British Social Attitudes* survey of adults found that a large part of the decline in turnout between 1997 and 2001 was accounted for by a sharp fall among those who were *least* interested in politics, a drop which can in turn be partly explained by their belief that little was at stake in the 2001 election, as well as by the perception that the outcome was rather obvious (Bromley *et al.*, 2004). Our findings suggest that the *children* of this particularly disinterested group might be responding to the political reality of the last five years by becoming less interested and more disenchanted themselves. In contrast, young people whose parents are more politically engaged appear to have been shielded from this process, no doubt partly because of the political stimulation they receive at home. As a result, a gulf is opening up between the attitudes expressed by young people living in the most and least politically engaged homes, and could potentially widen further still unless changes to current political reality convince their parents that politics has a purpose. Perhaps, for instance, if political competition was greater and there was an increased sense that different parties stand for very different things, willingness to vote, particularly among those who are less interested in politics, might increase substantially (Sparrow, 2003). And, if this takes place, we might reasonably expect to see levels of political engagement among the children of this group, those living in the least politically interested homes, increase too.

Conclusions

Is modern politics disenchanting young people? Certainly, since 1994 there has been a significant fall in the interest that young people express in politics, and an even sharper drop in the extent to which they favour *any* of Britain's political parties. There are hints of an increased disenchantment in their overall views about politics and voting, and it is clear that this applies particularly to those living in less politically interested homes. Moreover, while it is clear that both political interest and favouring a particular political party (rather than the 'no' party) increases as a person gets older, there is a question mark over the extent to which the engagement of current generations of young people will catch up with the generations which preceded them. And, unless they do, overall levels of political interest and party attachment in Britain are likely to fall gradually over time.

It also seems clear that current political reality plays a role in young people's engagement in politics, leaving open the possibility that, in a more stimulating political climate, their interest and willingness to favour a party rather than no party at all might increase. However, if this is to happen, it is those young people who receive little political stimulation at home who must be engaged, a group which has shown a marked decline in enthusiasm for politics over the last five years. That said, it is not *just* these groups of young people who need to be convinced; even those in the most politically engaged homes are less likely now to think it important that *everyone* vote, rather than just those who care about an election's outcome. To some extent, these issues might be addressed through endeavours in other arenas, most notably school. Indeed, the recent entry of Citizenship education onto the National Curriculum provides one example as to how this might be achieved. But it is also apparent that it is just as important to focus upon the political stimulation that young people receive at home. And the all important key to this must lie in the hands of those within British politics, and in their ability to convince the electorate, particularly its less interested components, that politics is indeed exciting. In this sense, then, their job is as much to attract *everybody* to politics as it is to engage young people in particular.

Notes

1. The final question in this series asked of adults differs slightly from that asked of young people. It asks "if there were a general election tomorrow, which party do you think you would be most likely to support" (rather than "which party would you hope would win").
2. This is in sharp contrast with adult views. When we last asked a similar question on *British Social Attitudes* in 2001, 65 per cent took the 'civic duty' view, 23 per cent the instrumental view, and 11 per cent thought that it was not worth voting.
3. Intriguingly, there has been a marked increase in the proportion who "neither agree nor disagree" with the statement "there isn't any real difference between the main political parties in Britain", or who did not know how to answer this question. In 1998, these responses accounted for 25 per cent of young people, compared with 38 per cent in 2003. It is unclear how this change should be interpreted, although it does imply that, for a substantial number of young people, the differences between Britain's political parties are far from clear.

4.   The bases for this table are as follows:

	1994	1998	2003
All 12–19 year olds	580	474	663
Cohort			
1975–1978	234	134	261
1979–1982	346	216	223
1983–1986	–	258	169
1988–1991	–	–	417

5.   This cohort was aged 17–20 in 2003. However, the *Young People's Social Attitudes* survey only interviews the 12–19 age group (meaning we can only consider the views of those aged 17–19 that year). A similar problem affects the *British Social Attitudes* survey of adults; as eligibility for this survey starts at the age of 18, we would be restricted to analysis of the views of 18–20 year olds.

6.   The bases for this table are as follows:

	1986	1996	2003
All	1548	3620	4432
Cohort			
1979–1985	*	*	348
1969–1976	*	473	749
1959–1968	310	812	879
1949–1958	303	621	759
1939–1948	294	527	669
1929–1938	248	450	550
1919–1928	187	468	*
1909–1918	133	*	*

7.   The bases for this table are as follows:

	1994	1998	2003
All 12–19 year olds	580	474	663
Cohort			
1975–1978	234	134	261
1979–1982	346	216	223
1983–1986	–	258	169
1988–1991	–	–	417

8. The bases for this table are as follows:

	1986	1996	2003
All	3100	3469	4432
Cohort			
1979–1985	*	*	348
1969–1976	*	344	749
1959–1968	582	788	879
1949–1958	608	596	759
1939–1948	578	523	669
1929–1938	508	477	550
1919–1928	414	430	*
1909–1918	288	*	*

9. These analyses, and Tables 2.11 to 2.13, are based only upon the 89 per cent of the sample of young people for whom parental information is available by way of the *British Social Attitudes* survey (in the remaining 11 per cent of cases, the adult interviewed was not the parent of the young person).

References

Advisory Group on Citizenship (1998), *Education for citizenship and the teaching of democracy in schools*, London: Qualifications and Curriculum Authority

Bentley, T. and Oakley, K. with Gibson, S. and Kilgour (1999), *The Real Deal: What young people really think about government, politics and social exclusion*, London: Demos

Bromley, C. and Curtice, J. (2002), 'Where have all the voters gone?', in Park, A., Curtice, J., Thomson, K., Jarvis, L. and Bromley, C. (eds.), *British Social Attitudes: The 19th Report*, London: Sage

Bromley, C., Curtice, J. and Seyd, B. (2004), *Is Britain facing a crisis of democracy?* London: *Centre for Research into Elections and Social Trends*

Bromley, C., Curtice, J. and Seyd, B. (2001), 'Political engagement, trust and constitutional reform', in Park, A., Curtice, J., Thomson, K., Jarvis, L. and Bromley, C. (eds.), *British Social Attitudes: The 18th Report – Public policy, social ties*, London: Sage

Butler, D. and Stokes, D. (1969), *Political Change in Britain*, London: Macmillan

Clarke, H., Sanders, D., Stewart, M. and Whiteley, P. (2004), *Political Choice in Britain*, Oxford: Oxford University Press

Crewe, I. and Thomson, K. (1999), 'Party loyalties: dealignment or realignment?' in Evans, G. and Norris, P. (eds.), *Critical Elections: British parties and voters in long-term perspective*, London: Sage

Egerton, M. (2002), 'Political partisanship, voting abstention and higher education: changing preferences in a British youth cohort in the 1990s', *Higher Education Quarterly*, **56(2)**: 156–177

Electoral Commission (2002), *Modernising elections – a strategic evaluation of the 2002 electoral pilot schemes*, London: Electoral Commission

Heath, A. and Park, A. (1997), 'Thatcher's children?', in Jowell, R., Curtice, J., Park, A., Brook, L., Thomson, K. and Bryson, C. (eds.), *British Social Attitudes: The 14th Report – The end of Conservative values?*, Aldershot: Ashgate

Park, A. (1995), 'Teenagers and their politics', in Jowell, R., Curtice, J., Park, A., Brook, L. and Ahrendt, D. (eds.), *British Social Attitudes – the 12th Report*, Aldershot: Dartmouth

Park, A. (1999), 'Young people and political apathy', in Jowell, R., Curtice, J., Park, A. and Thomson, K. (eds.), *British Social Attitudes: The 16th Report – Who shares New Labour values?*, Aldershot: Ashgate

Sparrow, N. (2003), 'The No party', *Reform, Autumn 2003* (www.reformbritain.com)

Acknowledgements

We are grateful to the Children, Young People and Families Directorate in the Department for Education and Skills for funding the 2003 *Young People's Social Attitudes* survey. Responsibility for analysis of this data lies solely with the author.

Appendix

The following tables show the results of the logistic regression models described in Figure 2.1 and the accompanying text.

The heading for each model defines the dependent variable – that is, the characteristic which the model seeks to predict, and the table shows the results for all variables that were significant in predicting the dependent variable. A negative B coefficient means that the characteristic is associated with the dependent variable being *less* likely than average; a positive characteristic means it is *more* likely than average. The table also shows the significance of the results; in all cases, our criteria for significance was 0.05. The order in which each characteristic was selected is listed at the foot of the table, as are those variables included in the model which did not emerge as significant.

1994: A great deal, quite a lot or some political interest

	B	S.E.	Wald	Sig.	Exp(B)
Age					
12-15	-.453	.139	10.598	.001	.636
16-19	.453	.139	10.598	.001	1.573
Parental education			11.526	.009	
Degree/HE	.720	.241	8.950	.003	2.054
A level	-.098	.347	.080	.777	.907
GCSE/O level	-.238	.242	.966	.326	.788
None	-.384	.218	3.099	.078	.681
Young person's party attachment					
No party attachment	-.643	.174	13.631	.000	.526
Party attachment	.643	.174	13.631	.000	1.903
Constant	-.809	.189	18.360	.000	.445

Base: 285

Variable(s) entered on step 1: young person's party attachment
Variable(s) entered on step 2: age
Variable(s) entered on step 3: parental education

Variables included but not selected as significant: sex, parental political interest, parental party attachment, household income

2003: A great deal, quite a lot, or some political interest

	B	S.E.	Wald	Sig.	Exp(B)
Parental political interest			13.097	.004	
A great deal/quite a lot	.550	.177	9.659	.002	1.733
Some	.069	.162	.180	.671	1.071
Not much	-.144	.200	.514	.473	.866
None	-.475	.251	3.570	.059	.622
Young person's party attachment					
No party attachment	-.669	.103	41.895	.000	.512
Party attachment	.669	.103	41.895	.000	1.952
Constant	-.850	.115	54.523	.000	.427

Base: 524

Variable(s) entered on step 1: young person's party attachment
Variable(s) entered on step 2: parental political interest

Variables included but not selected as significant: young person's sex, young person's age, parental party attachment, parental education, household income

1994: Has attachment to a political party

	B	S.E.	Wald	Sig.	Exp(B)
Parental party attachment					
No party attachment	.494	.179	7.597	.006	1.638
Party attachment	-.494	.179	7.597	.006	.610
Young person's political interest					
Not a lot, none	-.687	.171	16.077	.000	.503
A great deal, quite a lot, some	.687	.171	16.077	.000	1.988
Constant	.922	.203	20.531	.000	2.514

Base: 285

Variable(s) entered on step 1: young person's interest in politics
Variable(s) entered on step 2: parental party attachment

Variables included but not selected as significant: young person's sex, young person's age, parental political interest, parental education, household income

2003: Has attachment to a political party

	B	S.E.	Wald	Sig.	Exp(B)
Young person's age					
12-15	-.375	.104	12.958	.000	.687
16-19	.375	.104	12.958	.000	1.455
Parental education			9.602	.022	
Degree/HE	.343	.170	4.048	.044	1.409
A level	.235	.207	1.287	.257	1.265
O-level/GCSE	-.419	.169	6.163	.013	.658
None	-.159	.224	.501	.479	.853
Parental political interest			13.097	.004	
Great deal/quite a lot interest	.653	.191	11.721	.001	1.922
Some	-.154	.161	.916	.338	.857
Not very much	-.013	.194	.004	.947	.987
None	-.486	.250	3.781	.052	.615
Young person's sex					
Man	.266	.101	6.851	.009	1.304
Women	-.266	.101	6.851	.009	.767
Young person's political interest					
Not a lot, none	-.644	.107	36.300	.000	.525
A great deal, quite a lot, some	.644	.107	36.300	.000	1.904
Constant	-.148	.124	1.433	.231	.862

Base: 524

Variable(s) entered on step 1: young person's political interest
Variable(s) entered on step 2: parental political interest
Variable(s) entered on step 3: young person's age
Variable(s) entered on step 4: young person's sex
Variable(s) entered on step 5: parental education

Variables included but not selected as significant: parental party identification, household income

1998: Belief that it is everyone's duty to vote

	B	S.E.	Wald	Sig.	Exp(B)
Young person's party attachment					
No party attachment	-.357	.130	7.528	.006	.700
Party attachment	.357	.130	7.528	.006	1.429
Young person's political interest					
Not a lot, none	-.318	.123	6.647	.010	.728
A great deal, quite a lot, some	.318	.123	6.647	.010	1.375
Constant	-.619	.133	21.669	.000	.538
Base: 350					

Variable(s) entered on step 1: young person's party attachment
Variable(s) entered on step 2: young person's interest in politics

Variables included but not selected as significant: young person's sex, young person's age, parental political interest, parental party attachment, parental education, household income.

2003: Belief that it is everyone's duty to vote

	B	S.E.	Wald	Sig.	Exp(B)
Parental political interest			11.219	.011	
Great deal/quite a lot interest	.260	.183	2.026	.155	1.298
Some	.464	.158	8.629	.003	1.591
Not very much	-.083	.200	.172	.679	.921
None	-.642	.263	5.957	.015	.526
Young person's political interest					
Not a lot, none	-.335	.108	9.627	.002	.716
A great deal, quite a lot, some	.335	.108	9.627	.002	1.397
Young person's party attachment					
No party attachment	-.327	.106	9.515	.002	.721
Party attachment	.327	.106	9.515	.002	1.387
Constant	-.805	.121	44.506	.000	.447

Base: 517

Variable(s) entered on step 1: young person's political interest

Variable(s) entered on step 2: young person's party attachment

Variable(s) entered on step 3: parental political interest

Variables included but not selected as significant: young person's sex, young person's age, parental party attachment, parental education, household income

3 Teenagers on family values

Miranda Phillips [*]

The last two decades have seen a so-called 'revolution' in behaviour relating to gender roles and the family, marriage and sex. Women's employment rates are at their highest point since the First World War, a development which fundamentally challenges traditional gender roles – the notion of man as 'breadwinner' and woman as 'homemaker'. Indeed, the most recent increase in labour market participation has been concentrated among mothers with young children. Dramatic changes have also taken place in relation to marriage, cohabitation and divorce – changes which, according to some, signal a regrettable decline in 'family values'. And, the age at which young people have their first sexual experience appears to be markedly lower now than it was in previous decades (Wellings *et al.*, 2001).

Previous *British Social Attitudes Reports* have found that adult attitudes towards gender roles, marriage and sex have been moving hand in hand with social trends, towards increased tolerance and liberalism. The British public are now less attached to the idea of traditional gender roles, more supportive of working women, more accepting of cohabitation, and more permissive in their attitudes towards sexual behaviour. We know little, however, about young people's views – a group who are likely to have experienced the impact of these changes directly, without necessarily having yet been able to benefit personally from the increased choice and independence that some of them offer.

How might we expect young people's views on these issues to differ from those held by adults? Much of the literature asserts the *distinctiveness* of younger groups, with adolescence being seen as an important phase in an individual's life (Davis, 1990). Research among adults has found that the views of younger generations differ radically to those held by their elders (for example, Park, 2000; Crompton *et al.*, 2003). In general, the young appear to have more liberal, tolerant and unconventional attitudes than older groups,

---

[*] Miranda Phillips is a Senior Researcher at the *National Centre for Social Research*, and is Co-Director of the *British Social Attitudes* survey series.

though the findings are varied. Partly, this is likely to reflect the different circumstances within which particular generations have come of age, as well as current social reality. If this is the case, we might expect to find quite dramatic differences between the views of young people and adults on issues relating to gender roles, relationships and sex. After all, many more young people now than before have mothers in paid employment, will have experienced the breakdown of their parents' relationship, or live in a family headed by a single parent. Others argue that the distinctiveness of youth reflects their desire for independence, and their consequent challenging of adult norms and rules. This is often cited as an explanation for adolescent rebellion, risk-taking and deviant behaviour. This characterisation of young people is often seen in the media, which has a tendency to focus upon rather negative stereotypes, as suggested by reporting about 'yobs', 'tearaways', and more recent coverage of Anti-Social Behaviour Orders (ASBOs).

However, some suggest that young people are not quite as distinctive in their attitudes and values as we might imagine. Key cognitive and psychological developments occur during later childhood and teenage years, leading to increased cognitive ability and an increased capacity for weighing up sides of an argument, developing abstract thought, and empathising with other people's views (see, for instance, Coleman and Hendry, 1999). In this sense, young people's attitudes might be expected to crystallise during their teenage years, and then converge with those of young adults. Adolescence can thus be seen as a period of transition during which a young person leaves childhood behind and looks ahead to adult life. Some studies have found notable consensus between the attitudes and values of adults and young people (for example, McGrellis *et al.*, 2000), and have argued that the notion of a 'generation gap' has been overstated (Davis, 1990).

This chapter explores young people's attitudes towards three issues which broadly relate to families and relationships: gender roles and female employment; marriage and parenthood; and sexual behaviour. It makes use of data from the *Young People's Social Attitudes* surveys of 1994, 1998 and 2003, each of which involved interviews with young people aged between 12 and 19 who lived in the same households as adult *British Social Attitudes* respondents. This allows us to examine not only young people's views, and how they have changed over time, but also how they relate to those of their parents. The chapter begins by exploring whether teenagers and adults *really* do have markedly different views, allowing us to assess how distinctive young people's attitudes really are. It then considers how young people have responded to the dramatic societal changes of the last few decades, exploring whether their views, like those of adults, have become increasingly liberal, or whether they have remained static or even hardened.

Where we find differences between young people and adults, we explore whether this can best be seen as a response to the reality of growing up in modern Britain, teenage rebellion, or simply part of a smooth 'transition' to adulthood (although these three explanations are not, of course, mutually exclusive). To assess this, we are helped by the fact that we can compare young people's views with those of younger adults interviewed as part of the *British*

Social Attitudes survey. Moreover, on some issues, we can compare young people's views with those held by their parents, allowing us to see how much influence parental views have. The chapter also examines variations among young people, allowing us to assess whether the views of particular groups differ. In particular, we examine whether young people with direct experience of some of the issues in question (for example, those living in one-parent families or who have working mothers) have distinctive views, as well as whether there are differences between boys and girls, or those from different socio-economic and religious backgrounds.

Gender roles and working women

Female employment now stands at a record high level, following an increase of 1.39 million women in employment between 1992 and 2002 (Duffield, 2002). Moreover, the increased female participation in the labour market during the 1990s was entirely concentrated among women with children, and was particularly marked for women with very young children (Dench *et al.*, 2002). Indeed, women are now more likely to return to work after childbirth than at any time in the past. These labour market trends will clearly have an impact on family life, and also upon the traditional stereotype of man as 'breadwinner'; Crompton *et al.* (2003) found that the proportion of couples where the man was the sole breadwinner fell from a third in 1989 to a sixth in 2002. Such dramatic societal changes have been accompanied by changes in people's attitudes towards both working women generally and gender roles. However, Crompton *et al.* (2003) found that much of this change in people's views happened before the mid-1990s; since then, there is evidence of an apparent slowing down (or even reversal) of the trend towards more liberal views, leading them to speculate that we might be witnessing a very slight 'backlash' against working mothers. So we begin by exploring how young people have responded to this historically high rate of female employment and, in particular, whether the increased propensity of women to combine motherhood and paid work has had a positive or negative effect on the views of young people. Do young people's attitudes mirror those of adults, becoming more supportive over time, or can we find evidence of the possible backlash that has been suggested?

To assess this, we asked young people how much they agreed or disagreed with the four following statements – two which focus specifically on working mothers and the impact this might have on families and children, and two which concern women's employment more generally:

> *A working mother can establish just as warm and secure a relationship with her child as a mother who does not work*
>
> *All in all, family life suffers when the woman has a full-time job*
>
> *Having a job is the best way for a woman to be an independent person*
>
> *A man's job is to earn money; a woman's job is to look after the home and family*

In Table 3.1 we show the proportion of young people who take the most 'liberal' view of each of these statements, as well as the proportion of adults who took these views when we last asked these questions in 2002.[1] This shows that teenagers are clearly more liberal in their attitudes than adults; on three out of the four statements, the proportion of young people taking the most liberal view is around ten percentage points higher than it is among adults. The difference is most marked in relation to whether working mothers can have "just as warm and secure" a relationship with their children as mothers who do not have paid work – nearly eight in ten young people agree that they can, compared to 64 per cent of adults. The one exception to this pattern is in responses to the statement that "having a job is the best way for a woman to be an independent person", where the views of adults and young people do not really differ.

Table 3.1 Attitudes towards working women and gender roles, young people and adults

	12–19 (2003)	All adults (2002)
% agree		
Working mother can have as warm and secure a relationship with child as a non-working mother	78	64
Job is best way for woman to be independent	50	53
% disagree		
Family life suffers if woman has a full-time job	52	43
Man's job to earn money, woman's job to look after home and family	73	63
Base	*663*	*1960*

How have young people's views changed over the last decade? Here the pattern is mixed. Young people are *more* supportive now of working mothers and are less likely to see this as having a detrimental impact on family life. As Table 3.2 shows, there has been a nine percentage point increase in the proportion who think that a working mother can have just as good a relationship with her child as a mother who doesn't work, from 69 to 78 per cent. And more young people now *disagree* with the view that family life suffers if a woman has a full-time job. However, when it comes to the more general statements about women working, young people's opinions appear to have hardened somewhat. First, in relation to 'traditional' gender roles, fewer young people now disagree with the view that it is a man's 'job' to be breadwinner and a woman's to be homemaker than did so in 1994. And there has been an 11 percentage point decrease since

1994 in the percentage agreeing that a job is the best way for a woman to be independent, down from 61 to 50 per cent. However, this cannot necessarily be seen as an indication of a return to traditional views; rather, it is likely to reflect changing perceptions of what constitutes female independence.

Changes have also taken place among adults, though in a slightly different way. While the young have become increasingly supportive of working mothers since 1994, adult views have either been stable or become less liberal. And, while young people have become more conservative in their views about gender roles, adults have become more liberal. Despite this, young people remain more liberal in their outlook than adults.

Table 3.2 Attitudes towards working women and gender roles, young people and adults, 1994 and 2002/3

	12–19			18+		
	1994	2003	Change	1994	2002	Change
% agree						
Working mother can have as good a relationship with child as a non-working mother	69	78	+9	63	64	+1
Job is best way for woman to be independent	61	50	-11	59	53	-6
% disagree						
Family life suffers if woman has a full-time job	47	52	+5	50	43	-7
Man's job to earn money, woman's job to look after home and family	78	73	-5	58	63	+5
Base	*580*	*663*		*984*	*1960*	

Older teenagers, aged between 16 and 19, tend to express more liberal and egalitarian views about these matters than younger groups. As the next table shows, this difference is most marked in relation to the statement "family life suffers when the woman has a full-time job". Nearly two-thirds of 16–19 year olds *disagree* with this view, compared to under half of 12–15 year olds. The youngest group in our sample, those aged between 12 and 13 are the most conventional of all; 64 per cent *disagree* with the view that it's a man's job to earn money and a woman's job to look after home and family, compared to 76 per cent of 14–15 year olds and 81 per cent of 18–19 year olds. Table 3.3 also shows that although young people's views differ to those of adults overall, they are similar to those held by the youngest adults in our sample, those aged between 18 and 24.

Table 3.3 Young people's attitudes towards gender roles, by age

	12–15	16–19	18–24 (2002)
% agree			
Working mother can have as warm and secure a relationship with child as a non-working mother	79	75	67
Job is best way for woman to be independent	48	53	51
% disagree			
Family life suffers if woman has a full-time job	46	63	60
Man's job to earn money, woman's job to look after home and family	70	78	84
Base	*417*	*246*	*148*

One interpretation of these findings is that attitudes towards these issues develop during a person's adolescence and their early adulthood. As our surveys of young people did not involve interviewing the same groups of people in 1994, 1998 and 2003, we cannot use them to track how an individual's views might change as they get older. However, by combining information from the *Young People's Social Attitudes* survey with that from the adult *British Social Attitudes* surveys carried out in the same years we can track the attitudes of particular cohorts of young people (that is, people born during the same period). For example, we can examine how attitudes to gender roles have developed over time among those young people aged 12–15 in 1994 by looking at 16–19 year olds in 1998 and 21–24 year olds in 2003.

This analysis is shown in Table 3.4. Each cohort's years of birth are described in the first column of the table. Each row then shows the proportion of people who *disagree* with the view that family life suffers when a woman works in 1994, 1998 and 2003, in order to see whether, as they get older, their views change. Take the cohort born between 1979 and 1982 (who are highlighted in bold in the table). In 1994, when they were 12–15, 43 per cent disagreed with this statement. Four years later, in 1998, this proportion had grown to 50 per cent, rising to 57 per cent by the time they had reached their early twenties. An even more dramatic change took place among the next cohort; when they were 12–15, 41 per cent disagreed with the view that family life suffers when a women works, compared with 63 per cent of the same cohort at the age of 17–19.

Table 3.4 Family life suffers if woman has full-time job, cohort analysis, 1994-2003[2]

% disagree family life suffers	1994	1998	2003	Change (1994-2003)
All 12–19 year olds	47	45	52	+5
Cohort	(age in brackets)	(age in brackets)	(age in brackets)	
1975–1978	52 (16–19)	68 (20–23)	58 (25–28)*	+6
1979–1982	**43 (12–15)**	**50 (16–19)**	**57 (21–24)***	**+14**
1983–1986[3]		41 (12–15)	63 (17–19)	+22
1988–1991			46 (12–15)	n/a

* = data from 2002

A similar pattern emerges when we carry out the same exercise in relation to our statement about traditional gender roles, with the movement from one's late adolescence to early adulthood being associated with increasingly liberal views. However, when it comes to whether a working mother can have as good a relationship with her child as a non-working mother, there is little evidence of a change in view as young people age. On this issue, views appear to remain fairly fixed throughout one's teenage years and into one's early twenties.

The age of the young person was not the only characteristic associated with different views on these matters. In general, teenage girls emerge as being far more liberal and egalitarian on these matters than boys, particularly when it comes to views about 'traditional' gender roles. Around eight in ten (81 per cent) girls disagree with traditional views about the respective roles of men and women, compared with just over six in ten (63 per cent) boys. The same observations have been made elsewhere about men and women in their twenties and thirties (Crompton et al., 2003) and adolescents (Furnham and Gunter, 1989).

Those living in the most financially disadvantaged households have the *least* liberal views about the impact of a mother's paid employment on family life. To assess this, we divided our sample of young people into four income groups, based upon the information obtained about their household's income during the *British Social Attitudes* survey. Only four in ten young people living in the poorest households *disagree* with the view that family life suffers when a woman works, compared to nearly six in ten of those in other households. An even starker difference is shown in Table 3.5, which examines views about traditional gender roles. Just over half of those in the poorest households disagree with traditional notions of gender roles, compared to eight in ten of those in the richest homes. However, income was not clearly related to young people's views about the other two statements we considered. A range of other socio-economic characteristics were associated with differences of opinion on these issues, including class and parental education. However, if we examine the relative importance of a range of different factors using multivariate analysis, education and class cease to be significant once income is taken into account (and so we do not report them here).[4]

Table 3.5 Man's job to earn money, woman's job to look after home and family, by household income

	Household income quartile			
	Lowest	**2nd lowest**	**2nd highest**	**Highest**
	%	%	%	%
Agree	30	14	7	9
Neither agree nor disagree	15	11	6	10
Disagree	55	72	87	81
Base	*141*	*132*	*152*	*118*

Note: Based on all young people for whom parental data is available

The clearest relationship between young people's backgrounds and their views about gender roles and female employment relates to perhaps the most relevant consideration of all; whether the young person's mother works or not. Young people whose mothers are in paid work are far more supportive and liberal in their views than young people whose mothers do not work. As Table 3.6 shows, there is virtually a 20 percentage point gap between the views of these two groups on the assertions that family life "suffers" if a woman works, and that it is a man's job to earn money and a woman's to look after the home and family. In the latter case, for instance, nearly eight in ten of those whose mothers work disagree, compared with six in ten of those whose mothers do not work. The importance of this relationship, while taking into account differences in income, education and class, is confirmed by multivariate analysis.

Table 3.6 Young people's attitudes towards gender roles, by whether their mother has a paid job

	Mother not in paid work	Mother in paid work
% agree		
Working mother can have as warm and secure a relationship with child as a non-working mother	70	81
Job is best way for woman to be independent	47	53
% disagree		
Family life suffers if woman has a full-time job	40	58
Man's job to earn money, woman's job to look after home and family	60	79
Base	*203*	*388*

Note: Based on all young people for whom parental data is available

So far, therefore, we have found clear evidence that young people are considerably more liberal than adults in their views about gender roles and female employment. However, this does not reflect a huge generation gap; rather, teenagers' views are very similar to those held by younger adults (indeed, if we trace the development of young people's views as they age, we can see that their views about gender roles become increasingly liberal during their late teenage years, and into their early twenties).

We have also found that young people's views overall have changed over the last decade. This is particularly true as regards working mothers, of whom young people are more supportive now than before. By contrast, there has been little change of view among adults or, in the case of whether family life "suffers" if a women works, a hardening of view. And even young people are slightly *less* rejecting now of traditional gender roles than they were in 1994 (although they remain more liberal on this issue than adults). But it is hard to put this change down to a 'backlash' against increasing levels of female employment; young people with working mothers remain substantially more supportive of working women than are teenagers whose mothers do not work.

Relationships: cohabitation, marriage and lone parenthood

In 2001, marriages in Britain were at their lowest level since the First World War. The divorce rate increased steadily in the 1970s and 1980s, levelling off in the 1990s (Coleman, 2000; Barlow *et al.*, 2001). Cohabitation rates have increased, rising from five to 15 per cent between 1986 and 1999, and there has been a considerable rise in lone parenthood – more than doubling since 1971 (Barlow *et al.*, 2001). Around a quarter of dependent children now live with a lone parent (Dench *et al.*, 2002).

To assess young people's views about family formation and relationships, we asked them whether they agreed or disagreed with the following statements:

> *It is all right for a couple to live together without intending to get married*
>
> *It's a good idea for a couple who intend to get married to live together first*
>
> *One parent can bring up a child as well as two parents*
>
> *When there are children in the family, parents should stay together even if they don't get along*

In most cases, we can compare young people's responses to those of adults. And, as seen in Table 3.7, young people are notably more liberal in their views. Indeed, there is a gulf in attitudes between young and old on whether one parent can bring up a child as well as two; seven in ten young people agree that they can, nearly double the rate found among adults. Cohabitation is supported by the majority of both groups, but while 85 per cent of young people think it acceptable to live together without intending to marry, only 69 per cent of adults agree.

Table 3.7 Attitudes towards marriage, cohabitation, and family type, young people and adults

	12–19	18+ (2002)
% agree		
All right for a couple to live together and not marry	85	69
Good idea to live together first if intend to marry	73	61
One parent can bring up a child as well as two	70	39
% disagree		
When there are children, parents should stay together	66	n/a
Base	*663*	*1960*

n/a = not asked

Young people's views on lone parenthood have become more liberal over time. Table 3.8 shows that seven in ten now think that one parent can bring up a child as well as two, compared with just over half in 1994. They are also less likely to think that couples should stay together 'for the sake of the children'. However, a more mixed picture emerges in relation to cohabitation. Here we find a modest increase in the proportion agreeing that cohabitation is "all right", but a nine percentage point decline in the percentage who would recommend cohabitation to a couple before marriage. This suggests that, while young people are increasingly likely to *tolerate* a situation which is now widespread, they are less likely now to actively *advocate* it. That said, three-quarters of young people do advocate living together before marriage.

During the same period adult opinion about these issues has shifted in a consistently liberal direction. However, these changes are far more modest than those found among young people. Unfortunately, adults were not asked in 2002 about their views on relationship breakdown where children are involved, meaning that we cannot see how their views have changed alongside those of young people.

Table 3.8 Attitudes towards marriage, cohabitation, and family type, young people and adults, 1994 and 2002/3

	12–19			18+		
	1994	**2003**	**Change**	**1994**	**2002**	**Change**
% agree						
All right for a couple to live together and not marry	80	85	+5	64	69	+5
Good idea to live together first if intend to marry	82	73	-9	58	61	+3
One parent can bring up a child as well as two	55	70	+15	35	39	+4
% disagree						
When there are children, parents should stay together	59	66	+7	56	n/a	
Base	*580*	*663*		*984*	*1960*	

n/a = not asked

As we found with attitudes to gender roles, older teenagers generally have more liberal views than younger ones on cohabitation, marriage and relationships. The differences are generally fairly modest, though there is a large difference in relation to whether "when there are children in the family, parents should stay together even if they don't get along". On this issue, younger groups are more likely than older ones to think that parents should put their children first; seven in ten (72 per cent) 16–19 year olds disagree with this notion, compared to six in ten (62 per cent) 12–15 year olds (and, within this group, 56 per cent of 12–13 year olds).

To what extent do the views of teenagers tally with those of young adults (those aged 18 to 24)? The two groups do, in fact, have fairly similar views on cohabitation and marriage, but there is a large difference between their attitudes to lone parents. Only 55 per cent of 18–24 year olds think that one parent can bring up a child as well as two, compared to 70 per cent of 12–19 year olds. On this measure, then, teenagers' views are distinctive even when compared to those of young adults.

Earlier we found that girls were more likely than boys to have more liberal views about gender roles. The same applies to their views on marriage and cohabitation. Both our research, and that of others, finds young men to be more conventional and pro-marriage than young women (Sharpe, 2001). Table 3.9 shows that, as was the case with age, the difference is most marked in responses to the view that parents should stay together for their children's sake. Three-quarters of girls disagree with this, compared to 55 per cent of boys – a substantial difference. The only exception to this tendency for girls to be more liberal is that boys are more likely to advocate cohabitation for a couple intending to marry.

Table 3.9 Young people's attitudes towards marriage, cohabitation, and family type, by sex

	Boys	Girls
% agree		
All right for a couple to live together and not marry	83	86
Good idea to live together first if intend to marry	76	71
One parent can bring up a child as well as two	63	77
% disagree		
When there are children, parents should stay together	55	75
Base	*303*	*360*

Not surprisingly, perhaps, religion is strongly related to views about cohabitation. As shown in Table 3.10, nine in ten young people who do not belong to a religion think that this is "all right", compared to just seven in ten of their more religious counterparts.

Table 3.10 Young people's attitudes towards marriage, cohabitation, and family type, by whether belongs to a religion

	Does not belong to a religion	Belongs to a religion
% agree		
All right for a couple to live together and not marry	92	71
Good idea to live together first if intend to marry	76	68
One parent can bring up a child as well as two	73	66
% disagree		
When there are children, parents should stay together	67	63
Base	*430*	*231*

Perhaps the most relevant comparison is to examine the views of those young people who are themselves growing up within a lone-parent family. Table 3.11 shows that teenagers in this group are markedly more likely to think that one parent can bring up a child as well as two, nearly nine in ten doing so, compared to two-thirds of young people living in couple families. The former are also more likely to advocate cohabitation before marriage. Regression analysis shows that family type is significantly associated with views on these matters once other characteristics are taken into account.

Table 3.11 One parent can bring up a child as well as two, by family type

	Couple	Lone parent
	%	%
Agree	65	87
Neither agree nor disagree	14	7
Disagree	21	6
Base	*448*	*143*

Note: Based on all young people for whom parental data is available

Earlier we found that young people in more socio-economically 'advantaged' homes (whether measured by income, class or parental education) tended to have more liberal views about gender roles and female employment than young people in less advantaged ones. The same is *not* true in relation to views about single parenthood; here, young people with parents who are graduates or hold another higher education qualification are notably *less* approving. As seen in Table 3.12, eight in ten of those whose parent has no qualifications think that one parent can bring up a child just as well as two parents, compared to only six in ten of those whose parent has a higher education qualification. However, the latter are more likely than the former to *disagree* with the view that a couple with children should stay together if they don't get on. Half of those whose parent has no qualifications oppose this idea, compared to seven in ten young people whose parent has a higher education qualification. Similar differences apply when we consider young people's views in relation to their household income or their parent's class, with those in less advantaged homes being notably more likely to see single parenthood as acceptable, but more likely to think that parents should stay together for their children's sake. However, once parental education is taken into account, class and income do not emerge as significantly related to young people's views.

This relationship between young people's views about lone parenthood and their parent's education cannot solely be accounted for by the fact that lone parenthood is less common among those with more academic qualifications. Both parental education and family type are significantly associated with young people's views, even when their interrelationship is taken into account. A similar relationship between education and less 'liberal' attitudes towards relationships has been found among adults (Barlow *et al.*, 2001), suggesting that 'middle-class' values on marriage and parenthood are notably *less* liberal than they are in other areas.

Table 3.12 Young people's attitudes towards family type, by parental education

| | Parent's highest educational qualification | | | |
	Higher education	A Level or equiv.	GCSE or equiv.	None
% agree				
One parent can bring up a child as well as two	59	68	77	78
% disagree				
When there are children, parents should stay together	69	71	64	52
Base	*185*	*85*	*210*	*99*

Note: Based on all young people for whom parental data is available

As was the case with gender roles and female employment, young people are notably more liberal than adults in their views about families and relationships. Indeed, there is a considerable gulf in attitudes between young and old on whether one parent can bring up a child as well as two. On this issue, young people's views have become much more liberal over time. However, it appears that young people are *less* likely now to actively advocate cohabitation before marriage than they were in 1994 (even though they are increasingly likely to tolerate it).

The issue of single-parent families is one which divides teenagers even from young adults. Here, then, is a subject on which there truly does seem to be a generation gap; whereas 55 per cent of 18–24 year olds think one parent can bring up a child as well as two, 70 per cent of 12–19 year olds do so, 15 percentage points more than in 1994. To some extent, this is likely to reflect the different experiences of these groups and the increasing prevalence of lone-parent families. After all, as we have seen, teenagers who themselves grow up in a lone-parent family are much more accepting of lone parenthood than those who are living in a couple family.

Sexual behaviour

Unlike the previous two topics, there is less direct evidence as to how sexual behaviour has changed over the last few decades. Under-age sex, one of the issues we consider here, is notoriously hard to measure due to the lack of survey evidence for under 16s. However, that evidence which *does* exist suggests that teenagers are becoming sexually active at younger ages than in the past (Coleman, 2000). A recent report based on the *National Survey of Sexual Attitudes and Lifestyles* found that, among 16–19 year olds, 30 per cent of men and 26 per cent of women first had sex before they were 16 – a substantially higher proportion than that found among adults aged 35 and over (Wellings *et al.*, 2001). This suggests that younger groups are becoming sexually active at an earlier age than their predecessors. However, clear evidence exists of changing *attitudes* towards sexual behaviour. In particular, there has been a marked increase in permissiveness about pre-marital sex. For instance, the proportion of people who think there is "nothing wrong" with sex before marriage increased from 42 in 1984 to 62 per cent in 2000 (Barlow *et al.*, 2001).

We asked young people for their view on the rights and wrongs of two forms of sexual relationship, with the range of answer options distinguishing between extreme and more moderate views: "always wrong", "mostly wrong", "sometimes wrong", "rarely wrong" and "not wrong at all":

> *Now some questions about sexual relationships. Firstly, if a man and a woman have sexual relations before marriage, what would your general opinion be?*
>
> *What if it was a boy and a girl who were both still under 16?*

As Table 3.13 suggests, both young people and adults are far more permissive when it comes to pre-marital sex than they are about under-age sex. However, young people are notably more permissive about under-age sex than adults, with just a third thinking this is "always wrong", around half the rate found among adults. However, only small proportions of both groups think that it is "not wrong at all", though this view is held by more than twice as many young people as adults. Attitudes towards pre-marital sex do not vary to the same extent; in fact, more adults than young people say it is "not wrong at all" (63 compared to 54 per cent). This is, in fact, the only one of the measures considered in this chapter in which adults express *more* liberal views than young people!

The differences in attitudes towards the two contrasting situations is striking, and no doubt partly reflects the fact that under-age sex is illegal; while pre-marital sex might be considered immoral by those with conservative or traditional views, it is not against the law. However, the fact that young people are notably more liberal in their views about under-age sex suggests that this is an area about which they have formed views based less upon legality and more upon their own experiences and those of their peer-group. It has also been suggested that, on topics where communication within families is poor (which may be the case when it comes to under-age sex) attitudes between generations are most likely to diverge (Coleman and Hendry, 1999).

Table 3.13 Attitudes towards sexual relationships, young people and adults

	12–19	18+
Under-age sex	%	%
Always wrong	34	61
Mostly, sometimes or rarely wrong	56	34
Not wrong at all	5	2
Pre-marital sex	%	%
Always wrong	5	8
Mostly, sometimes or rarely wrong	36	25
Not wrong at all	54	63
Base	*663*	*2139*

Young people's views on these issues have changed little since 1998, when these questions were first asked. Over the same period, adults have become slightly more censorious about under-age sex (with a five point increase in the proportion saying this is "always wrong") and less censorious about pre-marital sex (with a five percentage point increase in the proportion saying that this is "not wrong at all").

Younger teenagers are notably *less* permissive in their views than older ones. As the next table shows, 16–19 year olds are both more likely to condone and less likely to condemn under-age and pre-marital sex. Indeed, the youngest teenagers in our sample, those aged 12–13, were the most condemning of both, with nearly half thinking that under-age sex is always wrong. When we compare older teenagers with young adults, aged 18–24, their views are notably similar in relation to pre-marital sex (with around a third seeing it as not wrong at all) but remarkably different in relation to under-age sex. Here, young adults were twice as likely to condemn it as older teenagers (50 and 27 per cent respectively). On this issue, therefore, it does seem that teenagers have notably distinctive views.

Table 3.14 Young people's attitudes towards sexual relationships, by age

	12–15	16–19	18–24
Under-age sex	%	%	%
Always wrong	39	27	50
Mostly, sometimes or rarely wrong	53	62	45
Not wrong at all	4	8	2
Pre-marital sex	%	%	%
Always wrong	6	4	8
Mostly, sometimes or rarely wrong	41	27	21
Not wrong at all	46	68	67
Base	*417*	*246*	*160*

Gender is not strongly related to views about sexual behaviour, with boys and girls having broadly similar views on the subject. That said, there is a small but consistent tendency for boys to take the most permissive view of all, that pre-marital or under-age sex is "not wrong at all". This difference is statistically significant in relation to under-age sex (eight compared to three per cent), but not for pre-marital sex (57 compared to 52 per cent). This tallies with other research which has found that teenage boys tend to be more liberal on these issues than girls (Sharpe, 2002) and that men are more liberal than women. It is notable, however, that this is the one area we have considered in which boys are more liberal in their views than girls (with the exception of the desirability of cohabitation).

Earlier we found that religious affiliation is linked to views about relationships. So it is not surprising that teenagers who are religious are more likely than those who are not to condemn under-age and pre-marital sex. As Table 3.15 shows, whereas six in ten teenagers with no religious affiliation say that pre-marital sex is "not wrong at all", just four in ten of their religious counterparts agree. A similar pattern exists in relation to under-age sex, with nearly half of religious young people saying this is "always wrong", compared to under a third of those with no religion. The importance of religion in explaining young people's views is confirmed by multivariate analysis.

Table 3.15 Young people's attitudes towards sexual relationships, by whether religious

	Does not belong to a religion	Belongs to a religion
Under-age sex	%	%
Always wrong	29	45
Mostly, sometimes or rarely wrong	61	48
Not wrong at all	6	3
Pre-marital sex	%	%
Always wrong	1	13
Mostly, sometimes or rarely wrong	32	45
Not wrong at all	63	39
Base	*430*	*231*

As levels of religiosity are higher among adults than young people, we also need to consider whether parental religious attachment plays any part in shaping attitudes among those young people who are not themselves religious. While young people with religious parents are more likely to have conservative views about sex, the relationship is less clear if the young person is not religious themselves. However, the relationship between young people's *own* religiosity (as opposed to their parents') and their views about sexual behaviour is far stronger.

A range of other characteristics are associated with differences of view about sexual behaviour. On the whole, young people in less socio-economically advantaged homes are less liberal in their views than those in more advantaged ones. Yet those living in a lone-parent household are more permissive about pre-marital sex than those living with a couple. Six in ten (61 per cent) think this is "not wrong at all", compared to half (51 per cent) of those living with a couple. However, parental education, income, class, and household type did not emerge as significantly related to views about sex once other factors such as religion and age were taken into account.

Many writers have discussed the likely influence of parents (and other family members) on young people's behaviour and attitudes towards sex (Coleman and

Hendry, 1999). To what extent, then, is there a correspondence between parental and teenage views on this issue? Table 3.16 groups young people according to their parent's view about pre-marital sex, and then examines the extent to which these groups of young people differ. It shows that there is a strong relationship between parental and teenage views, with six in ten young people whose parent thinks pre-marital sex is "not wrong at all" taking this view themselves, compared to just over three in ten of young people with parents who hold the alternative view.

Parental views about sex are also linked to young people's attitudes towards under-age sex, but the relationship is weaker than that shown in Table 3.16. This lower level of congruence between parental and teenage views on under-age sex might reflect the fact that young people's views on these matters are shaped more by personal experience and discussions with their peers than by family.

Table 3.16 Young people's attitudes towards pre-marital sex, by parent's view

	Parent's view	
	Always, mostly, sometimes, rarely wrong	Not at all wrong
Young person's view	%	%
Always wrong	16	2
Mostly, sometimes or rarely wrong	45	35
Not wrong at all	35	59
Base	*91*	*228*

Note: based on all young people for whom parental data is available

So, in contrast to our findings in relation to gender roles and family relationships, young people are slightly *less* liberal than adults about pre-marital sex. They are, however, notably more liberal when it comes to under-age sex, something which six in ten adults see as "always" wrong. This gulf between teenage and adult opinion holds true even when we compare teenagers with young adults, a half of whom take this view.

As we found earlier, older teenagers have more liberal views than younger ones, and those who describe themselves as religious are less liberal. And, as a sure sign that teenagers are not so rebellious as many would have us believe, it is clear that parental influences loom large. Teenagers with parents who hold liberal views about pre-marital sex are notably more liberal than those whose parents are more disapproving.

Conclusions

We began this chapter by asking whether young people's attitudes towards families and relationships are distinctive from those held by adults and, if so, why this might be. A number of patterns have emerged. Most importantly, it is clear that young people's views on gender roles, working women, family relationships and sex do differ from those held by adults. In some cases, these differences are very marked indeed. Teenagers are far more accepting of lone parents than are adults; a clear majority (seven in ten) of 12–19 year olds agree that one parent can bring up a child as well as two, compared to just four in ten adults. Under-age sex is another issue that clearly distinguishes between teenage and adult views, with a majority of adults thinking it to be "always" wrong, compared to just a third of young people. However, these marked differences of opinion are the exception rather than the rule. On most of the other measures we consider, the picture is more one of broad consensus, with differences in the *magnitude* of opinion rather than its direction. Moreover, differences of view between young people and adults tend to be reduced when the comparison is made with 18–24 year olds rather than with adults as a whole. There is also evidence of that young people's views about some issues, most notably sex, are closely related to those of their parents. In this sense, then, we have found little to suggest that young people's views are best explained by teenage rebellion and the rejection of adult views. Rather, they are likely to reflect the reality of their lives – lives which have been shaped by wide-ranging societal changes in relation to women's employment, marriage, cohabitation and lone parenthood. Meanwhile, although there is some evidence of a hardening of attitudes towards cohabitation and women working, the main picture painted by our findings is that young people have become more supportive of lone parents and working mothers over the last decade.

Differences *among* teenagers are considerable, complicating any notion of 'youth' as a homogenous group. Age, sex and religion are persistent factors affecting views. Older teenagers are generally more liberal or tolerant than younger groups. They are more permissive about pre-marital sex, with over two-thirds of 16–19 year olds saying this is "not wrong at all" compared to less than half of 12–15 year olds. There are similarly dramatic age differences in relation to views about whether family life "suffers" if a woman has a full-time job. Girls tend to be more liberal than boys. In particular, they are more opposed to the traditional view of gender roles; around eight in ten girls *disagree* that it's a man's job to be breadwinner and a woman's job to look after home and family, compared to just over six in ten boys. When it comes to relationships, too, boys are more likely to hold traditional views. Just over half (55 per cent) *disagree* with the view that parents should stay together for the sake of their children, even if they don't get along, compared to three-quarters of girls. And young people who are religious tend to be more traditional and conventional in their views than those who are not. This is particularly true in relation to attitudes to sex and cohabitation.

Personal experience appears to play an all-important role; teenagers who themselves live in a lone parent household are far more likely than those in couple families to think that one parent can bring up a child as well as two (nearly nine in ten agree, compared to two-thirds of young people living in couple families). There is also a clear relationship between personal experience and attitudes towards women and employment, with those who have working mothers being notably more supportive than those who do not. Indeed, six in ten young people whose mother works *disagree* that family life "suffers" if the woman works full-time, compared with just four in ten of those whose mother does not work. Other parental and household characteristics, including education, income and social class, play a minor role in shaping young people's views, although their relationship is not always consistent. Most notably, the highest level of liberalism towards lone-parents is found among those whose parents have few, or no, qualifications, despite the fact that this group are likely to have the most traditional attitudes towards gender roles.

What do our findings suggest might happen to societal attitudes over the next few decades? The fact that teenagers, like young adults, are so much more liberal than older groups suggests that British opinion overall will continue to become more liberal still, as younger generations, with their less traditional attitudes and values, gradually replace older generations, with their more traditional ones. This partly reflects the strong relationship we have found between religiosity and a person's attitudes; put simply, far more young people than adults do not define themselves as belonging to a particular religion (65 and 43 per cent respectively). Furthermore, the fact that personal experience is so closely related to attitudes, particularly towards lone parenthood and female employment, also points towards an increasingly liberal and tolerant view about these issues, as increasing numbers of young people grow up in homes in which mothers work, or which are headed by one parent.

The last few decades have been marked by considerable changes in family relationships, gender roles and sexuality. In most cases, young people appear to have responded to these changes by becoming more liberal still. There is certainly no sign that, in response to the increasing 'freedom' available to adults, young people wish to return to a more traditional view of the family and individuals' roles within it.

Notes

1. When comparing responses to questions in the *Young Person's Social Attitudes* survey (those of 12–19 year olds) with the same questions in the *British Social Attitudes* survey (18+) we need to be aware that there may be context effects. This may mean that apparent differences in opinion are, in fact, due to the impact of preceding questions. However, every effort has been made to ensure comparability in other ways – the same question wording, mode and answer options were used in the two surveys.

2.   The bases for this table are as follows:

	1994	1998	2003
All 12-19 year olds	580	474	663
Cohort			
1975–1978	227	31	117
1979–1982	346	216	80
1983–1986	–	258	169
1988–1991	–	–	417

Note: respondents who failed to give their age are excluded from the cohort breakdown.

3.   This cohort was aged 17–20 in 2003. However, the *Young People's Social Attitudes* survey only interviews the 12–19 age group (meaning we can only consider the views of those aged 17–19 that year).
4.   The findings reported in this chapter are informed by the results of a series of multivariate analyses carried out in order to identify the characteristics most strongly associated with views about families, gender roles and sex. The results of these analyses are not shown here; details are available from the author on request.

References

Barlow, A., Duncan, S., James, G. and Park, A. (2001), 'Just a piece of paper? Marriage and cohabitation', in Park, A., Curtice, J., Thomson, K., Jarvis, L. and Bromley, C. (eds.) *British Social Attitudes: the 18th Report – Public policy, Social ties*, London: Sage

Coleman, J. (2000), 'Young People in Britain at the Beginning of a New Century', *Children & Society*, **14**:230–224

Coleman, J. and Hendry, L. (1999), *The Nature of Adolescence*, London: Routledge

Crompton, R., Brockmann, M. and Wiggins, R.D. (2003), 'A woman's place … Employment and family life for men and women', in Park, A., Curtice, J., Thomson, K., Jarvis, L. and Bromley, C. (eds.), *British Social Attitudes: the 20th Report – Continuity and change over two decades*, London: Sage

Davis, J. (1990), *Youth and the Condition of Britain: Images of adolescent conflict*, London: The Athlone Press

Dench, S., Aston, J., Evans, C., Meager, N., Williams, M. and Willison, R. (2002), *Key Indicators of Women's Position in Britain*, Women and Equality Unit, London: Department of Trade and Industry

Duffield, M. (2002), 'Trends in female employment 2002', in *Labour Market Trends*, November

Furnham, A. and Gunter, B. (1989), *The Anatomy of Adolescence: Young People's Social Attitudes in Britain*, London: Routledge

McGrellis, S., Henderson, S., Holland, J., Sharpe, S. and Thomson, R. (2000), *Through the Moral Maze: a quantitative study of young people's values*, London: Tufnell Press

Park, A., (2000), 'The generation game', in Jowell, R., Curtice, J., Park, A., Thomson, K., Jarvis, L., Bromley, C. and Stratford, N. (eds.) *British Social Attitudes: the 17th Report – Focussing on diversity*, London: Sage

Sharpe, S. (2001), *More than just a piece of paper? Young people's views on marriage and relationships*, London: National Children's Bureau

Sharpe, S. (2002), '"It's Just Really Hard to Come to Terms With": young people's views on homosexuality', *Sex Education*, **2(3)**

Wellings, K., Nanchahal, K., Macdowall, W., McManus, S., Erens, B., Mercer, C.H., Johnson, A. M., Copas, A.J., Korovessis, C., Fenton, K.A. and Field, J. (2001), 'Sexual behaviour in Britain: early heterosexual experience', *The Lancet*, **358(9296)**: 1843

Acknowledgements

We are grateful to the Children, Young People's and Families Directorate in the Department for Education and Skills (formerly the Children and Young People's Unit) for funding the module of questions on which this chapter is based. Responsibility for analysis of this data lies solely with the author.

4 Can Britain close the digital divide?

Catherine Bromley [*]

The last few years have seen a marked increase in personal use of the internet. Now, 50 per cent of people use the internet (other than purely for their work), up from 33 per cent in 2000. Then, there was a significant 'digital divide' between those who did and did not use the internet, most notably in terms of their socio-economic backgrounds and their age (Gardner and Oswald, 2001), a pattern which has been identified in many other studies (Wilheim, 2000). A key aim of this chapter will be to examine whether the recent expansion of personal internet use has reduced these social differences.

We begin, however, by considering why a report on public attitudes should be interested in internet use in the first place. After all, it could be argued that the internet is just another technological innovation, on a par with the introduction of personal computers or mobile phones. If the internet was simply an extension of computer technology, then the case for analysing its reach and impact via public attitudes research would be weak. But the internet is not just a piece of software; it is a portal which has the potential to liberalise access to a whole host of resources and opportunities, and to increase social connections. Moreover, it is an important communication tool, much like newspapers, radio or television, all of which have been subjected to intense scrutiny by social scientists. It has the capacity to impart knowledge to groups which have tended to be excluded from traditional information sources, to provide new channels of communication, and to open up access to goods and services previously denied or impeded by older technologies or methods of exchange. Email has, for instance, vastly enhanced communication between people living on opposite sides of the globe, and has expanded access to all kinds of information, from travel times and weather forecasts to health advice. Indeed, the prolific extent to which the media makes reference to website and e-mail addresses could almost

[*] Catherine Bromley is a Senior Researcher at the *Scottish Centre for Social Research*, part of NatCen, and is Co-Director of the *British Social Attitudes* survey series.

lead a newcomer to Britain to conclude that the internet is *the* primary means of communication, rather than something to which just half the population has access.

From a global perspective, China provides an interesting case in point. Although its government is keen to exploit the economic gains that could accrue from internet access, the potential for it to have any wider socio-political impact is being carefully controlled through the use of surveillance, censorship and selective blocking of some services (*The Economist*, 2003). To the Chinese authorities, therefore, the internet is seen as having the potential both to create wealth and to foster critical thinking and dissent.

It is true that some of the more wildly optimistic hopes as to what the internet might deliver in terms of its potential to connect people politically and socially, most notably via the expansion of 'digital democracy' (Budge, 1996; Barber, 1999) have yet to be realised, and quite probably never will be. However, future historians will undoubtedly pinpoint the advent of widespread internet use as a key social development (see the chapter by Curtice and Norris in this volume for a detailed examination of the impact of the internet on political trust and engagement). Unless access to the internet is broadened – both within countries and cross-nationally – many millions will miss out on what the internet has to offer and, crucially, we could see the emergence of a digital underclass, excluded from all the possibilities which the majority will come to take for granted (Golding, 1998). In much the same way that literacy and numeracy empowered previous generations in the developed world (and has still to perform the same function in most of the developing world), internet access and the skills that accompany it could perform a similar function in the future.

The chapter begins by examining who uses the internet, focusing particularly on whether the recent expansion of internet use has reduced the social divisions that were so apparent in 2000. We then explore the different ways in which people use the internet, and their attitudes towards its functions and potential applications. Finally, we examine the attitudes and aspirations of *non*-users in order to better understand the reasons why large sections of the British population are not on-line. This allows us to assess the future prospects of reducing these stark social divisions in internet use.

Who is on-line?

The costs involved in internet use (such as buying the computer hardware and paying subscription fees to an internet provider) can be seen as a major barrier to internet use. Consequently, some have argued that one way of closing the digital divide is to expand public access through libraries, community centres and internet cafés. The last few years has indeed seen a vast expansion in the number of these kinds of public internet access points; in 2003 it was estimated that 89 per cent of the population lived within three kilometres of a public access point, while 99 per cent live within ten kilometres of one (Cabinet Office, 2004). However, as Table 4.1 shows, the growth in internet use between

2000 and 2003 has largely been fuelled by the growth of home access, rather than by increased take-up of more remote facilities. Between 2000 and 2003, the proportion of users with home internet access grew from 26 to 41 per cent, whereas the proportion who use the internet but who do not have access to it at home grew only two points, from seven to nine per cent.

Table 4.1 Home internet access and personal use, 2000 and 2003

	2000	2003	Change 2000–2003
Users	%	%	
Have internet access at home and use internet	26	41	+15
Do not have internet access at home but use internet elsewhere	7	9	+2
Non-users			
Have internet access at home but do not use internet	9	10	+1
Do not have internet access at home and do not use internet elsewhere	57	40	-17
Base	*2293*	*4432*	

It is also apparent that the growth of home internet access has partly been fuelled by parents. Between 2000 and 2003, home access and use amongst households with children grew from one in three (32 per cent) to over half (54 per cent), an increase of 22 percentage points. By contrast, the rate of growth amongst households without children was almost half this rate (from 23 to 35 per cent, 12 points). So, despite a mass expansion of public access sites, the story of Britain's escalating internet use largely goes hand in hand with increasing ownership of home computers – often, it would seem, at the behest of demanding children – rather than a stampede across the thresholds of libraries, internet cafés and other communal internet providers.

Rogers' theory of technological diffusion (1995) suggests that the first people to use new innovations such as telephones or radios are usually atypical in their social background, technical skills, and interests. However, as the costs of hardware fall and the skills required to operate the technology become more widespread, over time the user population gradually 'normalises'. Evidence from America suggests that these developments are already occurring in the United States, where more than two-thirds of the population are now on-line.[1] So, as internet access continues to spread across Britain, we might expect a diminishing of the 'digital divide' between different social use of the internet. We start by looking at whether this is in fact the case.

The reasons why the internet might be more attractive and less daunting to younger generations need little detailed exploration. But it is worth reflecting briefly on quite how rapid the pace of technological change has been over the past century. After all, 20 per cent of our respondents were born before the ballpoint pen was invented in 1938, over a half (55 per cent) before the first microchip was patented in 1959, and 71 per cent before the first handheld calculator was introduced in 1967. Just six per cent were born after IBM launched its first personal computer in 1981.

The marked age differences that exist in personal internet use are shown in Table 4.2, which examines how particular age groups differed in their use of the internet in 2000 and 2003. The 'digital divide' row shows the difference between the age groups most and least likely to use the internet (18–24 year olds and those aged 65 or over), and the third column shows the change in internet use between 2000 and 2003. This demonstrates that now, as in 2000, 18–24 year olds were markedly more likely than older groups to make personal use of the internet, and that the increase in internet use between 2000 and 2003 has actually *increased* the digital divide between these two groups, from 53 to 59 percentage points.

Table 4.2 Personal internet use, by age, 2000 and 2003

% who use the internet	2000	2003	Change 2000–2003	Base (2000)	Base (2003)
All	33	50	+17	2293	4432
Age					
18–24	58	74	+16	176	348
25–34	51	69	+18	410	749
35–44	40	65	+25	465	879
45–54	36	51	+15	339	759
55–59	23	41	+18	161	369
60–64	19	29	+10	198	300
65+	5	15	+10	538	1027
'Digital divide'	53	59	+6		

In 2000, we found that men were more likely to use the internet than women (Gardner and Oswald, 2001). Although this continues to be true, the rate of internet use by women has increased more than it has among men, meaning that the gap between these two groups is starting to close. So, while in 2000 there was a difference of 12 points between men's and women's use, by 2003 this had more than halved to just five points.[2]

Table 4.3 Personal internet use, by sex, 2000 and 2003

% who use the internet	2000	2003	Change 2000–2003	Base (2000)	Base (2003)
All	33	50	+17	2293	4432
Sex					
Men	40	53	+13	981	1959
Women	28	48	+20	1312	2473
'Digital divide'	12	5	-7		

Given the considerable financial costs involved of accessing the internet from home (as we have seen, by far the most popular form of access), and the degree of computer literacy required of users, it is unsurprising that socio-economic factors such as education, income and social class are all significant predictors of whether or not someone uses the internet. The next table illustrates this with reference to education. It shows that the growth in internet use has been greatest amongst the most qualified, with the proportion of graduates using the internet increasing by 12 percentage points between 2000 and 2003, from 72 to 84 per cent. Among those with no qualifications at all, however, internet use increased by only three points, from nine to 12 per cent. As a result, the digital divide associated with educational qualifications is now greater than ever before.

Table 4.4 Personal internet use, by highest educational qualification, 2000 and 2003

% who use the internet	2000	2003	Change 2000–2003	Base 2000	Base 2003
All	33	50	+17	2293	4432
Highest educational qualification					
Degree	72	84	+12	300	674
Higher education	47	68	+21	328	600
A level	49	69	+20	234	563
O level	30	53	+23	439	818
CSE or equivalent	21	38	+18	203	466
No qualifications	9	12	+3	740	1208
'Digital divide'	63	72	+9		

A similar pattern is evident in relation to household income and social class. Nearly eight in ten of those with a household income in the highest quartile (in 2003, those with incomes of £38,000 or above) use the internet, an increase of 18 points since 2000. Among those in the lowest income quartile (incomes of £11,999 or less), only 22 per cent use the internet, up 11 points since 2000. Consequently, the divide between these two groups now stands at 57 points, up seven points in three years. And, while 71 per cent of professionals and managers make personal use of the internet, up 18 points since 2000, the same applies to only 27 per cent of those in working-class occupations, up nine points since 2000. The digital divide between these two groups has grown from 35 to 44 points.

So, significant differences remain between the extent to which different groups use the internet. And, with the exception of gender, the recent expansion of internet use has not only failed to narrow Britain's digital divide – if anything it has exacerbated it. These findings support other analyses of the digital divide carried out cross-nationally (Norris, 2001), and also mirror the kinds of patterns evident in the US at the point when their internet use also stood at around half the population (US Department of Commerce, 2000). Of course, some of the five factors we have examined (age, sex, education, income and class) are themselves interrelated. Older people are, for instance, the most likely to have no formal education, meaning that the relationship we find between education and internet use might simply reflect the fact that older groups are the least likely to use the internet. To investigate this, we ran a multivariate logistic regression model (see Appendix I to this Report for more details of this method) which looked at the relationship between each of these five characteristics and internet use. This allows us to examine the contribution of each characteristic once the others are taken into account (see Model 1 in the appendix to this chapter for full results). This analysis reveals that all five factors are significant predictors of internet use. Even when we take account of a person's age, their level of education remains independently related to their internet use, as does their sex, social class and household income. In fact, the relationship between each factor and internet use is so significant that it is impossible to rank the factors in order of their relative contributions. The fact that these socio-demographic factors are so important in accounting for internet use underlines the extent to which the 'digital divide' is very much a social divide, and a divide which, as yet, shows no signs of diminishing.

How do people use the internet?

We now turn to examine the characteristics of those who *do* use the internet. We begin by considering where internet use most commonly takes place, and then examine the different ways in which the internet is used.

Location, location, location

As we have already discussed, the majority of internet users go on-line at home.[3] As the next table shows, the next most popular location for personal internet use is at work mentioned by 45 per cent of all users, and 59 per cent of all those actually in work (we do not include in this table people who only go on-line at work for work purposes). The least commonly mentioned places are the public access locations such as libraries and cafés, frequented by only one in fourteen users.

Table 4.5 Where do people use the internet?

	%
At home	83
At work	45
At a friend's or relative's house	15
At school / college / university	11
At an internet café	8
In a library or community centre	7
Base	*1527*

Note: Column does not sum to 100 as respondents could mention more than one location

The potential for public-access locations to increase internet use amongst those who cannot afford home access is self-evident. However, as demonstrated by Table 4.1, the impact of the dramatic expansion in the numbers of these remote locations has so far been limited, with the bulk of the recent increase in internet use reflecting an increase in access from home. But we might expect to find that, among internet users, public-access locations *are* important in enabling certain groups to go on-line. This is explored in the next table, which looks at the relationship between a range of socio-economic factors and reported use of the internet at home, work, and in libraries or community centres. It shows that the groups most likely to make use of internet facilities in a library or community centre (as well as being the least likely to have access at home), are the young (aged 18–24), those with the lowest household incomes and people in semi-routine and routine occupations. Indeed, these are the only groups among whom the use of public access facilities for internet use attains double figures. However, although public-access locations are an important source of access for these groups (two of whom, those on low incomes and in semi-routine and routine occupations, are amongst the *least* likely overall to be on-line), they remain less important than access at home or work.

Table 4.6 Location of personal internet use, by age, household income and social class

Use of the internet at ...		... home	... work[1]	... library or community centre	Base (All / all in work)
All	%	83	59	7	1527 / 1089
Age					
18–24	%	68	46	17	185 / 114
25–39	%	80	61	7	597 / 457
40–64	%	90	61	4	646 / 510
65+	%	92	(25)	2	98 / 7
Household income					
Highest quartile	%	91	79	7	428 / 327
Third quartile	%	83	57	7	570 / 420
Second quartile	%	80	44	7	439 / 298
Lowest quartile	%	66	(28)	3	87 /41
Social class					
Managerial/professional	%	88	70	4	476 /414
Intermediate	%	78	55	7	399 / 324
Self-employed	%	87	51	9	307 / 212
Lower supervisory/Technical	%	80	(24)	15	194 / 46
Semi-routine and routine	%	75	20	11	259 / 155

Notes:
1. This column is based only on those in work
Rows do not sum to 100 as respondents could mention more than one location
Cells with a base of fewer than 50 are in brackets

Table 4.6 also shows that, when it comes to personal use of the internet in the workplace, very clear social divisions exist. If we focus on social class (the factor which is, after all, most closely related to people's working environment) we find that three-quarters (76 per cent) of professionals and managers have the opportunity to use the internet at work for personal reasons, compared with just a fifth (20 per cent) of those in semi-routine and routine occupations.

What do people use the internet for?

So far we have seen that internet users have very different characteristics when it comes to *where* they access the internet. We now consider *what* people actually use the internet for. There are, of course, a vast number of different

Erratum:
Table 4.6 on page 80 contains incorrect figures. The correct figures can be found below

Table 4.6 Location of personal internet use, by age, household income and social class, 2003

Use of the internet at …		… home	… work[1]	… library or community centre	*Base (All / all in work)*
		Location of internet use			
All	%	83	59	7	*1527 / 1089*
Age					
18-24	%	68	46	17	*185 / 114*
25-39	%	80	61	7	*597 / 457*
40-64	%	90	61	4	*646 / 510*
65+	%	92	(25)	2	*98 / 7*
Household income					
Highest quartile	%	91	70	4	*476 /414*
Third quartile	%	83	55	7	*399 / 324*
Second quartile	%	80	51	9	*307 / 212*
Lowest quartile	%	66	(24)	15	*194 / 46*
Social class					
Managerial / professional	%	88	76	6	*774 / 596*
Intermediate	%	78	66	5	*189 / 141*
Self-employed	%	87	32	6	*99 / 79*
Lower supervisory / technical	%	80	38	8	*166 / 117*
Semi-routine and routine	%	75	20	11	*259 / 155*

Notes:
1.This column is based only on those in work
Rows do not sum to 100 as respondents could mention more than one location
Cells with a base of fewer than 50 are in brackets

things people can do on-line, and the possibilities no doubt grow exponentially by the day. To examine this, we presented respondents with a list of fifteen ways in which the internet might be used and asked them to say which, if any, applied to them. As Table 4.7 shows, the most common use of the internet was for e-mail, accounting for seven in ten internet users. Nearly half used the internet to access general information (the question did not spell out precisely what this might include), and around four in ten used it for travel and weather information, for shopping, and for banking.

Table 4.7 What people use the internet for

	%
E-mail	71
General information	48
Travel and weather information	44
Shopping	43
Banking and bill paying	37
Training, education and learning	31
News and current affairs	27
Job search	22
Sports information	17
Downloading music	16
Keeping in touch with groups I belong to	14
Games	11
Accessing local/central government information/services	11
Chat rooms	5
Something else	5
Median number of uses	4
Base (all who use the internet other than for work)	*1528*

Note: Table does not sum to 100 as respondents could mention more than one use

Of the fifteen different ways of using the internet presented in Table 4.7, the average number reported by respondents was four. A fifth (22 per cent) mentioned five or six and just over one in seven (14 per cent) picked seven or more. Younger people are the most likely to be fairly expansive users (with 44 per cent reporting five or more different uses of the internet), whereas older people are more likely to make quite limited use. In a similar vein, those with no qualifications, low household incomes, in routine occupations, and women are the least likely groups to be expansive users.

Some people regard the internet's capacity to expand people's access and exposure to information and resources from which they might otherwise be excluded from as one of its greatest advantages. Others question the extent to which its full potential will ever be properly realised, given the vast social divisions that exist not only between users and non-users but also amongst the different groups who use the internet. Indeed, the government is starting to shift its focus away from access targets towards encouraging existing users to make greater and more 'sophisticated' use of the internet (Cabinet Office, 2004).

To see whether particular reasons for using the internet are more common amongst some groups than others, we now focus upon four of the above examples of internet use: e-mail, shopping, news and current affairs, and downloading music. These items were selected to reflect some of the most and least common uses of the internet (ranging from the 71 per cent who use it to send e-mail to the 16 per cent who download music over the internet) and because they reflect four quite distinct uses of the internet: communication, commerce, information and exchange. To simplify the analysis, the table focuses upon the groups who were most and least likely to use the internet to do these things.

Table 4.8 Reasons for using the internet, by age, education, household income, social class and sex

Use of the internet for ...		Reasons for using the internet				
		... e-mail	... shop-ping	... news, current affairs	... down-loading music	Base
All	%	71	43	27	16	1528
Age						
18–24	%	71	41	28	42	185
65+	%	78	27	15	1	98
Highest educational qualification						
Degree	%	85	51	39	12	428
No qualifications	%	57	24	8	8	87
Household income						
Highest quartile	%	75	56	32	20	476
Lowest quartile	%	65	23	21	11	194
Social class (NS-SEC)						
Managerial/professional	%	79	49	33	14	771
Semi-routine and routine	%	60	35	19	21	256
Sex						
Women	%	72	41	22	13	778
Men	%	71	44	32	19	750

Notes: Rows do not sum to 100 as respondents could mention more than one reason

Some clear patterns emerge. With the exception of e-mail, older and younger people's use of the internet differs quite markedly. The over 65s are less likely to use the internet for shopping, are half as likely as 18–24 year olds to use it for news and current affairs, and just one per cent say they download music. Income, education and class are also related to the nature of people's internet use. Those on the lowest incomes, with no qualifications and who are in routine occupations are all less likely to make use of the internet for each of our four examples. The latter are, however, more likely to use the internet to download music (although this is likely to reflect the fact that the age profile of people in these jobs is younger to that found among professionals). Men's and women's use of e-mail and internet shopping is very similar, but men are more likely to use the internet for downloading music and for news and current affairs. Of course, men are also more likely than women to read a daily newspaper (59 and 48 per cent respectively), suggesting that patterns of internet use are likely to reflect both supply *and* demand, given that people's prior interests will greatly influence which activities they choose to pursue on-line. This suggests that, rather than being a mechanism for smoothing out social divisions and exposing marginalised groups to information and resources traditionally denied them, internet use can often mirror – and in some circumstances exacerbate – pre-existing differences and inequalities.

Why aren't more people on-line?

As we saw in Table 4.2, internet use is clearly associated with a range of social characteristics. Consequently, there is little need to present an exhaustive picture of the *non*-user population, a half of our respondents. Put simply, the highest proportions of non-users are found among those aged over 65 (85 per cent), with no formal qualifications (89 per cent), with household incomes in the lowest quartile (78 per cent), or in semi-routine or routine occupations (70 per cent). Among these groups, therefore, those who do *not* use the internet are very much the majority.

Likely internet use in the future

To what extent do non-users actually *want* to use the internet? To assess this, we asked those who did not currently make personal use of the internet whether they expected, or wanted, to use the internet in this way:

> *How likely do you think it is, if at all, that you will start using the*
> *internet one day (other than for work) ...*
> *... very likely,*
> *fairly likely,*
> *not very likely,*
> *or, not at all likely?*

> *Regardless of whether you think you ever will, would you like to use*
> *the internet (other than for work) one day, or not?*

The majority said it was "not very" (20 per cent) or "not at all likely" (43 per cent) that they would start to use the internet one day. Just over a third (37 per cent) thought it likely they would use the internet in future. However, opinion was more evenly split when it came to the question of whether they would *like* to use it, with 46 per cent saying they would and 53 per cent saying they would not. This suggests that there is sizeable pool of potential future internet users. We shall return to this group towards the end of this chapter to examine what impact their joining the ranks of current internet users would have on the digital divide.

Certain groups of non-users are much more likely than others to say they would like to use the internet one day. The most striking relationship is, unsurprisingly, with age. Three-quarters (75 per cent) of 18–24 year olds who don't currently use the internet would like to, compared with just one in four (24 per cent) of those aged 65 and over. Education is also an important factor; seven in ten (71 per cent) of non-users with a degree want to use the internet, compared with just three in ten (31 per cent) of people with no qualifications. Perhaps surprisingly, the relationship between people's future aspirations and social class is not so stark; among those who are not currently on-line, 53 per cent of professionals and 40 per cent of working-class people want to use the internet one day. Logistic regression confirms that age, education, household income, class and gender are all independently linked to the likelihood of current non-users saying they would like to use the internet in the future (Model 2 in the appendix to this chapter). So, just as the digital divide between users and non-users reflects broader social inequalities, so too does the divide between those who would, and would not, like to use the internet in future.

Why don't people use the internet?

Of course, knowing *who* does not use the internet is not the same as knowing *why* this might be so. A number of possible reasons present themselves. As we might imagine, the barriers associated with social and economic resources cannot be underestimated. The internet might be *physically* accessible in libraries and community centres to all but a handful of the population, but significant problems still remain for those who don't have the skills or confidence to use or seek assistance in using a computer. Other barriers might be related more to people's initial *motivation* – if you feel you have no need for what the internet has to offer, you will, quite understandably, be less likely to try it out. Finally it could be that people are mistrustful or fearful of what the internet has to offer; after all, a lot of the coverage the internet gets in the press centres on the more nefarious uses to which it can be put, such as fraud or child sexual abuse. These distinctions are important. After all, if internet access among hitherto excluded groups is to increase, any attempt to promote access must be based on a proper understanding of the factors that currently inhibit internet use.

To explore this, we presented respondents with a list of nine possible reasons which might explain why they do not use the internet and asked which, if any, applied to them. As the next table shows, the most commonly cited reason was a lack of interest, chosen by just over a half of internet non-users, followed by a lack of need. Of course, that someone has no interest in, or feels no need for, the internet is arguably more a matter of personal taste than of any specific socio-economic barrier to access. However, more explicit barriers to access were also frequently mentioned, most notably lack of knowledge (mentioned by 28 per cent) or lack of hardware (25 per cent). In this sense, therefore, the government's success in establishing a comprehensive network of public internet access points is diminished by the fact that one in four non-users still feel that they need their own computer in order to make use of the internet. Furthermore, the range of reasons people give for not using the internet suggest that any attempt to increase internet use amongst people for whom home access is not a reality will be no easy feat. That so many non-users see very little point in using the internet means that access to resources such as training, as well as the physical hardware to go on-line, needs to be complemented by concerted efforts to ignite people's interest as well. To be fair, government and other organisations have directed resources towards increasing skills, as well as targeting groups for whom the benefits of the internet might not be immediately obvious (for example, Age Concern has been involved with initiatives to introduce older people to the internet, promoting benefits such as making contact with distant relatives or friends as an incentive). So it seems that as internet use becomes more and more widespread, the kind of action required to help increase its uptake even further will need constant re-evaluation as the nature of the barriers to access shift over time.

Table 4.9 Reasons for not using the internet

	%
No interest	51
Don't need to	28
Don't know how to	28
Don't have or can't afford a computer	25
Don't like using the internet / computers	11
Other reason	5
Takes too long	4
Has computer – but can't afford internet connection	4
Has computer – but too old to connect to internet	2
Base (all who do not use the internet)	*1519*

Of course, we should not assume that these reasons for not using the internet apply equally to all social groups. This again has implications when it comes to attempting to promote internet use among different groups. We consider this by examining how a range of social groups differ in the extent to which they cite three of the most commonly mentioned reasons for not using the internet: lack of interest, lack of knowledge and lack of hardware. As Table 4.10 shows, lack of interest has a very clear and predictable social pattern. The older you are, the fewer qualifications you hold, and the lower your household income, the less likely you are to be interested in the internet. Men are also more likely than women to give this response. However, when it comes to lack of knowledge or technical skills the pattern is far less predictable. Whereas there are clear age differences in the extent to which lack of knowledge is mentioned as a barrier, there are few differences between the extent to which this is mentioned by different income or education groups, or by men and women. Not surprisingly, those in the lowest income households are the most likely to say that a lack of resources is an important factor in explaining their non-use of the internet. In addition, men significantly are more likely to give this response than women.

Table 4.10 Reasons for not using the internet by age, education, income, gender, and desire to use the internet in future

% of non-users who say ...	Reason for not using the internet			
	... not interested	... don't know how to use internet / computers	... don't have / can't afford a computer	Base
All	51	28	25	1519
Age				
18–24	41	8	38	71
25–39	34	22	31	300
40–64	50	29	19	748
65+	64	31	28	653
Highest educational qualification				
Degree	38	26	19	88
Higher education / A level	42	21	21	309
GCSE / O level or below	45	28	29	557
No qualifications	61	32	24	804
Household income				
Highest quartile	39	26	10	120
Third quartile	43	25	16	230
Second quartile	55	32	26	381
Lowest quartile	54	30	34	753
Sex				
Women	48	26	22	1044
Men	55	29	27	728
Future internet use				
Would like to use it one day	29	32	30	769
Would not like to	71	25	20	984

This table also looks at the very important distinction between those who actually *want* to use the internet one day and those who do not. Understandably, this shows that lack of interest is a very significant factor among the latter group, seven in ten of whom say the internet does not interest them, compared with just one in three of those keen to go on-line. Those who *would* like to go on-line are more likely to say they lack skills or resources than are those who don't want to use it in the first place.

Earlier we wondered whether the kinds of initiatives used to increase internet access might need to change over time as the reasons people give for not going on-line shift. The findings in Table 4.10 suggest that such strategies will also have to use a multi-layered rather than 'one-size-fits-all' approach. Not only do different subsections of the non-user population give different reasons for not using the internet, but also we cannot take for granted that when someone aged 18–24 says they have no interest in using the internet, this has the same meaning as it does for someone over 65.

Attitudes towards the internet

In order to understand the concerns of non-users, it is important to look not only at their social characteristics, but also at their attitudes towards the internet. This would seem particularly important given the fact that a lack of interest in the internet is so commonly cited by non-users, as it might allow us to gain a better understanding of what lies behind such thinking.

To examine attitudes towards the internet, we presented respondents with the statements shown in Tables 4.11 and 4.12. These were designed to tap a range of views about the internet, including its potential to foster social isolation, its potential dangers, and whether it contains information not available elsewhere. Both tables contrast the responses of current users with two groups of non-users: those who would like to use the internet (who we shall refer to as 'potential future users') and those who would not like to use it ('non-users').

The statements shown in Table 4.11 attracted very different responses from our three groups of interest. Thus, just over a third of potential users and a half of non-users agree that "the internet is too complicated for me to use fully", compared with just one in ten of current users. A belief that those who do not use the internet "miss out" was most prevalent among current users, and was least common among non-users. Meanwhile, potential users and non-users were the most likely to be concerned about the safety of payment over the internet. Only a minority in each of the three groups felt that the dangers posed to children by the internet were exaggerated. These patterns are hardly surprising, but it is instructive that the attitudes of potential users and non-users differ on a number of items, as it suggests that people's attitudes might help account for some of their resistance to the internet.[4]

Table 4.11 Attitudes towards the internet by current and future usage (i)

% who agree	Current user	Potential future user	Non-user
The internet is too complicated for someone like me to use fully	9	36	49
People miss out on important things by not using the internet or e-mail	37	26	13
It's much safer to use a credit card in a shop than on the internet	38	55	50
Many people exaggerate the dangers children can come across using the internet	16	18	21
Base	*1290*	*642*	*803*

A slightly different pattern emerges in Table 4.12. For example, when it comes to the issue of whether the internet is the *only* source of certain kinds of information, the views of current and potential users are very similar (with around a half agreeing), while non-users stand out as being far less likely to agree. The group of potential users thus clearly sense that they are missing out on something by not using the internet, a feeling that does not appear to be shared by non-users. In contrast, when it comes to the potential for the internet to promote social isolation, it is current users whose views stand out, with potential users and non-users being more likely to hold the view that using the internet reduces people's likelihood of going out and talking to people. Finally, as the last row in the table demonstrates, the same proportion (three in ten) in all three groups agree that using the internet is too expensive, which suggests that financial concerns about internet use might not be as pressing a reason for non-internet use as perhaps thought.

Table 4.12 Attitudes towards the internet by current and future usage (ii)

% who agree	Current user	Potential future user	Non-user
Most information on the internet cannot be found elsewhere	50	47	30
Using the internet makes people less likely to go out and talk to other people	42	53	52
Using the internet is too expensive	30	31	31
Base	*1290*	*642*	*803*

Earlier we saw that lack of interest is a major reason cited by people as to why they do not use the internet. Of course, it is always possible that people use this rationale to mask other concerns, perhaps related to a perceived lack of skills or general confidence. There is some evidence that this might be the case. As the next table shows, half (48 per cent) of those who say they have no interest in using the internet also say it is "too complicated" for them to use fully. They were less likely than those who cited lack of knowledge or resources as a barrier to think that people who don't use the internet "miss out on important information", and to think that most information on the internet "cannot be found elsewhere". Of course it could simply be that those who say they are not interested are offering a realistic assessment of their likely aptitude when it comes to internet technology. But it does suggest that, among some people at least, more could be done both to promote the advantages of internet use and to allay fears about how difficult the internet is. For some, this might help alleviate their apparent lack of interest.

Table 4.13 Attitudes towards the internet by reasons for not using it

% who agree	Reason for not using the internet			
	Not interested	Don't know how to use internet/ computers	Don't have/ can't afford a computer	All non-users
The internet is too complicated for someone like me to use fully	48	59	41	43
People miss out on important things by not using the internet or e-mail	13	20	22	19
Most information on the internet cannot be found elsewhere	32	39	38	38
Using the internet is too expensive	30	29	37	31
Base	*758*	*415*	*412*	*1458*

Another concern voiced about the internet is the extent to which – given the unregulated nature of much of its content – the information it contains can be trusted. The following table looks at our three groups of users' responses to questions about how trustworthy the internet is as a source of information about, firstly, news and current affairs, and secondly, health (see also the chapter by Curtice and Norris in this volume). By way of contrast, we also asked people to judge newspapers on the same criteria. Two key findings emerge. Firstly, current users are equally trusting of the internet and newspapers when it comes to news and current affairs (65 per cent doing so), whereas they are *more* trusting of the internet on health matters than they are of newspapers (47 and 39 per cent respectively). It is also notable that both sources of information are seen as less reliable about health than they are about news and current affairs. So, even amongst the internet savvy, levels of trust are not blind to the context or nature of the information. Secondly, potential users are *more* likely to trust the internet (on either matter) than non-users, which confirms our earlier finding that potential users and non-users have quite distinct views about the internet. True, potential users are not as trusting as current users, but they are, on balance, closer in their attitudes to current users than non-users. We can counter the suggestion that those who do not use the internet are possibly less trusting of information sources in general by pointing to the fact that, for both news and current affairs and health issues, the attitudes of the three groups towards the trustworthiness of newspapers is identical.

Table 4.14 Trust in the internet as a source of information by current and future usage

% who say	Current users	Potential future user	Non-user
Newspapers are a reliable source of information about news and current affairs	65	62	59
The internet is a reliable source of information about news and current affairs	65	43	19
Newspapers are a reliable source of information about what is best for your health	39	41	39
The internet is a reliable source of information about what is best for your health	47	34	14
Base	*1527*	*769*	*984*

These findings suggest that general attitudes towards, and trust in, the internet are associated with the likelihood of a person wanting to use the internet in future. This is confirmed by a logistic regression model which, in addition to including the 'traditional' factors driving the digital divide (age, education, social class, income and sex) also included people's attitudes towards the internet (see Model 3 in the appendix to this chapter for full results). This analysis confirms that, even when socio-demographic factors are taken into account, a person's attitudes towards the internet, and their trust in it as a source of information, are significantly related to their desire to use the internet in future.[5] So while the digital divide is very much related to broad socio-economic inequalities, the gulf between those who do and do not use the internet, and between those who would and would not like to use it one day also has subtle attitudinal dimensions.

Can the digital divide ever be closed?

As we have seen, the recent increase in internet usage has done very little to reduce the stark divide between those who are and are not on-line. We turn now to examining the future prospects for reducing these social divisions. Of course, given the age profile of the internet's current users, we can expect to see internet use increase gradually over time, as older generations (who are less likely to use the internet) die and new generations are born. However, if such generational change is to be the internet's sole source of new recruits, it will take decades for the existing social divisions in internet use to decline (and will not necessarily eradicate socio-economic differences associated with education, income and class). Consequently, if internet use is to increase in the near future, it will have to do so by drawing in groups who have hitherto proved unwilling or unable to access the internet. So we turn now to examine what would happen if all those who would *like* to use the internet were to start doing so. Would existing divisions in internet access narrow, widen or stay the same? The first column in the next table presents the current prevalence of internet use among different social groups [6], while the second column shows, for the same groups, the proportion who would use the internet if potential users (defined as those who *would like* to use the internet) are included alongside those who currently *do* use it. This gives us a picture of what the social distribution of internet use might look like in the future, assuming that all those who desire it were to gain access to the internet.

When we take account of potential internet users as well as current users, internet use overall grows from half to almost three-quarters of the population (73 per cent). Indeed, among some groups – in particular, the young (18–24 year olds), graduates, and those in professional occupations – internet use would become almost universal.

As before, the table shows the size of the 'digital divide' between the groups who are most and least likely to access, or want to access, the internet. Comparing these figures allows us to see whether, if all potential users were to gain access to the internet, the digital divide would increase or shrink. We begin with age. Among 18–24 year olds, three-quarters currently use the internet, and a further 19 per cent do not but would like to do so. If all of these people were to gain access to the internet, 94 per cent of young people would be on-line. Among those aged 65 and over, however, only 15 per cent currently access the internet, while a further 20 per cent do not but would like to do so. If all these people were to gain access, just over a third (35 per cent) of those aged 65 and over would be on-line. This makes little difference to the gulf between different generations, with just a small decrease in the digital divide of one percentage point. In order for this divide to narrow, a far larger proportion of older people than younger people would need to want to gain access to the internet in the future.

However, taking account of potential users as well as actual ones *does* narrow the digital divide between different education, social class and income groups. Table 4.15 illustrates this with regard to education. It shows that, while only 11 per cent of those with no qualifications use the internet, 28 per cent would like to do so, resulting in a combined total of actual and potential internet users of 39 per cent. This potential increase results in the digital divide between the most and least educated shrinking by 16 points. Despite this, however, the differences that remain are still quite large. For instance, 95 per cent of those with a degree are either current or potential users, compared with the 39 per cent found among those with no qualifications. Similar findings apply in relation to household income and social class, with the inclusion of potential as well as actual users resulting in a smaller, but still substantial, digital divide.

Earlier we noted that the social composition of those who would *like* to use the internet in future was very similar to its existing user profile (for example, both groups are mainly young, well educated and middle class). The fact that their addition to our existing group of users in Table 4.15 results, in some instances, in the digital divide narrowing might thus seem slightly odd. This reflects the fact that the absolute numbers of non-users within the more socially advantaged groups are now quite small, because so many of them are already internet users.

Table 4.15 Current and potential internet users, by age, education and sex

	Current users	All potential users	Base	Change
All	50	73	*3299*	+23
Age				
18–24	75	94	*256*	19
25–39	67	90	*897*	23
40–64	47	74	*1394*	27
65+	15	35	*751*	20
'Digital divide'	60	59		-1
Highest educational qualification				
Degree	83	95	*516*	12
Higher education / A level	67	87	*879*	20
O level or below	47	76	*996*	29
No qualifications	11	39	*891*	28
'Digital divide'	72	56		-16
Sex				
Men	54	74	*1477*	20
Women	46	72	*1822*	26
'Digital divide'	8	2		-6

Taking account of potential users as well as actual ones almost eradicates the current digital divide between men and women (though admittedly the gap between men and women's current internet use is smaller than for any of the other factors).

These findings suggest that, in the short term at least, the potential to close the digital divide is greatest where the divide is at its smallest, and that the most significant challenge is the generational digital divide.

Conclusions

This chapter began by asking if the recent increase in internet use has done anything to reduce the sharp social divisions in internet use identified in *The 18th Report*. So far, we find, it has not. Broadly speaking, if you are young, well educated, well paid, male or a manager / professional then the chances are you are also an internet user. Furthermore, most of this growth in internet use has been fuelled by an increase in home access, rather than through greater use of public-access locations.

We also found that, as well as there being a digital divide between users and non-users, there is also a divide amongst users in terms of where they use the internet, what they use it for and the degree of sophistication of their use. Certain patterns start to become familiar: younger people, those with degrees, and high household incomes are more likely to make extensive use of the internet than are older internet users or those with fewer educational or economic resources (whose use tends to be restricted to just one or two different applications). It is therefore perhaps more apposite to talk of digital *divides* rather than simply referring to it as a singular phenomenon.

Nearly a half of non-users would like to use the internet one day, and familiar divides once again appear – these potential internet users tend to be young, well educated or middle class. The most common reasons given for not using the internet are lack of interest (51 per cent), lack of need (28 per cent), lack of suitable skills (28 per cent) and lack of a computer (25 per cent). This latter finding is significant given the government's recent drive to extend public internet access locations to the extent that most of the population now lives within a few miles of somewhere to log on. For a significant minority, however, it seems that home access will be the key to their joining the digital age, rather than trips to libraries, community centres or internet cafés. For others, it would appear that the most significant barrier to use is their own lack of interest. Whether this is compounded by their lack of knowledge as to what the internet could offer is unclear, but is certainly worthy of future investigation.

In addition to more traditional socio-demographic factors, we also explored general attitudes towards, and trust in, the internet. This reveals some noticeable differences between potential users (that is, non-users who would like to use the internet) and non-users who have no desire to go on-line. The former are more likely to feel they are missing out on something by not surfing the web, and are less concerned about their ability to master the requisite skills for using the internet than non-users who profess no interest in ever going on-line. Potential users are also more trusting of the web as an information source.

We found that by combining current users and potential users the social profile of the digital divide becomes less stark, though it far from disappears altogether. Most notably, it seems that the digital divide between men and women looks likely to evaporate within a short period.

The internet has the potential to offer a great deal in terms of access to information that was hitherto the reserve of a small elite, as well as innumerable opportunities for communication between and across communities. As more and more services in both the public and the private sectors, from filling in tax returns to booking cinema tickets, become commonplace, one significant challenge that remains is to ensure that those who for various reasons cannot or will not ever use the internet in future are not disadvantaged by their lack of engagement with this new technology. A further challenge will be to ensure that those who register some interest in using the internet in the future are supported in that aim, be it through boosting their skills or confidence or by continuing to ensure that the costs of internet access are not overly prohibitive. The greatest challenge, of course, will be in persuading those who claim no interest in ever using the internet that they may have something to gain from adjusting their view.

Notes

1. *Pew Internet and American Life* monthly tracking survey (www.pewinternet.org).
2. This increase is almost entirely accounted for by an increase in women having internet access at home rather than through any greater use of the internet elsewhere; the proportion of women who use the internet but do not have home access was eight per cent in 2000 and nine per cent in 2003.
3. The use of items such as televisions and mobiles phones has been mooted as a potential way of expanding access amongst those without the means to buy a home computer, so we also asked people *how* they accessed the internet. The overwhelming majority used a PC or laptop (97 per cent), just three per cent mentioned accessing it via their television, and seven per cent use a mobile phone.
4. It should be noted, however, that a large proportion of the non-users (and, to a lesser extent, potential users) said 'don't know' in response to the statements.
5. The inclusion in Model 3 of responses to the statement "using the internet is too expensive" results in household income no longer being a significant predictor of potential internet use (though age, sex, education and social class remain significant).
6. The figures for current users in Table 4.15 differ slightly to those in Tables 4.2 and 4.3. The earlier tables are based on all respondents to the survey whereas Table 4.15 is based only on those respondents who were asked the module of questions about the internet (two-thirds of the sample).

References

Barber, B. (1999), 'Three scenarios for the future of technology and strong democracy', *Political Science Quarterly*, **113**: 573–590

Budge, I. (1996), *The New Challenge of Direct Democracy*, Oxford: Polity Press

Cabinet Office (2004), *UK Online Annual Report 2003*, London: Office of the e-Envoy, http://e-government.cabinetoffice.gov.uk/assetRoot/04/00/60/69/04006069.pdf

The Economist (2003), 'Caught in the net', 23rd January

Gardner, J. and Oswald, A. (2001), 'Internet use: the digital divide', in Park, A., Curtice, J., Thomson, K., Jarvis, L. and Bromley, C. (eds.), *British Social Attitudes – the 18th Report: Public policy, Social ties*, London: Sage

Golding, P. (1998), 'Global Village or Global Pillage? The Unequal Inheritance of the Communication Revolution', in McChesney, R.W., Meiksins Wood, E. and Foster, J.B. (ed.), Capitalism and the Information Age: The Political Economy of the Global Information Revolution, New York: Monthly Review Press

Norris, P. (2001), *Digital Divide: Civic Engagement, Information Poverty and the Internet Worldwide*, New York: Cambridge University Press

Rogers, E. (1995), *Diffusion of Innovations*, New York: Routledge

US Department of Commerce (2000), *Falling through the net: toward digital inclusion*, http://www.ntia.doc.gov/ntiahome/digitaldivide/

Wilheim, A.G. (2000), *Democracy in the Digital Age: Challenges to Political Life in Cyberspace*, New York: Routledge

Acknowledgements

We are grateful to the Economic and Social Research Council's (ESRC) E-Society Programme for funding the module of questions on which this chapter is based (grant number 335250010). We are also grateful to the Department for Education and Skills for supporting the question about what people use the internet for. Responsibility for analysis of this data lies solely with the author.

Appendix

The three models referred to in the text are presented below. All the variables entered in the first model were significant and are shown in the first table. All the items shown in the table below were entered into Model 3, as well as the two statements about trust in the internet as a source of information which proved significant and are therefore shown in the second table.

Logistic regression: Internet use

Model 1	Demographics	
	B	Exp(B)
Age		
18–24	1.10	3.001**
25–39	0.50	1.652**
40–64	-0.20	0.820**
65+	-1.40	0.246**
Education		
Degree	1.04	2.825**
HE / A level	0.45	1.568**
O level	-0.16	0.853**
None	-1.33	0.265**
Household income		
Lowest quartile	-0.58	0.559**
2nd quartile	-0.13	0.880
3rd quartile	0.36	1.437**
Highest quartile	0.74	2.093**
Ref / DK	-0.39	0.676**
Social class		
Prof / manager	0.56	1.747**
Intermediate	0.29	1.331**
Small employers	-0.46	0.630**
Lower supervisory	-0.19	0.831
Semi & routine	-0.32	0.725**
Unable to classify	0.13	1.134
Sex		
Men	0.17	1.181**
Women	-0.17	0.847**
Constant	0.02	1.023

Number of cases in model: 4395
* Significant at the 5% level
**Significant at the 1% level

Logistic regression: Would like to use internet one day

	Model 2		Model 3	
	Demographics		Demographics and attitudes	
	B	Exp(B)	B	Exp(B)
Age				
18–24	0.868	2.383**	0.43	1.536
25–39	0.571	1.770**	0.60	1.815**
40–64	-0.227	0.797*	-0.25	0.777*
65+	-1.211	0.298**	-0.77	0.462**
Education				
Degree	0.720	2.054**	0.71	2.030**
HE / A level	0.021	1.021	0.02	1.022
O level	-0.066	0.936	-0.16	0.856
None	-0.675	0.509**	-0.57	0.563**
Household income				
Lowest quartile	-0.099	0.906	ns	ns
2nd quartile	0.295	1.343**	ns	ns
3rd quartile	0.161	1.175	ns	ns
Highest quartile	0.120	1.127	ns	ns
Ref / DK	-0.477	0.621**	ns	ns
Social class				
Prof / manager	-0.045	0.956	-0.14	0.865
Intermediate	0.271	1.311	0.32	1.375
Small employers	0.463	1.590**	0.47	1.608*
Lower supervisory	-0.309	0.735*	-0.48	0.618**
Semi & routine	-0.237	0.789*	-0.40	0.672**
Unable to classify	-0.143	0.867	0.23	1.259
Sex				
Men	-0.132	0.877*	-0.18	0.832**
Women	0.132	1.141*	0.18	1.202**

continued on next page

	Model 2 (cont..)		Model 3 (cont..)	
	Demographics		Demographics and attitudes	
How reliable is internet news & current affairs?				
Reliable			0.40	1.488**
Neither			-0.08	0.924
Unreliable			-0.59	0.554*
DK			0.27	1.312
How reliable is internet health information?				
Reliable			0.28	1.317
Neither			0.17	1.191
Unreliable			-0.13	0.878
DK			-0.32	0.727
"Using the internet is too expensive"				
Agree			0.00	0.996
Neither			0.15	1.159
Disagree			0.50	1.656**
DK			-0.65	0.523**
"Most info on internet can't be found elsewhere"				
Agree			0.31	1.358**
Neither			-0.05	0.949
Disagree			-0.15	0.857
DK			-0.10	0.905
"Internet is too complicated for me to use fully"				
Agree			-0.18	0.836
Neither			-0.29	0.749*
Disagree			0.51	1.666**
DK			-0.04	0.959
"People who don't use the internet miss out on important information"				
Agree			0.51	1.663**
Neither			0.03	1.029
Disagree			-0.32	0.727**
DK			-0.22	0.805
Constant	0.531	1.700	0.44	1.554

Number of cases in Model 2: 1755
Number of cases in Model 3: 1345
* Significant at the 5% level
**Significant at the 1% level
ns = not significant

5 e-politics? The impact of the internet on political trust and participation

John Curtice and Pippa Norris [*]

The internet has only been widely available for a few short years. Yet it has already radically changed the way that we undertake everyday tasks. Many now send an e-mail rather than make a phone call or send a letter. They look for information on the web rather than in a reference book or a library. And they order goods or organise their financial affairs over the web rather than trotting into town to shop or bank.

But while the internet has undoubtedly changed *how* we do things, this does not necessarily mean that it has changed *what* we do. For what we do depends not just on technological availability but also on motivation. The web may make it easier for us to organise our financial affairs, but this will make little difference to our behaviour if we lack the motivation to keep them in order. E-mail might make it easier for us to keep in touch with distant friends and relatives, but this may matter little if we are unwilling to invest in the emotional energy required to maintain such relationships. Nowhere would motivation seem to matter more than when we consider the possible impact of the internet on people's involvement in politics. The internet would certainly appear to have the *potential* to make a difference, making it easier both for citizens to become involved in political activity and for governments to strengthen the bonds between themselves and those they seek to serve. Getting involved simply becomes easier (Budge, 1996; Bimber, 1998). People can get involved without crossing their front door, by signing up to an e-petition or sending an e-mail to their MP. They can use the internet to find others with similar political instincts and values to themselves, without being constrained by where they live (Negroponte, 1995; Dertouzous, 1997). Political organisations with limited resources can mobilise their members in a manner that would otherwise have

[*] John Curtice is Research Consultant at the *Scottish Centre for Social Research*, part of NatCen, Deputy Director of the *Centre for Research into Elections and Social Trends*, and Professor of Politics and Director of the Social Statistics Laboratory at Strathclyde University. Pippa Norris is the McGuire Lecturer in Comparative Politics at the John F. Kennedy School of Government, Harvard University.

been beyond them (Bimber, 2002). Meanwhile, by placing information about its activities on the internet and making it possible to access government services and personnel electronically, governments can make themselves appear more transparent and accessible, qualities that they might hope would be translated into greater trust and confidence in what they do (Grossman, 1995; Rainie, 2002).

But while the internet may make it easier for people to get involved in politics or find out what government is doing, it does not necessarily follow they will choose to do so. If they do not care about any particular political cause or subject, they are unlikely to use the internet to seek out those of like mind. And if they have little interest in the details of governmental policy, ministerial speeches or party political statements, they can happily give these a miss as they surf through the wide range of resources available on the net. Rather than making more citizens active, the internet may simply make it easier for those who are *already* politically active to pursue their interests with greater ease and more vigour (Margolis and Resnick, 2000). Instead of producing a more active citizenry, the internet might even simply enable the minority of already active citizens to become even more active while allowing everybody else to bypass politics entirely.

Meanwhile, as the chapter by Catherine Bromley in this volume discusses, only half the adult population currently has access to the internet. Moreover, the half with access disproportionately includes those sections of the population that are already relatively likely to be politically active (see also Davis, 1999; Norris, 2001). So far, then, the internet largely misses those parts of the population that will have to be reached if it is to have much impact on overall levels of political participation in Britain or on the degree of trust and confidence in government. However, if the internet has facilitated political engagement amongst those who do have access to it, there would appear to be potential for it to have a yet greater impact if and when it spreads to the rest of the population.

This chapter attempts to discern which of these perspectives appears to be the more correct. Is there any evidence that the new opportunities for involvement created by the internet make it more likely that people will participate politically? Does the availability of government information on the internet instil greater confidence amongst the public in how they are governed? Or is the internet simply a tool that is used by those who are *already* interested and engaged in the political process and confident in the manner in which it works, at most increasing their already relatively high levels of trust and participation yet further?

Uses of the web

Clearly, the internet is unlikely to stimulate political activity or enhance trust and confidence in government if people do not actually use it to find out or communicate about politics. So we begin by looking at how much use is made of the web for political purposes. Table 4.7 in Bromley's chapter shows the uses to which the web is put by those who do have access (other than the small minority who only have access to it for work purposes). Finding out about news and current affairs appears to be in the middle rank of uses, engaged in by around one in four; this makes it decidedly less common than, for example, shopping or paying bills but more common than finding out about sport or downloading music. However, using the web to access local or central government information or services is undertaken by only just over one in ten. Indeed, of all the uses we asked about, only chat rooms appear to be less popular.

Of course, not all web users are the same. Not surprisingly, some activities are more popular with certain kinds of users than others (see also Table 4.8 in Bromley's chapter). Most importantly, the groups most likely to use the web to find out about the news or to access government services are precisely that section of the population, the better educated, that has long been the most likely to be involved in politics (Parry *et al.*, 1992; Curtice and Seyd, 2003). For example, among those with internet access, nearly two in five of graduates use it to find out about news and current affairs, compared with just one in five of those with no qualifications. When it comes to accessing government information, the educational divide is even more stark. While 17 per cent of graduates use the internet for this purpose, only two per cent of those without any educational qualifications do so.

However, the pattern of uses of the web for political purposes does not simply replicate traditional patterns of political participation. In general, political participation is relatively low amongst the young, highest amongst the middle aged, and then starts to fall off again amongst older groups. Despite this, 18–24 year olds with internet access are just as likely to use it to find out about news and current affairs as are adults in general, and are far *more* likely to do so than those aged 55 or over. Such use is actually highest of all amongst those aged 25–34, over a third of whom (35 per cent) use the internet in this way. However, we have to bear in mind that young people with internet access tend to make greater use of the web in general. When we examine the different ways in which this group uses the web, we find that accessing information about news and current affairs comes no higher on its list of activities than it does for adults in general. Moreover, 18–24 year olds actually rarely use the web to access government information and services – just six per cent do so, making this the least popular use of the web amongst this age group. So while the web may be a particularly effective means of reaching young people, politics faces a crowded market for their attention as they exploit the resources of cyberspace.

Political trust

So the internet does indeed appear to be used, to some degree, to acquire political information (albeit more so to find out about the news than to access government information and services). So we cannot simply dismiss out of hand the possibility that it might stimulate political activity or help engender greater trust in the political process. In this section we examine whether those with internet access have greater trust and confidence in government, while in the next section we consider whether they are more likely to become involved in political activity.

In order to measure trust and confidence, we asked:

> *How much do you trust British governments of any party to place the needs of the nation above the interests of their own political party?*

> *And how much do you trust politicians of any party in Britain to tell the truth when they are in a tight corner?*

For each question, the answer options ranged from "just about always" to "almost never". In both cases, Table 5.1 shows the proportion answering either "just about always" or "most of the time" among those with *no* internet access, and then among relatively new and more long-standing internet users. We make this latter distinction as there is no reason to believe that any impact internet access might have on people's political outlooks occurs the *moment* they get connected; rather it would only be expected to emerge over a period of time as people ascertain, use, and respond to the political resources that the internet offers. In any event, the table shows that those with internet access appear to be a little more trusting of governments, albeit only marginally. It also appears that those who have had access to the internet the longest are also the most likely to trust politicians. So the pattern in Table 5.1 is precisely what we should expect to find if the internet is helping to restore trust and confidence in government.

Table 5.1 Political trust by length of internet use

		Length of internet use		
% trust just about always/mostly	**Non-user**	**Less than 3 years**	**3–5 years**	**Over 5 years**
Governments to put national needs above party interest	16	18	18	22
Politicians to tell truth in a tight corner	6	4	5	11
Base	*1656*	*756*	*478*	*407*

However, we have to be careful in our interpretation of these findings. Perhaps the higher level of trust exhibited by those who have had internet access the longest is a reflection, not of their use of the internet, but of their highly distinctive social profile? As we might anticipate from Tables 4.2 to 4.4 of Bromley's chapter, long-term internet users are distinctly young, well educated and affluent. Nearly half (45 per cent) of long-standing internet users (those who have used it for more than five years) are aged under 35, compared with just 14 per cent of non-users. A similar proportion (46 per cent) are graduates (compared with just four per cent of non-users) and over half (55 per cent) live in a household with an income in the top income quartile (compared with just eight per cent of non-users). Perhaps this relatively well-educated and affluent group of people has *always* had a relatively high level of trust? Certainly, previous research has indicated that those with higher levels of educational attainment are more likely to have trust in governments (Bromley and Curtice, 2002). Clearly we need to dispose of this possibility before we can conclude that access to the internet encourages trust and confidence in the political process.

Dealing with this possibility is, however, not entirely straightforward. We have two strategies open to us. The first is the more conventional one. This is to construct a multivariate model of trust in which we include not only a measure of how long someone has had access to the internet but one or more 'control' variables that measure the distinctive social and attitudinal profile of long-term internet users. The key limitation of this strategy, however, is that we cannot always be sure that our controls have adequately identified what was distinctive about long-term internet users prior to their becoming long-term users.[1]

This problem arises of course because we are trying to use a single survey to examine a process that we would expect to take place over a period of time. Ideally, we should examine this process by looking at how attitudes have changed over time. Fortunately we have the means to do this, as we asked similar questions on the 2000 *British Social Attitudes* survey. This provides our second strategy. If we assume, as would seem reasonable, that most of those who had internet access in 2000 *still* did so in 2003, then those who have now been using the internet for three or more years should be the same people as all those who were internet users in 2000. So, if long-term access to the internet increases trust in government, we should find that levels of trust should have increased more (or fallen less) among this group than it has among those with less experience of the internet.

Of course, there are some limitations to this strategy too. Perhaps, for some internet users, the beneficial impact of the internet on political trust was already apparent by 2000, while some of its benefit might already be being enjoyed now by those who have had access to the internet for less than three years. Consequently, this strategy may underestimate somewhat the overall impact of the internet on levels of trust over the past three years. But even so, if the internet *has* had any impact, there should be a discernible difference between long-term users and the rest of the population.

We begin by pursuing our first strategy, using multivariate analysis techniques to examine the relationship between political trust and internet use after taking into account the impact of just one 'control', education (which, as we have discussed, is linked to both internet use and trust). The results are shown in Model 1 in the appendix to this chapter. They confirm that graduates are significantly more likely to trust governments to put "the needs of the nation" above those of their party than are those without any qualifications at all. Moreover, once we take account of this relationship, there is no link between political trust and the length of time that a person has used the internet. So the apparent relationship in Table 5.1 between the length of time that someone has been on-line and their trust in government is simply a reflection of the fact that long-term internet users are more highly educated than those who have come on-line more recently or do not use the internet at all.

There is also a relationship between educational attainment and the level of trust a person has in politicians to "tell the truth in a tight corner". But here we find too that non-users of the internet are significantly *less* likely to trust politicians than are those who have used the internet for five years or more, even after differences in their levels of educational attainment are taken into account. However, the relationship is a relatively weak one and accounts for very little of the overall variance in levels of trust.

What happens when we pursue our second strategy, and examine whether levels of trust among longer-term users have changed differently from those among other groups? As Table 5.2 shows, neither measure of trust shows a clearly divergent pattern between 2000 and 2003. True, there has been a three percentage point increase since 2000 amongst longer-term users in the proportion trusting governments to put national above party interest "just about always" or "most of the time", up from 17 to 20 per cent. But there has also been a three percentage point increase amongst the remainder of the population as well. And there is little difference between the two groups when it comes to whether their views about politicians' ability to tell the truth in a tight corner have changed.

Table 5.2 Trends in political trust by internet use, 2000–2003

	Non-user, 2000	Non-user or recent user, 2003		User, 2000	Longer-term user, 2003	
% trust just about always / most of time	**2000**	**2003**	**Change**	**2000**	**2003**	**Change**
Governments to put national needs above party interest	15	18	+3	17	20	+3
Politicians to tell truth in a tight corner	11	10	-1	6	7	+1
Base	*1595*	*2412*		*684*	*885*	

'Recent users' are defined as those who, in 2003, had used the internet for under three years. Longer-term users are defined as those who had used the internet for three years or more in 2003.

So far it seems that access to the internet and the information it can provide has little or no impact on levels of trust in the political process. But there is a second set of attitudes towards the political process that we can also examine; political efficacy. By this we mean both the degree to which someone feels able to pursue their political interests effectively (sometimes known as 'personal efficacy') and the degree to which they feel the political system is willing and able to respond to the demands they might make of it ('system efficacy'). After all, we might well expect that access to political information on the web enhances people's belief in their ability to express their political views effectively, as well as enabling them to understand better the way in which the political system attempts to respond to the demands that are made of it.

Table 5.3 shows how each of six measures of political efficacy (three system and three personal) vary according to length of internet use. In each case, the table shows the proportion strongly agreeing with our propositions and thus the proportion who feel the *least* confident, either in the ability of the system to respond to public demands or in their own ability to influence the political process. For the most part, those with internet access, even if it has been for a relatively short time, are *less* likely to feel unconfident about these matters (and thus have higher levels of political efficacy). Moreover, the differences between the columns of the table are rather bigger than those we saw when we examined political trust. Here, at first glance at least, there seems more reason to believe that access to the internet might make a difference.

Table 5.3   Political efficacy by length of internet use

% strongly agree	Length of internet use			
System efficacy	Non-user	Less than 3 years	3–5 years	Over 5 years
Parties are only interested in people's votes, not in their opinions	30	19	17	18
Generally speaking, those we elect as MPs lose touch with people pretty quickly	29	18	16	16
It doesn't really matter which party is in power, in the end things go on much the same	23	15	13	13
Personal efficacy				
People like me have no say in what the government does	27	19	17	17
Sometimes politics and government seem so complicated that a person like me cannot really understand what is going on	20	11	11	7
Voting is the only way people like me have any say about how the government does things	18	15	12	12
Base	*1656*	*756*	*478*	*407*

Multivariate analysis in which we take into account the effect of age and education leads to a similar conclusion. Model 2 in the appendix shows the results of two examples of such analyses, one focusing on system efficacy (whether MPs are thought to lose touch "pretty quickly") and one on personal efficacy (whether politics and government seem too complicated for "a person like me" to understand). The results reveal that, in both cases, someone's level of educational attainment clearly makes a difference to their degree of political efficacy. The better qualified someone is, the more efficacious they feel. Age also matters. Those aged 18–24 are significantly less likely to feel personally efficacious than are those aged 65 or over, though so far as our measure of system efficacy is concerned, it is those aged 45 to 64 who prove to be least efficacious. But of most concern to us here is the fact that, even once these two relationships are taken into account, those who currently have no access to the internet are significantly *less* likely to feel efficacious than are those who have had access for five years or more. In addition, when it comes to our measure of personal efficacy, levels of efficacy are also significantly lower amongst those who have been using the web for three years or less.

These results are largely typical of all of the measures included in Table 5.3. In each case, those without internet access are significantly less likely to feel confident about the responsiveness of the political system, or their own ability to influence it, than those who have been using the web for five years or more – even after we take account for differences in the educational and age profile of these groups. Moreover, this relationship between length of internet use and political efficacy appears to be robust even if we add further controls to our analysis.[2]

But what of our second analytic strategy? If access to the internet *really* enhances political efficacy we should find that trends in political efficacy amongst those who have had access to the internet throughout the last three years have been more favourable than they have amongst those who have not. Table 5.4 presents the evidence, some of which at least provides some support to the notion. In at least three cases (whether MPs lose touch, whether people "like me" have any say, and whether voting is the only way to influence government actions), the proportion strongly agreeing with the proposition has fallen by three points or more amongst those who have had long-term internet access while changing little amongst the rest of our sample. For instance, the proportion of longer-term users agreeing with the view that MPs quickly lose touch with the electorate has fallen three points, from 19 to 16 per cent, while it has remained constant, at 25 per cent, among those who either do not use the internet at all, or have been using it for under three years.

Table 5.4 Trends in political efficacy by internet use, 2000–2003

	Non-user, 2000	Non-user or recent user, 2003		User, 2000	Longer-term user, 2003	
% strongly agree	2000	2003	Change	2000	2003	Change
Parties only interested in votes, not people's opinions	28	26	-2	21	17	-4
MPs lose touch pretty quickly	25	25	0	19	16	-3
Doesn't matter who's in power, things go on the same	21	20	-1	14	13	-1
People like me have no say in what the government does	26	24	-2	22	17	-5
Politics and government seem so complicated	20	17	-3	11	9	-2
Voting is the only way people like me have any say	18	17	-1	17	12	-5
Base	*1595*	*2412*		*684*	*885*	

'Recent users' are defined as those who, in 2003, had used the internet for under three years. Longer-term users are defined as those who had used the internet for three years or more in 2003.

So both of our tests provide some evidence to support the argument that the internet may help to increase levels of political efficacy, through the access it offers to political information. But if this process is at work, we should be able to demonstrate one further pattern – that it is those who actually *use* the internet to access government information who are largely responsible for the higher level of political efficacy found amongst internet users. To test this, we repeated the analysis described in our second multivariate model but added a measure of whether or not respondents use the web to access government information. If the increase in efficacy that we have seen reflects access to this sort of information, we would expect to find that introducing this measure makes little difference to the impact of either education or age on political efficacy, but that it substantially reduces the impact of not having access to the internet.

This is indeed precisely what we find (see appendix for details of Model 3). Whether or not someone uses the web to access government information is significantly associated with their political efficacy. Once this is taken into account, the length of time for which they have used the internet becomes less important (and, in the case of the question of whether MPs lose touch too quickly, actually becomes insignificant) while the importance of age and education is largely unchanged.

Of course, there are other ways of interpreting these results. It could be, for instance, that those who have been using the web the longest have *always* been an unusually politically efficacious group, happy to find their way around a myriad of government websites, a quality that our model has not been able to take into account. So our results do not *prove* that it is access to government information provided by the web that makes long-term internet users more confident in the responsiveness of government or in their own ability to get involved. But the results are consistent with this argument and, together with the results of our earlier analyses, it appears reasonable to conclude that some such process has been at work, at least among some longer-term internet users.

Political participation

We now turn to our second question; whether or not access to the internet makes it more likely that someone will participate in politics. Certainly, as Table 5.5 shows, those who have had access to the internet the longest tend to be the most likely to have undertaken some form of political action in their lives, or to be members of a political party, trade union or pressure group. There is but one exception to this picture; those who have used the internet the longest are somewhat *less* likely to claim to have voted in the last general election.

Moreover, many long-term users also report reasonably high use of e-mail or the web to undertake one or more of the activities described in the first part of Table 5.5. A quarter of those who have used the internet for five years or more have used it for at least one of these activities, twice the proportion found amongst those who have used the internet between three and five years, and the just four per cent of those who have used it for less than three years (see also Ward *et al.*, 2003). Equally, no less than one in three (33 per cent) long-term internet users say they have received an e-mail at some point asking them to join in a protest or a campaign, as have one in five (19 per cent) of those who have used the internet for between three and five years (though only seven per cent of those whose internet career has been shorter than this, report receiving this sort of e-mail). In short, the internet does appear to be being used both as a means of mobilising people and as a way of taking part in political activity, especially among longer-term users.

Table 5.5 Political action by length of internet use

	Length of internet use			
% ever done	Non-user	Less than 3 years	3–5 years	Over 5 years
Signed a petition	36	44	50	51
Contacted MP	14	15	21	21
Gone on a protest or demonstration	8	11	12	19
Spoken to an influential person	4	4	7	8
Contacted the media	3	4	9	11
Contacted a government dept.	3	4	6	9
Raised issue in an organisation	2	4	4	6
Formed a group of like-minded people	2	2	2	3
% who				
Voted in 2001 election*	74	70	69	65
Belong to political party/trade union	6	10	14	15
Belong to a pressure group	1	2	4	8
Base	1656	756	478	407
* Base	1564	703	451	380

* Based on respondents aged 21 or over

But of course none of this *proves* that access to the internet makes it more likely that someone will get involved in politics. Perhaps those who have had access to the internet the longest have always been relatively politically active? While they might well use the internet in the course of their political activity, this might simply be an alternative way of doing something they would be doing anyway. After all, long-term internet users have far higher levels of interest in politics than do the remainder of the population – no less than half (51 per cent) of those who have used the internet for five years or more have "a great deal" or "quite a lot" of interest in politics compared with a quarter (24 per cent) of non-users. So, once again, we need to deploy our two analytic strategies to assess whether the levels of political participation we have found amongst long-term internet users are, in fact, an indication that access to the internet really does have an impact.

Certainly, the results of logistic regressions that simply take into account the impact of age, educational attainment and internet use on levels of political participation give some pause for thought. True, they indicate that length of use of the internet is clearly related to the chances that someone is a member of a political party or trade union, or of a pressure group. But, when we focus on reported political activities, at least some of the associations we saw in Table 5.5 start to disappear. Multivariate analysis of the six most commonly undertaken forms of political activity reveal that in three cases there is no significant relationship between long-term internet use and participation once differences in educational attainment and age are taken into account.[3] Only in the case of signing a petition, contacting the media, or speaking to an influential person do long-term internet users remain distinctive. Meanwhile, in all but one case (contacting the media), even this distinctiveness vanishes once the high level of political interest expressed by internet users is taken into account.

There is also no consistent evidence of a marked increase in political participation amongst longer-term internet users over the last three years. The only form of activity where the trend since 2000 has differed between longer- and shorter-term users is contacting the media. As Table 5.6 shows, while this has actually declined among non-users and those who have used the internet for less than three years, it has slightly increased among long-term users. As our modelling also suggested that this form of political participation might be stimulated by access to the internet (even when we take account of political interest), it does appear that here the internet may indeed make a difference, perhaps reflecting the now widespread practice in the media of inviting viewers, listeners and readers to make their views known via the internet. But otherwise there are more instances of political participation having increased more over the last three years amongst those who are *not* long-term users of the internet than there are amongst long-term users. So, in general, it appears that we cannot safely conclude that use of the internet encourages or stimulates political activity.

Table 5.6 Trends in political participation by length of internet use, 2000–2003

	Non-user, 2000	Non-user or recent user, 2003		User, 2000	Longer-term user, 2003	
% ever done	2000	2003	Change	2000	2003	Change
Signed petition	37	39	+2	52	51	-1
Contacted MP	13	14	+1	23	21	-2
Gone on a protest	7	9	+2	14	16	+2
Spoken to influential person	3	4	+1	6	7	+1
Contacted media	5	3	-2	8	10	+2
Contacted government dept.	3	4	+1	6	8	+2
Raised issue in an organisation	3	2	-1	8	5	-3
Formed a group	1	2	+1	3	2	-1
Base	*1595*	*2412*		*684*	*885*	

'Recent users' are defined as those who, in 2003, had used the internet for under three years. Longer-term users are defined as those who had used the internet for three years or more in 2003.

However, perhaps there is a more subtle argument that we need to investigate. We have already suggested that the internet might increase political efficacy amongst the minority who have the motivation to use the internet to acquire government information. Maybe, in a similar way, the internet increases the range and intensity of political activity of those who are *already* interested in politics. If so, then we might expect to find that being both a longer-term user of the internet *and* being interested in politics makes more difference to the number of political actions in which someone has engaged than does either characteristic on its own.

Table 5.7 suggests that this is indeed the case. Longer-term users of the internet who do *not* have a lot of interest in politics are only slightly more likely to report having undertaken one of the activities detailed in Table 5.6 than are shorter-term or non-users with similarly low levels of interest. However, the average number of political actions reported by longer-term users of the internet who *do* have a substantial interest in politics is significantly higher than the average number reported by non-users or shorter-term users with the same level of interest. Moreover, more formal modelling of this result (which also takes into account the impact of educational attainment and age) confirms that *both* being a longer-term internet user and being interested in politics results in significantly higher levels of political activity than does either characteristic alone.

Table 5.7 Number of political actions undertaken, by length of internet use and political interest, 2003

	Mean number of political actions			
Interest in politics	Non-user or user for less than 3 years		User for more than 3 years	
		Base		Base
A great deal/quite a lot	1.3	593	1.7	389
Some	0.8	799	0.9	302
Not very much/none at all	0.5	1018	0.6	193

However, if this result means that internet access enables those who are already interested in politics to become more active (rather than indicating that early adopters of the internet have *always* been unusually politically active) we should find that this result is not replicated when we undertake a similar analysis on data from our 2000 survey. But, as Table 5.8 shows, a similar pattern was also evident that year too, a conclusion that is supported by more formal modelling of the data. Moreover, the table also shows that the total number of political activities reported by politically interested longer-term internet users was just as high three years ago as it is now. In short, we cannot in fact be sure that long-term access to the internet does encourage those with a prior interest in politics to become yet more politically active.

Table 5.8 Number of political actions undertaken, by length of internet use and political interest, 2000

	Mean number of political actions			
Interest in politics	Non-user		User	
		Base		Base
A great deal/quite a lot	1.2	438	1.8	293
Some	0.7	503	0.9	232
Not very much/none at all	0.4	653	0.8	159

We can also investigate a rather different claim. As we noted earlier, younger people are particularly likely to use the internet to find out about news and current affairs, as well as being more intensive users of the web in general. Perhaps, as sometimes has been argued (see, for example, Ward *et al.*, 2003), the internet is particularly effective at getting younger people involved in politics. If this were the case, we should find that access to the internet is more strongly associated with the reported level of political participation amongst 18–24 year olds than it is amongst the population in general. Although the sample sizes available to examine this are small, there is nothing to suggest that this is the case. For example, in Table 5.9, which looks at the reported incidence of the three most common forms of political participation (other than voting), the differences across the rows are much the same as those in the equivalent rows of Table 5.5. Equally, if we undertake more formal modelling of the number of political actions a person reports, we find no evidence that being both young *and* a longer-term internet user makes a significant difference to the range of political activities in which someone has been engaged.

Table 5.9 Political action, by length of internet use amongst 18–24 year olds

	Length of internet use			
% ever done	Non-user	Less than 3 years	3–5 years	Over 5 years
Signed a petition	26	31	35	40
Contacted MP	3	3	4	3
Gone on a protest or demonstration	0	6	3	10
Base	64	89	56	47

Conclusions

In recent years, politicians have been concerned about the alleged apathy and cynicism of the electorate. So the possibility that the internet might help reconnect the public with their political system has been eagerly grasped by those in power. Indeed, current government policy requires *all* government services to be accessible via the web by 2005, and for it to be possible to use the internet as a way of voting in national elections some time after 2006.

Our analysis suggests that this policy might have some success. In particular, it appears that the easy availability of government information on the web does appear to help increase people's sense that they can have some influence on what government does. However, relatively few people actually use the internet in this way. So, although the internet may help increase the level of political efficacy amongst a minority, it is unlikely to transform levels of political efficacy amongst the public as a whole. Certainly, as Table 5.10 shows, there is no evidence that the spread of the internet in recent years has been accompanied by an increased sense of political efficacy amongst the public as a whole. Meanwhile, there appears to be no evidence that having access to a wide range of government information on the web encourages people to be more trusting of those in power.

Table 5.10 Trends in political efficacy, 1998–2003

% strongly agree	1998	2000	2001	2002	2003
Parties are only interested in people's votes, not in their opinions	21	26	27	29	25
Generally speaking, those we elect as MPs lose touch with the people pretty quickly	20	23	25	28	23
It doesn't really matter who's in power, in the end things go on much the same	17	19	18	22	20
People like me have no say in what the government does	17	25	22	26	23
Sometimes politics and government seem so complicated that a person like me cannot really understand what is going on*	15	18	n/a	17	15
Voting is the only way people like me can have any say about how the government does things*	14	17	n/a	17	16
Base	*2071*	*2293*	*1099*	*2287*	*4432*
* Base					*3299*

At the same time, although those with access to the internet might use it to facilitate their political activity, for the most part it does not yet appear that the internet encourages people to become more politically active. Those who have had access to the internet for some time are undoubtedly particularly active politically. But it seems that they were just as active *before* they secured access to the internet (see also Hill and Hughes, 1998; Selnow, 1998; Toulouse and Luke, 1998). Meanwhile, we have not uncovered any evidence at all that access to the internet makes the young more likely to become politically active. The one exception to these generalisations appears to be that access to the internet does encourage people to contact television, radio or a newspaper when they are upset about what government is doing.

Still, perhaps we should not overload the internet with exaggerated expectations. Even if it has simply been added to the litany of ways in which people can get politically involved, there is no sign that the spread of the internet has in anyway *discouraged* people from getting involved in politics. And, if it does not make the already active yet more active, then at least this means the internet is not helping to make those who do get involved in politics any more unrepresentative of their fellow-citizens than they are already. We should also bear in mind that, even if the internet does not result in more people becoming more politically active, it could still have important consequences if it makes the political activity that does take place more *effective*, something we have not been able to consider here. In short, the internet may not ensure we become any better connected with our politicians, but it does at least provide another means through which we can attempt to make our voice heard when we feel the need.

Notes

1. At the same time, we also have to try and avoid being overzealous in our controls, that is, to include as a control something on which internet use might also have an influence and so factor out the very impact that we are trying to measure.
2. These include controls, such as political interest and the extent to which someone identifies with a particular political party that might in themselves be thought to be affected positively by an ability to access political information via the internet.
3. These models are available from the author on request.

References

Bimber, B. (1998), 'The Internet and Political Transformation: Populism, Community and Accelerated Pluralism', *Polity*, **21**: 133–160
Bimber, B. (2002), *Information and American Democracy*. New York: Cambridge University Press

Bromley, C. and Curtice, J. (2002), 'Where have all the voters gone?', in Park, A., Curtice, J., Thomson, K., Jarvis, L. and Bromley, C. (eds.), *British Social Attitudes: the 19th Report.* London: Sage

Budge, I. (1996), *The New Challenge of Direct Democracy.* Oxford: Polity Press

Curtice, J. and Seyd, B. (2003), 'Is there a crisis of political participation?', in Park, A., Curtice, J., Thomson, K., Jarvis, L. and Bromley, C. (eds.), *British Social Attitudes: the 20th Report – Continuity and Change over Two Decades,* London: Sage

Davis, R. (1999), *The Web of Politics,* New York: Oxford University Press

Dertouzous, M. (1997), *What Will Be: How the New Information Marketplace will Change our Lives,* San Francisco: Harper

Grossman, L. (1995), *The Electronic Commonwealth,* New York: Penguin

Hill, K. and Hughes, J. (1998), *Cyberpolitics: Citizen Activism in the Age of the Internet,* Lanham, Md: Rown & Littlefield

Margolis, M. and Resnick, D. (2000), *Politics as Usual: The Cyberspace Revolution,* Thousand Oaks: Sage

Negroponte, N. (1995), *Being Digital,* New York: Knopf

Norris, P. (2001), *Digital Divide: Civic Engagement, Information Poverty and the Internet Worldwide,* New York: Cambridge University Press

Parry, G., Moyser, G. and Day, N. (1992), *Political Participation and Democracy in Britain,* Cambridge: Cambridge University Press

Rainie, L. (2002), *The Rise of the E-Citizen: How People Use Government Agencies' Web Sites,* Washington, DC: Pew Internet and American Life Project (available at www. pewinternet.org)

Selnow, G. (1998), *Electronic Whistle-Stops: The Impact of the Internet on American Politics,* Westport, Conn.: Praeger

Toulouse, C. and Luke, T. (eds.) (1998), *The Politics of Cyberspace.* London: Routledge

Ward, S., Gibson, R. and Lusoli, W. (2003), 'Online Participation and Mobilisation in Britain: Hype, Hope and Reality', *Parliamentary Affairs,* **56**: 652–668

Acknowledgements

We are grateful to the Economic and Social Research Council's (ESRC) E-Society Programme for funding the module of questions on which this chapter is based (grant number 335250010). We are also grateful to the Department for Education and Skills for supporting the question about the purposes for which people use the internet. Responsibility for analysis of this data lies solely with the authors.

Appendix

The multivariate analyses referred to in the text are presented below. All are ordinal logistic models. The reference category for each variable in the model is shown in brackets (for example, the reference category in Model 1 for internet use comprises those with five or more years of internet access and the model shows the impact of being in each category of internet user as compared with being in this group). The entries in each cell are the parameter coefficients, and the entries in brackets their associated standard errors.

Model 1 Political trust

	Dependent variables	
	Trust governments	**Trust politicians**
Educational level		
Degree	.40 (.12) *	.31 (.13) *
HE below degree	.14 (.12)	.06 (.12)
A level	.12 (.12)	.02 (.13)
O level/GCSE	.13 (.11)	.03 (.11)
CSE	.10 (.13)	.04 (.13)
(None / foreign)		
Length of internet use		
Non-user	-.16 (.12)	-.26 (.12) *
0–3 years	-.06 (.12)	-.01 (.12)
3–5 years	-.07 (.12)	-.13 (.13)
(Over 5 years)		
Cox and Snell R^2	0.8%	0.7%

* Significant at the 5% level

Model 2 Political efficacy

	Dependent variables	
	MPs lose touch pretty quickly	Politics seems complicated for me to understand
Educational level		
Degree	1.13 (.13)*	1.50 (.12) *
HE below degree	.48 (.12) *	.94 (.12) *
A level	.47 (.13) *	.71 (.12) *
O level/GCSE	.47 (.11) *	.43 (.11) *
CSE	.21 (.13)	.32 (.13) *
(None / Foreign)		
Age		
18–24	-.01 (.14)	-.82 (.12) *
25–34	-.22 (.12)	-.36 (.12)
35–44	-.16 (.12)	-.13 (.12)
45–54	-.28 (.11) *	-.07 (.11)
55–64	.35 (.12) *	-.03 (.11)
(65+)		
Length of internet use		
Non-user	-.44 (.12) *	-.82 (.14) *
0–3 years	-.01 (.12)	-.39 (.11) *
3–5 years	-.01 (.12)	-.15 (.12)
(Over 5 years)		
Cox and Snell R^2	7.0%	12.9%
Base	*3241*	*3260*

* Significant at the 5% level

Model 3 The impact of accessing government information on political efficacy

	Dependent variables	
	MPs lose touch pretty quickly	Politics seems complicated for me to understand
Educational level		
Degree	1.07 (.13) *	1.42 (.12) *
HE below degree	.45 (.12) *	.92 (.12) *
A level	.45 (.12) *	.68 (.12) *
O level/GCSE	.48 (.11) *	.44 (.11) *
CSE	.22 (.13)	.33 (.13) *
(None / Foreign)		
Age		
18–24	-.01 (,14)	-.80 (.12) *
25–34	-.24 (.12)	-.39 (.12)
35–44	-.19 (.12)	-.17 (.12)
45–54	-.28 (.11) *	-.07 (.11)
55–64	.35 (.12) *	-.03 (.11)
(65+)		
Length of internet use		
Non-user	-.22 (.13)	-.55 (.13) *
0–3 years	.12 (.12)	-.24 (.12) *
3–5 years	.05 (.13)	-.10 (.12)
(Over 5 years)		
Ever access government information on-line		
Yes	.43 (.10) *	.55 (.10) *
(No)		
Cox and Snell R^2	7.5%	13.8%
Base	*3241*	*3260*

* Significant at the 5% level

6 Genomic science: emerging public opinion

Patrick Sturgis, Helen Cooper, Chris Fife-Schaw and Richard Shepherd [*]

It is five decades since the landmark discovery of DNA, the so-called 'blueprint for life'. Scientists have now completed decoding the entire human genome, our unique hereditary code. Our increasing understanding of genes and their function in humans, plants and animals has already begun to revolutionise progress in biomedical and agricultural sciences, with the rapid development of genetic technologies ranging from genetically modified (GM) food to genetic testing and cloning.

Grand claims have been made about the future potential of genetic technologies to transform key aspects of our lives. Advocates of genetically modified food predict improved food safety and nutritional quality. Crops genetically modified to tolerate harsh environmental conditions are proposed as a remedy for hunger, poverty and disease in developing countries. Future cures for life-threatening illnesses are predicted to lie in developing medical applications of genetic technology, such as stem-cell and gene therapy. Together with genetic testing, these developments promise to improve our understanding of how genes influence susceptibility to illnesses, so allowing early medical diagnosis and treatment. Viewed from this perspective, it would appear that the dawn of a 'genomic society', where the information in genes is readily obtained and utilised, has much to offer in terms of human longevity, opportunity and choice. Indeed, our future stake in a genomic society is already underpinned by substantial government investment in the delivery of genetic technologies within key public services including, most notably, policing and health (Department of Health, 2003).

However, while the transformative potential of genetic science has acquired increasing prominence in both the media and academia, it has been accompanied by high levels of public controversy and resistance. Perhaps more than any other area of scientific and technological research, it is framed by the

[*] Patrick Sturgis is Lecturer in Sociology; Helen Cooper is a Research Fellow in Psychology; Chris Fife-Schaw is Senior Lecturer in Psychology; and Richard Shepherd is Professor of Psychology – all at the University of Surrey.

complex moral, political and ethical questions it raises. For example, whilst genetic testing can be used to inform an individual about their risk of developing an inherited disorder, the same information is of predictive value for biological blood relations (who may carry the same gene), for insurers who wish to calculate premiums based on future health risks, and for employers making decisions about recruitment and retention of staff. Social and ethical concerns about privacy and protection against unfair treatment on the basis of genetic characteristics are inextricably linked to the development of gene-based technology (Human Genetics Commission, 2000, 2002).

In the British media, the past few years have seen extensive and, at times, sensational reporting about a number of new genetic technologies. This includes speculation about whether or not scientists have succeeded in cloning a human, the potentially deleterious effects of genetically modified crops on wild-life, and the birth of a baby genetically selected to have body tissues that match those of a seriously ill sibling.[1] Such coverage has prompted sustained discussion and debate about 'designer babies', reproductive choice and the ways in which genetic science is conducted and regulated (Human Genetics Commission, 2004).[2] So, concerns that society will abandon traditional morality and ethics at the altar of 'scientific advancement', widely articulated through the popular media, counterbalance the utopian optimism which underlies the development of much genetic science.

In light of these conflicting discourses concerning the future direction of genetic science, calls have come from politicians and scientists for a more 'balanced' debate about the role of science in society. In a recent speech to the Royal Society (2002), the Prime Minister, Tony Blair, emphasised the need to:

> ... ensure government, scientists and the public are fully engaged together in establishing the central role of science in the world we want.

To meet this need requires that scientists and policy makers engage in more and better-quality dialogue with the public, fostering an informed debate about the merits of scientific research programmes (House of Lords, 2000). A number of large-scale opinion canvassing exercises, most notably on GM crops and food, have taken place under the general banner of consultation and debate (Food Standards Agency, 1999; Department of Trade and Industry, 2003).[3] The impetus for such exercises can be traced to a move in science communication towards engaging with public anxieties, rather than denigrating them as irrational and based on scientific ignorance (Bodmer, 1985; Irwin and Wynne, 1996; House of Lords, 2000).

However, despite the proliferation of such attempts to engage 'the public' in some kind of 'genetic dialogue', their success in creating any real impact on public consciousness is far from clear-cut. The government-sponsored 'GM Nation?' debate is undoubtedly the most prominent example in this regard. Charged with fostering a nationwide public dialogue on the merits of GM crops and food, it ultimately attracted a small and unrepresentative sample of mainly anti-GM campaigners (Campbell and Townsend, 2003), while the broader population largely ignored it (Poortinga and Pidgeon, 2004). Despite the organising committees' attempts to define the exercise as a debate rather than an opinion poll, their use of a standardised questionnaire as a centre-piece of the exercise inevitably (and unsurprisingly) led to media reports focusing on percentages for and against GM. While we make no claims to having fostered a public dialogue by administering the questions in this survey, we believe that our findings are a good deal more robust and representative of public preferences on these issues than can ever be produced by such exercises in public 'consultation'.

We begin the chapter by describing public opinion toward a broad range of genetic technologies. As questions about some of these issues have been asked in previous *British Social Attitudes* surveys, we can also examine how public opinion toward such technologies has changed over the last few years. We then consider to what extent the proliferation of information and news stories about genes and genetics has influenced people's attitudes and beliefs. Does, for instance, growing familiarity with genetic technologies result in more or less opposition toward their development and application in society? Or does this depend, as previous research suggests, on the precise nature of the technology in question? Alternatively, are new genetic technologies still perceived as a rather distant and abstract concept, of which the average person is only dimly aware? Is there evidence to suggest that – as this area of scientific inquiry gains more prominence in the public sphere – we are becoming increasingly 'geneticised' in our thinking about the role that genes might play in the development of particular character traits and dispositions?

Next, we move on to examine the antecedents and consequences of interest in, and engagement with, genetic science and technology. Being more attentive to genetic issues has been shown to be linked to more positive general appraisals of genetic science (Pardo *et al.*, 2002; Gaskell *et al.*, 2003a). Others, however, argue that being attentive and knowledgeable can have the opposite effect by cultivating more critical expectations (Midden *et al.*, 2002). At a time when facilitating public dialogue and debate about this area of science is high in the minds of scientists and policy makers alike, we identify the socio-demographic characteristics associated with being 'attentive' to debates surrounding genetic science and technology. Finally, we move on to use multivariate models to explore the extent to which attentiveness underpins attitudes to genomics.

The shape of public opinion toward genomics

GM foods

Of all genomic technologies, the genetic modification of crops and food has been the most widely discussed and investigated. During the 1990s, the general trajectory of public opinion about GM food was one of strong and increasing opposition (Gaskell *et al.*, 2003a). Table 6.1 compares public attitudes towards GM in 1999 – a time when anti-GM sentiment and negative media coverage was at something of a high water mark (Gaskell *et al.*, 2003b) – with public attitudes in 2003. That year saw a great deal of coverage of GM crop trials in the UK, speculation about a government decision on the commercialisation of GM crops and, of course, the 'GM Nation?' public debate on the pros and cons of this technology. A key finding of 'GM Nation?' was that a huge majority of participants in the debate rejected any benefits of GM technology (Department of Trade and Industry, 2003), prompting headlines in the media such as "Five to one against GM crops in biggest ever public survey".[4] However, our findings suggest that to characterise current public opinion in this way presents a highly misleading picture. At the end of the 1990s, only one in ten people supported the view that Britain should grow GM foods "in order to compete with the rest of the world", with a majority (around two-thirds) opposing. At the same time, over half agreed with an outright ban on GM foods and rejected the view that "the advantages of GM food outweigh any dangers". By 2003, however, the same statements elicit significantly less opposition. The prospect of Britain growing GM foods is no longer rejected by a majority, whilst the proportion in favour of a GM food ban fell from 52 per cent to 29 per cent over the same period. Similarly, only one-third of the British public now disagree that the benefits of GM foods outweigh any dangers.

Table 6.1 Attitudes towards GM foods, 1999 and 2003

		Agree	Neither	Disagree	Base
In order to compete with the rest of the world, Britain should grow GM foods					
1999	%	10	18	65	833
2003	%	15	30	45	2649
GM foods should be banned, even if food prices suffer as a result					
1999	%	52	22	20	833
2003	%	29	33	26	2649
On balance, the advantages of GM foods outweigh any dangers					
1999	%	12	22	57	833
2003	%	14	38	33	2649

It is important to note that this shift away from outright opposition is underpinned not so much by increased public *support* for GM food, as by a considerable rise in the proportion of people who neither agree nor disagree with these propositions. In line with other recent survey research (Horlick-Jones *et al.*, 2004), the attitudes of the general public towards GM foods appear increasingly ambivalent in nature, with people simultaneously perceiving benefits and risks associated with the technology rather than opting for a clear 'pro' or 'anti' position. As Table 6.1 shows, for each of our questions approximately a third of Britons can now be characterised as neither for nor against GM foods, a sizeable increase over a four-year period.

Attitude change over the same time period is also evident from people's appraisals of the risks associated with GM foods. As Table 6.2 shows, in 1999 approximately three-quarters of the British public thought that growing GM foods presented a "definite" or "probable" danger to other plants and wildlife. Four years later, a majority still share this view but the proportion is much lower, at 55 per cent. The public in 2003 are also more willing to accept the safety of GM foods available in the shops than they were in 1999. In sum, these differences show that public opinion about the risks associated with GM food has become more evenly divided over time; although opposition remains the predominant response, it is substantially lower than it was four years earlier.

Table 6.2 Appraisals of GM food risks, 1999 and 2003

% saying definitely or probably	1999	2003
Growing GM foods poses a danger to other plants and wildlife	73	55
All GM foods already available in the shops are safe to eat	34	47
Base	*833*	*2649*

Genetic databases

The use of population databases of genetic information in a wide range of different contexts is predicted by some to be the next big issue of genomic controversy. To date, the use of such databases has largely been limited to the mandatory requirement for individuals investigated for a serious criminal offence to provide a DNA sample to the police. Recent amendments to the law, however, have broadened the criteria which determine who can be asked to provide the police with a genetic sample to be stored indefinitely on a national DNA database. DNA 'success stories' in high-profile criminal cases feature regularly in the media, alongside arguments for the criminal genetic database to be compulsory nationwide, and for individual biometric information to be used on a national identity card scheme. In addition, it has long been recognised that databases of genetic information have the potential to transform traditional practices in the insurance industry, in the recruitment and retention of employees, and beyond.

As genetic databases proliferate and become more familiar to the public, so might public anxieties about the social ramifications of their wider use evolve. As the final column in Table 6.3 shows, attitudes towards establishing genetic databases vary considerably according to their stated purpose. Nearly nine in ten are in favour of databases to better understand human illness and disease, with a similar proportion endorsing the use of genetic databases to identify serious criminal offenders.[5] Genetic databases for purposes other than health improvement or crime reduction are much less well received by the public. Support for their use to trace ancestry is evenly divided, but a majority reject the development of genetic databases used to establish health or life insurance premiums, or a person's suitability for employment; fewer than two people in ten support the use of databases for these purposes.

Levels of support vary between different groups. As we shall explore in more detail later in this chapter, a person's educational attainment is linked to their views about the acceptability of genetic databases. As Table 6.3 shows, this is particularly evident in relation to their less popular potential uses, with support highest amongst those with lower levels of educational attainment. Just over a quarter of adults without any formal qualifications are in favour of a database used for insurance purposes, more than double the support found among graduates or those with an equivalent qualification.

Table 6.3 Support for the use of databases for human genetic information

% strongly in favour or in favour of a database used to ...	Degree/ higher	A level or equiv	O level or equiv	No qualific- ations	All
... improve our understanding of illness and disease	86	90	88	80	86
... identify people who have committed serious crimes	84	88	91	81	85
... find out more about where people's ancestors came from	49	50	56	50	51
... judge a person's suitability for getting health and life insurance	11	19	21	26	19
... judge a person's suitability for getting a job they've applied for	8	12	14	21	14
Base	943	421	940	894	3272

The manner in which public support for genetic databases varies according to their proposed use suggests that public concerns, particularly among the most well-educated groups, might centre on the use of genetic data by third parties for commercial gain, which could adversely affect individuals' quality of life.

Although a clear majority oppose the use of databases for insurance or employment purposes, a majority believe it likely that this will eventually happen, in the longer term at least. Table 6.4 shows that seven in ten believe that genetic information will be used to determine health or life insurance premiums within the next 25 years, a similar proportion as did in 1996. A lower proportion believe that genetic information will be used to judge job applicants, but this view has become more prevalent since 1996.

Table 6.4 Perceived likelihood that insurance companies and employers will use genetic data within the next 25 years, 1996, 2000 and 2003

% saying it is very or quite likely that genetic information will be used to judge a person's suitability for getting ...	1996	2000	2003
... health and life insurance	72	76	70
... a job they've applied for	43	58	52
Base	*2096*	*1963*	*2649*

Public trust

We turn now to examine how far members of the public are trusting of the different stakeholders involved in genetic science. As Table 6.5 suggests, mistrust appears to be more prevalent than trust. Thus, only a quarter trust those in charge of "new developments" in genetic science to act in society's interests, while a third do not. And, while just under a quarter think that government legislation will protect the public from any risks linked to modern genetic science, nearly double this proportion disagree. Such mistrust extends particularly to genetic scientists, with six in ten agreeing that they only tend to report what their employers want to hear. Only 15 per cent rejected this statement. Of particular concern to those policy makers eager to engage the public in some kind of scientific dialogue may be the fact that only around a quarter of Britons see public involvement in policy decisions as a feasible option, with half thinking that such involvement is unrealistic, owing to the complexity of the underlying science.

Table 6.5 Trust in modern genetic science

		Agree	Neither	Disagree	*Base*
Those in charge of new developments in genetic science cannot be trusted to act in society's interests	%	34	36	25	*3272*
Rules set by government will keep us safe from any risks linked to modern genetic science	%	23	27	45	*3272*
Genetic scientists only tend to tell us what the people paying their wages want us to hear	%	60	21	15	*3272*
Modern genetic science is so complex that public involvement in policy decisions is not realistic	%	50	18	27	*3272*

Human genomics

With the completion of the human genome sequence in 2001, much attention
has focused on genetic approaches to health improvement and diagnosis. The
complex role that genes can have in many human illnesses and diseases is now
becoming better understood by scientists and, it would seem, attracting a large
measure of public support; nearly half (47 per cent) of the British public in 2003
disagree that "research into human genes will do more harm than good".

However, when research into the genetic basis of human characteristics and
disease are communicated to a general audience, media headlines, perhaps
inevitably, tend to focus on discoveries of "the gene for" particular health
conditions and, more controversially, the origins of complex personality or
behavioural traits.[6] As a result, some have argued that the public are
increasingly likely to take a deterministic view of genetics, that is, to ascribe
particular character traits or dispositions to a person's genetic make-up
(Lippman, 1993).

To examine whether the increasingly detailed scientific delineation of the
genetic basis of human behaviour and morbidity have led to more genetic
determinism amongst the public, we asked a series of questions about the
'causes' of a range of different traits. The questions were introduced as follows:

> Some things about a person are caused by their **genes**, which they
> inherit from their parents. Others may be to do with **the way they are
> brought up**, or **the way they live**. Some may happen just **by chance**.
> Using this card, please say what **you** think decides each of the
> [following] things. If you don't know, please just say so.

Respondents could choose from six different answer options: "all to do with
genes"; "mostly to do with genes"; "mostly to do with upbringing or lifestyle";
"all to do with upbringing or lifestyle"; "an equal mixture of genes and
upbringing or lifestyle"; and "just chance". Table 6.6 shows the proportions of
people who thought that the different traits were "all" or "mostly to do with
genes", and how this has changed over time. Just under a third of Britons
believe that intelligence is mainly a genetic trait, a proportion that has shown a
slight but consistent decrease since 1998. Genes are also perceived by around
one-third of the British public as having a major role in determining sexuality, a
figure which has remained unchanged over the last five years. Far fewer
individuals see genes as mainly responsible for aggressive or violent behaviour;
since 1998, a consistent nine-tenths of the public have opposed this view. This
stability contrasts with the slight increase over time in the proportion attributing
a strong genetic component to medical conditions. This applies most strongly to
breast cancer where a majority (55 per cent) now attribute "all" or "most" of the
cause to genes, compared to 48 per cent in 1998. Genes are also now likely to
be perceived as a dominant cause of heart disease, but to a far lesser extent than
breast cancer, with just a third of the public endorsing this view. On the whole,
then, there is little evidence to support the notion that the public are becoming
increasingly likely to see the underlying causes of human behaviour and disease

as mainly genetic, although this is clearly rather a short time frame within which to evaluate the hypothesis.

Table 6.6 Extent to which various traits are perceived as genetically determined, 1998, 2000 and 2003

% saying all or mostly to do with genes ...	1998	2000	2003
... intelligence	36	34	30
... being gay or lesbian	34	n/a	35
... chances of being aggressive or violent	9	11	10
... chances of getting heart disease	29	29	33
... chances of getting breast cancer	48	n/a	55
Base	*2112*	*2267*	*3272*

n/a = not asked

In order to examine the acceptability of gene therapy, we also asked whether, for each of these traits, gene therapy *should* be allowed:

> *Suppose it was discovered that a person's genes could be changed. Taking your answers from this card, do you think this should be allowed or not allowed to ...*

Although a majority of the British public reject the view that a person's genes determine complex behavioural traits such as aggression or violence, Table 6.7 shows that more than half would favour genetic intervention to make someone less aggressive, were this possible, a proportion that has remained largely unchanged since 1998. The overall trend during this period, however, is of reduced support for this kind of intervention. What has remained consistently unacceptable over the last five years is changing a person's genes so that they become heterosexual rather than gay or lesbian, or to determine an unborn child's sex; around 80 per cent think neither of these should be allowed. However, the use of gene therapy to reduce a person's chance of developing breast cancer is much more popular and has attracted increasing public support, up from 72 per cent in 1998 and 2000 to 81 per cent in 2003.

For the first time, the 2003 survey distinguished between *somatic* gene therapy, where genetic material is transferred to normal body tissue, and *germ-line* gene therapy, where genetic material is also transferred to cells that produce eggs or sperm. The key difference is that the results of somatic gene therapy are restricted to the patient treated, while for germ-line gene therapy these modifications are passed from the patient to any children they may subsequently have. In both cases, we asked how acceptable these forms of therapy would be for "someone in their 20s who has a life-threatening medical condition"; around eight in ten thought that these two treatments should be allowed (although support for germ-line therapy was slightly lower than support for somatic gene therapy, at 79 and 85 per cent respectively). Thus, when its purpose is clearly defined as medical treatment, gene therapy receives widespread public support, be it of the somatic or germ-line variety.

Table 6.7 Attitudes towards gene therapy, 1998, 2000 and 2003

% saying that changing a person's genes should definitely or probably be allowed to ...	1998	2000	2003
... make a person less aggressive or violent	59	56	56
... make a person straight, rather than gay or lesbian	18	18	18
... determine the sex of an unborn baby	12	16	15
... reduce a person's chances of getting breast cancer	72	72	81
... treat someone in their 20s with a life-threatening medical condition if the new genes would <u>not</u> be passed on to any children they might have	n/a	n/a	85
... treat someone in their 20s with a life-threatening medical condition if the new genes <u>would</u> be passed on to any children they might have	n/a	n/a	79
Base	*2112*	*2267*	*3272*

n/a = not asked

Much opposition to human genetic intervention is underpinned by its potential to select for 'desirable' physical or cognitive characteristics in children. This has prompted fears about a generation of 'designer babies', with characteristics such as sex, height, eye colour and even intelligence chosen by parents, as if from a shopping list. More realistically, concerns have focused on prenatal testing for an ever-increasing range of genetic conditions, leading to the termination of pregnancies that, for a variety of social and historical reasons, are not considered 'normal' or desirable. To examine attitudes towards these issues, we asked about the acceptability of prenatal testing in the five different circumstances shown in Table 6.8:

> *Genetic tests can also be carried out on an unborn child. Do you agree or disagree with parents using such tests to help them decide whether or not to have a child that ...*

As it is often argued that religious beliefs about the sanctity and protection of human life underpin debate on these issues, the table also shows how public opinion about parental use of prenatal genetic testing varies according to religious affiliation.

Overall, around two-thirds agree that it should be permissible for parents to use a genetic test to help decide whether or not to have a child with a mental or physical disability serious enough to mean the child would never be able to live an independent life. A similar proportion are in favour of genetic testing that selects a child whose body tissues are a genetic match for a seriously ill sibling (and could hence be used to provide medical treatment or a cure). Public endorsement of parental use of prenatal testing is markedly lower if its purpose is to decide whether to have a healthy child with a reduced life expectancy. This suggests that perceived quality of life is an important factor in determining the moral acceptability of this type of genetic intervention. Finally, there is very little support for prenatal testing in order to help parents decide a child's sex, with less than one in ten in favour of genetic testing for this purpose. This is consistent with previous research by the Human Fertilisation and Embryology Authority which found widespread public opposition to the idea that parents should have the right to choose the sex of their child (HFEA, 2003).

Views about these matters vary significantly according to a person's religious affiliation. Those who are not religious, or who belong to the Church of England, are the most supportive of prenatal testing, while those who belong to other religious groups are less in favour. Thus, while seven in ten Anglicans support prenatal tests to help parents decide whether to have a child with a serious mental disability, only just over a half of Catholics agree. It is notable, however, that for the three most serious conditions described in the next table, majorities among *all* religious groups agree with the use of prenatal tests. Religious affiliation makes no difference to attitudes about genetic testing to have a child on the premise that its body tissues could be used to provide medical treatment for a sibling; nor does it relate to views about the acceptability of prenatal tests to determine a child's sex.

Table 6.8 Attitudes towards prenatal genetic testing, by religious affiliation

% agree with genetic tests to help decide whether to have a child with ...	Church of England	Catholic	Other Christian	Non-Christian	No religion	All
... a serious mental disability and would never be able to live an independent life	71	54	62	57	69	66
... a serious physical disability and would never be able to live an independent life	68	51	62	57	67	64
... the same types of body tissues needed to treat a brother or sister who is seriously ill	68	62	60	57	64	63
... a condition that means it would live in good health but then die in its 20s or 30s	43	34	35	32	42	40
... one sex rather than another	9	10	7	12	10	9
Base	*872*	*300*	*494*	*153*	*1421*	*3272*

The cloning of human embryos is, in many ways, a lightning rod for public resistance and hostility to the moral and ethical problems of human genetic research. With its frightening sci-fi images and associations of 'playing God', cloning goes right to the heart of what it is to be human. The few large-scale surveys that have included questions on attitudes to human cloning have found substantial opposition to the idea of creating cloned human embryos, on both moral and religious grounds (Singer *et al.*, 1998; Nisbet, 2004). In-depth qualitative investigations, however, have found the public to be less opposed towards the use of cloned embryos in medical research (Wellcome Trust, 1998).

Clearly, therapeutic human cloning is not an easy subject to ask about in a survey questionnaire. So we began by describing it to respondents as follows:

> *You might have heard of something called human cloning. One type of cloning would be if a person's genes were copied exactly and used to make an embryo. Cells from the embryo could be used to supply the person with tissues or organs that would be a perfect match for them, meaning their body would not reject them. Do you think this should be allowed or not allowed ...?*

We then asked about the acceptability of cloning in three specific circumstances: organ transplantation; the treatment of Parkinson's disease; and to prolong a healthy person's life. Of these, the two applications with clear medical benefits – organ transplantation and treatment for Parkinson's disease – are supported by a majority of the public, echoing findings from other studies (Gaskell *et al.*, 2003a). However, public opinion about using the same cloning technology in order to extend the life expectancy of someone in good health is rejected by a sizeable majority; less than one in five adults think that this should be allowed, while nearly three-quarters disagree.

We also asked about reproductive human cloning:

> *Another type of human cloning might be used to treat a young couple who are infertile and cannot have a child. Suppose that the genes from one of them were copied exactly and used to make an embryo with exactly the same genetic make up as that parent. Do you think this should be allowed or not allowed ...?*

Just under four in ten people think such reproductive cloning should be allowed, while just under half think it should not. This suggests that human reproductive cloning does not meet with quite as strong a level of public opposition as might, perhaps, be expected. However, support for this technology is substantially lower than support for therapeutic cloning for clear medical purposes.

Nine per cent of our sample had been advised by a doctor of a serious genetic condition in their family, or knew of another family member who had been told of this. This group were slightly more supportive than average of cloning for organ transplantation or the treatment of Parkinson's disease, although their small sample size meant that these differences were not statistically significant.

Table 6.9 Attitudes towards human cloning

		Should be allowed	Should not be allowed
... if a person needs an organ transplant	%	64	24
... if a person needs treatment for Parkinson's disease	%	64	23
... if a person is generally in good health and wants to live longer	%	15	73
... to treat a young couple who are infertile and cannot have a child	%	38	48

Base: 2649

Our results so far have shown that a majority of the British public approve of human genetic intervention where there is a clear medical benefit. Even reproductive human cloning attracts less outright public opposition than might be expected. It is also clear that attitudes towards the same genetic technology vary substantially according to the *context* within which that technology is applied. Meanwhile, clear majorities are favourable towards genetic databanks where there is a societal benefit in terms of health or crime control, although the use of individual genetic data in a way that might adversely affect the person concerned attracts little public support.

A second key finding to emerge so far is that some attitudes towards genomics have changed substantially over a relatively short time frame. Change is most evident in relation to GM foods; the public in 2003 are far less opposed to these than they were just four years earlier.

How attentive are we to modern genetic science?

We now turn our attention to an examination of the antecedents and consequences of public attentiveness towards this new and rapidly evolving area of science and technology. Here we pursue a long-standing tradition in models of public opinion which calls into question the notion of a unitary and homogenous 'public' with respect to issues of social controversy. Rather, the population as a whole is seen as comprising a number of distinct subgroups, each with differing levels of interest, engagement and familiarity with the issue in question (Le Bon, 1895; Park, 1904; Blumer, 1946). Although the make-up of these groups is conceived as fluid and subject to change as an issue evolves, only a small proportion of the general population are likely to constitute the most attentive group, on most issues, at any one time. By contrast, the majority of the public will be disinterested, uninformed and disconnected from any ongoing public debate. As a consequence, it is argued that only a relatively small proportion of the public will be able to provide an 'informed' opinion on any given issue.

Such a model can be usefully applied to our understanding of public attitudes towards genomics, a fast-moving area of scientific enquiry which is clearly still an 'emergent' object of public opinion. We are not the first to adopt this stratified approach to understanding public opinion toward science (Miller, 1998; Pfister *et al.*, 2000). Most prominently in relation to genetic science, Gaskell and colleagues (2003a) combine measures of factual knowledge of biology and genes, with behavioural intentions towards, and awareness of, new genetic technologies into an index of public engagement with biotechnology. According to the Gaskell index, only around a quarter of Britons constituted the 'engaged public', with the remaining three-quarters not discussing biotechnology with any regularity, nor anticipating taking part in any public discussion on the subject in the future. Using this approach Gaskell and colleagues find the typical 'engaged' European citizen to be male, university educated and below 55 years of age.

Who do our results suggest are the most attentive when it comes to genomics? We measured attentiveness by asking whether people were interested in "issues to do with genes and genetics". Nearly a quarter (24 per cent) had "a great deal" or "quite a lot" of interest in the area, a quarter had "some" interest, another quarter (24 per cent) "not very much" interest, and 27 per cent had "none at all". We also asked about the extent to which they had recently heard or read about these issues, talked about them or simply thought about them. As Table 6.10 shows, just over a third had *heard* or *read* "a great deal" or "quite a lot" about genes and genetics, and just under a third had heard or read "a small amount". One in five had *thought* about genetics at least quite a lot in the past few months, and one in seven had talked about these issues.

Table 6.10 Attentiveness to genes and genetics

Over the past few months, how much, if at all, have you ...		A great deal, quite a lot	A small amount	Not very much, not at all
... *heard* or *read* about issues to do with genes or genetics	%	36	30	33
... *thought* about issues to do with genes or genetics	%	21	26	53
... *talked* about issues to do with genes or genetics	%	14	27	59

Base: 2649

We combined responses to these four questions to identify those who were particularly more, or less, likely to be attentive to genetic issues. In order to identify the groups who are the *most* attentive we ran a multivariate analysis, the results of which are summarised in Figure 6.1 (see Model A in the appendix to this chapter for further details). The advantage of this form of analysis is that it takes account of relationships that exist between particular groups of interest (for example, the fact that older people tend to have lower educational qualifications than younger ones). Counter to previous research which shows that men tend to be most engaged with new scientific advancements, including biotechnology (Gaskell *et al.*, 2003a), we find that women are more attentive to issues involving genes and genetics. Such issues encompass a variety of genetic technologies relevant to health and family formation which may be of particular salience for women. There is no simple linear relationship between attentiveness and age; older people (in their mid- to late 50s) are the most attentive and younger people (between 18 and 24 years) are the least attuned to issues relevant to modern genetic science. Education and knowledge of genetics are also important predictors of attentiveness. Those without formal qualifications are the least attentive to modern genetic science. More specifically, having a qualification in a biological science is associated with greater attentiveness. In addition, even once education is taken into account, people who score highly on a four item knowledge quiz about genes and genetics are also the most engaged with debates surrounding this area of science (further information about these knowledge questions can be found in the appendix to this chapter).

Interest in politics is positively correlated with genomic attentiveness, a finding consistent with previous research (Gaskell *et al.*, 2003a), and likely to result from a general engagement with news and current affairs. Newspaper readership is also related to attentiveness. The most attentive, unsurprisingly, are broadsheet readers, though those who read no paper at all are significantly more attentive than readers of tabloid newspapers. Internet users also score significantly higher on the genomics attentiveness scale than do non-users. As these latter findings apply even when education and a person's factual knowledge of genetics are taken into account, they suggest that the contexts and channels through which information about genomics is obtained may be important in shaping people's attentiveness. Equally, however, it is likely that attentiveness itself influences when and how people seek out information.

Figure 6.1 Groups more likely to be attentive towards modern genetic science

Attentive public

Age 55 to 59 years

Women

Politically engaged

Broadsheet reader

Internet user

O level/GCSE qualifications or above

Biology qualification

Higher genetic knowledge

Reported genetic condition in family

In sum, prior and current levels of formal knowledge appear to play a role in shaping people's ongoing interest in, and awareness of, genes and genetics. Increased information-seeking may explain why the attentive public is more likely to include people who report having had a serious genetic illness diagnosed in their family – not only may such a diagnosis prompt people to find out more, but it is also likely to increase the salience of information about genes and genetics in the public domain.

Attentiveness and enthusiasm about genomics

This evidence has helped us identify those most likely to be attentive to modern genetic science. The more important question, however, is whether the *attitudes* of this group towards genomics are in some senses distinct. After all, it is often anticipated that increasing public awareness and understanding about technological innovation will lead to opinion becoming more informed by "fact and reason" than by "unfounded fear and emotion" (Blair, 2002). There is reason to believe that, as simple familiarity grows with what was initially a novel and alien concept, resistance and hostility will decline as the object becomes anchored and assimilated into existing public discourses and cognitive schemas. Indeed, this could offer an explanation as to why attitudes to GM foods have changed since 1999, with no particular event or 'shock' appearing to underlie the general softening of opinion that has been apparent.

In order to investigate whether the attentive public have distinctive views about genomics, we carried out a series of multivariate analyses to assess how a range of factors relate to views about GM crops and foods, trust in the regulation of modern genetic research, therapeutic cloning, and genetic science in general (the construction of these models is described in detail in the appendix to this chapter). Our particular interest is in examining the joint influence of three key 'cognitive' factors: education, genetic knowledge and attentiveness. Do these, *in and of themselves*, make a difference to a person's views on these matters, even when background characteristics such as age and sex are taken into account?

Each model includes a broad range of background variables measuring social and demographic characteristics, most notably age, gender, social class and educational qualifications (including whether the person has any qualification in a biological science). Factual knowledge of biology is measured *via* our four item knowledge quiz. We also include a self-reported measure of whether a serious genetic condition has been diagnosed within a family as an indicator of the personal salience of issues related to genes and genetics. Measures of internet use and newspaper readership capture differential access or exposure to information relevant to genetic science and the broader context in which this information is conveyed. Additionally, internet use may be indicative of acceptance and adoption of new technologies and, therefore, positively correlated with attitudes to genomics. Self-reported interest in politics is included as a measure of broader political engagement. Finally, religious denomination is included as we earlier found this to be an important predictor of views about genetic issues. The full results for these models are presented in the appendix to this chapter.

Figure 6.2 summarises, for each issue, the direction and statistical significance of the effects of education, genetic knowledge and attentiveness, taking account of all the demographic characteristics listed earlier. We report in the text cases where these other characteristics emerge as significant once attentiveness, education and knowledge are taken into account.

This analysis confirms that an individual's level of knowledge about, and attentiveness towards, genetic science are important in understanding their attitudes, as is their educational background. The results, however, are far from uniform, with quite different patterns of significance and direction of effect, depending on the particular subject area being considered. We start with attitudes towards GM foods. The negative association between public attentiveness and attitudes to GM food in Figure 6.2 shows that those who are the *most* attentive to genomics are *less* likely to be supportive of GM foods. Factual knowledge about genes and genetics, perhaps a better indicator of public familiarity than self-reported interest and engagement, is, however, predictive of *more* favourable attitudes towards GM foods. The most knowledgeable are, in other words, the most positive about this form of genetic technology. The model also shows that, even once these factors are taken into account, a person's age, sex, and their interest in politics are significantly related to their views about GM foods. Younger age groups tend to be more favourable than older ones, men more favourable than women, and the politically interested *less* favourable than those with lower levels of interest.

When it comes to trust in the regulation of genetic science, attentiveness is associated with *lower* levels of trust in the way genomics is managed and regulated. This runs counter to the expectation that attentive individuals should have greater confidence in the competence and trustworthiness of those charged with managing modern genetic science, as they are better able to appreciate the constraints within which they have to operate (Sturgis and Allum, 2004). However, education is positively associated with trust, meaning that the most well educated tend to be the most trusting of current arrangements as regards the management and regulation of genomics. Even when these factors are taken into account, tabloid readers and those who read no newspaper are less trusting than broadsheet readers. Social class also matters, with those in managerial and professional occupations and the self-employed being more trusting than those in skilled manual positions.

Attentiveness proves to be unrelated to attitudes towards human cloning for the purposes of medical treatment or organ transplantation, despite this being a genetic technology that has attracted public controversy. When it comes to education and genetic knowledge, we find their impact appears to operate in opposite directions, with knowledge being associated with *less* favourable attitudes and higher qualifications associated with *more* favourable attitudes to therapeutic cloning. There were also significant differences of opinion associated with age, sex, newspaper readership, religion and class. Men were more favourable than women, tabloid readers more favourable than broadsheet readers, the non-religious more favourable than the religious, and those in intermediate non-manual occupations less favourable than those in skilled manual positions.

The final area we examine relates to a person's general attitude towards human genetic research. This is the only model in which both attentiveness and genetic knowledge prove to be significantly related to people's attitudes in the same way; those who are more attentive and knowledgeable about genes and genetics express *more* favourable general attitudes towards human genetic research than those who are not. The only other characteristic to emerge as significantly associated with responses to this question was sex, with men being more favourable than women.

Figure 6.2 Relationship between attitudes to genomics and education, knowledge and attentiveness

	GM food and crops	Trust	Therapeutic cloning	General attitude to genetic research
Education	—	Positive	Positive	—
Genetic knowledge	Positive	—	Negative	Positive
Attentiveness	Negative	Negative	—	Positive

— = relationship is not statistically significant

We can conclude from these findings that attentiveness does appear to influence public attitudes towards genomics. However, this must be qualified in two important respects. First, attentiveness is not a *uniform* predictor of genomic attitudes as it is unrelated to attitudes towards therapeutic cloning. Second, our findings show that it is misleading to assume that a more attentive and knowledgeable public is necessarily more supportive of genetic science and its associated technologies. Indeed, attentive individuals are *more* critical of GM foods, and are *less* trusting of those conducting and regulating modern genetic science. At the same time, however, they are significantly less likely to believe that, on balance, human genetic research will do more harm than good. Thus, while these factors are clearly important to our understanding of the shape and trajectory of public opinion in this area, they are not related to attitudes in any simple or straightforward manner.

Further analysis also shows that the views that people hold about these four different areas are not strongly related, providing further evidence that public appraisals of specific areas of genetic science are, to a large degree, independent of one another. Although we may see these applications as falling under the general umbrella of 'genomics', by dint of their common relation to modern genetic science, it is questionable whether this homogenous classification has any resonance in the public mind. People seem to evaluate technology on the basis of its specific application in society, rather than on the common underlying science. Further details of this analysis can be found in the final table in the appendix to this chapter.

Conclusions

A key finding to emerge from these analyses is that some attitudes towards genomics have changed over a relatively short time frame. Change is most evident in relation to GM crops and foods; the public in 2003 are far less opposed to these than they were just four years ago. It is worth emphasising again the substantially different picture we have obtained of current public opinion towards GM than that which emerged from the 'GM Nation?' debate. In our analysis, we find opinion towards GM to be broadly ambivalent. By ambivalence we mean, in this context, that most questions attract a significant amount of both support and opposition, with even larger proportions 'sitting on the fence'. Opinion in Britain towards genetically modified crops and food cannot, on this evidence, be described as overwhelmingly hostile.

Our findings also show that a majority of the British public approve of human genetic intervention where there is a clear medical benefit. This applies when that benefit is intended for another person, such as an ill sibling, and even when it will be passed on to future generations, as in the case of germ-line gene therapy. When considered in the context of treating infertility, even reproductive human cloning garners less outright public opposition than might be expected. A key finding of this research, then, is that attitudes towards the *same* genetic technology vary substantially according to the context in which that technology is applied. The public are far less accepting of genetic intervention for the purposes of sex selection, increasing healthy life expectancy or determining characteristics such as sexuality. Similarly, a sizeable proportion of the public are favourable towards genetic databanks where there is a clear societal benefit in terms of improved health or crime reduction, but the use of individual genetic data in a way that might adversely affect the person concerned attracts little public support.

Our analysis also identifies certain groups as being particularly attentive towards genes and genetics. Amongst the characteristics which are most important in determining level of attentiveness are those that relate to educational qualifications, knowledge of genetics and exposure to information in the public domain (whether through newspapers or the internet).

We find some evidence to support the idea that people who are more interested in, and pay more attention to, genomics have distinct attitudinal profiles. Importantly, however, levels of public attentiveness do not have a uniform effect on attitudes across different areas of genetic science. Public attentiveness does not help us discriminate between different views about cloning and, for attitudes towards GM food and trust in modern genetic science, attentive individuals are more opposed and resistant than non-attentive ones. This suggests that it may be overly simplistic to consider public engagement in genetic science as a means to foster greater public confidence and support in new technological developments. Only when it comes to very general attitudes to human genetic research do our results show attentiveness to be linked to a more favourable attitude. A similar conclusion can be extended to our measure of genetic knowledge, commonly used with awareness measures to examine public engagement in science.

Modern genetic science is still in its infancy. Public opinion towards its technological applications is, perhaps as a consequence, cautious, guarded and sometimes outright oppositional. Are we now though, perhaps, beginning to see some signs of growing familiarity and acceptance, with the earliest and most prominent genomic technology – GM crops and food – showing clear signs of a softening of opinion in Great Britain? In truth, it is too early to tell. Other evidence in this chapter questions the whole idea of the different genomic technologies being considered, in the public mind, as strongly related. Rather, people seem to evaluate these technologies as independent entities, on the basis of the costs and benefits they each bring for individuals and society. Only through continued, high-quality public opinion measurement over a sustained period will such questions really become amenable to empirical enquiry.

Notes

1. 'Contamination in Canada sounds warning to UK', *The Guardian*, 18 June 2003; 'The designer baby created to save his brother's life...', *Daily Mail*, 19 June 2003, headline; 'GM crops "could carpet Britain with superweed"', *Daily Mail*, 10 July 2003, p. 17; 'Playing God? Ethical storm as first human clone is created', *Daily Mail*, 13 February 2004, headline.
2. Also 'The designer baby myth', *The Guardian*, 5 June 2003; 'Fears over genetic profiles for all', *The Observer*, 17 August 2003.
3. Other canvassing exercises have been undertaken in relation to the genetic selection of embryos (HFEA, 2001, 2003; Human Genetics Commission, 2004), the use of human genetic information (Human Genetics Commission, 2001; People Science and Policy, 2002) and predictive genetic testing (Royal Society, 2003).
4. *The Guardian*, 25 September 2003.
5. To check levels of support for the specific use of genetic databases in order to help solve crime, we also asked:

    Some people think everyone in Britain should have to give a sample of their genetic information to a database that would help identify people who have committed serious crimes. Would you be in favour of, or against, this happening?

    When put in these terms, public support falls slightly, to just under seven in ten (69 per cent).
6. 'Prostrate cancer gene identified', BBC News online, 8 June 2004, http://news.bbc.co.uk/1/hi/health/3787033.stm;
    'Genes may be to blame for infidelity', BBC News online, 7 June 2004, http://news.bbc.co.uk/1/hi/health/3783031.stm

References

Blair, A. (2002), Science Matters, Speech to the Royal Society, 10 April 2002

Blumer, H. (1946), 'Collective behaviour', in Lee, A.M. (ed.), *New outlines of the principles of sociology*, New York: Barnes and Noble

Bodmer, W. (1985), *The public understanding of science*, London: Royal Society

Campbell, S. and Townsend, E. (2003),'Flaws undermine results of UK biotech debate', *Nature*, **425:**559, 9 October)

Department of Health (2003), *Our Inheritance, our future – realising the potential of genetics in the NHS*, White Paper, Cmd 5791, London: HMSO

Department of Trade and Industry (2003), *GM Nation? The findings of the public debate*, London: HMSO

Food Standards Agency (1999), *Consumer views of GM food*, London: FSA

Gaskell, G., Allum, N. and Stares, S. (2003a), *Europeans and Biotechnology in 2002, Eurobarometer 58.0*, A report to the EC Directorate General for Research from the project 'Life Sciences in European Society', Brussels: European Commission

Gaskell, G., Allum, N., Bauer, M., Jackson, J., Howard, S. and Lindsey, N. (2003b), *Ambivalent GM Nation? Public attitudes to biotechnology in the UK, 1991–2002*, Life Sciences in European Society report, London: London School of Economics

Horlick-Jones, T., Walls, J., Rowe, G., Pidgeon, N., Poortinga, W. and Riordan, T. (2004), *A Deliberative Future? An independent evaluation of the GM Nation? Public debate about the possible commercialisation of transgenic crops in Britain*, Understanding Risk Working Paper 04-02, Norwich: Centre for Environmental Risk

House of Lords (2000), *Science and Society: Third report*, Science and Technology Select Committee, London: HMSO

Human Fertilisation and Embryology Authority, (2001), *Outcome of the public consultation on preimplantation genetic diagnosis*, London: HFEA

Human Fertilisation and Embryology Authority, (2003), *Sex selection: options for regulation*, London: HFEA

Human Genetics Commission (2000*), Whose hands on your genes?* London: HGC

Human Genetics Commission (2001), *Public attitudes to human genetic information*, London: HGC

Human Genetics Commission (2002), *Inside information: balancing interests in the use of personal genetic data*, London: HGC

Human Genetics Commission (2004), *Choosing the future: genetics and reproductive decision making*, London: Department of Health

Irwin, A. and Wynne, B. (eds.) (1996), *Misunderstanding Science? The Public Reconstruction of Science and Technology*, Cambridge: Cambridge University Press

Le Bon, G. (1895), *The crowd: a study of the popular mind*, New York: Macmillan

Lippman, A. (1993), 'Prenatal genetic testing and geneticization: mother matters for all', *Fetal Diagnosis and Therapy*, **8:**175–188

Midden, C., Boy, D., Einsiedel, E., Fjæstad, B., Liakopoulos, M., Miller, J.D., Öhman, S. and Wagner, W. (2002), 'The structure of public perceptions', in Bauer, M., Durant, J. and Gaskell, G. (eds.), *Biotechnology: the making of a global controversy*, Cambridge: Cambridge University Press

Miller, J. (1998), 'The measurement of civic scientific literacy', *Public Understanding of Science*, **7:**203–223

Nisbet, M.C. (2004), 'Public opinion about stem cell research and human cloning', *Public Opinion Quarterly*, **68(1)**: 131–154

Pardo, R., Midden, C. and Miller, J. (2002), 'Attitudes towards biotechnology in the European Union', *Journal of Biotechnology*, **98**: 9-24

Park, R.E. (1904), *The Crowd and the Public and Other Essays*, Elsner, H. Jr (ed.), Chicago: Chicago University Press

People Science and Policy (2002), *BioBank UK: a question of trust. A consultation exploring and addressing questions of public trust*, Report for the Medical Research Council and the Wellcome Trust, London: People Science and Policy

Pfister, H., Böhm, G. and Jungermann, H. (2000), 'The cognitive representation of genetic engineering: knowledge and evaluations', *New Genetics and Society*, **19(3)**: 296–316

Poortinga, W. and Pidgeon, N.F. (2004), *Public Perceptions of Genetically Modified Food and Crops, and the 'GM Nation?' Public Debate on the Commercialisation of Agricultural Biotechnology in the UK*, Understanding Risk Working Paper 04-01, Norwich: Centre for Environmental Risk

Royal Society (2003), *Genetic Testing – which way forward?* Report from the Royal Society National Forum for Science, People's science summit, London: Royal Society

Singer, E., Corning, A. and Lamias, M. (1998), 'Trends: genetic testing, engineering and therapy: awareness and attitudes', *Public Opinion Quarterly*, **62(4)**: 633–664

Sturgis, P. and Allum, N. (2004), 'Science in Society: Re-evaluating the Deficit Model of Public Understanding', *Public Understanding of Science*, **13(1)**: 55–75

Wellcome Trust (1998), *Public perspectives on human cloning*, London: Wellcome Trust

Acknowledgements

The support of the Economic and Social Research Council (ESRC) is gratefully acknowledged. The work arises from the ESRC Attitudes to Genomics project L145251005 (www.surrey.ac.uk/shs/genomics). The authors wish to acknowledge the co-investigators on this project at the University of Surrey for their contribution to this paper: Julie Barnett, Adrian Coyle, Jo Moran-Ellis, Victoria Senior and Chris Walton. We would also like to extend our gratitude to the members of the project Advisory Board.

Appendix

Structural Equation Modeling (SEM) in MPlus 2.14 was used for all the models detailed below. All figures shown in the table are parameter estimates. Variables obtaining statistical significance at the $p<0.05$ level are marked with a single asterisk (*). Background characteristics entered as independent variables into all models were: age, gender, interest in politics, newspaper readership, whether or not internet user, highest educational qualification, biology qualification, religion, individual social class (NS-SEC), reported serious genetic illness in the family, attentiveness (models B to E only) and genetic knowledge. The genetic knowledge measure is derived from the following battery of four true/false items: it is possible to transfer animal genes into plants; ordinary tomatoes do not contain genes, while genetically modified tomatoes do; it is the father's genes that determine whether a child is a girl; genetically modified animals are always bigger than ordinary ones. Correct answers were scored +1, and all other answers coded zero, before items were summed to produce a 5-point scale ranging from 0 to 4. This scale is included in the model as a continuous variable.

Model A: Predictors of attentiveness to modern genetic science
The dependent variable was a single factor of attentiveness based on the aggregation of four items:

> *How much interest, if any, do you have in issues to do with genes and genetics? [A great deal, Quite a lot, Some, Not very much, None at all]*

> *Over the past few months, how much, if anything, have you heard or read about issues to do with genes and genetics? [A great deal, Quite a lot, A small amount, Not very much, Nothing at all]*

> **And over the past few months, how much, if at all, have you talked about issues to do with genes and genetics?*

> **Over the past few months, how much, if at all, have you thought about issues to do with genes and genetics?*

> **[A great deal, Quite a lot, A small amount, Not very much, Not at all]*

The table shows how much more or less likely the various groups are to be attentive to modern genetic science. Positive parameter estimates in the table indicate the independent variable is associated with greater attentiveness towards modern genetic science.

Model B: Predictors of attitudes towards GM foods
The dependent variable was a single factor of attitude towards GM foods based on the aggregation of the following four agree/disagree items:

> *In order to compete with the rest of the world, Britain should grow genetically modified (GM) foods*

> *Genetically modified (GM) foods should be banned, even if prices suffer as a result*

On balance, the advantages of genetically modified (GM) foods outweigh any dangers

It is important for me to check whether or not foods contain genetically modified ingredients.

Two other attitude items were included:

In general, do you think growing genetically modified (GM) foods poses a danger to other plants and wildlife?

Do you think that all genetically modified (GM) foods already available in the shops are safe to eat?

[Definitely, Probably, Probably not, Definitely not, Can't choose]

The table shows how much more or less likely the various groups are to be in favour of GM foods. Positive parameter estimates in the table indicate the independent variable is associated with greater opposition about GM food.

Model C: Predictors of trust
The dependent variable was a single factor of trust towards modern genetic science based on the aggregation of three agree/disagree items:

Those in charge of new developments cannot be trusted to act in society's interests

Rules set by government will keep us safe from any risks linked to modern genetic science

Genetic scientists only tend to tell us what the people paying their wages want us to hear.

The table shows how much more or less likely the various groups are to display a trusting attitude towards modern genetic science. Positive parameter estimates in the table indicate the independent variable is associated with greater trust.

Model D: Predictors of attitudes towards therapeutic cloning
The dependent variable was a single factor of attitude towards therapeutic cloning based on the aggregation of two items about whether or not this form of cloning should be allowed or not if "a person needs an organ transplant" and if "a person needs treatment for Parkinson's disease".

The table shows how much more or less likely the various groups are to be in favour of therapeutic cloning. Positive parameter estimates in the table indicate the independent variable is associated with greater opposition towards therapeutic cloning.

Model E: Predictors of general attitude
The dependent variable was a single measure of general attitude towards modern genetic science based on agreement with the statement "research into human genes will do more harm than good". The table shows how much more or less likely the various

groups are to adopt a favourable stance towards this area of science. Positive parameter estimates in the table indicate the independent variable is associated with more favourable attitudes towards human genetic research.

Parameter estimates from Attentiveness Model

Model Predictor	A **Attentiveness** (higher scores >attentive)	B **Attitude to GM food** (higher scores >favourable)	C **Trust** (higher scores >trust)
Age: 18-24	-0.12	0.18*	ns
25-34	0.00	0.10*	ns
45-54	0.06	-0.10	ns
55-59	0.20*	-.011	ns
60-64	0.12	-0.03	ns
65+	0.08	0.00	ns
ref=age 35-44			
Gender: Male	-0.19*	0.17*	ns
Interest in politics: yes	0.29*	-0.05*	ns
Newspaper readership: None	-0.20*	ns	-0.12*
Tabloid	-0.34*	ns	-0.17*
Other newspaper	-0.08	ns	-0.07
Ref=broadsheet			
Internet user: yes	0.25*	ns	ns
Highest qualification: degree	0.08	ns	0.11*
No qualifications	-0.23*	ns	-0.07
Ref=O or A Levels			
Biology qualification: yes	0.34*	ns	0.11*
Religion: Church of England	ns	ns	ns
Catholic	ns	ns	ns
Non-Christian	ns	ns	ns
None	ns	ns	ns
Ref= Other Christian			
Socio-economic Class:			
IManagerial/professional	ns	ns	0.14*
Intermediate	ns	ns	0.06
Self-employed	ns	ns	0.14*
Routine occupations	ns	ns	0.01
Other social class	ns	ns	0.21*
Ref=supervisory & technical			
Genetic knowledge: high score	0.13*	0.06*	ns
Reported genetic condition in family: yes	0.35*	ns	ns
Attentiveness	-	-0.11*	-0.05*
Base	*2299*	*2299*	*2299*

ns = variable parameters not statistically significant, p>0.05.
* = significant at the p<0.05 level

Model Predictor	D Therapeutic Cloning (higher scores >favourable)	E General Attitude (higher scores >favourable)
Age: 18-24	-0.05	-0.01
25-34	0.00	-0.18*
45-54	-0.14*	0.03
55-59	-.006	0.01
60-64	-0.15	0.03
65+	-0.14	-0.12
ref=age 35-44		
Gender: Male	0.12*	0.13*
Interest in politics: yes	ns	ns
Newspaper readership: None	-0.01	ns
Tabloid	0.16*	ns
Other newspaper	0.18	ns
Ref=broadsheet		
Internet user: yes	ns	ns
Highest qualification: degree	-0.07	ns
No qualifications	0.17*	ns
Ref=O or A Levels		
Biology qualification: yes	ns	ns
Religion: Church of England	0.09	ns
Catholic	-0.09	ns
Non-Christian	0.17	ns
None	0.13*	ns
Ref= Other Christian		
Socio-economic Class:		
Managerial/professional	-0.01	ns
Intermediate	-0.18*	ns
Self-employed	-0.08	ns
Routine occupations	-0.05	ns
Other social class	0.06	ns
Ref=supervisory & technical		
Genetic knowledge: high score	-0.04*	0.07*
Reported genetic condition in family: yes	ns	ns
Attentiveness	ns	-0.15*
Base	*2299*	*2299*

ns= variable parameters not statistically significant, p>0.05.
* = significant at the p<0.05 level

Correlations between attitudes to different genetic applications

	GM food	Trust	Therapeutic cloning	General attitude
GM Food	**1.00**			
Trust	.37*	**1.00**		
Therapeutic Cloning	.26*	0.10*	**1.00**	
General Attitude	.18*	0.30*	0.21*	**1.00**

* Statistically significant p<0.05

7 Dimensions of British identity

James Tilley, Sonia Exley and Anthony Heath *

Much of the literature on national identity draws a distinction between 'civic' and 'ethnic' conceptions. The former is supposed to place importance on aspects such as respect for political institutions, possessing national citizenship and speaking the national language. The latter is associated with a greater emphasis on bloodlines, ancestry and cultural assimilation, leading to a concern with people having been born and brought up in a country, and is therefore thought to be associated with weaker support for multiculturalism and potentially higher levels of worry about immigration. As is described below, French and German conceptions of national identity are generally recognised in literature as fitting neatly into this 'civic' and 'ethnic' typology respectively. This chapter seeks to explore the extent to which the typology is adequate in describing dimensions of British national identity. What do the British perceive as the things that make a person 'truly British'?

Using data from the 1995 and 2003 *International Social Survey Programme* modules which were administered as part of the *British Social Attitudes* series, the chapter begins by exploring the literature surrounding different dimensions of national identity. In order to assess how appropriate the civic/ethnic distinction is in a British context, we examine the extent to which people in Britain fall into different 'types' in terms of the way they conceptualise national identity. After this, we explore the differing social characteristics of those who conceptualise national identity in different ways. In particular, we are interested in the effect of generational changes on the types of national identity that are prevalent in Britain. Lastly, the relationship between people's differing conceptions of national identity and their degree of patriotism is explored.

* James Tilley is Lecturer in Quantitative Political Science and Fellow of Jesus College, Oxford; Sonia Exley is Research Assistant in the Department of Sociology and a member of Nuffield College, Oxford; Anthony Heath is Professor of Sociology at the University of Oxford.

The concept of national identity

The historical background

The origins of national identity as a concept and unifying human force in society can be traced back to the development of states and the centralisation of political power in the post-Reformation, pre-industrial era. Anderson describes the concept of a nation as "an imagined political community – and imagined as both inherently limited and sovereign" (Anderson, 1983: 6). He argues that this "deep horizontal comradeship" felt by citizens within certain territorial confines arose at a time when Enlightenment thought was questioning the notion of divinely ordained authority and a feeling of enlarged community 'belonging' was needed in order to gain legitimacy for centralised state power. Indeed, this rejection of the 'primitive' theory of nationalism (i.e. that nations have always existed) and the idea that nations are in fact ideological creations has been supported by commentators such as Gellner (1983), Hutchinson and Smith (1994) and Miller (1995). Hutchinson and Smith cite the importance of academic elites in this process: "movements of intelligentsia and opposition groups calling for the vernacular mobilisation of 'the people' against a variety of evils" (Hutchinson and Smith, 1994: 8). Mobilisation of this kind in the eighteenth and nineteenth centuries took the form of developing national cultures through national literary and cultural traditions and the standardisation of languages and education systems in an attempt to achieve three central goals of 'autonomy', 'unity' and 'identity' within sovereign states. The rise of a mass economy during the Industrial Revolution required mass communication and a reorganisation of humans from their fragmented and local social groupings into nations as the "natural social unit" (Gellner, 1983: 143).

However, the extent to which nations and national identity are viewed in this imaginary sense is a matter of some disagreement between theorists. While Gellner has tended to claim that nations are entirely invented entities, Anderson believes this goes too far, arguing that *all* communities larger than those of immediate localities might be considered 'imagined' in that members do not personally know each other, and that to imagine an identity does not necessarily constitute the fabrication of such an identity. Similarly, Miller has raised fundamental questions regarding the way that feelings of national identity are repressed in society and the way in which it is considered "a mark of civilisation not to be affected by the vulgar emotions that nationality evokes" (Miller, 1995: 15).

Hutchinson and Smith have drawn attention to the difficulty of defining nationalism as a concept compared with other forms of collective identity. Competing conceptions of national identity are evident in comparative studies of the phenomenon. While some theories focus on nostalgia relating to cultural heritage, others focus on language and geographical boundaries. Miller (1995) has made use here of the arguments of Hans Kohn, who draws a distinction between Western, liberal conceptions of national identity based on civic attachment to the state and Eastern conceptions of nationalism based on more mystical, quasi-tribal and 'backward' notions of identity. Smith has argued that the Eastern "ethnic genealogical" conception of nationality, with its focus on shared descent and ancestral culture, can tend towards the authoritarian and culturally repressive (Miller, 1995). However, this might be viewed as culturally relativist, particularly given arguments which draw attention to historic repression inherent in certain Western states such as France during the Napoleonic empire. Such arguments are difficult to resolve through comparative studies as there will only ever be a few countries that fall into each type. Each nation's development tends towards a unique path, and general rules will always be subject to exceptions.

Civic versus ethnic dimensions

Debates about the nature of nationality are often centred on a division of national identity into two overarching types of a civic, or 'inclusive', conceptualisation and an ethnic, or 'exclusive', conceptualisation. The civic 'inclusive' conception is perhaps best characterised by France after the 1789 Revolution. This idea stemmed from the creation of a republic and the Declaration of the Rights of Man, a reduction in the influence of the church and an end to feudal power structures (Safran, 1998).

The ethnic 'exclusive' form is characterised by the approach taken by Germany after unification in 1870. It has been argued that the ethnic nature of German national identity stems from an issue of national borders. The French national boundaries were clearly defined so that a territorial identity (*ius soli*) was feasible, but this was not the case in Germany. Here, conceptions of national identity were based more along bloodlines (*ius sanguinis*), with the focus on the notion of German people as an ethnic group. Fifty years of cultural advancement preceding unification in Germany had led to strong national sentiment, particularly in reaction to French developments, and unification marked the culmination of nationalist ideology whereby the German 'volk' were destined to unify and lead from the centre.

Much academic literature has been devoted to creating refined typologies of national identity in comparative politics. In addition to the broad conceptions of civic and ethnic identity as typified in France and Germany, factors such as ascriptive ideology (as in the US experience), religion and levels of cultural tolerance can come into play. Bryant (1997) has argued that civic and ethnic definitions of nationality can be subdivided according to their accommodation of difference, and that these definitions can be broadly applied to approaches taken in key societies. While Germany has an ethnic conception of citizenship, it is also exclusive in terms of cultural tolerance. The French civic identity is made more complicated by the expectation of cultural assimilation. This contrasts with the Dutch approach of civic identity and cultural pluralism. Bryant describes British national identity as being civic and also 'pragmatic'.

This notion of pragmatism in British identity is added to by Hjerm (1998), who discusses multicultural approaches to nationality, defined as tolerance without the need for cultural assimilation. Hjerm draws a distinction between British 'laissez-faire', non-interventionist pluralism and the multicultural policies of 'new world' countries such as Australia where active policies for the integration of minority cultures are adopted. The relationship between national identity and tolerance of immigration is discussed in more detail in the chapter by McLaren and Johnson.

This discussion suggests that definitions of national identity, and the relative importance of cultural indicators in defining identity, vary strongly between countries. In *The 15th Report*, McCrone and Surridge (1998) use data from the *International Social Survey Programme* specifically to examine which aspects of national identity tend to be viewed as important among survey respondents in four countries (Britain, Germany, Sweden and Spain). While they do find clear international differences (Spain, for example, places a higher value on religious identity – undoubtedly a feature of its Catholic and autocratic history), commonality, rather than difference, of experience seems to emerge. There is a focus in all four countries on language and respect for political institutions, which leads the authors to conclude that "overall, considerable national consensus exists with regard to the importance of the basic building blocks that make up national identity" (McCrone and Surridge, 1998: 7). One must be careful, therefore, not to overstate the importance of typologies of identities in comparative work on nationality.

Where does Britain fit in?

Whilst national identities in countries such as Germany and France seem relatively easy to categorise into overarching civic and ethnic definitions, the British experience might be considered more difficult. Cohen (1994) has described the notion of Britishness as "fuzzy" in that British identity has evolved gradually over time (as opposed to being defined through a distinct geo-political event such as a revolution or unification). It is more a result of continuous processes such as rising democracy, industrialisation and welfare state creation, not to mention the complicating factors of sub-state ethno-cultural identities. McCrone and Surridge (1998) suggest that in many ways the British tend to be defined, not in terms of who they are, but in terms of who they are *not*. High levels of post-colonial immigration and the lack of a clear extreme nationalist presence in Britain might suggest an ideology of civic multicultural tolerance as defining the British experience. However, this might equally suggest an *absence* of clear British identity. If we think about the two 'ideal' types of national identity as intersecting with one another, then we have four possibilities that Figure 7.1 illustrates.

Figure 7.1 The two dimensions of national identity

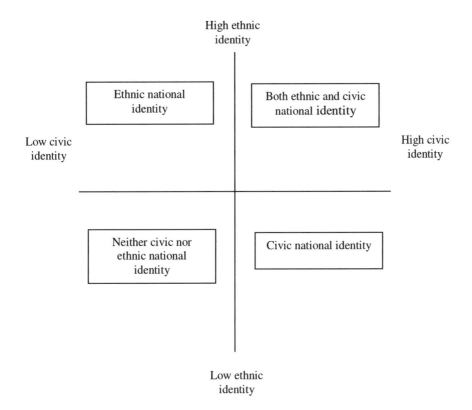

In general, it might be argued that German national identity could be located in the top left-hand quadrant, whereas French national identity resides in the bottom right-hand quadrant. If Britain fits neither of these, there are still two other possibilities: that British people may have little national feeling of either ethnic or civic origin (bottom left-hand quadrant), or that Britishness is actually a composite of ethnic *and* civic ideas of national identity (top right-hand quadrant). We turn now to the survey data to try to resolve this issue.

Just how 'fuzzy' is British national identity?

As part of the 1995 and 2003 ISSP surveys, respondents were asked the following question:

> *Some people say that the following things are important for being truly British. Others say that they are not important. How important do you think each of the following is?*

> *To have been born in Britain*
> *To have British citizenship*

To have lived in Britain for most of one's life
To be able to speak English
To be a Christian
To respect Britain's political institutions and laws
To feel British
To have British ancestry (this was asked in 2003 only)

This series of items was combined with a question that attempts specifically to address issues of ethnicity:

Now a few questions about minority groups in Britain. ... how much do you agree or disagree [that] ...

... It is impossible for people who do not share Britain's customs and traditions to become fully British

Defining civic and ethnic national identity in the British context

Table 7.1 shows proportions rating each of the above items as being "very" or "fairly important" in 'being British', broken down by year.[1]

Table 7.1 Importance of different aspects of 'being British', 1995 and 2003

% who say "very" or "fairly important"	1995	2003
	%	%
Speak English	85	87
British citizenship	83	83
Respect laws/institutions	82	82
Born in Britain	76	70
Feel British	74	74
Lived life in Britain	71	69
Have British ancestry	n/a	46
Be a Christian	32	31
Sharing customs/traditions*	50	52
Base	*1058*	*873*

n/a = not asked
* = % who "agree" or "strongly agree" with the statement "it is impossible for people who do not share Britain's customs and traditions to become fully British"

From the table, it is clear that there is general agreement that most of these items are important. This is particularly the case for speaking English, having British citizenship, and respecting British political institutions and laws, all of which were thought important by over four-fifths of respondents. There are only two items where there is not a clear majority in favour of their importance: having British ancestry and being a Christian – the latter being chosen by less than a third of respondents. The table also shows that there has been little change over time, with the exception of being born in Britain, where the proportion saying this was important fell six percentage points between 1995 and 2003.

We used a statistical technique called factor analysis to explore the different dimensions in the responses. The results of this analysis are shown in more detail in the appendix to this chapter. In summary, the items fell into two distinct groups which seem to correspond to ethnic and civic conceptions rather well. The first group, which we term the ethnic dimension, contained the items about birthplace, ancestry, living in Britain, and sharing British customs and traditions. The second, or civic group, contained the items about feeling British, respecting laws and institutions, speaking English, and having British citizenship.

The analysis also showed that the item on the necessity of being a Christian in order to be truly British did not fit neatly into either dimension, forming instead a separate factor. Given that we might expect this item to associate strongly with Christian belief, this item has been dropped from our analysis.[2]

It should be noted that our definition of civic *versus* ethnic national identity differs from the traditional *ius soli* and *ius sanguinis* conceptions. In particular, birthplace would normally be interpreted as a feature of *ius soli*, but we have it as part of the ethnic conception. Our categorisation relies rather on a distinction between 'choice' and ascriptive characteristics of national identity. While individuals can choose to do things such as learn English, respect British laws and institutions, and gain British citizenship, they cannot choose their ancestors and nor can they choose where they were born and raised.

The distribution of civic and ethnic national identity in Britain

Using the questions associated with each of the civic and ethnic dimensions, we assigned respondents a civic and an ethnic 'score' of between one and five depending on how important they had considered each of the items, where one represented low importance and five high importance.[3] Table 7.2 shows the distribution of respondents along both scales. We can see an emerging pattern of three key groups. Around two-thirds of respondents score highly on *both* civic and ethnic conceptions of identity (the bottom right-hand cells of the table). This is the only group to have an ethnic component to their conception of national identity. Around a quarter score highly on the civic identity scale but lowly on the ethnic identity scale (top right quarter). A small number of respondents seem to believe neither dimension of national identity is important for 'true' Britishness (top left quarter). (Although they make up only about three per cent of the population, they form a disproportionately large group among the young, as we shall see.) But there is practically no one in the bottom left quarter of the table, i.e. scoring high on the ethnic dimension and low on the civic one.

Table 7.2 Distribution of scores on the ethnic and civic national identity scales

		Civic national identity			
		2 or less	**2.01–3**	**3.01–4**	**4.01–5**
Ethnic national					
identity	2 or less	*	1	1	7
	2.01–3	*	2	4	13
	3.01–4	*	2	8	27
	4.01–5	*	*	3	29

Base: 796

Table percentages are shown
* = less than 1%

These findings can be mapped onto Figure 7.1. Thus, there is evidence in Britain of a stand-alone civic national identity, a civic coupled with ethnic identity, and a conception of identity that appears based on neither. The final cell remains rather empty, however; there appear to be few people who claim a stand-alone ethnic national identity.

We can define these groups more rigorously using a statistical technique called cluster analysis which brings together individuals with similar scores on items.[4] This technique has been used to create three 'clusters' – or groups – with similar meaning as the three groups identified in Table 7.2. As seen in Table 7.3, the 'civic *and* ethnic identity' group is the largest, although it has been slightly in decline between 1995 and 2003. The group who see neither civic nor ethnic dimensions of national identity as important is the smallest. But perhaps the most interesting findings relate to the 'civic identity only' group. They see the importance in British citizenship, speaking English and respect for British laws and institutions, but tend to view having been born and lived one's life in Britain and sharing British customs and traditions as considerably less important. This group has grown from less than a quarter of the population in 1995 to around a third in 2003.

Table 7.3 Distribution of conceptions of national identity, 1995 and 2003

Conception of national identity	1995	2003	Both years pooled
	%	%	%
Civic and ethnic	63	58	61
Civic only	23	32	27
Neither civic nor ethnic	13	10	12
Base	*961*	*772*	*1733*

Although there have been changes over time in the relative size of the groups shown in Table 7.3, a point to which we shall return, there is no reason for thinking that the factors associated with each group have changed. Therefore – and in order to make our statistical analysis more powerful – we pool the data from 1995 and 2003 in the analysis presented in the rest of this chapter.[5]

National identity and generational change

Having identified three distinct groups of individuals with quite different conceptions of what Britishness means, we now turn to examining the social characteristics of those falling into each group.

One common feature emerging from analysis of national sentiment in many countries is that older generations tend to feel a stronger sense of patriotism and national identity than do the young (Rose, 1985; McCrone and Surridge, 1998). A comparative study of Britain and Germany found that pride in the British welfare state was felt more strongly among older age groups in Britain, just as pride in German economic achievements was felt more strongly among older age groups in Germany (Topf *et al.,* 1989). Clearly, one important question to address, then, is whether or not older cohorts hold different views to younger cohorts on their conceptions of national identity. Drawing some conclusions about this allows us to attempt to predict future trends in the strength and importance of civic/ethnic identities as older generations die out and are gradually replaced by newer generations.

Table 7.4 gives evidence of a clear difference in views between generations born before and after 1945. Broadly speaking, there is in the more recent generations a rise in the exclusively civic conception of national identity which is matched by a decline in the combined ethnic and civic conception. While only around one in seven of the pre-1945 generation are members of the 'civic only' group, around a third of later generations are members of this group. Conversely, membership of the 'ethnic and civic' group is most extensive among the older generation. Although 'civic and ethnic' is the most common group among all generations, the figure is just over half for the 1945 to 1964 generation and just under half for the youngest group, compared with four-fifths of those born before 1945.

Lastly, there are clear generational differences in the 'neither civic nor ethnic' group. While only around one in sixteen of those born before 1945 fall into this category, the comparable figures are over one in ten for those born between 1945 and 1964 and one in five for those born after that. This may reflect a growing apathy amongst younger cohorts towards *all* types of national sentiment, not just differing conceptions of national identity.

Table 7.4 Conception of national identity by generational group

Conception of national identity	Born pre-1945	Born 1945–1964	Born 1965+
	%	%	%
Civic and ethnic	80	55	47
Civic only	14	34	33
Neither civic nor ethnic	6	11	20
Base	*611*	*641*	*479*

Source: *British Social Attitudes* surveys, 1995 and 2003

It should be noted that whilst we have identified these differences as generational in nature, it is possible that they are actually related to the ageing process. That is, as people become older they may change their conception of national identity. This seems rather implausible, though. Whilst it seems reasonable to argue that differing formative experiences (the decline of Empire and the increased ethnic mix of the population, for example) have led to generations with different conceptions of national identity, it is much more difficult to think of a mechanism that could explain why growing older makes one less likely to adopt an inclusive idea of Britishness.[6]

Different formative experiences of the cohorts are still not the only possible explanation for the patterns seen in Table 7.4. However, these generational differences could, for example, be due to compositional changes. Ideas of national identity are linked to a number of other important individual characteristics. Levels of education, libertarian *versus* authoritarian views and religiosity are linked in important ways to aspects of national identities. More highly educated citizens with socially liberal attitudes are thought to have more inclusive ideas of national identity (see Dowds and Young, 1996 for a detailed discussion of this phenomenon). And these other characteristics are also linked to generation. For example, older generations tend to be less well educated – while only seven per cent of those aged between 18 and 24 in 2003 have no formal qualifications, the comparable figure for those aged between 45 and 54 is 25 per cent, and 55 per cent for those aged 65 and over. Older generations are also more religious (Tilley, 2003). It may be therefore that differences between generations are simply due to differences in their education, religiosity and so forth.

Equally there have been large shifts in the composition of the British population in terms of parental origins. People born before the Second World War are overwhelmingly likely to be born of British parents. By contrast, with the mass immigration from former Empire countries in the 1960s and 1970s and more recently from Central and Eastern Europe, newer generations of British-born individuals are much more likely to have non-British born parents. By 2001, 8.3 per cent of the British population was born overseas compared with just 4.2 per cent in 1951. Moreover, this proportion rose faster between 1991 and 2001 than in any previous decade (Rendell and Ball, 2004). Clearly we would expect this to have an effect on conceptions of national identity that focus on ancestry, ethnicity and birthplace.

Thus, we need to use more sophisticated statistical techniques which allow all these factors to be taken into account at the same time. The detailed results of this analysis are reported in the appendix to this chapter. In summary, it confirms many of our expectations regarding the impact of social factors. There is a clear effect of education: those with degrees are significantly more likely to belong to the civic only group (or to the 'neither civic nor ethnic' group), as compared with those who have no formal qualifications. In addition, there is also an effect of religion: those who describe themselves as belonging to the Church of England are *less* likely to have a civic only or a 'neither' conception (i.e. more likely to have an ethnic component to their conception of identity) than those with no religion, or for that matter those with a non-Christian or non-state Christian religion. Also, as might be expected, those whose parents are or were not British citizens are also more likely to belong to the civic only group (or to the 'neither civic nor ethnic' group).

However, even after all these other factors are taken into account, the clearest pattern is the continued significance of generational differences in determining membership of the three different groups. The pattern shown previously in Table 7.4 still holds: there is a substantial split between those born *before* the 1940s and those born *during* and particularly *after* the 1940s. Younger generations, starting from those born in 1940, are strongly and significantly more likely to support a civic only conception, eschewing any ethnic component. There is a similar pattern for the 'neither civic nor ethnic' group, with those born after 1960 being strongly and significantly more likely to fall into this category.

The standard accounts of generational change emphasize the role of formative experiences when people are growing up and entering adulthood. It is by no means difficult to link the differences that we have found to events that happened in these cohorts' youth. The emergence of generations that experienced their adolescence and early adulthood during the 1960s and later on with more inclusive national identities fits with events of the time. The 1960s saw a number of changes to Britain's place in the world and the composition of citizens in Britain. The decline of British imperial power in the post-war period and the final end of Empire in the early 1960s, coupled with mass immigration from former colonial holdings, are both likely to have affected how individuals experienced Britishness when growing up.

A number of theorists have also emphasized the role of international conflict in fostering national consciousness. The historian Linda Colley (1992) has shown how a sense of Britishness was in large part a consequence of the wars with Napoleonic France in the late eighteenth and early nineteenth centuries and the conflicts between Protestant Britain (with its constitutional monarchy) and Catholic and absolutist European countries. More recent conflicts with Germany in the two world wars will have maintained this sense of a shared British endeavour that joined the different nations of Britain in a shared project against a common enemy. But the latter decades of the twentieth century have not seen Britain pitted on its own against other nations (with the exception of the Falklands War). Britain now tends to take part in broader international coalitions, whether in military, economic or political conflicts, and these will not have the same implications for national identity as did earlier conflicts. It is not surprising then that for the youngest generations British identity does not have the same resonance as it did for older generations.

However, although we have discounted the effect of ageing on attitudes, there is always the possibility that external events will act as a shock to change attitudes across generations, a so-called period effect. Recent years, with the resurgence of the debate about immigration (discussed in more detail in the chapter by McLaren and Johnson), may have had an impact on conceptions of British national identity. There is, in fact, a hint of this in our analysis: even after all the factors discussed above were taken into account, there were significantly fewer people who professed neither a civic nor an ethnic conception of national identity in 2003 than in 1995. If, as we have argued earlier, the views of this group are effectively an expression of apathy on the issue, then recent events may have jolted them to take sides. However, there is no similar reduction in the numbers espousing a 'civic only' conception of identity, so even this possible period effect seems to contribute to conceptions of national identity moving in a civic direction.

Conceptions of national identity and patriotic views

Heath *et al.* have shown the continued importance of British national sentiment as a notion which should be "conceptualised as an autonomous principle in its own right" for its explanatory power in determining views on issues such as Europe, nuclear defence, devolution and Irish unification (Heath *et al.*, 1999: 158). Similarly, Hutchinson and Smith have stated that "what is often conceded is the power, even primacy, of national loyalties and identities over those of even class, gender and race" (Hutchinson and Smith, 1994: 4). Therefore, we are also interested in whether conceptions of national identity are related to national sentiment.

To examine this, we use a battery of questions from the 1995 and 2003 *British Social Attitudes* surveys designed to measure how 'patriotic' individuals are. They might to some extent be best thought of as a measure of "my country right or wrong" – how much people think that Britain is superior to other countries. Respondents were asked to agree or disagree with the following statements:

> *I would rather be a citizen of Britain than of any other country in the world*

> *There are some things about Britain today that make me feel ashamed of Britain*

> *The world would be a better place if people from other countries were more like the British*

Generally speaking, Britain is a better country than most other countries

People should always support their country, even if the country is in the wrong

When my country does well in international sports, it makes me feel proud to be British

We used the answers to these six items to give respondents a score from one to five on a 'patriotism scale', where one represented a low level and five a high level of patriotism.[7] Table 7.5 shows scores on the patriotism scale broken down by the different conceptions of national identity. It is clear from the table that those who hold a 'civic and ethnic' conception of national identity (i.e. the only group that have an ethnic component to their view of national identity) are substantially more patriotic than those in other groups. Those with a 'civic only' conception hold the lowest level of patriotism, while the 'neither civic nor ethnic' group fall somewhere in the middle. This pattern has been stable over time.

Table 7.5 Patriotism score by conception of national identity

	Civic and ethnic		Civic only		Neither civic nor ethnic		All	
	1995	2003	1995	2003	1995	2003	1995	2003
	%	%	%	%	%	%	%	%
2 or less	*	*	5	6	15	10	4	3
2.01–3	25	26	60	58	53	63	37	40
3.01–4	61	61	33	34	28	23	50	49
4.01–5	12	11	3	*	3	*	9	7
Base	*618*	*462*	*222*	*236*	*121*	*74*	*961*	*772*

* = less than 1%

In order to untangle the relationship between conceptions of national identity and patriotism, we carried out a multivariate analysis that allowed us to take other factors such as sex, education, race, religion, class, region and parental citizenship into account. We also included respondents' underlying libertarian–authoritarian and left–right economic values. For this, we used the *British Social Attitudes* libertarian–authoritarian and left–right scales which are described in the Appendix to this Report (see Heath *et al.*, 1994; Evans *et al.*, 1996). The reason for including these values is that they are possible alternative sources of patriotic feeling. In particular, given that libertarian–authoritarian values are also related to generational group (Tilley, 2005), it is important to see whether the conception of national identity has any use in explaining the level of patriotism over and above that provided by libertarian–authoritarian values.

The results of this analysis are presented in detail in the appendix to this chapter. As we might expect, there is a negative relationship between patriotism and education – those with degrees are significantly less likely than their less-educated counterparts to espouse patriotic views. Equally religion, social class and parental citizenship all have some effect on patriotism scale scores. Most notable is the generational differences, however. Less patriotic cohorts born after 1940 appear to be replacing older, more patriotic generations (see Model 1 in the appendix to this chapter).

When we add libertarian–authoritarian values to the model, they also show a clear relationship to patriotism: libertarian views are significantly negatively correlated with pro-patriotic sentiments, and their introduction into the model tends to reduce the effect of some of the social characteristics, notably education, suggesting that some of the effect of education was mediated by libertarian values (see Model 2). The explanatory power of the model is increased from 20 per cent of the variation to 27 per cent. (Left–right values had no significant effect.)

Finally, when we add in our measure of conception of national identity, we find that people whose conception of national identity does not include an ethnic component are much less patriotic than those in the majority 'ethnic and civic' group (see Model 3). Libertarian–authoritarian values retain a (slightly reduced) importance of their own, as does generation and education. The explanatory power of the model increases further to 34 per cent of the variation. Thus we are not simply reducing the effect of values and social characteristics by including conception of national identity, although this is certainly true, but are also adding a substantial new factor to the model.

Conclusions

The literature on national identity has tended to focus on a general typology of 'civic' *versus* 'ethnic' conceptions, where the former concerns itself with citizenship rights and respect for laws and political institutions, and the latter with issues of ancestry and cultural assimilation. It has been argued that civic and ethnic ideas correspond broadly with French and German approaches to membership of the nation, and in our analysis we sought to examine the extent to which Britain might fit into this (rather simplistic) typology.

We find that the British cannot easily be categorised as either 'civic' or 'ethnic' nationalists. Instead there are three main groups. First, there is a group which combines both civic *and* ethnic conceptions of identity. This is the only group for whom ethnic considerations play any part in their conception of national identity. Although they make up the majority of the population, they are more numerous in the older generations, and we can surmise that this view is therefore in decline within the population as whole.

The second largest group are those who reject ethnic conceptions in favour of a purely civic approach. They make up around a third of people born after the second world war, and there seems every prospect that this group will grow in size as younger generations replace older ones.

Lastly, there a group who believe that there is very little at all that matters in making a person 'truly British'. Although much smaller, this group does make up around a fifth of the generation born since 1965. Might the growth in Britain of a younger generation which rejects both civic and ethnic identities signal a potential decline in British nationalist sentiment? It is possible, and commentators such as Dogan (1994) have long argued the arrival of a 'post-nationalistic' era in Western European politics. However, the extent to which national identities will shrink in importance over time is a matter of some speculation. Increasing migration, European enlargement and the broader processes of globalisation must be balanced against the persistence of nationalist conflicts throughout the world. Indeed, Miller has asserted that "the majority of people are too deeply attached to their inherited national identities to make their obliteration an intelligible goal" (Miller, 1995: 184). In fact, there is some evidence that events since 1995 may have caused this last group to shrink, perhaps as people take sides on the national identity issue in the climate of a more polarised debate about immigration.

Within Great Britain, continuation of strong national identity might be a good thing. While nationality can be a source of division between countries it can also promote a sense of community and belonging, collective loyalty and shared mutual responsibility. However, distinctions must be drawn between different types of national identity. We find in our analysis that those who include ethnic elements in their conception of national identity tend towards authoritarian values and greater patriotism. We also find evidence showing the replacement of older generations who hold 'exclusive' ethnic conceptions of identity with younger, more 'inclusive' cohorts. Indeed, the existence of multiple models of national identity seems to capture the prevailing mood. To borrow from Partridge (1999), it is "a thoroughly post-modern, post-national solution, in keeping with our mongrelised and global times".

Notes

1. In order to combine the two types of questions and make them comparable it was necessary to combine "can't choose" and "neither agree nor disagree" into a single middle category for all nine items.
2. Religion is included as a controlling variable in the later analysis.
3. The civic identity scale was a simple summation of the responses to items about citizenship, ability to speak English, respect for political institutions and laws, and feeling British, divided by four. It was coded 1 to 5 so that higher scores mean individuals think civic elements of national identity are more important. Unfortunately 'to have British ancestry' was only asked in 2003. Thus, in order to enable us to pool data from both surveys, the ethnic identity scale was created summing only the items on having been born in Britain, having lived in Britain all

one's life, and sharing British customs and traditions, and dividing by three. Again this scale was coded 1 to 5, where 5 indicated that ethnic elements of national identity were deemed most important. Both scales proved to be fairly internally coherent, with a Cronbach's alpha of 0.70 for the civic scale and 0.67 for the ethnic scale. The scales also correlated together, with the majority of respondents scoring above four on both scales.

4. Under this procedure (K-means cluster analysis) the number of clusters has to be fixed in advance. A visual inspection of the data in Table 7.2 suggested three groups. The addition of more clusters tends to give very small clusters with few individuals. The three clusters are thus similar to the ones that could be seen by eye from Table 7.2, with one main group with high scores on all items (a civic-cum-ethnic cluster), one smaller group which has high scores on the civic items but not on the ethnic, and the smallest group with comparatively low scores on all items. The next table shows the mean scores for each cluster.

Mean scores of importance for 'being British' by cluster membership

	Civic and ethnic cluster	Civic only cluster	Neither civic nor ethnic
Born in Britain	4.65	2.67	2.99
British citizenship	4.65	3.79	2.93
Lived life in Britain	4.51	2.84	2.47
Speak English	4.78	4.52	1.97
Respect laws/institutions	4.45	4.19	2.81
Feel British	4.53	3.23	2.64
Sharing customs/traditions	3.69	2.98	2.79
Base	*1080*	*458*	*195*

Source: *British Social Attitudes* surveys, 1995 and 2003

5. All the analysis in this paper has been replicated using only the 2003 data and including the item on British ancestry, and the results of this are consistent with those presented here.
6. Indeed, there appears little relationship between conventional social ageing landmarks such as marriage, childbirth and national identity.
7. These items scale extremely well with a Cronbach's alpha of 0.78

References

Anderson, B. (1983), *Imagined Communities*, London: Verso

Bryant, C.G.A. (1997), 'Citizenship, national identity and the accommodation of difference: reflections on the German, French, Dutch and British cases', *Journal of Ethnic and Migration Studies*, **23**(2): 157–172

Cohen, R. (1994), *Frontiers of Identity: the British and Others*, Oxford: Oxford University Press

Colley, L. (1992), *Britons: Forging the Nation 1707–1837*, New Haven: Yale University Press

Dogan, M. (1994), 'The decline of nationalisms within Western Europe', *Comparative Politics*, **26**: 281–305

Dowds, L. and, Young, K. (1996), 'National Identity', in Jowell, R., Curtice, J., Park, A., Brook, L. and Thomson, K. (eds.), *British Social Attitudes: the 13th Report*, Aldershot: Dartmouth

Evans, G.A., Heath, A.F. and Lalljee, M.G., (1996), 'Measuring left–right and libertarian–authoritarian values in the British electorate', *British Journal of Sociology*, **47**: 93–112

Gellner, E. (1983), *Nations and Nationalism: New Perspectives on the Past*, Oxford: Blackwell

Heath, A.F., Evans G.A. and Martin J., (1994), 'The measurement of core beliefs and values: The development of balanced socialist/laissez faire and libertarian/ authoritarian scales', *British Journal of Political Science*, **24**: 115–158

Heath, A.F., Taylor, B., Brook, L. and Park, A. (1999), 'British National Sentiment', *British Journal of Political Science*, **29**: 155–175

Hjerm, M. (1998), 'National Identities, National Pride and Xenophobia: A Comparison of Four Western Countries', *Acta Sociologica*, **41**: 335–347

Hutchinson, J. and Smith, A. (eds.) (1994), *Nationalism*, Oxford: Oxford University Press

McCrone, D. and Surridge, P. (1998), 'National Identity and National Pride', in Jowell, R., Curtice, J., Park, A., Brook, L., Thomson, K. and Bryson, C. (eds.) *British – and European – Social Attitudes: The 15th Report*, Aldershot: Ashgate

Miller, D. (1995), *On Nationality*, Oxford: Clarendon

Partridge, S. (1999), The British–Irish Council: the trans-islands symbolic and political possibilities. Paper presented to the British Council 'Looking into England' conference, 16th December 1999,
http://www.britishcouncil.org/studies/england/partridge.htm

Rendall, M.S. and Ball, D.J. (2004), 'Immigration, emigration and the ageing of the overseas-born population in the United Kingdom', *Population Trends*, **116**: 18–27

Rose, R. (1985), 'National pride in cross-national perspective', *International Social Science Journal*, **37**: 85–96

Safran, W. (1998), 'The context of French politics', in Donald-Hancock, M., Conradt, D.M., Peters, G., Safran, W. and Zariski, R. (eds.) *Politics in Western Europe*, London: MacMillan

Tilley, J.R. (2003), 'Secularisation and ageing in Britain: Does family formation cause greater religiosity?', *Journal for the Scientific Study of Religion*, **42**: 269–278

Tilley, J.R. (2005 forthcoming),'The generational basis of libertarian–authoritarian values in Britain', *Political Studies*

Topf, R., Mohler, P. and Heath, A. (1989), 'Pride in One's Country: Britain and West Germany', in Jowell, R., Witherspoon, S. and Brook, L. (eds.) *British Social Attitudes: Special International Report*, Aldershot: Gower

Acknowledgements

The *National Centre for Social Research* is grateful to the Economic and Social Research Council (grant number RES-000-22-0326) for their financial support which enabled us to ask the *International Social Survey Programme* questions reported in this chapter.

Appendix

Factor analysis of dimensions of British national identity: scores for maximum likelihood factor analysis with varimax factor rotation

	Civic dimension	Ethnic dimension
Born in Britain		.81
British citizenship	.44	
Lived life in Britain		.56
Speak English	.49	
Respect laws/institutions	.56	
Feel British	.68	*
British ancestry		.70
Sharing customs/traditions		.49
Initial Eigen values	1.29	3.23
Base: 770		

* Scores below 0.4 not reported

Multinomial logistic model predicting national identity cluster membership for 1995 and 2003 (relative to "civic and ethnic")

	Civic only		Neither civic nor ethnic	
	B	SE	B	SE
2003	.19	.13	-.76***	.19
Women	-.24*	.13	-.17	.19
Degree	1.26***	.25	.80**	.36
Some education	.49***	.18	.29	.25
Ref: No qualifications	0.00		0.00	
Non-white	.18	.41	-.13	.55
Church of England	-.32**	.16	-.83***	.24
Other Protestant	.05	.20	-.30	.28
Catholic	-.06	.23	-.06	.29
Non-Christian	-.01	.50	.38	.62
Ref: No religion	0.00		0.00	
Salariat	.30*	.18	.26	.25
Routine non-man	.01	.18	-.07	.24
Petty bourgeoisie	.27	.24	-.07	.37
Ref: Working class	0.00		0.00	
Born 1970+	1.15***	.30	2.27***	.47
Born 1960–69	1.46***	.28	2.02***	.45
Born 1950–59	1.21***	.38	1.26***	.46
Born 1940–49	.78***	.29	.27	.53
Born 1930–39	.22	.31	.99**	.48
Ref: Born pre-1930	0.00		0.00	
Scotland	.37*	.22	.50*	.29
Wales	-.32	.27	.04	.36
Ref: England	0.00		0.00	
Parents non-citizens	1.23***	.32	1.54***	.40
Constant	-2.34***	.29	-3.17***	.46
Base	*409*		*173*	

* $p<.10$; ** $p<.05$; *** $p<.01$. Relative to "civic and ethnic" (N = 987)
R-square (Cox and Snell) = .17

Linear (OLS) models predicting patriotism score

	Model 1		Model 2		Model 3	
	B	SE	B	SE	B	SE
2003	.04	.03	.03	.03	.02	.03
Sex	-.06**	.03	-.05*	.03	-.06**	.03
Degree	-.45***	.06	-.28***	.06	-.23***	.05
Some education	-.19***	.04	-.15***	.03	-.13***	.03
Ref: No quals	0.00		0.00		0.00	
Non-white	-.16*	.09	-.16*	.09	-.15*	.08
Church of England	.16***	.03	.09***	.03	.07**	.03
Other Protestant	.07	.04	.02	.04	.01	.04
Catholic	-.08	.05	-.10**	.05	-.10**	.05
Non-Christian	.18	.12	.12	.11	.13	.10
Ref: No religion	0.00		0.00		0.00	
Salariat	-.15***	.04	-.11***	.04	-.09***	.04
Routine non-man	-.11***	.04	-.08**	.04	-.08**	.04
Petty bourgeoisie	-.10*	.05	-.10*	.05	-.08*	.05
Ref: Working class	0.00		0.00		0.00	
Born 1970+	-.39***	.06	-.34***	.05	-.23***	.05
Born 1960–69	-.43***	.05	-.37***	.05	-.26***	.05
Born 1950–59	-.35***	.05	-.27***	.05	-.21***	.05
Born 1940–49	-.29***	.05	-.27***	.05	-.23***	.05
Born 1930–39	-.07	.05	-.05	.05	-.02	.05
Ref: Born pre-1930	0.00		0.00		0.00	
Scotland	-.12**	.05	-.10**	.05	-.07	.05
Wales	-.02	.06	-.03	.06	-.04	.05
Ref: England	0.00		0.00		0.00	
Parents non-citizens	-.18***	.07	-.18***	.07	-.09	.07
Authoritarian–libertarian			-.29***	.02	-.23***	.02
Left–right			.01	.02	.01	.02
NI – neither					-.46***	.04
NI – civic					-.34***	.03
NI – civic and ethnic					0.00	
Constant	3.74***	.05	4.26***	.07	4.21***	.07
R-square (adjusted)	.20		.27		.34	

Base: 1502

* p<.10; ** p<.05; *** p<.01.

8 Understanding the rising tide of anti-immigrant sentiment

Lauren McLaren and Mark Johnson [*]

Britain, like many of her European neighbours, has experienced considerable uneasiness at being a country of immigration. Although policy makers tend to express pride in Britain's comparative success at multiculturalism ('however bad things are in Britain, Europe is surely worse' goes the thinking – see Favell, 2001), Britain's experiment with multiculturalism was, in fact, an unwanted consequence of her desire to retain her Empire at the end of the Second World War.

Immigration policy prior to 1962 was primarily determined by the concern for maintaining subjecthood linkages with the Old Commonwealth of Canada, Australia and New Zealand. This meant the creation of a citizenship status that treated all Commonwealth citizens as subjects and thus allowed the free movement of both Old and New Commonwealth citizens to the United Kingdom. Even in the face of increasing numbers of migrants from the West Indies after the Second World War and pressure from backbench politicians who were, in turn, under pressure from their constituents to put a halt to black immigration, Conservative governments preferred a quasi-open-door policy[1] so that Britain might preserve Commonwealth linkages. What is more, in the face of 'race riots' (arguably mild by comparative standards) in August 1958 and public demands to restrict new migration from the West Indies, politicians preferred to leave the issue alone and continue to uphold the symbolic nature of a common status across the Commonwealth.

It was not until the adoption of the 1962 Commonwealth Immigrants Act – when there were already an estimated 400,000+ immigrants from the West Indies, India and Pakistan in Britain – that the government finally attempted to close the doors to immigration (see Layton-Henry, 1992). The 1962 Act was

---

[*] Lauren McLaren is Lecturer in Comparative Politics at the University of Nottingham. Mark Johnson is a Researcher at the *National Centre for Social Research* and Co-Director of the *British Social Attitudes* survey series.

primarily concerned with halting the flow of new immigrants, but by the time Britain tried to put a stop to immigration, she already had a multicultural society, whether she liked it or not.

From the time of the 1962 Act, there was a consensus across both the Conservative and the Labour parties that strict controls were desirable and necessary. Along with strict controls, however, it was thought that conditions for migrants already in Britain would need to be improved. Indeed, this has been the mantra of Conservative and Labour governments alike since 1962. Still, while the UK has been far more successful than her European counterparts at restricting immigration, and is less vulnerable to the immigrant-related effects of globalisation and to legal restrictions on political action in the realm of restricting migration (see Hansen, 2000), further immigrants have indeed come. Some of these are individuals from former colonies who have come to join family members, but many others are from countries that were never British colonies, like those who have come from Central Europe or Iraq[2] with the initial purpose of seeking asylum. While legal scholars make a clear distinction between asylum seekers and immigrants, it is unlikely that ordinary citizens – who are the focus of this chapter – see such a clear distinction. Indeed, British policy itself – until recently – has tended to conflate the two (see Favell, 2001).

Given past restrictive policies, it is reasonable to ask how it is that migration figures have recently increased so dramatically, particularly between 1998 and 2000. Prior to 2000, the UK was known for having one of the most restrictive immigration and asylum regimes in all of Europe, but by the end of 2002, even the United Nations – which had previously been critical of Britain's (non-existent) asylum policy – contended that the country was taking more than its fair share of refugees.[3] How did such a dramatic change come about? It seems to have started in 1993, with the Asylum and Immigration Appeals Act, which for the first time introduced the right of appeal to those with failed applications for asylum. Subsequent legislation, however, made it increasingly difficult to be accepted as an asylum claimant in the first place and appeared to keep a cap on the slowly increasing number of claims. In 1998, however, the Labour government decided for the first time to incorporate the European Convention on Human Rights and Fundamental Freedoms (ECHR) into British law via the Human Rights Act, and Figure 8.1 shows a jump in both asylum applications and new settlements shortly after this. We can only speculate that this new introduction of human rights legislation into statutory law sent a signal to asylum seekers that they would indeed get fairer treatment (as promised by the new Labour government when it took power in 1997) than previously. It definitely seems to have spawned more court cases related to immigration and asylum (the number of cases included in the law reports of *The Times* tripled between 1994 and 2002). Moreover, while hostility to new entries is quite high in the UK, it is also known as being a far friendlier place to migrants than many continental European countries (see, for instance, Nielsen, 2004). This, combined with improved statutes related to the treatment of asylum seekers, is thus likely to have contributed to the increase in applications. While this point may lead some to the conclusion that the legislation in question ought to be repealed, it is highly unlikely that any British government could do so without a huge outcry from the international community.

Figure 8.1 Immigration: the statistics

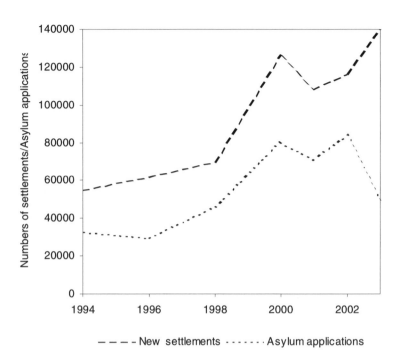

In this chapter we focus on the period between 1995 and 2003. As Figure 8.1 shows, the number of both asylum applications and new settlements clearly increased over this period (although there was a large decrease in asylum applications between 2002 and 2003). The number of asylum applications is not overwhelmingly large, and the bulk of the increase is reflected in the number of new settlements. Again, it is likely that some of this increase was the result of the passage of the Human Rights Act in 1998, and the subsequent possibility for UK courts to then interpret the act in a way that would be favourable to the families of established migrants. Previous immigration legislation had aimed at severely curbing family reunification, but given that one of the provisions of the ECHR is the right to family life, it is possible that courts in the UK have been able to use this provision to allow extended family members of established migrants to move to the UK. At the same time, the New Labour government is promoting the economic benefits of importing skilled labour from abroad and some of the increase in settlements very likely results from this new approach to solving labour shortages in certain sectors of the economy and health service.

Given the traditional uneasiness with its multicultural status and with the idea of immigration (particularly non-white immigration), continued exploration of attitudes to immigration in Britain today is of utmost importance. To do this we use questions from the *International Social Survey Programme* asked as part of the *British Social Attitudes* survey in 1995 and 2003.

Are anti-immigration sentiments increasing?

We begin by investigating whether 'anti-immigration' views have increased over time. There are two questions that serve as summary measures of general attitudes towards immigration. The first considers immigrants generally:

> *Do you think the number of immigrants to Britain nowadays should be ... increased a lot, increased a little, remain the same as it is, reduced a little, or reduced a lot?*

As can be seen in Table 8.1, the views of the British public have shifted quite considerably between 1995 and 2003. In 1995, around two-thirds of the population thought the number of immigrants should be reduced, but by 2003 this had jumped to three-quarters. Further, all of this increase was among those who thought that the number of immigrants should be reduced "a lot". Meanwhile, the proportion who thought that immigration should stay at the same level or be increased has fallen from just under a third to a fifth. Where there was previously some degree of ambivalence there now seems to be more conviction, and the conviction is overwhelmingly against immigration. (Those who are not citizens and whose parents were not citizens when they were born are removed from the analyses because it is expected that citizenship status would confound the effects of all variables analysed here.)[4]

Table 8.1 Views on whether the number of immigrants should be increased or reduced, 1995 and 2003

	1995	2003	% change
	%	%	
Increased a lot + a little	3	5	+2
Remain as is	26	15	-12
Reduced a little	24 } 65	23 } 74	-1
Reduced a lot	41 }	51 }	+10
Base	*970*	*793*	

Base: Respondents who are British citizens and whose parents were British citizens at the time of the respondent's birth

Of course, this change has happened against a backdrop of increased immigration, so the *status quo* has changed. It is not necessarily the case that people want less immigration than they did in 1995 – if they want immigration to be brought back to 1995 levels, they might logically have moved from the "remain as it is" to the "reduced" camp. Nevertheless, the increase in the "reduced a lot" category would appear to signify a hardening of attitudes against immigration. That this is the case is supported by the weaker but still significant increase in our second measure of attitudes to immigration:

> *Do you agree or disagree that Britain should take stronger measures to exclude illegal immigrants?*[5]

Whilst the increase may be less than that found for our first measure, the initial level of opposition to illegal immigration is perhaps more important. As shown in Table 8.2, already in 1995 over three-quarters of respondents wanted stronger measures to exclude illegal immigrants. With such a high level already, further large changes are hardly likely. The question clearly illustrates the high anti-immigrant sentiment prevalent in Britain.

Table 8.2 Views on whether Britain should take stronger measures to exclude illegal immigrants, 1995 and 2003

	1995	2003	% change
	%	%	
Agree strongly	49 } 78	53 } 82	+5
Agree	29 }	28 }	-1
Neither agree nor disagree	13	10	-4
Disagree/disagree strongly	6	5	-1
Base	*970*	*793*	

Base: Respondents who are British citizens and whose parents were British citizens at the time of the respondent's birth

We turn now to a discussion of *why* the British public has grown more hostile to immigration over this eight-year period. Apart from the objective increase in immigration levels, commentators have suggested a number of reasons why this has happened, and we examine six hypotheses (see, for example, Hjerm, 1998; McCrone and Surridge, 1998):

- that national pride has increased;
- that there is increasing conservatism in conceptions of the key components of Britishness;
- that racial prejudice is on the increase;
- that there is a new, increased concern about Muslims in particular which has spilled over into attitudes towards immigration;
- that perceptions of the economic and social consequences associated with

immigrants are changing; and
- that politicians and the media have flagged up the immigration issue more often and/or in a different manner to previously.

For each of the hypotheses, two conditions need to hold in order to confirm the link with increases in anti-immigration sentiment. The first is that the measure must be related to attitudes towards immigration, and the second is that the measure must itself show an increase over the relevant time period.

National pride

Our first hypothesis is that the shift in attitudes to immigration is the result of rising levels of national pride. There are strong grounds for expecting this to be the case: pride in one's own country may mean one resents change to a greater extent, but also it is likely to mean less identification with people from elsewhere. Immigrants may be seen as posing a threat to the basic functioning of the political system, as well as the social and economic systems. Given that most immigrants to the UK come from polities with very different systems of governance (in comparison to that of the UK), it may be perceived that these newcomers do not understand the basic functioning of British democracy. Further, specific types of immigrants – namely those from Muslim-based countries – may be perceived as having extremely non-democratic goals like the replacement of secular British democracy with a religiously based fundamentalist government. In addition, those who are more proud of the British system of government may, in turn, feel the threat from immigrants more acutely. Even things like extreme pride in the treatment given to various minority groups may be associated with increased concerns about immigration: people may feel pride in the way current groups are treated but may also worry that the country will no longer be able to accommodate various groups equally if more immigrants come into the country. In the realm of economy, immigrants are often perceived as being a drain on national economic resources, and so those who feel greater pride in the British economy may have concerns that immigrants are a threat to the economic achievements of the country.

Respondents were asked to say how proud they were of Britain in each of the following respects:

> *The way democracy works*
> *Its political influence in the world*
> *Britain's economic achievements*
> *Its social security system*
> *Its scientific and technological achievements*
> *Its achievements in sports*
> *Its achievement in the arts and literature*
> *Britain's armed forces*
> *Its history*
> *Its fair and equal treatment of all groups in society*

The first stage is to examine whether pride in one's country is indeed related to attitudes towards immigration. The results are summarised in Table 8.3.[6] This shows separately for respondents who were either proud or not proud of each achievement, the proportion who agreed that the level of immigration should be reduced. The final column shows the difference in the level of hostility towards immigration between those who were proud and not proud of each achievement. Throughout this chapter, this figure has been calculated so that it is positive if the variable in question is related to a wish to reduce immigration and zero or negative if it is not – in this case, column 1 minus column 2.

Table 8.3 National pride and anti-immigration hostility

Pride in ...	% who want to reduce number of immigrants				
	Proud	Base	Not proud	Base	% diffe-rence
... armed forces	77	692	52	61	+25
... history	77	662	57	84	+20
... achievements in sports	77	510	69	229	+8
... scientific and technological achievements	74	612	73	99	+2
... achievement in the arts and literature	73	537	72	136	+1
... economic achievements	73	484	76	221	-3
... fair and equal treatment of all groups in society	73	418	76	290	-3
... social security system	73	374	76	347	-3
... political influence in the world	72	415	76	297	-4
... the way democracy works	72	487	79	224	-7

Base: Respondents who are British citizens and whose parents were British citizens at the time of the respondent's birth

The table shows a mixed picture. Most aspects of national pride are either unrelated to attitudes towards immigration or correlated in the 'wrong' direction. For example, pride in the way British democracy works, which we had hypothesised might be related to opposition to further immigration that could dilute its effectiveness, is in fact significantly related to *not* wanting to reduce immigration. However, there are three aspects of national pride which *are* related to opposition to immigration: pride in Britain's armed forces, pride in its history, and – to a lesser extent – pride in its sporting achievements.

The particular importance of pride in the armed forces and in Britain's history is confirmed by these being the measures that also show the closest relationship to wanting to take stronger measures against illegal immigrants. Pride in sport did not show a clear relationship to this measure, but there was a significant but weaker relationship with pride in scientific achievements, economic achievements and political influence.

However, if a rise in national pride is responsible for the change in views on immigration, we would also need to establish that levels of national pride have themselves increased since 1995. As Table 8.4 shows there has been relatively little increase in national pride over the period. Indeed, for one of the sources of pride of interest – in sporting achievements – there has been a significant *fall* in pride. In fact, only two of the statements show a significant increase, namely in Britain's economic achievements and in the fair and equal treatment of all groups in society. Since these were only inconsistently associated with hostility to immigrants or not at all, this does not look promising for the hypothesis. The two aspects of national pride that were clearly and consistently linked to hostility to immigration – armed forces and history – show no significant change over time.

Table 8.4 Sources of national pride, 1995 and 2003

% who have pride in ...	1995	2003	% change
... Britain's economic achievements	38	62	+24
... its fair and equal treatment of all groups in society	49	54	+5
... its political influence in the world	49	53	+4
... Britain's armed forces	84	86	+3
... its social security system	45	47	+2
... the way democracy works	61	62	+1
... its scientific and technological achievements	80	78	-3
... its achievement in the arts and literature	70	67	-3
... its history	86	83	-3
... its achievements in sports	71	63	-8
Base:	*970*	*793*	

Base: Respondents who are British citizens and whose parents were British citizens at the time of the respondent's birth

In a final attempt to rescue the hypothesis, we looked at change over time in the proportion of people who said they were "very proud" of the various achievements. It could perhaps be argued that this is the real group of interest for our purposes. This analysis added a few further relatively small but significant increases – in Britain's economic achievement (up from five to 13 per cent), in its armed forces (up from 46 to 51 per cent), in its social security system up from seven to ten per cent, and in its political influence in the world (up from six to nine per cent) – all of which are related to attitudes to immigration on one or other of the measures (except pride in the social security system).

The best that can be said is perhaps that changes in national pride could have had some limited influence on the increase in anti-immigration sentiment, but could hardly be the main factor. We continue our search for an explanation, turning next to notions of 'Britishness'.

Conceptions of Britishness

In many ways, traditional elite discourse on British citizenship is likely to have led to comparatively liberal perceptions of what it means to be British. The key historical precedent here is the British Nationality Act of 1948, which contained an extraordinarily inclusive citizenship norm. This norm was maintained until it was finally dismantled by the 1981 British Nationality Act. The original notion of citizenship in Britain as outlined in the 1948 Act was one that provided citizens of the UK and its colonies with a common citizenship. Even in the face of ever-increasing migration, and even during a Conservative government administration in the 1950s, elite discourse on the issue remained inclusive.

However, this conception of British citizenship became increasingly conservative over time – under both Labour and Conservative governments. It moved from exclusion based on the place from which one's passport was issued (1962 Commonwealth Immigrants Act) to quasi-ancestry (Commonwealth Immigrants Bill of 1968)[7] to clear ancestry with the new concept of patriality (1971 Immigration Act). Plus, there were increasing restrictions between 1971 and 1974 as the rhetoric of Enoch Powell contributed to moving the Conservative Party into a more restrictionist mode. Thus, an initially liberal conception of citizenship was converted into one that made clear the importance of ancestry and heritage (and in particular, the heritage of the stock of people who had initially migrated to the Old Commonwealth).

Finally, in keeping with the need to bring citizenship law in line with migration law and with the acceptance of the near-collapse of direct colonial/Commonwealth ties, the 1981 British Nationality Act completely revamped the notion of citizenship and, presumably, the official notion of what it meant to be British. While all previous legislation held onto the category of Citizen of the UK and Commonwealth (CUKC) and to the notion of subjecthood, the 1981 Act abolished the former and almost completely abolished the latter as well. A new category, UK citizen, was established and specified a more standard form of citizenship. Essentially, a child born in the UK would be granted British citizenship if either its mother or its father was a British citizen or settled in the UK, and naturalisation for those without kinship linkages was made relatively easy (and short).[8] As discussed above, however, it was expected that this liberal citizenship regime would coincide with a very strict initial entry policy (see Hansen, 2000).

Given the history of citizenship and immigration policies in the UK, it is difficult to know what ordinary citizens' views might be on what it takes to be British. Fortunately, we have survey questions in 1995 and 2003 which do precisely that. The results of these are discussed in more detail in the chapter by Tilley, Exley and Heath. Our interest here is in exploring whether the increase in hostility towards immigration might lie in increasingly conservative notions of what it means to be British. But we must first determine whether conservative notions of being British are indeed related to attitudes to immigration.

There are several different components of Britishness investigated in the 1995 and 2003 *British Social Attitudes* surveys, and their relationship to attitudes to immigration are shown in Table 8.5. We can see from the final column, that four of these components of Britishness are strongly related to hostility towards further immigration – being born in Britain, having British ancestry, having lived most of one's life in Britain and agreeing that "it is impossible for people who do not share Britain's customs and traditions to become fully British". These are in fact the four components that Tilley, Exley and Heath identify in their chapter as the ethnic, or exclusive, dimension of national identity.

Table 8.5 Components of Britishness and anti-immigration hostility

	% who want to reduce number of immigrants				
Components of Britishness	Important	*Base*	**Not important**	*Base*	**% diffe-rence**
Be born in Britain	80	*589*	56	*183*	+24
Have British ancestry	85	*400*	63	*348*	+22
Have lived most of life in Britain	80	*560*	59	*197*	+20
Be able to speak English	76	*687*	63	*68*	+13
Be a Christian	82	*257*	70	*483*	+12
Respect British political institutions and laws	75	*652*	69	*101*	+5
Hold British citizenship	75	*662*	71	*92*	+4
Feel British	75	*594*	73	*152*	+2
	Agree	*Base*	**Disagree**	*Base*	
People who do not share British customs can never be fully British	88	*424*	52	*138*	+36

Base: Respondents who are British citizens and whose parents were British citizens at the time of the respondent's birth

Other components of Britishness – such as respect for political institutions and laws, holding British citizenship and feeling British – which Tilley, Exley and Heath include in their civic, or inclusive, dimension of national identity, do not have a significant relationship to hostility to further immigration.[9] A middle position is held by the items on being able to speak English and being a Christian. These have a significant relationship with wishing to reduce immigration, but it is weaker than for the items of the ethnic dimension of national identity.

Having established a relationship between some aspects of Britishness and attitudes to immigration, we turn now to look at whether change in these variables could have caused the rise in anti-immigration feeling. As seen in Table 8.6, in stark contrast to the fairly short/easy naturalisation process in Britain, vast majorities in both 1995 and 2003 thought that in order to be truly British a person really must have been born on British soil. However, as also shown in the chapter by Tilley, Exley and Heath the 'ethnic' components of Britishness have tended to decrease, not increase, over time. This is especially true of the requirement to have been born in Britain in order to be truly British. (The question on having British ancestry was not asked in 1995.)

Table 8.6 Components of Britishness, 1995 and 2003

% who say important for being truly British	1995	2003	% change
Be born in Britain*	79	73	-6
Have lived most of life in Britain*	74	71	-3
Hold British citizenship*	85	84	-2
Be a Christian*	33	31	-1
Respect British political institutions and laws*	83	82	-1
Feel British*	75	75	0
People who do not share British customs can never be truly British**	52	53	0
Be able to speak English*	86	87	+1
Have British ancestry*	n/a	48	–
Base	*970*	*793*	

* Per cent responding 'very' or 'fairly important'
** Per cent responding 'strongly agree' or 'agree'
n/a = not asked
Base: Respondents who are British citizens and whose parents were British citizens at the time of the respondent's birth

We looked also at those who thought each of the components of Britishness were "very important" only to find that, on this measure, *all* the components of Britishness have declined over time. In summary, then, although certain elements of the conception of Britishness are related to hostility towards further immigration, we have to dismiss the hypothesis that this has caused the observed increase in anti-immigration sentiments as there has been no increase in these elements. We turn next to another potential explanation: that racial prejudice is on the rise.

Racial prejudice

To what degree has the increase in preference for the exclusion/restriction of migrants been a result of increased levels of prejudice? Before considering this hypothesis, however, it is necessary first to determine whether self-reported levels of prejudice are related to attitudes towards immigrants.[10] As shown in Table 8.7, this is indeed the case. Among the, admittedly very small, group who describe themselves as "very prejudiced" against people of other races, an astonishing 100 per cent would like to reduce the number of immigrants. Among the larger (and therefore more reliable) group who describe themselves as "a little prejudiced", the figure is still almost nine out of ten. But it falls to two-thirds among those who say they are "not at all prejudiced". There is a similar but weaker relationship with the desire to be tougher on illegal immigrants (88 per cent of those who are a little prejudiced want stronger measures, compared with 80 per cent of those who claim not to be prejudiced at all).

Table 8.7 Perceptions of prejudice and anti-immigrant hostility

	% who want to reduce number of immigrants	Base
Self-reported prejudice		
Very prejudiced	100	23
A little prejudiced	88	224
Not at all prejudiced	67	539

Base: Respondents who are British citizens and whose parents were British citizens at the time of the respondent's birth

As with our previous hypotheses, we need to show also that racial prejudice has increased over the time period in order to be able to conclude that this may have caused the increase in hostility to immigration. In *The 20ᵗʰ Report*, Rothon and Heath (2003) charted the long-term decline in self-reported racial prejudice. Between 1983 and 2001, for instance, the proportion of respondents who reported that they were either very or a little prejudiced dropped from 35 per cent to 25 per cent. However, they also note that this increased to 31 per cent in 2002. As seen in Figure 8.2, this has now levelled off at 30 per cent.

Figure 8.2 Self-reported racial prejudice: per cent who see themselves as "very prejudiced" or "a little prejudiced", 1983–2003

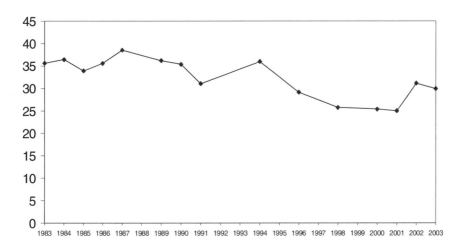

Although the 2003 figure represents an increase from 2001, it is no higher than in the mid-1990s. The question was not asked in 1995, but in 1994, reported racial prejudice was even higher than in 2003, at 36 per cent. By 1996, this figure had dropped to 29 per cent, indicating that the 1995 figure would have likely been somewhere between these two. It is thus impossible to conclude that there has been an increase in racism in the 1995–2003 period as a whole.

However, before we write off the effect of racism completely, we should look beyond self-rated racism at perceptions of racism in society more generally. Perhaps some respondents who will not themselves admit to being racist, will oppose immigration on the grounds that it will cause more racism in others. We have two questions to consider here: whether it is perceived there is more or less racial prejudice in Britain now than there was five years ago, and whether it is thought there will be more or less in five years' time. And these measures do indeed correlate with views on immigration: 79 per cent of people who think there is more prejudice now would like to reduce the number of immigrants, compared with 71 per cent of those who see less prejudice or the same. Similarly, 81 per cent of those who think there will be more prejudice in five years' time would like to reduce immigration, compared with 68 per cent of those who expect there to be less or the same prejudice. Clearly, interpretation of this latter question is complicated by the fact that we do not know whether respondents think that levels of immigration *will* be reduced or not, but there is nevertheless a relationship there.

And in this case we do find a change since the mid-1990s, as seen in Table 8.8. Back in 1994 around a third of respondents thought there had been a rise in prejudice, whereas this figure is now almost half. Similarly, two-fifths predicted a rise in prejudice and this now stands at over half.

Table 8.8 Perceptions of prejudice in society, 1994–2003

	1994	1996	2003
Prejudice now compared to five years ago	%	%	%
More now	34	29	45
About the same	42	48	32
Less now	22	20	20
Prejudice in five years compared to now	%	%	%
More in 5 years' time	39	32	52
About the same	35	43	26
Less in 5 years' time	20	20	18
Base	*2302*	*2399*	*4432*

Thus, while people do not seem to perceive themselves to be any more prejudiced now than in the mid-1990s, they increasingly think that their countrymen – and women – are becoming more prejudiced, perhaps as a result of increased immigration.

Prejudice against Muslims

We have thus found mixed support for our explanation invoking increasing racial prejudice as an explanation for increased hostility towards immigration. We look next at an area likely to be related to racism – increasing hostility towards Muslims. There are good grounds to believe that prejudice against this particular group will have increased over the eight years of interest.

Arguably the most significant event to have occurred between 1995 and 2003 was the September 11th terrorist attacks in America. This and the resulting "war on terror" have left much tension and suspicion between Islam and the West.

Such suspicion of 'others' from different backgrounds is likely to have been influential in shaping people's attitudes towards immigration (because both involve the same notion of 'other' in many people's minds). Indeed one of the key reasons people may be anti-immigration is because of their fears for security, which are likely to be linked to perceived terrorist threats.

Here we speculate on the role that anti-Muslim sentiment may have had on immigration attitudes. Unfortunately this cannot be properly explored because the questions were only asked in 2003 and we have no data on change over time. Nevertheless, we can look at the extent to which anti-Muslim sentiment relates to anti-immigration views.

A sequence of questions were asked in 2003 about various aspects of people's attitudes to Muslims. As shown in Table 8.9, there is a strong relationship between answers to these questions and anti-immigration views – indeed stronger than any of the relationships we have examined previously. In keeping with work that emphasises the importance of symbols in explaining attitudes to particular policies (Kinder and Sears, 1981; Sears and Funk, 1991), this is particularly the case for 51 per cent of the population who agree that England (or Scotland or Wales) would start to lose its identity if more Muslims came to live here. They are 40 percentage points more likely to think that immigration should be reduced than the 30 per cent who do not think that their country would lose its identity. This close correlation is hardly surprising given that the question is specifically about Muslim immigration, and it would be hard to claim that one sentiment *causes* the other – rather, we should conclude that they are closely related views. None of the other questions reported in Table 8.9 are *as* closely related to views on immigration, but they all still show a very strong relationship with anti-immigration views. For example, among the 25 per cent of respondents who would be unhappy if a close relative married a Muslim, almost nine out of ten would like to see a reduction in immigration, whereas the figure among the 29 per cent who would be happy to see such a marriage, the figure is three-fifths. (The figures reported in this section exclude Muslim respondents.) A slightly less strong, but still significant, relationship is also found between all these items and the desire for stronger measures against illegal immigrants.

It is unfortunate that we do not have a reading on these Muslim questions before 2003 and can therefore say nothing with any certainty about their effect on the increase in hostility to immigrants. However, it is widely thought that hostility towards Muslims has increased in the wake of September 11th, and the very close relationship between these views and hostility towards immigration certainly suggest that this has been part of the story why opposition to immigration has hardened since 1995.

Table 8.9 Anti-Muslim hostility and anti-immigration hostility

| | % who want to reduce number of immigrants | | | | |
	'Pro'-Muslim view	Base	'Anti'-Muslim view	Base	% difference
England (Scotland/Wales) would begin to lose its identity if more Muslims came to live in England (Scotland/Wales)	50	226	90	413	+40
How would you feel if a close relative of yours married or formed a long-term relationship with a Muslim	59	213	88	211	+29
Some people think that Muslims living in Britain are really committed to Britain ... Other people feel that Muslims living in Britain could never be really committed to Britain	62	215	89	354	+27
Some people think that Muslims who come to live in Britain take jobs, housing and health care from other people in Britain ... Other people feel that Muslims in Britain contribute a lot in terms of hard work and much needed skills	61	278	88	251	+27
British Muslims are more loyal to other Muslims around the world than they are to other people in this country	57	77	83	463	+26
Muslims living in Britain have done a great deal to condemn Islamic terrorism	60	183	85	291	+25

Base: Respondents who are British citizens and whose parents were British citizens at the time of the respondent's birth. Muslims are also excluded

Economic and social consequences of immigration

So far none of our hypotheses have allowed us to answer satisfactorily our question of why anti-immigration feelings have increased since the mid-1990s. Increases in some aspects of national pride and in certain forms of racism may hold part of the answer, but we have not found anything that is clearly at the root of the development. We turn next to look at perceptions of the consequences of immigration: are people increasingly hostile to immigration because they have come to associate immigrants who are already in the country with economic and social problems?

As discussed above, British immigration policy since the mid-1960s has emphasised the combination of tight immigration controls, along with improvement of social and economic conditions of immigrants already living here. Thus, via the Race Relations Act of 1965 and later government policies, a strategy of improving housing, education, and health care for immigrants was pursued indirectly by addressing general issues of poverty and development (Joppke, 1999). With such policies, it was presumably hoped that new settlers would be allowed to adopt a lifestyle similar to more established British citizens and become full participants in society. However, although there is no affirmative action policy in Britain, some British people may come to feel that minorities and immigrants draw too heavily on the social and economic resources of the country.

One important point to note is that although the nature of immigration has changed since the end of the British Empire and the near collapse of the Commonwealth, British citizens tend to conflate various types of immigration into a single category. While the majority of movement into the UK through the early to mid-1980s was Commonwealth-related, from the 1990s onward, migration has tended to be less related to former colonial status and is increasingly asylum-related. However, according to one analysis, ordinary British citizens do not make these distinctions between types of migration (Saggar, 2003), so it is not unreasonable for us to expect that any changes in attitudes to established minorities will help to explain the changes in attitudes to further immigration.

Economic consequences of immigration

Turning first to views on the economic implications of immigrants, respondents were asked to agree or disagree with the following statements:

Immigrants are generally good for Britain's economy

Immigrants take jobs away from people who were born in Britain

Government spends too much money assisting immigrants

Table 8.10 Perceived economic consequences of immigration and anti-immigration hostility

	% who want to reduce number of immigrants				
	Agree	*Base*	**Disagree**	*Base*	**% difference**
Government spends too much on immigrants	91	*522*	36	*95*	+55
Take jobs from people born in Britain	92	*357*	46	*205*	+46
Immigrants are good for Britain's economy	47	*151*	92	*330*	+45

Base: Respondents who are British citizens and whose parents were British citizens at the time of the respondent's birth

As shown in Table 8.10, views on these matters are strongly related to attitudes
to immigration. Indeed, among people who see adverse economic consequences
of immigration, there is near unanimity that it should be reduced. They also
hold similarly implacable views on the need for stronger measures against
illegal immigrants. However, among people who do not perceive adverse
economic consequences, only a minority want to reduce the number of
immigrants.

Have we at last found the key source of the increase in anti-immigration
sentiment? Well, no, as it turns out, because this explanation fails at the second
hurdle – that there should have been change since 1995. As seen in Table 8.11,
there has, if anything, been a polarisation of views on whether immigration is
good for the economy, with both the agree camp and the disagree camp
increasing by five percentage points at the expense of those who said they held
neither view. In line with our findings for the two summary measures, there
seems less ambivalence on these matters in 2003 than in 1995. On the question
of whether immigrants take jobs from British-born workers, there has been a
small but significant *increase* in the proportion who disagree with this, perhaps
in line with improvements in the economy in general over the period.

Table 8.11 Perceived economic consequences of immigration, 1995 and 2003

	1995	2003	% change
Good for British economy	%	%	
Agree	14	19	+5
Neither agree nor disagree	47	37	-10
Disagree	37	42	+5
Base	*970*	*793*	
Take jobs from British	%	%	
Agree	49	45	-4
Neither agree nor disagree	28	27	-1
Disagree	22	27	+5
Base	*970*	*793*	
Govt spends too much assisting immigrants	%	%	
Agree	n/a	64	–
Neither agree nor disagree	n/a	23	–
Disagree	n/a	12	–
Base	–	*793*	–

n/a = not asked
Base: Respondents who are British citizens and whose parents were British citizens at
the time of the respondent's birth

The question about government giving too much assistance to immigrants was,
unfortunately, not asked in 1995, so we have no measure of change over time.

However, it should be noted that almost two-thirds of respondents agreed with this sentiment. This distribution was by far the most negative of any on the perceived economic consequences of immigration, and it was also the most polarised of the three, having the lowest proportion in the middle. It is perhaps even more surprising given the probable lack of actual knowledge on the amount of government spending. One reason for this may be the press attention given to spending on asylum seekers, which respondents perhaps had in mind when answering. We shall return to this point. Another may be the traditional emphasis of UK governments on improving the conditions of migrants accepted to the country (as outlined above). The lack of time-series on this question is unfortunate because it means we are unable to interpret the role of perceptions of government spending on immigrants in explaining the rise in anti-immigration sentiment. Nonetheless the high level of people agreeing leads us to suspect it is important.

Social consequences of immigration

Since perceptions of the economic consequences of immigration were not fruitful in explaining the increasingly negative views about immigration, we turn now to perceptions of the social consequences.

Respondents were asked to agree or disagree with the following statements:

Immigrants increase crime rates

Immigrants improve British society by bringing in new ideas and cultures

Are perceived negative social consequences of immigration related to feelings about reducing or excluding immigrants in the future? The effects shown in Table 8.12 indicate that they are. As with the economic consequences, there is near unanimity among those who perceive adverse social consequences that immigration should be reduced, while only half the respondents who perceive no such consequences want a reduction. Again, the effect is not quite as strong when we consider attitudes to illegal immigrants, but it is still quite powerful.

Table 8.12 Perceived social consequences of immigration and anti-immigration hostility

	% who want to reduce number of immigrants				
	Agree	*Base*	**Dis-agree**	*Base*	**% diffe-rence**
Immigrants make Britain open to ideas	50	240	95	244	+45
Immigrants increase crime rates	93	310	50	204	+43

Base: Respondents who are British citizens and whose parents were British citizens at the time of the respondent's birth

Have perceptions of the social consequences of immigration become more negative over the 1995–2003 period, however? As seen in Table 8.13, both measures have shown a net shift in the anti-immigrant direction. In the case of increased crime rates, the most common answer in 1995 was "neither agree nor disagree", now it is agreement. Such a dramatic reversal of opinion is a promising candidate in helping us determine why there was an increase in preference for restrictions on the entry of new immigrants.

Table 8.13 Changes in perceived social consequences of immigration, 1995 and 2003

	1995	2003	% change
Make Britain open to ideas and cultures			
Agree	51	31	-20
Neither agree nor disagree	31	39	+8
Disagree	17	29	+12
Base	*970*	*793*	
Increase crime rates			
Agree	25	39	+14
Neither agree nor disagree	38	34	-4
Disagree	36	26	-10
Base	*970*	*793*	

Base: Respondents who are British citizens and whose parents were British citizens at the time of the respondent's birth

Clearly, the increases in negative perceptions regarding the social consequences of immigration are prime candidates to explain the overall rise in negative perceptions about immigration. However, to stop there does not provide a completely satisfactory understanding of the processes involved. We really need to ask *why* these perceptions have changed because it seems highly unlikely that they are endogenous – that is, other things must be fuelling them. To address this we turn to the role of politicians and the media.

The portrayal of immigration by politicians and in the media

We now consider the question of where it is that survey respondents are likely to find information on immigration that would lead them to be either more positive or more negative about it. Since many people will have had no personal experience of immigrants, their sources of information must come from somewhere else. It is expected that the primary source of information related to political affairs is the mass media (Lazarsfeld and Merton, 1948; Funkhouser, 1973; MacKuen, 1981, 1984; Iyengar and Kinder, 1987).

Although the media cannot sway the entirety of a population, they generally can have considerable influence over people who do not have strongly anchored opinions – or those who had no/little opinion on an issue in the first place (see Levin *et al.*, 1998). One of the now seminal works on public opinion formation contended many years ago that people with unformed ideas tend to reach for 'top-of-the-head' responses to survey questions while being interviewed (Taylor and Fiske, 1978), and later work elaborated this idea by showing that people are likely to draw these top-of-the-head responses from things they have heard or seen lately about the issue at hand (Zaller, 1992). In addition, it is well known that the media can have an impact on perceptions of particular issues by the way in which they frame these issues (see Druckman, 2001). What this means is that – at least in the short term – the media can have a tremendous effect on perceptions of topics like immigration.

In *The 20th Report*, Rothon and Heath (2003) compiled information on the number of immigration-related articles presented in *The Times*. As the authors point out, information from reports in additional newspapers would have been helpful as well since *The Times*' circulation is rather low and its emphasis is likely to be somewhat different from other more widely circulated papers like *The Sun* and the *Daily Mail*. Unfortunately, other newspaper indices are not freely available. Thus, like these authors, we shall depend on the count of stories related to immigration from this index, bearing in mind the potential problems with doing so. Figure 8.3 presents these counts over the period from 1994. What is clear from this figure is that between the mid-to-late 1990s and 2000, the number of articles related to immigration more than tripled. Moreover, by the year before our most recent *British Social Attitudes* survey, this number had quadrupled from the mid-1990s baseline. If we can take this as a general representation of coverage of immigration-related issues in the press, it is clear that the increased reporting on the issue is likely to have had an impact on making people think more about the issue. Naturally, it may be that *The Times* and other newspapers are simply reporting on what they perceive to be the major concerns of their readers, but as discussed above, many people will not have encountered immigrants personally and are dependent on news sources to inform them as to what is happening on this front – not the other way around.

Why did the media suddenly take up the issue of immigration in full force in the late 1990s and 2000? To some degree, this shift in coverage is likely to be related to the actual numbers of immigrants entering and settling in the country. We saw earlier in Figure 8.1 the increase in this period in the numbers of people settling in the UK and in the number of new asylum applications received. Clearly, the number of *Times* articles on immigration is partly a reflection of the increase in immigration as a whole (i.e. immigration + asylum seekers). Thus, it appears that our causal chain may look something like the following:

Increased immigration→Increased news coverage→Increased anti-immigration hostility

Figure 8.3 *The Times* **immigration-related articles**

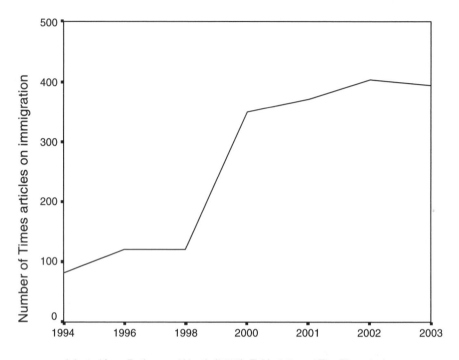

Adapted from Rothon and Heath (2003), Table 9.5, and The Times Index

On the other hand, it may be useful to consider whether this news coverage is to scale with the increase in migration? That is, does there appear to be a one-to-one correspondence between the increase in numbers and the rise in coverage of the issue? In comparing Figure 8.1 and Figure 8.3 we see that, while the number of articles related to immigration tripled and then quadrupled over this period, the number of new asylum applications and new settlements merely doubled. It is important to note, of course, that after 2000, the numbers of new settlements and asylum applications remained at the higher level, and so the overall numbers of new individuals in the country was compounded over time.

One explanation for this disproportionate increase in coverage has to do with where the media gets its information. While sources of information are numerous, a key source is, of course, the British government. Thus, UK government ministers can set the media's agenda to some degree, and increases in government ministers' statements about an issue like immigration can change the nature of media coverage of the issue, both quantitatively and qualitatively. It seems that by the year before our 2003 survey, government ministers and agencies were indeed setting the media's agenda to a greater degree than previously. In 1994, there were only four *Times* articles centred around the reporting of restrictive government policies or negative government statements regarding immigration. By 2002, however, this number had approached 40.

Moreover, the nature of the messages coming out of government offices, particularly the Home Office, appears to have changed as well. In the mid-1990s, the Home Office clearly favoured restriction, and most of the reports in *The Times* stemming from Home Office announcements were related to decisions on deportations[11] and refusal to allow certain individuals into the country on asylum grounds[12], along with a story about Prime Minister John Major supporting the introduction of identity cards[13]. By 2002, there were equally restrictive statements, but apparently more of them, plus the introduction of novel ways of approaching the issue of immigration. Specifically, this was the year in which the new Home Secretary, David Blunkett, suggested that immigrants speak English in their own homes[14], proposed adding an oath of allegiance to citizenship provisions[15], advised Asians to stop making arranged marriages in their home countries and make them within the UK instead[16], and compared Muslim forced marriages with practices of medieval England[17]. That is, the traditional acceptance of multicultural practices in Britain seemed to come under sustained direct attack from the Labour government, aided and abetted by the Conservative opposition. This, along with the announcements of the creation of new detention centres[18], of sending asylum seekers back to their home countries en masse[19], and even tipping off television crews as to times and locations of deportations so they could be filmed[20], may have contributed to the overall impression of the citizenry that immigration needed to be stopped. But can this be supported by the survey data?

Newspapers

One obvious way in which we may be able to detect a role of the media is by comparing attitudes to immigration and their change among those who read different types of newspapers and those who do not read a newspaper. Indeed, of all forms of media, the newspapers are probably the most influential in stimulating debate. Clearly, if newspapers are responsible for the rise in anti-immigration sentiment, those who do read 'anti-immigration' newspapers should have a higher level of hostility to immigrants and have experienced a greater increase in hostility, than those who read 'pro-immigration' newspapers or do not read newspapers at all. The analysis is not perfect, as people may choose a newspaper to fit their views rather than the other way round. However, it is hardly likely that immigration looms so large in people's minds that there has been wholesale switching of newspapers on this issue alone, but to the extent that this happens, it will tend to inflate any media effect in the data.

In order to get to the bottom of this, we classify the newspapers into two groups which broadly summarises their overall coverage of immigration into 'pro-immigration' and 'anti-immigration'.[21] Unsurprisingly, the first part of our prediction is correct, with readers of anti-immigration papers being substantially more anti-immigration than readers of pro-immigration papers and non-readers. However, with large majorities of readers of pro-immigration papers and non-readers also being anti-immigration, the role of the media must be considered to be rather small.

When we consider the change over time we find an even bigger problem with the media-effect hypothesis. The group which has had the largest increase in opposition to further immigration is actually non-readers, and this holds also for the desire for stronger measures against illegal immigrants. The increase in anti-immigration sentiments among readers of pro- and anti-immigration papers is rather similar, thus failing to display any newspaper effect.

Table 8.14 Anti-immigration hostility by stance of newspaper, 1995 and 2003

	% saying number of immigrants should be reduced				
	1995	*Base*	**2003**	*Base*	**% change**
Pro-immigration	60	*157*	71	*70*	+11
Anti-immigration	74	*349*	84	*266*	+10
Does not read paper	65	*353*	79	*359*	+14

Base: Respondents who are British citizens and whose parents were British citizens at the time of the respondent's birth

We are forced to conclude that if the media have played a role, it is not in the direct way that may be expected, and newspapers may not be the most important source of information on this. However, one aspect that we cannot examine is that newspapers may have an indirect effect. They may influence people who do not actually read them – for example, people may see headlines and form opinions on the basis of them (see Taylor and Fiske, 1978, cited previously concerning 'top-of-the-head' responses), they may hear summaries of newspaper stories on the television or radio, or friends may tell them about what they have read.

Interest in politics

Another factor that may be important in understanding the change in attitudes to immigration is how interested people are in politics. Clearly, this is related to reading a newspaper (more specifically a broadsheet newspaper) – of those who read a newspaper 39 per cent are interested in politics and 26 per cent are not, compared to 27 per cent and 41 per cent among those who do not read a paper. Among broadsheet readers 72 per cent are interested in politics and six per cent are not, compared to 30 per cent and 33 per cent among tabloid readers.

Looking at interest in politics rather than newspaper readership has the advantage that we can take into account, albeit in an indirect way, those who get more of their information from news and current affairs programmes on television and radio than from a newspaper. Given the role of politicians in initiating debate, and how they have seemingly become more negative in their presentation of immigration issues, one expectation would be that those people interested in politics would be more anti-immigration than those not, as they will be the ones paying most attention to the discourse. On the other hand, it is possible that those with a deep interest in politics could take a more considered approach to political issues, whereas those who are disinterested will only see or hear the headlines.

In Table 8.15, we find that the latter of these two propositions is supported – those people with more interest in politics are indeed less likely to say the number of immigrants should be reduced than are those with less interest. However, the percentage change since 1995 is similar among all levels of interest in politics, with all groups becoming more hostile to immigration.

Table 8.15 Anti-immigration hostility by interest in politics, 1995 and 2003

	% saying number of immigrants should be reduced				
Interest in politics	**1995**	*Base*	**2003**	*Base*	**% change**
Great deal/quite a lot	59	*337*	67	*217*	+8
Some	68	*331*	76	*277*	+9
Not very much/none	68	*302*	77	*299*	+9

Base: Respondents who are British citizens and whose parents were British citizens at the time of the respondent's birth

These are interesting findings because not only do they suggest that things other than the media and politicians influence attitudes to immigration, but they also show that those most concerned about immigration are likely to be those least well armed with the facts.

Education

A key factor that is highly likely to be related both to reading a newspaper and to having an interest in politics is education. Education is known to be critical in the formation of attitudes (Stouffer, 1955; Prothro and Grigg, 1960; Nunn *et al.*, 1978; but see Jackman, 1978; Sullivan *et al.*, 1982; Jackman and Muha, 1984).

Our survey is no exception and we see a clear education gradient in hostility to immigration, as seen in Table 8.16. In 1995, around a third of graduates wanted a reduction in the numbers of immigrants, compared with over four-fifths of those with no qualifications. But the changes between 1995 and 2003 are unexpected and revealing. The group whose attitudes towards immigration has changed the most is actually the most educated, particularly those with degrees. The proportion believing the number of immigrants should be reduced rose by 21 percentage points among graduates, compared to the next highest increase of 12 percentage points among those with O level or equivalent. Of course, the less highly educated groups already had high levels of anti-immigration feelings in the first place and so had less 'room' to become even more hostile.

Table 8.16 Anti-immigrant hostility by education, 1995 and 2003

	% saying number of immigrants should be reduced				
	1995	*Base*	**2003**	*Base*	**% change**
Degree	35	*94*	56	*112*	+21
HE below degree	64	*140*	71	*107*	+7
A level	65	*151*	68	*113*	+3
O level or equivalent	71	*280*	83	*242*	+12
No qualification	82	*295*	81	*212*	-1

Base: Respondents who are British citizens and whose parents were British citizens at the time of the respondent's birth

Given that better-educated people are thought to be less easily persuaded and influenced by newspapers and politicians, this is further evidence that the role of politicians and the media on attitudes to immigration is unlikely to be direct. Rather, it seems they may have had an effect pervasive throughout society. On the other hand, the results presented here could indicate media and politicians have accomplished a rather impressive feat of convincing even the well educated that immigration must be halted, combined, of course, with the actual increase in immigration over the period.

Party identification

If politicians have stirred up this anti-immigration sentiment then another group who we would predict to have had a disproportionate increase in anti-immigration sentiments would be Conservative supporters, because this is the party that has traditionally been the most hostile toward new immigration. In fact, as already described, part of Labour's platform in the 1997 election included the desire to create kinder, fairer policies, particularly regarding asylum seekers.

But Table 8.17 shows that, whilst Conservatives are the most likely of any party supporters to think immigration should be reduced, the extent to which they increased in such views over the eight years is the same as Labour supporters and greater than those without a party identification. In fact, in percentage terms, among Labour supporters anti-immigration views increased by 22 per cent, whereas among Conservatives it was by only 18 per cent. As with education, this may in part be due to a 'ceiling effect' – Conservative supporters were already so opposed to immigration that there was less 'room' for further increases.

Table 8.17 Anti-immigration hostility by party identification, 1995 and 2003

	% saying number of immigrants should be reduced				
	1995	*Base*	**2003**	*Base*	**% change**
Conservative	71	*257*	84	*209*	+13
Labour	58	*415*	71	*292*	+13
Liberal Democrat	66	*144*	62	*98*	-4
No party identification	71	*85*	81	*122*	+10

Base: Respondents who are British citizens and whose parents were British citizens at the time of the respondent's birth

Perhaps, though, it is the change among Labour supporters which can actually be argued to support the thesis that the pronouncements of politicians have an effect. Over the eight years there can be no doubt that Labour has become more right-wing in its views on immigration. Therefore, supporters are increasingly hearing ministers speaking in negative and restrictionist terms about immigration described above and may have been influenced in that direction.

A more complex picture

Perhaps the reason that we do not find more of a direct effect is that the role of the media and politicians is really a mediating one. We have already noted the relationship between views on the social consequences of immigration and hostility to further immigration. Where does newspaper readership fit into this? Among newspaper readers there was a 17 percentage point increase in the proportion who thought immigrants increase crime rates, whereas amongst non-readers there was only a 12 percentage point increase. So perhaps this is the way the media has played a significant role in this change. Further, among tabloid readers this increase was actually 20 per cent, so that virtually half of all tabloid readers now think that immigrants increase crime, compared to around a quarter of broadsheet readers. It was also the least educated who experienced the greatest rise in this view with an 18 percentage point rise among those with no qualifications (but there was a 12 percentage point increase among those with degrees as well).

On whether immigrants improve society, the increase in proportion disagreeing was the same among readers and non-readers of newspapers (14 percentage points). Tabloid readers, however, increased by 15 percentage points compared to the 11 percentage point increase among broadsheet readers. And those with little interest in politics experienced a higher rise than those with quite a lot or some interest in politics (16 points compared to 11 and eight respectively). Among those with no qualifications this view increased by 23 per cent, and by 29 per cent among those with O level equivalent qualifications, whereas those with degrees remained roughly stable.

Conclusions

As we have discussed, Britain has seen a large increase in anti-immigration sentiment since 1995. Back then, two-thirds of respondents wanted the number of immigrants reduced, whereas by 2003 almost three-quarters held this view. Seventy eight per cent wanted stronger measures to be taken to exclude illegal immigrants, which increased to 82 per cent in 2003. This is surprising for two reasons – firstly, these levels were already very high, and secondly, because a dominant trend found over the last twenty years of the *British Social Attitudes* survey is an increasing liberalism on social issues.

We found partial support for the prediction that the change was due to rising national pride. There was no support for the idea that the increase was caused by notions of Britishness becoming increasingly conservative, however. Nor were we able to establish conclusively that it was due to increasing racial prejudice – the picture is complicated because levels of self-rated prejudice for the two years in question were very similar, but at the same time respondents reported that prejudice in society as a whole had increased. We speculated about the possible role of attitudes towards Muslims in particular, but lack of data prevents us from coming to any firm conclusions. Nor have people become more wary of immigration because of perceived economic threats posed by migrants, perhaps because we are looking at a period of rising economic prosperity. However, there is good evidence that people are increasingly concerned about the perceived social consequences of immigration, and this is certainly related to anti-immigration hostility.

The best explanation we could find for this change related to the overall increase in numbers of immigrants, which appears to have stimulated a rise in media coverage of immigration, and perhaps more importantly produced an increase in government statements and proclamations on the subject, many of which were quite negative in tone and content. This was a far from perfect explanation, however. Rather than the increased hostility being particularly associated with people exposed to the anti-immigration newspapers, it seems to have affected everyone, suggesting either that newspapers have a power beyond their own readership or that there are other forces behind the change. It seems as though there has been a 'culture shift' throughout society. Indeed, change has been greatest among groups such as graduates, Labour supporters and those with a substantial interest in politics, who were previously relatively pro-immigration.

Given the barrage of news reports and government statements and coupled with actual increases in immigration, it is perhaps no wonder that British citizens became less open to the idea of immigration. In fact, given all of these components – the increase in immigration, increase in government pronouncements, plus the increase in media coverage of the issue – it is perhaps surprising that hostility did not increase even more than it did. Possibly this is due to the fact that hostility was already so high.

This would appear to be a fertile area for future research. In particular, one point worthy of further investigation is the changing interpretation of survey questions and especially the word 'immigrant' by respondents, in the light of the current political debate. Another is the specific role played by the media and politicians in framing the immigration issue and shaping public opinion towards immigrants and immigration.

Notes

1. Informal controls were used in the 1950s to discourage immigration. These included having colonial overseas offices explain to potential migrants that their lives in the UK would be difficult, as well as indefinitely holding the passports of those who attempted to migrate (Hansen, 2000).
2. Although Britain did indeed conquer Iraq at the end of the First World War, the intention did not appear to be the setting up of colonial power there.
3. *The Times*, 28 December 2002, p.18.
4. Ideally, we would investigate the effect of citizenship status on these variables, but we fear that this would take the chapter rather far afield from its main concern. The removal of these observations represents a loss of approximately eight per cent of the 1995 sample and nine per cent of the 2003 sample.
5. This is a different format of question compared to our first summary measure – it was asked in an agree–disagree format, whereas our first measure had answer options ranging from increased a lot to reduced a lot. Clearly, then, comparing the two should be done with caution.
6. We use the 2003 survey only to ease interpretation; we have no reason to suspect that the bivariate relationships discussed here differed in 1995.
7. Only individuals who had a 'qualifying connection' to the UK could enter, with this meaning individuals, their children, and grandchildren who were born, naturalised, or adopted in the UK (see Hansen, 2000).
8. The Act also incorporated British Dependent Territories Citizenship and British Overseas Citizenship, but neither of these included an automatic right of entry to the UK.

9. It should be noted, however, that *all* the various measures of Britishness – with the sole exception of being a Christian – are positively correlated with wishing to take stronger measures against illegal immigrants.
10. We acknowledge the likely problems with political correctness related to this particular survey question. Unfortunately, measuring racial prejudice directly is extraordinarily difficult (if not impossible) in the current day, and so we are dependent on this rather direct approach.
11. *The Times*, 8 June 1995, p.2g.
12. e.g. *The Times*, 27 November 1995, p.1/7f; 28 November 1995, p.2a.
13. *The Times*, 29 April 1995, p.2g.
14. *The Times*, 16 September 2002, p.1g.
15. *The Times*, 8 February 2002, p.1a.
16. *The Times*, 1 June 2002, p.2e.
17. *The Times*, 15 January 2002, p.8f.
18. *The Times*, 28 January 2002, p.4g.
19. *The Times*, 24 May 2002, p.1a.
20. This division was done on the basis of the authors' impressions of coverage and was not 'scientific' in any sense. Newspapers assigned as 'pro-immigration' were *Daily Mirror, The Guardian, The Independent* and *The Financial Times*; 'anti-immigration' were *Daily Express, Daily Mail, Daily Star, The Sun, Daily Telegraph*, and *The Times*.

References

Druckman, J.N. (2001),'The implications of framing effects for citizen competence', *Political Behavior*, **23(3)**: 225–256

Favell, A. (2001), 'Multi-ethnic Britain: an exception in Europe?', *Patterns of Prejudice* **35(1)**: 35–57

Funkhouser, G.R. (1973), 'The issues of the sixties: an exploratory study in the dynamics of public opinion', *Public Opinion Quarterly*, **37**: 620–675

Hansen, R. (2000), *Citizenship and Immigration in Post-War Britain*, Oxford: Oxford University Press

Hjerm, M. (1998), 'National Identities, National Pride and Xenophobia: A Comparison of Four Western Countries', *Acta Sociologica*, **41**: 335–347

Home Office (2003), 'Control of Immigration: Statistics United Kingdom 2002', London: The Stationary Office

Iyengar S. and Kinder D. (1987), *News That Matters: Television and American Opinion*, Chicago: University of Chicago Press

Jackman, M. (1978), 'General and Applied Tolerance: Does Education Increase Commitment to Racial Education?', *American Journal of Political Science*, **22**:302–324

Jackman, M. and Muha, M. (1984), 'Education and Intergroup Attitudes: Moral Enlightenment, Superficial Democratic Commitment, or Ideological Refinement?', *American Sociological Review,* **49**:751–769

Joppke, C. (1999), 'How Immigration is Changing Citizenship', *Ethnic and Racial Studies,* **22(4)**: 629–652

Kinder, D.R. and Sears, D.O. (1981), 'Prejudice and Politics: Symbolic Racism versus Racial Threats to the Good Life', *Journal of Personality and Social Psychology,* **40(3)**: 414–431.

Layton-Henry, Z. (1992), *The Politics of Immigration: Immigration, Race and Race Relations in Post-War Britain,* Oxford: Blackwell

Lazarsfeld P.F. and Merton R.K. (1948), 'Mass communication, popular taste, and organized social action', in Bryson, L. (ed.), *The Communication of Ideas,* New York: Harper; Urbana: University of Illinois Press

Levin, I.P., Schneider, S.L. and Gaeth, G.J (1998), 'All frames are not created equal: a typology and critical analysis of framing effects', *Organizational Behavior and Human Decision Processes,* **76**: 149–188

McCrone, D. and Surridge, P. (1998), 'National Identity and National Pride' in Jowell, R., Curtice, J., Park, A., Brook, L., Thomson, K. and Bryson, C. (ed.), *British and European Social Attitudes: The 15th Report,* Aldershot: Ashgate

MacKuen, M. (1981), 'Social communication and the mass policy agenda', in MacKuen, M.B. and Coombs, S.L. (ed.), *More than News: Media Power in Public Affairs,* Beverly Hills, Calif. Sage

MacKuen M. (1984), 'Exposure to information, belief integration and individual responsiveness to agenda change', *American Political Science Review,* **78**:372–391

Nielsen, K.B. (2004), *Next Stop Britain: The Influence of Transnational Networks on the Secondary Movement of Danish Somalis,* Working Paper no. 22, March, Brighton: Sussex Centre for Migration Research

Nunn, C.Z. Crockett, H.J. and Williams, J.A. (1978), *Tolerance for Nonconformity,* San Francisco: Jossey-Bass

Prothro, J.W. and Grigg, C.W. (1960), 'Fundamental Principles of Democracy: Bases of Agreement and Disagreement', *Journal of Politics,* **22**:276–294

Rothon, C. and Heath, A. (2003), 'Trends in racial prejudice', in Park, A., Curtice, J., Thomson, K., Jarvis, L. and Bromley, C. (eds.) *British Social Attitudes: the 20th Report – Continuity and change over two decades,* London: Sage

Saggar, S. (2003), 'Immigration and the Politics of Public Opinion', *The Political Quarterly,* **74**: 178–194

Sears, D.O. and Funk, C. (1991), 'The Role of Self-Interest in Social and Political Attitudes', *Advances in Experimental Psychology,* **24**: 1–91

Stouffer, S. (1955), *Communism, Conformity, and Civil Liberties,* New York: Doubleday

Sullivan, J.L., Pierson, J. and Marcus, G.E. (1982), *Political Tolerance and American Democracy,* Chicago: University of Chicago Press

Taylor, S.E., and Fiske, S.T. (1978), 'Salience, attention and attribution: top of the head phenomena', in Berkowitz, L. (ed.), *Advances in experimental social psychology, Vol 11,* New York: Academic Press

The Times Index (2003), Reading: Newspaper Archive Developments Ltd.

Zaller, J. (1992), *The Nature and Origin of Mass Opinion,* Cambridge: Cambridge University Press

Acknowledgements

The *National Centre for Social Research* is grateful to the Economic and Social Research Council (grant number RES-000-22-0326) for their financial support which enabled us to ask the *International Social Survey Programme* questions reported in this chapter. We are also grateful to the Nuffield Foundation (grant number OPD-00213-6) for funding the module on 'Public attitudes towards minorities in post-devolution Scotland' which included the questions covered in the section about attitudes to Muslims.

9 Does England want devolution too?

John Curtice and Mark Sandford [*]

The current Labour government has introduced a substantial programme of devolution since it was first elected in 1997. Scotland has been granted her own parliament with substantial law-making powers, while Wales has an assembly that has administrative and secondary law-making responsibility for a significant range of public services. A further attempt to restore devolved powers to Northern Ireland has been made, while a form of city-wide government has been re-established in London in the form of a mayor and assembly. Although various forms of territorial administration had existed before in the UK, what is significant about these developments is that in each case those responsible for running the new institutions are directly elected by the electorates that they seek to serve, thereby giving them a mandate separate from that of the UK government at Westminster.

But this programme of devolution is asymmetric. Each of the four new sets of institutions has a different set of powers and responsibilities. More importantly, England seems largely to have been left out, a situation that has created some apparent anomalies. For example, while the law in Scotland on health and education can be determined within Scotland without any interference from English MPs, the law on such matters for England is still made at Westminster, where Scottish MPs continue to have both a voice and a vote. Moreover, this privilege has been granted while Scotland (and indeed Wales) still enjoys a higher level of public expenditure per head than England. For some commentators the people of England could not be expected to tolerate such apparent inconsistency and unfairness for long. Marquand and Tomaney, for example, have claimed that "it is logically impossible to devolve power to part

[*] John Curtice is Research Consultant at the *Scottish Centre for Social Research*, part of NatCen, Deputy Director of the *Centre for Research into Elections and Social Trends*, and Professor of Politics and Director of the Social Statistics Laboratory at Strathclyde University. Mark Sandford is a Research Fellow in the Constitution Unit at University College, London.

of a hitherto unitary state without impacting on the governance of the remaining parts" (2000: 4; see also McLean, 2000).

Yet, so far, little has happened in provincial England. True, a regional development agency has been established in each region of England, an agency which is charged with the task of promoting the region's economy and whose work is overseen by a regional chamber or assembly. But the agencies are staffed by civil servants while the members of the assemblies are unelected nominees (for further details, see Tomaney, 2002). Neither set of bodies enjoys the independent authority that can come from being directly elected. Only in May 2002 did the government set out proposals for the introduction of elected regional assemblies (DTLR/Cabinet Office, 2002). And it was not until November 2004 that it finally gave some people in provincial England a chance to have a say in a referendum on whether they would like their own elected regional institutions. Even then, it scaled down its original ambition of holding a referendum in all three of the northernmost regions of England to doing so in just one, the North East.[1]

There are two possible explanations why so little has happened. One is that those commentators who were critical of asymmetrical devolution overestimated the impact it would have on the public in England. Perhaps people in England were largely content to be ruled by Westminster before devolution was introduced elsewhere in the UK, and they simply continue to be content to be ruled in that way now. The other interpretation is that the government has been too circumspect. Perhaps there *is* a strong demand in England to be allowed to enjoy the benefits of devolution, a demand that the current government has simply been too slow to recognise, let alone respond to. In this chapter we consider first of all whether there really is a demand for devolution in England, and then proceed to try to account for the patterns that we find.

Levels of support for devolution

It might be thought that it would be relatively straightforward to ascertain whether there is a clear demand for devolution. Presumably, if we ask people in a survey a suitably worded question as to whether or not they favour devolution, we would discover whether a majority are in favour or opposed. If a majority say they are in favour, then we can conclude there is indeed a real demand for devolution. If a majority are opposed, then we should draw the opposite conclusion.

In practice it is not so simple. A number of surveys designed to tap people's attitudes towards devolution have been conducted in recent years. For the most part, however, they do not present the clear picture that we might have anticipated. Typically, they fail to find either a majority in support or a majority in opposition to devolution. For example, a survey conducted by ICM for the County Councils Network in January 2003 found that while only 21 per cent of people in provincial England said they would vote in a referendum against creating a "regional government" for their region, just 44 per cent said that they would vote in favour (ICM, 2003). Meanwhile a poll conducted by MORI the following month found only 27 per cent of people in provincial England were against their region having its own assembly, but equally only 44 per cent were in favour (MORI, 2003). In both cases relatively large numbers of people said "don't know", that they would not vote, or said that they were "neither in favour nor opposed", an answer that can sometimes be a surrogate for "don't know". In the MORI poll 27 per cent fell into one of these categories, while in ICM's case as many as 35 per cent did so. In short it appears that for many people in England devolution is a subject on which they simply do not have a clear view one way or the other.

Further doubt about the extent of support in England for creating elected regional assemblies is cast by the most recent State of the Nation poll conducted for the Joseph Rowntree Reform Trust by ICM in the summer of 2004 (Joseph Rowntree Reform Trust, 2004; see also Dunleavy *et al.*, 2001 for details of the results of earlier surveys in this series). This survey asked respondents which they thought was the best way "of deciding how to generate new jobs, develop major road and public transport, and other similar issues". Just 34 per cent of people in England said they favoured investing responsibility for these matters in the hands of "an elected regional assembly". As many as 40 per cent backed one of two options that feature in the current *status quo*: giving the decision either to "appointed business and local government representatives" (24 per cent) or to "government officials meeting at regional level" (16 per cent). Meanwhile a further 14 per cent were quite happy to leave matters in the hands of government ministers in Whitehall.

Indeed, of all the independent attempts to measure public opinion on this subject since 1997, only one has ever found a majority in favour of English devolution. This was a poll conducted by Opinion Research Business for the BBC in March 2002. Here, no less than 63 per cent of respondents said they were in favour of creating a regional assembly in their region, while just 22 per cent were opposed. However, this poll failed to offer people explicitly the option of saying that they neither agreed nor disagreed with the idea.[2] And, strikingly, no less than 44 per cent said they were "somewhat in favour" rather than "strongly in favour". Discouraged from expressing indifference, it appears that respondents opted for the next closest option – lukewarm support.

We should bear in mind two features of the surveys we have examined so far. First, just because someone is willing to indicate support for the creation of a regional assembly, it does not follow that they necessarily think that this is the *best* arrangement for England. Only the State of the Nation poll offered respondents a range of possible options for governing England. Second, not even the State of the Nation survey included one of the clear and logically possible solutions to the alleged difficulties of an asymmetric devolution settlement – that England as a whole should have its own parliament in much the same manner as Scotland already has. While regional assemblies may be the form of devolution favoured by the current government, it is not the only possible form of English devolution.

Given the apparently lukewarm support for devolution registered by other polls, it should come as no great surprise that we failed to find majority support in the 2003 *British Social Attitudes* survey for any of the devolution options. First, we asked the following question, offering a clear set of alternatives for how England might be governed:

> *With all the changes going on in the way the different parts of Great Britain are run, which of the following do you think would be best for England ...*
>
> *... for England to be governed as it is now, with laws made by the UK parliament,*
>
> *for each region of England to have its own elected assembly that makes decisions about the region's economy, planning and housing,*
>
> *or, for England as a whole to have its own new parliament with law-making powers?*

Only just over a quarter (27 per cent) of respondents in England picked creating regional assemblies, while a little under a fifth (19 per cent) said they preferred an English parliament. The combined level of support for these two options (46 per cent) is actually a little less than the 48 per cent who say they wanted England to continue to be governed as it is now.

Even if we focus just on the possibility of creating elected regional assemblies, and remind respondents of the devolution already enjoyed by Scotland and Wales, we still find that support falls well short of a majority. We asked people whether they agreed or disagreed with the following statement:

> *Now that Scotland has its own parliament and Wales its own assembly, every region of England should have its own assembly too*

Only 30 per cent indicated they agreed with this proposition, with most (24 per cent) saying they simply "agreed" rather than "agreed strongly". This group was actually slightly outnumbered by the 33 per cent who said that they disagreed (though again only 7 per cent actually disagreed strongly). As we might by now have come to expect, the largest group, 36 per cent, either said they "neither agreed nor disagreed" or were unable to choose an answer at all.

It appears, then, that five years after its introduction in Scotland and Wales, devolution fails to ignite much excitement in England. Sometimes surveys find more people saying they are in favour of the creation of elected devolved institutions than say they are opposed, sometimes the opposite. Much depends on just how the question is posed. But it seems that no adequately designed poll secures a majority for either option. For many people in England, devolution is just not a subject on which they have much of a view at all. English devolution is not so much supported or opposed, as greeted with an air of indifference.

Nevertheless, there is some sign that public opinion has actually become somewhat more favourable towards regional devolution in recent years. The *British Social Attitudes* survey has regularly tracked attitudes towards devolution in England since the advent of the Scottish Parliament and the Welsh

Assembly in 1999, using a slightly different version of the first of the two questions introduced earlier.[3] In this version, the wording of the regional devolution option reflects the kind of devolution implemented in Wales, rather than that currently proposed by the government, and reads:

> *Each region of England to have its own assembly that runs services like health*

As Table 9.1 shows, worded in this way, support for regional devolution has increased from just 15 per cent in 1999 to a little under a quarter now. Meanwhile around one in six persistently opt for an English parliament. Even so, despite the increase in support for regional devolution, it remains the case that on this version of the question over half say they are in favour of the *status quo*.

Table 9.1 Attitudes towards different ways of governing England, 1999–2003

	1999	2000	2001	2002	2003
	%	%	%	%	%
England be governed as it is now, with laws made by the UK parliament	62	54	57	56	55
Each region of England to have its own assembly that runs services like health	15	18	23	20	24
England as a whole to have its own new parliament with law-making powers	18	19	16	17	16
Base	*2718*	*1928*	*2761*	*2897*	*975*

We should, of course, bear in mind that public opinion might vary from one part of England to another. Perhaps those living further away from London, where economic growth is less strong and more people have a sense of regional identity, are more likely to want regional devolution (Heath *et al.*, 2002). In particular, most though not all of the polls to which we have referred so far suggest that support for devolution is rather higher in the north of England and especially so in the North East. Our own survey provides some support for this view. For example, as Table 9.2 shows, as many as one in three people in the North East say they favour a regional assembly over either the *status quo* or an English parliament, more than in any other region, including London which already as an elected assembly.[4] Support for regional devolution is also relatively high in Yorkshire and the Humber and (to some extent) the North West. Much the same is true as well of our alternative question that simply invited respondents to say whether they agreed or disagreed with creating assemblies in each region. But even in the North East, neither question elicits anything like a majority expressing positive support for a regional assembly.

Table 9.2 Attitudes towards different ways of governing England, by region

	NE	NW	YH	EM	WM	SW	E	GL	SE
	%	%	%	%	%	%	%	%	%
As now	48	50	48	49	47	49	55	52	50
Regional assemblies	32	27	30	26	29	27	21	24	21
English Parliament	18	18	16	20	20	18	19	15	21
Base	218	444	380	381	420	367	438	489	573

NE: North East. NW: North West. YH: Yorkshire & the Humber. EM: East Midlands. WM: West Midlands. SW: South West. E: East of England. GL: Greater London. SE: South East

So, whichever way we look at it, there does not appear to be a strong demand for devolution in England, more a mixture of lukewarm support and indifference. The government's apparent timidity in introducing regional devolution appears to have been a more accurate reading of public opinion than the expectations of those commentators who anticipated that asymmetric devolution would generate an 'English backlash'. But why is this so? How can we account for the apparent lack of enthusiasm for devolution in England?

Why so little enthusiasm?

Knowledge and awareness

The first, and perhaps simplest, explanation as to why devolution generates so little excitement in England is that, for whatever reason, people in England have little awareness or knowledge of the subject. Perhaps the existing unelected regional institutions are too remote and have failed to achieve a sufficiently high profile in their region for people to be aware of what regional government might be able to achieve. Perhaps too, people in England simply know too little about the asymmetric devolution settlement that is already in place to want to rebel against it. In short, while students of the British constitution regard the institutional developments of recent years as significant, if not indeed revolutionary, perhaps they have simply failed to register with the wider English public (Sandford, 2002).

Table 9.3 certainly suggests that the existing unelected regional chambers or assemblies have for the most part had little impact. Only in the North East do a majority of people say they have heard at least something about the work of their regional assembly. Even here, most say they have not heard very much. The chambers in the other two northern regions, together with the East of England region, also have a relatively high public profile, but elsewhere three-fifths or more say they have heard nothing at all of their work. Meanwhile, awareness of the work of the regional development agencies is only a little higher, with 57 per cent of people outside of London saying they have not heard anything at all about them.

Table 9.3 Awareness of work of regional chamber or assembly, by region

How much heard about:	NE	NW	YH	EM	WM	SW	E	SE	All
	%	%	%	%	%	%	%	%	%
A great deal/ quite a lot	4	8	5	6	6	4	3	1	5
Not very much	51	39	39	23	24	34	39	22	32
Nothing at all	45	52	55	69	70	62	58	75	62
Base	*217*	*444*	*380*	*381*	*420*	*367*	*438*	*573*	*3220*

NE: North East. NW: North West. YH: Yorkshire & the Humber. EM: East Midlands. WM: West Midlands. SW: South West. E: East of England. SE: South East
Note: Greater London is excluded from this table

At the same time, the level of objective knowledge of the current asymmetric devolution settlement also appears to be low, certainly as judged by the answers given when respondents were asked whether each of four statements was true or false. The statements were:

*Scottish MPs in the UK House of Commons **cannot** vote on laws that only apply in England.* (FALSE)

It has been decided to cut the number of Scottish MPs in the UK House of Commons. (TRUE)

*The Scottish parliament **can** increase the level of social security benefits in Scotland.* (FALSE)

London is the only region in England with its own elected regional assembly. (TRUE)

As seen in Table 9.4, none of these statements attracted correct answers from anywhere near half of the respondents. Knowledge was highest on whether Scottish MPs can continue to vote on laws that only apply in England, but even here only 38 per cent correctly identified this statement as true. Meanwhile, over half of English respondents incorrectly believed that the Scottish Parliament has the power to increase social security benefits north of the border. Many respondents did not even attempt to guess whether a statement was true or false; on none of the items did much less than a third simply say they did not know the answer. Indeed, on the issue of the reduction of the number of Scottish MPs, regarded by some as a key reversal of an unfairness that existed prior to devolution, nearly half said "don't know".

Table 9.4 Responses to knowledge quiz about devolution

		Correct	Incorrect	Don't know
Scottish MPs cannot vote on English laws	%	38	25	37
London only region with elected assembly	%	27	29	44
Cut number of Scottish MPs	%	18	34	48
Scottish Parliament can increase social security	%	13	56	32

Base: 975

So people in England appear to be largely unaware of the existing institutions in their region and they have little knowledge of the current devolution settlement. However, it is not clear that this is an important explanation of their lack of enthusiasm for devolution. If that were the case, we should find that those who are more aware or more knowledgeable should show a greater level of support for devolution. But of this there is no sign. The small proportion who have heard a great deal or quite a lot about their regional assembly are no more likely to prefer an elected assembly than are those who have heard nothing at all. Equally, they are only two percentage points more likely to agree with our proposition that every region of England should now have its own assembly. Meanwhile, the balance of opinion amongst those able to answer at least two of the knowledge questions correctly is no more favourable towards regional devolution (or indeed an English parliament) than it is amongst those who could not answer any of them correctly.

One obvious explanation for this lack of relationship between awareness, knowledge and support is that awareness and knowledge may bring with them an appreciation of the disadvantages of devolution as well as its advantages (see, for example, MORI, 2003). In fact, in our survey those who are most knowledgeable are both more likely to agree with the creation of regional assemblies and more likely to disagree too.

For familiarity to lead to support, people may need not only to be aware but also to have formed a favourable impression of the work of the existing regional institutions. And indeed, as Tables 9.5 and 9.6 show, those who think that the existing regional assemblies are giving ordinary people more say or will make their region's economy better, are far more likely to back the idea of regional assemblies. However, relatively few people fall into these two groups. Less than one in five feel that having a regional assembly gives ordinary people more say in how they are governed, while less than a quarter think it will make their economy better. In both cases the predominant view, shared by around three in five is that the existing regional assemblies simply make no difference. Only in the North East is the picture at all notably different, but even here only around a third think that their assembly is giving people more say or will make their economy better. Evidently, then, one reason for the lack of enthusiasm for devolution is that the existing regional structures are not thought to be making a perceptible difference to people's lives.

Table 9.5 Attitudes towards regional devolution, by whether assemblies give people more say

	Perceived impact of regional assembly on giving ordinary people a say		
	More say	**No difference**	**Less say**
	%	%	%
As now	43	52	51
Regional assembly	39	23	23
English parliament	15	20	21
Base	*720*	*2288*	*162*
% agree every region should have its own assembly	44	27	27
Base	*591*	*1903*	*116*

Table 9.6 Attitudes towards regional devolution, by whether assemblies improve region's economic prospects

	Perceived impact of regional assembly on region's economic prospects		
	Better	**No difference**	**Worse**
	%	%	%
As now	43	53	57
Regional assembly	41	22	11
English parliament	15	21	27
Base	*820*	*2126*	*159*
% agree every region should have its own assembly	42	28	18
Base	*664*	*1764*	*129*

Are the arguments in favour of devolution getting through?

A second possible explanation for the apparent lack of enthusiasm for devolution in England is that the arguments used by proponents are failing to make an impact. For example, a common argument in favour of regional institutions is that they can provide a focus and a symbol for the pride that people feel in their particular part of England.[5] If this argument resonates with the public at large, then we would expect those who feel a strong sense of regional identity to be more supportive of regional assemblies. Another important argument often used in favour of regional government, and the one which the current government has tended to emphasise, is that it can help overcome some of the economic inequalities that are created by differences in the economic performance of different regions (Morgan and Nauwelaers, 1999; Labour Party, 2001; Adams and Tomaney, 2002; DTLR/Cabinet Office, 2002). That should mean that those living in less affluent economic circumstances, or those who are ideologically inclined to support greater equality in society, should be more in favour of devolution (Hechter, 1975; Rokkan and Urwin, 1982, 1983). Finally, it is often argued that regional government can improve the way that Britain is governed, not least by increasing the opportunities for people to get involved in decision making and by increasing the accountability of government to the people it seeks to serve (Adams and Tomaney, 2002). If this argument cuts ice with the public, we would expect those who are critical of the way Britain is governed at present to be more supportive of devolution than those who are happy with our current system.

The first of these expectations – that those who have a strong sense of regional identity should be more likely to favour devolution – is largely unfulfilled. As Table 9.7 shows, those who say they are very proud of being someone who lives in their particular region are effectively no more likely to prefer a regional assembly to an English parliament or the *status quo* than are those who say they have little or no pride in their region. Meanwhile, there is only a small difference between these two groups in their response to our second question about every region having its own assembly. Only amongst those who say they do not think of themselves as someone who lives in their particular region does support for regional assemblies fall away somewhat, but even here the relationship cannot be described as anything other than modest.[6]

Table 9.7 Attitudes towards different ways of governing England, by regional pride

	Regional pride			
	Very proud	Somewhat	Not very/ not at all	Don't think that way
	%	%	%	%
As now	52	50	41	50
Regional assembly	27	29	26	24
English parliament	17	16	21	20
Base	*836*	*902*	*191*	*1765*
% agree every region should have its own assembly	36	32	32	27
Base	*675*	*739*	*147*	*1451*

Perhaps, however, this is a dimension where the arguments for an English parliament have an appeal, even if those for regional assemblies do not. But, in fact, there is little sign that support for an English parliament is embedded in a strong sense of Englishness. For example, support for an English parliament is only seven percentage points higher amongst those who describe themselves as "English" than it is amongst those who consider themselves to be "British". And those who say they are "very proud" of being English are no more likely to support an English parliament than are those who say they are not very proud or not proud at all.

On the other hand, there is some limited evidence that devolution has a greater appeal to those who are less well off and those who have an ideological commitment to greater equality. For example, as Table 9.8 shows, less than two in five of those who say they are finding it difficult to cope on their current income support the *status quo*, compared with over half of those who say they are living comfortably. However, it is not clear that economic dissatisfaction fuels greater support for regional assemblies as opposed to an English parliament. Rather, support for both is a little higher amongst the economically dissatisfied. A not dissimilar result is found if we compare the attitudes of those in routine occupations with the views of those in professional and managerial positions. The former are rather more likely to back some form of devolution and oppose maintenance of the *status quo*, though the relationship is no more than a moderate one.

Table 9.8 Attitudes towards different ways of governing England, by subjective income

	Feelings about current household income		
	Comfortable	Coping	Difficult
	%	%	%
As now	55	49	38
Regional assembly	24	27	28
English parliament	18	17	25
Base	*1562*	*1614*	*527*
% agree every region should have its own assembly	27	32	34
Base	*1307*	*1309*	*404*

Rather more striking, however, are the differences of view between those who hold different ideological outlooks. Here we have divided our sample into four groups according to where they stand on a set of items that tap the degree to which people favour greater economic equality and government action to secure it. The quarter or so of our sample who are most inclined towards this view can be considered 'left-wing' while the quarter or so who are least so inclined can be described as 'right-wing', with similarly sized groups on the 'centre–left' and the 'centre–right' in between. (Further details about this left–right scale can be found in Appendix I to this book.) As Table 9.9 shows, those on the left are notably less likely to support the *status quo* and to favour the creation of regional assemblies than are those on the right. Moreover, this pattern of higher support for regional assemblies amongst those on the left is found on both of the questions we have been analysing.

Table 9.9 Attitudes towards different ways of governing England, by position on left–right scale

	Position on Left-Right scale			
	Left	Centre-Left	Centre-Right	Right
	%	%	%	%
As now	42	50	54	57
Regional assembly	32	26	26	20
English parliament	21	19	16	18
% agree every region should have its own assembly	41	30	25	23
Base	*907*	*631*	*817*	*596*

Left: those with a score of between 1 and 2 on the left–right scale described in the technical appendix. Centre–Left: those with a score of more than 2 but no more than 2.4. Centre–Right: those with a score of more than 2.4 but no more than 3. Right: those with a score of more than 3.

There is also some evidence to support the view that regional assemblies are relatively popular with those who are dissatisfied with the way that Britain is governed at present. As shown in Table 9.10, only two in five of those who think that the system of governing Britain needs a great deal of improvement favour the *status quo* rather than regional assemblies or an English parliament. This compares with nearly two-thirds of those who reckon that no more than small changes are needed. However, it appears that dissatisfaction with the governance of Britain as a whole is as likely to translate into increased support for an English parliament as it is for regional assemblies. The latter are evidently not regarded as a particularly apposite solution for the alleged inadequacies in the way that Britain is currently governed.

Table 9.10 Attitudes towards different ways of governing England, by perceptions of how well British government works

	System of governing Britain could be improved		
	Not at all/ in small ways	Quite a lot	A great deal
	%	%	%
As now	63	46	40
Regional assembly	21	27	32
English parliament	13	21	21
Base	*1256*	*1566*	*836*
% agree every region should have its own assembly	26	32	34
Base	*1033*	*1292*	*672*

Our investigation of who does and does not support devolution has, then, thrown up an interesting pattern. Few show much awareness of the existing regional institutions in England, while the idea of regional assemblies or even an English parliament has so far failed to tap into the emotional loyalties that people feel towards their region in particular or to England as a whole. Those who are relatively keen on devolution are those who have doubts about the degree of economic inequality in society or about how well the country is governed. At the same time, it is those who think that having a regional assembly would actually improve their region's economy or how much say ordinary people have in government who particularly back devolution. In short, it appears that support for devolution in England is – at present at least – primarily instrumental. People back it if they think it will bring about some kind of material improvement, but not because they feel it might be a way of symbolising and expressing their sense of regional or even English identity. In this respect it is clearly not anchored in the nationalist sentiment that helped foster the demand for – and opposition to – devolution in Scotland (Curtice, 1999) or indeed explains why any proposed constitutional arrangement for Northern Ireland generates such fierce debate. Lacking this emotional force, and with relatively few convinced as yet of the instrumental benefits that devolution might bring, it is perhaps unsurprising that devolution largely fails to excite the passions of many English hearts.

The political debate

So far, however, we have left aside one other potentially important shaper of public opinion – the political parties. It is often argued that political parties can mould public opinion by persuading their supporters of the merits of the policy platforms they have adopted (Butler and Stokes, 1974; Evans, 1999; Curtice and Fisher, 2003). Even if a party's supporters are initially reluctant to back a particular policy, the fact that it is promulgated by the party for which they normally vote and with which they may identify means that they are persuaded to change their minds. If indeed the various political parties have had any influence on public opinion on devolution, we should find a considerable difference between the views of, on the one hand, Conservative supporters and, on the other, those of both Labour and Liberal Democrat supporters. After all, the Conservative Party has signalled its opposition to the creation of elected regional assemblies in England, just as it initially opposed the creation of the Scottish Parliament and the National Assembly for Wales, while both Labour and the Liberal Democrats are in favour.

Yet, as Table 9.11 shows, the differences between the views of different parties' supporters are not particularly strong. Asked to choose between the *status quo*, an English parliament and regional assemblies, Conservative identifiers are the most likely to support the *status quo* and least likely to support a regional assembly, while Liberal Democrat supporters are at the other end of the spectrum. Even so, the differences between them are no more than a dozen percentage points or so. But even this gap disappears when respondents are simply asked whether they support or oppose regional assemblies and it is now Labour identifiers rather than Liberal Democrats who exhibit a touch more enthusiasm. It appears that the various stances taken by the political parties have had little impact on the electorate.

Table 9.11   Attitudes towards different ways of governing England, by party identification

	Party identification			
	Conservative	Labour	Lib Dem	None
	%	%	%	%
As now	57	52	45	41
Regional assembly	20	26	33	28
English parliament	21	18	19	18
Base	*1010*	*1372*	*428*	*575*
% agree every region should have its own assembly	28	34	28	25
Base	*872*	*1093*	*365*	*440*

Interestingly, however, there are rather sharper differences between the parties' supporters in the three northernmost regions of England. Here, Liberal

Democrat identifiers are around twenty percentage points more likely than Conservative identifiers to support regional assemblies, irrespective of how the question is asked. It appears that voters in the north of England have taken rather more notice of the political debate between the parties about devolution than they have elsewhere, not least because the debate has been more intense there. Here perhaps is an indication that the government has been correct in suggesting that this part of England is more ready to hold a referendum on the subject.

Table 9.12   Attitudes towards different ways of governing England, by party identification in the north of England

	Party identification			
	Conservative	**Labour**	**Lib Dem**	**None**
	%	%	%	%
As now	61	52	36	38
Regional assembly	21	30	42	27
English parliament	17	16	17	23
Base	*208*	*463*	*111*	*179*
% agree every region should have its own assembly	23	36	41	29
Base	*184*	*372*	*98*	*146*

Note: Table based on respondents in the North East, North West and Yorkshire & the Humber

But at the same time, Table 9.12 also contains one other striking feature, as indeed does its predecessor. Labour identifiers do not appear to be particularly keen on regional assemblies, even though it is their government that is promoting them. Asked to choose between the *status quo*, regional assemblies and an English parliament, Labour identifiers are at best only midway between Conservative and Liberal Democrat supporters in their degree of support for regional assemblies. And in the north of England at least, they also emerge as somewhat less keen on regional assemblies than Liberal Democrat identifiers in response to our specific question about regional devolution. This pattern is in sharp contrast to the position in Scotland where, as Table 9.13 shows, not only are there are sharper differences in general between the constitutional preferences of the various parties' supporters, but Labour identifiers are as much in favour of Scotland having her own parliament, either independent or devolved, as are Liberal Democrat identifiers.

Table 9.13 Attitudes towards different ways of governing Scotland, by party identification

	Party identification				
	Conser-vative	Labour	Lib Dem	SNP	None
	%	%	%	%	%
Independence	7	20	12	58	27
Devolution	56	66	75	38	67
No parliament	34	9	14	1	13
Base	230	483	163	254	181

Source: *Scottish Social Attitudes*, 2003

Thus, the relative lack of enthusiasm for devolution amongst Labour supporters in England suggests that while the government's reading of public opinion on devolution may have been more accurate than the expectations of those who anticipated an 'English backlash', its apparently circumspect approach may also have incurred a price. The government's relatively *sotto voce* approach may well have resulted in its message not being heard by many of its supporters. And, if indeed that is the case, it will doubtless have contributed to the apparent lack of enthusiasm with which regional devolution is still greeted in England. Whether the decision now to hold the first referendum in the North East means that its message will finally secure more attention, remains to be seen.

Conclusions

As its critics have long pointed out, asymmetric devolution is full of apparent anomalies and logical flaws. Yet the success of government institutions is not necessarily determined by rational logic. Rather, a crucial ingredient is that the public agree with their very existence in the first place. Institutions that lack such legitimacy will always find it difficult to persuade the public that their decisions and laws should be obeyed, as many years of civil strife in Northern Ireland testify. Creating public institutions that the public does not want is unlikely to be a recipe for good government.

Evidently the public in Scotland and in Wales could not now conceive of life without devolution (Curtice, 2004). Any attempt to scrap the existing devolved institutions would be regarded as illegitimate. However, public opinion in England is very different. Here it seems there is still little interest in devolution despite the examples set by Scotland, Wales or even London. Asymmetric devolution may be illogical, but it apparently reflects the varied contours of public opinion across the UK.

Our investigation has, of course, found that England is currently indifferent rather than hostile to devolution. So the difficulty that currently faces attempts to introduce elected regional government in England is not that such institutions would be considered illegitimate, but rather that people will simply not think that they are worth bothering with at all. Even so, creating elected regional assemblies in such a climate could still be a recipe for institutions whose elections produce low turnout and whose politicians have little authority or influence. If English regional government is ever to enjoy widespread public support then its advocates will at some point need the courage to argue their case.

Notes

1. This chapter was completed before the result of this referendum was known.
2. The eight per cent of people who were recorded by this survey as being "neither for nor against" comprised respondents who gave this response even though it was not offered by the interviewer.
3. The older question was framed in 1999 in the light of the introduction of the Scottish Parliament and Welsh National Assembly. The new question was introduced in 2003 to reflect what is now government policy for England (DTLR/Cabinet Office, 2002). The 2003 survey asked both questions of different random sub-samples of respondents so that the impact of the different wording could be assessed.
4. In this table and in the rest of this chapter we have combined the answers given by those 975 respondents who were asked the older version of our question with the answers of the 2,734 who were asked the newer one. As will be apparent by now, the two questions secured a broadly similar pattern of response.
5. For example, the 2001 Labour manifesto stated that, "For some regions this degree of regional representation [i.e. unelected Regional Chambers] will be sufficient. However, in other parts of the country there may be a stronger sense of regional identity and a desire for a regional political voice."
6. We might also note that these generalisations are also true within the three northernmost regions of England. Thus the fact that levels of regional pride are notably higher in these three regions than they are in the rest of England does nothing to increase support for regional devolution in those regions (Curtice, forthcoming).

References

Adams, J. and Tomaney, J. (2002), *Restoring the Balance: Strengthening the Government's proposals for elected regional assemblies,* London: IPPR

Butler, D. and Stokes, D. (1974), *Political Change in Britain,* 2nd edition, London: Macmillan

Curtice, J. (1999), 'Is Scotland a Nation and Wales Not?', in Taylor, B. and Thomson, K. (eds.), *Scotland and Wales: Nations Again,?* Cardiff: University of Wales Press

Curtice, J. (2004), 'Restoring Confidence and Legitimacy? Devolution and Public Opinion', in Trench, A. (ed.), *Has Devolution Made a Difference? The State of the Nations 2004*, Exeter: Imprint Academic

Curtice, J. (forthcoming), 'What the People Say – If Anything', in Hazell, R.(ed.), *The English Question*, Manchester: Manchester University Press

Curtice, J. and Fisher, S. (2003), 'The power to persuade? A tale of two Prime Ministers', in Park, A., Curtice, J., Thomson, K., Jarvis, L. and Bromley, C. (eds.), *British Social Attitudes: the 20th Report – Continuity and change over two decades,* London: Sage

DTLR/Cabinet Office (2002), *Your Region, Your Choice: Revitalising the English Regions*, London: DTLR

Dunleavy, P., Margetts, H., Smith, T. and Weir, S. (2001), *Voices of the People: Popular attitudes to democratic renewal in Britain*, London: Politicos

Evans, G. (1999), 'Europe: A New Electoral Cleavage?', in Evans, G. and Norris, P. (eds.), *Critical Elections: British Parties and Voters in Long-Term Perspective*, London: Sage

Heath, A., Rothon, C. and Jarvis, L. (2002), 'English to the core?', in Park, A., Curtice, J., Thomson, K., Jarvis, L. and Bromley, C. (eds.) *British Social Attitudes: the 19th Report*, London: Sage

Hechter, M. (1975), *Internal Colonialism*, London: Routledge and Kegan Paul

ICM (2003), *Regional Assembly Research*. Available at: http://www.icmresearch.co.uk/reviews/2003/CCN%20report4.pdf

Joseph Rowntree Reform Trust (2004), *State of the Nation Poll 2004: Summary of Main Findings*. Available at: http://www.jrrt.org.uk/findings.pdf

Labour Party (2001), *Ambitions for Britain*, London: Labour Party

McLean, I. (2000), 'Getting and Spending: can (or should) the Barnett formula survive?', *New Economy* **7**: 76–80

Marquand, D. and Tomaney, J. (2000), *Democratising England*, Oxford: Regional Policy Forum

Morgan, K and Nauwelaers, C. (eds.), (1999), *Regional Innovation Strategies: The challenge for less favoured regions*, London: Taylor and Francis

MORI (2003), *Regional Government in England 2003: A Synthesis of Research*, London: MORI

Rokkan, S. and Urwin, D. (1982), *The Politics of Territorial Identity: Studies in European Regionalism*, Beverley Hills: Sage

Rokkan, S. and Urwin, D. (1983), *Economy, Territory, Identity: Politics of European peripheries*, Beverley Hills: Sage

Sandford, M. (2002), 'What place for England in an asymmetrically devolved UK?', *Regional Studies*, **36**: 789–796

Tomaney, J. (2002), 'New Labour and the evolution of regionalism in England', in Tomaney, J. and Mawson, J. (eds.), *England: The State of the Regions*, Bristol: Policy Press

Acknowledgements

The survey work reported in this chapter was funded by the Economic and Social Research Council as part of its Devolution and Constitutional Change Research Programme (grant number L219 25 2018), by the Leverhulme Trust as part of its Nations and Regions Research Programme, and by the Office of the Deputy Prime Minister. We are grateful to all three bodies for their generous support. However, responsibility for the interpretations offered and views expressed here lies solely with the authors.

Appendix I
Technical details of the survey

In 2003, the sample for the *British Social Attitudes* survey was split into three sections: versions A and B made up a random quarter each and version C half of the sample. Depending on which versions it was included in, each 'module' of questions was thus asked either of the full sample (4,432 respondents) or of a random three-quarters, half or one-quarter of the sample. (In most years, the *British Social Attitudes* sample is around 3,300 in size and split into three versions. Thus versions A and B in 2003 are the equivalent of a third of the sample in a normal year; version C is the equivalent of two-thirds of the sample in a normal year; and version C plus either A or B is the equivalent of the full sample in a normal year.)

The structure of the questionnaire is shown at the beginning of Appendix III.

Sample design

The *British Social Attitudes* survey is designed to yield a representative sample of adults aged 18 or over. Since 1993, the sampling frame for the survey has been the Postcode Address File (PAF), a list of addresses (or postal delivery points) compiled by the Post Office.[1]

For practical reasons, the sample is confined to those living in private households. People living in institutions (though not in private households at such institutions) are excluded, as are households whose addresses were not on the PAF.

The sampling method involved a multi-stage design, with three separate stages of selection.

Selection of sectors

At the first stage, postcode sectors were selected systematically from a list of all postal sectors in Great Britain. Before selection, any sectors with fewer than 500 addresses were identified and grouped together with an adjacent sector; in Scotland all sectors north of the Caledonian Canal were excluded (because of the prohibitive costs of interviewing there). Sectors were then stratified on the basis of:

- 37 sub-regions
- population density with variable banding used, in order to create three equal-sized strata per sub-region
- ranking by percentage of homes that were owner-occupied in England and Wales and percentage of homes where the head of household was non-manual in Scotland.

Two hundred and sixty-six postcode sectors were selected, with probability proportional to the number of addresses in each sector.

Selection of addresses

Thirty-one addresses were selected in each of the 266 sectors. The issued sample was therefore 266 x 31 = 8,246 addresses, selected by starting from a random point on the list of addresses for each sector, and choosing each address at a fixed interval. The fixed interval was calculated for each sector in order to generate the correct number of addresses.

The Multiple-Output Indicator (MOI) available through PAF was used when selecting addresses in Scotland. The MOI shows the number of accommodation spaces sharing one address. Thus, if the MOI indicates more than one accommodation space at a given address, the chances of the given address being selected from the list of addresses would increase so that it matched the total number of accommodation spaces. The MOI is largely irrelevant in England and Wales as separate dwelling units generally appear as separate entries on PAF. In Scotland, tenements with many flats tend to appear as one entry on PAF. However, even in Scotland, the vast majority of MOIs had a value of one. The remainder, which ranged between three and 12, were incorporated into the weighting procedures (described below).

Selection of individuals

Interviewers called at each address selected from PAF and listed all those eligible for inclusion in the *British Social Attitudes* sample – that is, all persons currently aged 18 or over and resident at the selected address. The interviewer then selected one respondent using a computer-generated random selection procedure. Where there were two or more households or 'dwelling units' at the selected address, interviewers first had to select one household or dwelling unit using the same random procedure. They then followed the same procedure to select a person for interview.

Weighting

Data were weighted to take account of the fact that not all the units covered in the survey had the same probability of selection. The weighting reflected the relative selection probabilities of the individual at the three main stages of selection: address, household and individual.

Table A.1 Distribution of unscaled and scaled weights

Unscaled weight	Number	%	Scaled weight
0.08	2	0.0	0.0459
0.10	1	0.0	0.0550
0.11	1	0.0	0.0612
0.13	3	0.1	0.0688
0.17	3	0.1	0.0918
0.22	1	0.0	0.1223
0.25	1	0.0	0.1376
0.40	1	0.0	0.2202
0.50	2	0.0	0.2752
0.83	1	0.0	0.4587
1.00	1587	35.8	0.5504
2.00	2266	51.1	1.1009
3.00	384	8.7	1.6513
4.00	142	3.2	2.2017
5.00	19	0.4	2.7521
6.00	12	0.3	3.3026
7.00	6	0.1	3.8530

Base: 4432

First, because addresses in Scotland were selected using the MOI, weights had to be applied to compensate for the greater probability of an address with an MOI of more than one being selected, compared to an address with an MOI of one. (This stage was omitted for the English and Welsh data.) Secondly, data were weighted to compensate for the fact that dwelling units at an address which contained a large number of dwelling units were less likely to be selected for inclusion in the survey than ones which did not share an address. (We use this procedure because in most cases of MOIs greater than one, the two stages will cancel each other out, resulting in more efficient weights.) Thirdly, data were weighted to compensate for the lower selection probabilities of adults living in large households compared with those living in small households. The weights were capped at 7.0 (causing three cases to have their weights reduced).

The resulting weight is called 'WtFactor' and the distribution of weights is shown in Table A.1.

The mean weight was 1.82. The weights were then scaled down to make the number of weighted productive cases exactly equal to the number of unweighted productive cases (n = 4,432).

All the percentages presented in this Report are based on weighted data.

Questionnaire versions

Each address in each sector (sampling point) was allocated to either the A, B or C portion of the sample. If one serial number was version A, the next was version B and the next two after that version C. Thus each interviewer was allocated seven or eight cases from each of versions A and B and 15 or 16 cases from version C. There were 2,062 issued addresses for versions A and B and 4,122 for version C.

Fieldwork

Interviewing was mainly carried out between June and September 2003, with a small number of interviews taking place in October and November.

Table A.2 Response rate on *British Social Attitudes*, 2003

	Number	%
Addresses issued	8,246	
Vacant, derelict and other out of scope	753	
In scope	7,493	100.0
Interview achieved	4,432	59.1
Interview not achieved	3,061	40.9
Refused[1]	2,357	31.5
Non-contacted[2]	309	4.1
Other non-response	395	5.3

1 'Refused' comprises refusals before selection of an individual at the address, refusals to the office, refusal by the selected person, 'proxy' refusals (on behalf of the selected respondent) and broken appointments after which the selected person could not be recontacted

2 'Non-contacted' comprises households where no one was contacted and those where the selected person could not be contacted

Fieldwork was conducted by interviewers drawn from the *National Centre for Social Research*'s regular panel and conducted using face-to-face computer-assisted interviewing.[2] Interviewers attended a one-day briefing conference to familiarise them with the selection procedures and questionnaires.

The mean interview length was 68 minutes for version A of the questionnaire, 72 minutes for version B and 65 minutes for version C.[3] Interviewers achieved an overall response rate of 59 per cent. Details are shown in Table A.2.

As in earlier rounds of the series, the respondent was asked to fill in a self-completion questionnaire which, whenever possible, was collected by the interviewer. Otherwise, the respondent was asked to post it to the *National Centre for Social Research*. If necessary, up to three postal reminders were sent to obtain the self-completion supplement.

A total of 811 respondents (18 per cent of those interviewed) did not return their self-completion questionnaire. Version A of the self-completion questionnaire was returned by 84 per cent of respondents to the face-to-face interview, version B by 77 per cent and version C by 83 per cent. As in previous rounds, we judged that it was not necessary to apply additional weights to correct for non-response.

Advance letter

Interviewers were supplied with letters describing the purpose of the survey and the coverage of the questionnaire, which they posted to sampled addresses before making any calls.[4]

Analysis variables

A number of standard analyses have been used in the tables that appear in this Report. The analysis groups requiring further definition are set out below. For further details see Exley *et al.* (2003).

Region

The dataset is classified by the 12 Government Office Regions.

Standard Occupational Classification

Respondents are classified according to their own occupation, not that of the 'head of household'. Each respondent was asked about their current or last job, so that all respondents except those who had never worked were coded. Additionally, if the respondent was not working but their spouse or partner *was* working, their spouse or partner is similarly classified.

With the 2001 survey, we began coding occupation to the new Standard Occupational Classification 2000 (SOC 2000) instead of the Standard Occupational Classification 1990 (SOC 90). The main socio-economic grouping based on SOC 2000 is the National Statistics Socio-Economic Classification (NS-SEC). However, to maintain time-series, some analysis has continued to use the older schemes based on SOC 90 – Registrar General's Social Class, Socio-Economic Group and the Goldthorpe schema.

National Statistics Socio-Economic Classification (NS-SEC)

The combination of SOC 2000 and employment status for current or last job generates the following NS-SEC analytic classes:

- Employers in large organisations, higher managerial and professional
- Lower professional and managerial; higher technical and supervisory
- Intermediate occupations
- Small employers and own account workers
- Lower supervisory and technical occupations
- Semi-routine occupations
- Routine occupations

The remaining respondents are grouped as "never had a job" or "not classifiable". For some analyses, it may be more appropriate to classify respondents according to their current socio-economic status, which takes into account only their present economic position. In this case, in addition to the seven classes listed above, the remaining respondents not currently in paid work fall into one of the following categories: "not classifiable", "retired", "looking after the home", "unemployed" or "others not in paid occupations".

Registrar General's Social Class

As with NS-SEC , each respondent's Social Class is based on his or her current or last occupation. The combination of SOC 90 with employment status for current or last job generates the following six Social Classes:

I	Professional etc. occupations	
II	Managerial and technical occupations	'Non-manual'
III (Non-manual)	Skilled occupations	
III (Manual)	Skilled occupations	
IV	Partly skilled occupations	'Manual'
V	Unskilled occupations	

They are usually collapsed into four groups: I & II, III Non-manual, III Manual, and IV & V.

Socio-Economic Group

As with NS-SEC, each respondent's Socio-Economic Group (SEG) is based on his or her current or last occupation. SEG aims to bring together people with jobs of similar social and economic status, and is derived from a combination of employment status and occupation. The full SEG classification identifies 18 categories, but these are usually condensed into six groups:

- Professionals, employers and managers
- Intermediate non-manual workers
- Junior non-manual workers
- Skilled manual workers
- Semi-skilled manual workers
- Unskilled manual workers

As with NS-SEC, the remaining respondents are grouped as "never had a job" or "not classifiable".

Goldthorpe schema

The Goldthorpe schema classifies occupations by their 'general comparability', considering such factors as sources and levels of income, economic security, promotion prospects, and level of job autonomy and authority. The Goldthorpe schema was derived from the SOC 90 codes combined with employment status. Two versions of the schema are coded: the full schema has 11 categories; the 'compressed schema' combines these into the five classes shown below.

- Salariat (professional and managerial)
- Routine non-manual workers (office and sales)
- Petty bourgeoisie (the self-employed, including farmers, with and without employees)
- Manual foremen and supervisors
- Working class (skilled, semi-skilled and unskilled manual workers, personal service and agricultural workers)

There is a residual category comprising those who have never had a job or who gave insufficient information for classification purposes.

Industry

All respondents whose occupation could be coded were allocated a Standard Industrial Classification 1992 (SIC 92). Two-digit class codes are used. As with Social Class, SIC may be generated on the basis of the respondent's current occupation only, or on his or her most recently classifiable occupation.

Party identification

Respondents can be classified as identifying with a particular political party on one of three counts: if they consider themselves supporters of that party, as closer to it than to others, or as more likely to support it in the event of a general election (responses are derived from Qs.199–201). The three groups are generally described respectively as *partisans, sympathisers* and *residual identifiers*. In combination, the three groups are referred to as 'identifiers'.

Attitude scales

Since 1986, the *British Social Attitudes* surveys have included two attitude scales which aim to measure where respondents stand on certain underlying value dimensions – left–right and libertarian–authoritarian.[5] Since 1987 (except 1990), a similar scale on 'welfarism' has been asked. Some of the items in the Welfare scale were changed in 2000–2001. The current version of the scale is listed below.

A useful way of summarising the information from a number of questions of this sort is to construct an additive index (DeVellis, 1991; Spector, 1992). This approach rests on the assumption that there is an underlying – 'latent' – attitudinal dimension which characterises the answers to all the questions within each scale. If so, scores on the index are likely to be a more reliable indication of the underlying attitude than the answers to any one question.

Each of these scales consists of a number of statements to which the respondent is invited to "agree strongly", "agree", "neither agree nor disagree", "disagree", or "disagree strongly".

The items are:

Left–right scale

> Government should redistribute income from the better-off to those who are less well off. *[Redistrb]*

> Big business benefits owners at the expense of workers. *[BigBusnN]*

> Ordinary working people do not get their fair share of the nation's wealth. *[Wealth]*[6]

> There is one law for the rich and one for the poor. *[RichLaw]*

> Management will always try to get the better of employees if it gets the chance. *[Indust4]*

Libertarian–authoritarian scale

> Young people today don't have enough respect for traditional British values. *[TradVals]*

People who break the law should be given stiffer sentences. *[StifSent]*

For some crimes, the death penalty is the most appropriate sentence. *[DeathApp]*

Schools should teach children to obey authority. *[Obey]*

The law should always be obeyed, even if a particular law is wrong. *[WrongLaw]*

Censorship of films and magazines is necessary to uphold moral standards. *[Censor]*

Welfarism scale

The welfare state encourages people to stop helping each other. *[WelfHelp]*

The government should spend more money on welfare benefits for the poor, even if it leads to higher taxes. *[MoreWelf]*

Around here, most unemployed people could find a job if they really wanted one. *[UnempJob]*

Many people who get social security don't really deserve any help. *[SocHelp]*

Most people on the dole are fiddling in one way or another. *[DoleFidl]*

If welfare benefits weren't so generous, people would learn to stand on their own two feet. *[WelfFeet]*

Cutting welfare benefits would damage too many people's lives. *[DamLives]*

The creation of the welfare state is one of Britain's proudest achievements. *[ProudWlf]*

The indices for the three scales are formed by scoring the leftmost, most libertarian or most pro-welfare position, as 1 and the rightmost, most authoritarian or most anti-welfarist position, as 5. The "neither agree nor disagree" option is scored as 3. The scores to all the questions in each scale are added and then divided by the number of items in the scale giving indices ranging from 1 (leftmost, most libertarian, most pro-welfare) to 5 (rightmost, most authoritarian, most anti-welfare). The scores on the three indices have been placed on the dataset.[7]

The scales have been tested for reliability (as measured by Cronbach's alpha). The Cronbach's alpha (unstandardized items) for the scales in 2002 are 0.81 for the left–right scale, 0.82 for the 'welfarism' scale and 0.74 for the libertarian–authoritarian scale. This level of reliability can be considered "very good" for the left–right and welfarism scales and "respectable" for the libertarian–authoritarian scale (DeVellis, 1991: 85).

Other analysis variables

These are taken directly from the questionnaire and to that extent are self-explanatory. The principal ones are:

Sex (Q.39)
Age (Q.40)
Household income (Q.1191)
Economic position (Q.706)
Religion (Q.866)

Highest educational qualification
obtained (Q.1018)
Marital status (Q.133)
Benefits received
(Qs.1122-1139)

Sampling errors

No sample precisely reflects the characteristics of the population it represents, because of both sampling and non-sampling errors. If a sample were designed as a random sample (if every adult had an equal and independent chance of inclusion in the sample) then we could calculate the sampling error of any percentage, p, using the formula:

$$s.e.\ (p) = \sqrt{\frac{p(100\text{-}p)}{n}}$$

where n is the number of respondents on which the percentage is based. Once the sampling error had been calculated, it would be a straightforward exercise to calculate a confidence interval for the true population percentage. For example, a 95 per cent confidence interval would be given by the formula:

$$p \pm 1.96 \times s.e.(p)$$

Clearly, for a simple random sample (srs), the sampling error depends only on the values of p and n. However, simple random sampling is almost never used in practice because of its inefficiency in terms of time and cost.

As noted above, the *British Social Attitudes* sample, like that drawn for most large-scale surveys, was clustered according to a stratified multi-stage design into 266 postcode sectors (or combinations of sectors). With a complex design like this, the sampling error of a percentage giving a particular response is not simply a function of the number of respondents in the sample and the size of the percentage; it also depends on how that percentage response is spread within and between sample points.

The complex design may be assessed relative to simple random sampling by calculating a range of design factors (DEFTs) associated with it, where

$$\text{DEFT} = \sqrt{\frac{\text{Variance of estimator with complex design, sample size n}}{\text{Variance of estimator with srs design, sample size n}}}$$

and represents the multiplying factor to be applied to the simple random sampling error to produce its complex equivalent. A design factor of one means that the complex sample has achieved the same precision as a simple random sample of the same size. A design factor greater than one means the complex sample is less precise than its simple random sample equivalent. If the DEFT for a particular characteristic is known, a 95 per cent confidence interval for a percentage may be calculated using the formula:

$$p \pm 1.96 \text{ x complex sampling error (p)}$$

$$= p \pm 1.96 \text{ x DEFT x } \sqrt{\frac{p(100\text{-}p)}{n}}$$

Calculations of sampling errors and design effects were made using the statistical analysis package STATA.

Table A.3 gives examples of the confidence intervals and DEFTs calculated for a range of different questions. Most background variables were fielded on the whole sample, whereas attitudinal variables were mainly asked only of three-quarters, half or a quarter of the sample; some asked on the interview questionnaire and some on the self-completion supplement. It shows that most of the questions asked of all sample members have a confidence interval of around plus or minus two to three per cent of the survey proportion. This means that we can be 95 per cent certain that the true population proportion is within two to three per cent (in either direction) of the proportion we report. Variables with much larger variation are, as might be expected, those closely related to the geographic location of the respondent (e.g. whether living in a big city, a small town or a village). Here the variation may be as large as six or seven per cent either way around the percentage found on the survey.

It should be noted that the design effects for certain variables (notably those most associated with the area a person lives in) are greater than those for other variables. For example, the question about benefit levels for the unemployed has high design effects, which may reflect differing rates of unemployment across the country. Another case in point is housing tenure, as different kinds of tenures (such as council housing, or owner-occupied properties) tend to be concentrated in certain areas; consequently the design effects calculated for these variables in a clustered sample are greater than the design effects calculated for variables less strongly associated with area, such as attitudinal variables. Also, sampling errors for proportions based only on respondents to just one of the versions of the questionnaire, or on subgroups within the sample, are larger than they would have been had the questions been asked of everyone.

Table A.3 Complex standard errors and confidence intervals of selected variables

	% (p)	Complex standard error of p	95% confidence interval	DEFT	Base
Classification variables					
Q202 Party identification (full sample)					*4432*
Conservative	25.2	1.1	23.1 – 27.3	1.65	
Labour	37.2	1.0	35.2 – 39.3	1.43	
Liberal Democrat	10.8	0.6	9.6 – 12.0	1.32	
Q848 Housing tenure (full sample)					*4432*
Owns	71.8	1.2	69.4 – 74.2	1.80	
Rents from local authority	12.6	0.9	10.8 – 14.3	1.80	
Rents privately/HA	14.0	0.9	12.2 – 15.8	1.75	
Q866 Religion (full sample)					*4432*
No religion	43.0	1.0	41.2 – 44.9	1.29	
Church of England	26.6	1.1	24.5 – 28.8	1.63	
Roman Catholic	8.9	0.6	7.7 – 10.0	1.39	
Q930 Age of completing continuous full-time education (full sample)					*4432*
16 or under	58.5	1.3	55.8 – 61.1	1.80	
17 or 18	18.5	0.7	17.1 – 19.9	1.22	
19 or over	22.3	1.1	20.1 – 24.5	1.78	
Q264 Home internet access (full sample)					*4432*
Yes	51.2	1.1	49.2 – 53.3	1.40	
No	48.7	1.1	46.6 – 50.8	1.40	
Q852 Urban or rural residence (full sample)					*4432*
A big city	31.0	2.7	25.6 – 36.4	3.95	
A small city/town	50.8	2.6	45.7 – 55.9	3.45	
Village/countryside	17.2	2.1	13.1 – 21.3	3.65	
Attitudinal variables (face-to-face interview)					
Q219 Benefits for the unemployed are ... (3/4 of sample)					*3272*
... too low	24.9	0.9	23.1 – 26.7	1.39	
... too high	29.8	0.9	28.1 – 31.5	1.26	
Q510 NHS should be available to those with lower incomes (half sample)					*2293*
Support a lot	10.6	0.7	9.2 – 11.9	1.07	
Support a little	16.5	0.9	14.7 – 18.3	1.19	
Oppose a little	14.6	0.9	12.9 – 16.3	1.17	
Oppose a lot	56.9	1.3	54.3 – 59.6	1.29	
Q778 Sexual relations between two adults of the same sex are ... (half sample)					*2193*
Always wrong	31.4	1.2	29.0 – 33.8	1.21	
Mostly wrong	8.7	0.6	7.4 – 9.9	1.03	
Sometimes wrong	9.2	0.9	7.8 – 10.5	1.10	
Rarely wrong	6.7	0.6	5.5 – 8.0	1.14	
Not wrong at all	36.5	1.2	34.2 – 38.9	1.14	

	% (p)	Complex standard error of p	95% confidence interval	DEFT	
					Base

Attitudinal variables (self-completion)

A22a
B56a **Government should redistribute income from**
C45a **the better off to those who are less well off**
(full sample)   *3621*

	% (p)		95% CI	DEFT
Agree strongly	10.3	0.6	9.1 – 11.4	1.13
Agree	31.7	0.9	30.0 – 33.5	1.17
Neither agree nor disagree	23.7	0.7	22.3 – 25.2	1.03
Disagree	26.0	0.8	24.4 – 27.7	1.14
Disagree strongly	5.9	0.5	4.9 – 6.8	1.24

B44b **GM foods should be banned even if food prices**
C34b **suffer as a result (3/4 of sample)**   *2649*

Agree strongly	8.2	0.6	7.0 – 9.5	1.18
Agree	21.1	0.9	19.2 – 22.9	1.18
Neither agree nor disagree	32.7	1.1	30.4 – 35.0	1.25
Disagree	22.9	0.9	21.1 – 24.7	1.10
Disagree strongly	3.0	0.3	2.3 – 3.6	0.98

A13a **I would worry if housing were provided near my home for people**
B31b **with mental problems leaving hospital (half of sample)**   *1845*

Agree strongly	12.8	1.0	10.8 – 14.8	1.29
Agree	31.0	1.2	28.8 – 33.3	1.07
Neither agree nor disagree	29.8	1.3	27.3 – 32.3	1.19
Disagree	16.8	1.0	14.9 – 18.7	1.11
Disagree strongly	4.6	0.6	3.5 – 5.7	1.17

A18a **How important to cut down on the number of**
cars (1/4 of sample)   *972*

Very important	26.4	1.6	23.2 – 29.6	1.15
Fairly important	43.9	1.7	40.6 – 47.2	1.05
Not very/not at all important	21.9	1.4	19.1 – 24.7	1.07

Analysis techniques

Regression

Regression analysis aims to summarise the relationship between a 'dependent' variable and one or more 'independent' variables. It shows how well we can estimate a respondent's score on the dependent variable from knowledge of their scores on the independent variables. It is often undertaken to support a claim that the phenomena measured by the independent variables *cause* the phenomenon measured by the dependent variable. However, the causal ordering, if any, between the variables cannot be verified or falsified by the technique. Causality can only be inferred through special experimental designs or through assumptions made by the analyst.

All regression analysis assumes that the relationship between the dependent and each of the independent variables takes a particular form. In *linear regression*, it is assumed that the relationship can be adequately summarised by a straight line. This means that a one percentage point increase in the value of an independent variable is assumed to have the same impact on the value of the dependent variable on average irrespective of the previous values of those variables.

Strictly speaking the technique assumes that both the dependent and the independent variables are measured on an interval level scale, although it may sometimes still be applied even where this is not the case. For example, one can use an ordinal variable (e.g. a Likert scale) as a *dependent* variable if one is willing to assume that there is an underlying interval level scale and the difference between the observed ordinal scale and the underlying interval scale is due to random measurement error. Often the answers to a number of Likert-type questions are averaged to give a dependent variable that is more like a continuous variable. Categorical or nominal data can be used as *independent* variables by converting them into dummy or binary variables; these are variables where the only valid scores are 0 and 1, with 1 signifying membership of a particular category and 0 otherwise.

The assumptions of linear regression cause particular difficulties where the *dependent* variable is binary. The assumption that the relationship between the dependent and the independent variables is a straight line means that it can produce estimated values for the dependent variable of less than 0 or greater than 1. In this case it may be more appropriate to assume that the relationship between the dependent and the independent variables takes the form of an S-curve, where the impact on the dependent variable of a one-point increase in an independent variable becomes progressively less the closer the value of the dependent variable approaches 0 or 1. *Logistic regression* is an alternative form of regression which fits such an S-curve rather than a straight line. The technique can also be adapted to analyse multinomial non-interval level dependent variables, that is, variables which classify respondents into more than two categories.

The two statistical scores most commonly reported from the results of regression analyses are:

A measure of variance explained: This summarises how well all the independent variables combined can account for the variation in respondent's scores in the dependent variable. The higher the measure, the more accurately we are able in general to estimate the correct value of each respondent's score on the dependent variable from knowledge of their scores on the independent variables.

A parameter estimate: This shows how much the dependent variable will change on average, given a one unit change in the independent variable (while holding all other independent variables in the model constant). The parameter estimate has a positive sign if an increase in the value of the independent variable results in an increase in the value of the dependent variable. It has a negative sign if an increase in the value of the independent variable results in a decrease in the value of the dependent variable. If the parameter estimates are standardised, it is possible to compare the relative impact of different independent variables; those variables with the largest standardised estimates can be said to have the biggest impact on the value of the dependent variable.

Regression also tests for the statistical significance of parameter estimates. A parameter estimate is said to be significant at the five per cent level, if the range of the values encompassed by its 95 per cent confidence interval (see also section on sampling errors) are either all positive or all negative. This means that there is less than a five per cent chance that the association we have found between the dependent variable and the independent variable is simply the result of sampling error and does not reflect a relationship that actually exists in the general population.

Factor analysis

Factor analysis is a statistical technique which aims to identify whether there are one or more apparent sources of commonality to the answers given by respondents to a set of questions. It ascertains the smallest number of *factors* (or dimensions) which can most economically summarise all of the variation found in the set of questions being analysed. Factors are established where respondents who give a particular answer to one question in the set, tend to give the same answer as each other to one or more of the other questions in the set. The technique is most useful when a relatively small number of factors are able to account for a relatively large proportion of the variance in all of the questions in the set.

The technique produces a *factor loading* for each question (or variable) on each factor. Where questions have a high loading on the same factor then it will be the case that respondents who give a particular answer to one of these questions tend to give a similar answer to the other questions. The technique is most commonly used in attitudinal research to try to identify the underlying ideological dimensions which apparently structure attitudes towards the subject in question.

International Social Survey Programme

The *International Social Survey Programme* (*ISSP*) is run by a group of research organisations, each of which undertakes to field annually an agreed module of questions on a chosen topic area. Since 1985, an *International Social Survey Programme* module has been included in one of the *British Social Attitudes* self-completion questionnaires. Each module is chosen for repetition at intervals to allow comparisons both between countries (membership is currently standing at 40) and over time. In 2003, the chosen subject was National Identity, and the module was carried on the B version of the self-completion questionnaire (Qs.1–15).

Young People's Social Attitudes survey

As in 1994 and 1998, we fielded in parallel a survey of young people aged between 12 and 19. In 2003, the *Young People's Social Attitudes* survey was funded by the Children and Young People's Unit.

Sample design

All young people aged 12–19 living in the same household as an adult *British Social Attitudes* respondent were eligible for interview on the *Young People's* survey, except any 18 or 19 year old who had already been interviewed as part of the main study. The *Young People's* data can thus be linked to the *British Social Attitudes* responses given by an adult within the household – normally a parent of the young person.

The questionnaire

Unlike the main *British Social Attitudes* survey, there was only one version of the questionnaire administered to 12-19 year olds, and no self-completion supplement. Some of the questions were also asked on one or more versions of the adult survey, allowing direct comparisons to be made between the adult and the young people's samples. The rest were unique to the *Young People's* survey.

The topics covered were:

- Gender differences
- Problems at school
- Views about education and work
- Politics and decision-making
- Prejudice and morality
- Fulfilment
- Friends and social networks
- Household tasks

A number of demographic and other classificatory questions were also included (such as age, sex, religion, current economic activity, and educational experience and expectations). Other background variable, (such as tenure) can be derived from the adult *British Social Attitudes* responses.

Weighting

As with the adult data, the *Young People's Social Attitudes* data were weighted to take account of the relative selection probabilities of the adult respondent at the address and household stage. However, the young people's data do not need to be weighted further to take account of the differential selection probabilities within the household: since all 12–19 year olds in the household were eligible for inclusion in the survey, there is no need for further weighting.

Fieldwork

The *Young People's Social Attitudes* questionnaire was implemented in computer-assisted personal interviewing (CAPI). Interviews were carried out by the same interviewers who worked on the *British Social Attitudes* survey. During the interview with the adult respondent, the interviewer established the number of eligible young people living in the household. At the end of the BSA interview, they asked permission to approach these young people. The median interview length was 32 minutes. Out of a sample of 4,432 BSA respondents, 997 eligible young persons were identified, which represents a response rate of 66%. The final response achieved is shown in Table A.4.

Table A.4 Response rate on the *Young People's Social Attitudes* survey

	Number	%
In scope	997	100.0
Interview achieved	663	66.5
Interview not achieved	334	33.5
Refused	240	24.1
Non-contact	39	3.9
Other	55	5.5

Notes

1. Until 1991 all *British Social Attitudes* samples were drawn from the Electoral Register (ER). However, following concern that this sampling frame might be deficient in its coverage of certain population subgroups, a 'splicing' experiment was conducted in 1991. We are grateful to the Market Research Development Fund for contributing towards the costs of this experiment. Its purpose was to investigate whether a switch to PAF would disrupt the time-series – for instance, by lowering response rates or affecting the distribution of responses to particular questions. In the event, it was concluded that the change from ER to PAF was unlikely to affect time trends in any noticeable ways, and that no adjustment factors were necessary. Since significant differences in efficiency exist between PAF and ER, and because we considered it untenable to continue to use a frame that is known to be biased, we decided to adopt PAF as the sampling frame for future *British Social Attitudes*

surveys. For details of the PAF/ER 'splicing' experiment, see Lynn and Taylor (1995).

2. In 1993 it was decided to mount a split-sample experiment designed to test the applicability of Computer-Assisted Personal Interviewing (CAPI) to the *British Social Attitudes* survey series. CAPI has been used increasingly over the past decade as an alternative to traditional interviewing techniques. As the name implies, CAPI involves the use of lap-top computers during the interview, with interviewers entering responses directly into the computer. One of the advantages of CAPI is that it significantly reduces both the amount of time spent on data processing and the number of coding and editing errors. There was, however, concern that a different interviewing technique might alter the distribution of responses and so affect the year-on-year consistency of *British Social Attitudes* data.

   Following the experiment, it was decided to change over to CAPI completely in 1994 (the self-completion questionnaire still being administered in the conventional way). The results of the experiment are discussed in *The 11th Report* (Lynn and Purdon, 1994).

3. Interview times of less than 20 minutes were excluded as these were likely to be errors.

4. An experiment was conducted on the 1991 *British Social Attitudes* survey (Jowell *et al.*, 1992), which showed that sending advance letters to sampled addresses before fieldwork begins has very little impact on response rates. However, interviewers do find that an advance letter helps them to introduce the survey on the doorstep, and a majority of respondents have said that they preferred some advance notice. For these reasons, advance letters have been used on the *British Social Attitudes* surveys since 1991.

5. Because of methodological experiments on scale development, the exact items detailed in this section have not been asked on all versions of the questionnaire each year.

6. In 1994 only, this item was replaced by: Ordinary people get their fair share of the nation's wealth. *[Wealth1]*

7. In constructing the scale, a decision had to be taken on how to treat missing values ('Don't knows,' 'Refused' and 'Not answered'). Respondents who had more than two missing values on the left–right scale and more than three missing values on the libertarian–authoritarian and welfare scale were excluded from that scale. For respondents with just a few missing values, 'Don't knows' were recoded to the midpoint of the scale and 'Refused' or 'Not answered' were recoded to the scale mean for that respondent on their valid items.

References

DeVellis, R.F. (1991), 'Scale development: theory and applications', *Applied Social Research Methods Series*, **26**, Newbury Park: Sage

Exley, S., Bromley, C., Jarvis, L., Park, A., Stratford, N. and Thomson, K. (2003), *British Social Attitudes 2000 survey: Technical Report*, London: *National Centre for Social Research*

Jowell, R., Brook, L., Prior, G. and Taylor, B. (1992), *British Social Attitudes: the 9th Report*, Aldershot: Dartmouth

Lynn, P. and Purdon, S. (1994), 'Time-series and lap-tops: the change to computer-assisted interviewing', in Jowell, R., Curtice, J., Brook, L. and Ahrendt, D. (eds.), *British Social Attitudes: the 11th Report*, Aldershot: Dartmouth

Lynn, P. and Taylor, B. (1995), 'On the bias and variance of samples of individuals: a comparison of the Electoral Registers and Postcode Address File as sampling frames', *The Statistician*, **44**: 173–194

Spector, P.E. (1992), 'Summated rating scale construction: an introduction', *Quantitative Applications in the Social Sciences*, **82**, Newbury Park: Sage

Appendix II
Notes on the tabulations in chapters

1. Figures in the tables are from the 2003 *British Social Attitudes* survey unless otherwise indicated.
2. Tables are percentaged as indicated.
3. In tables, '*' indicates less than 0.5 per cent but greater than zero, and '–' indicates zero.
4. When findings based on the responses of fewer than 100 respondents are reported in the text, reference is made to the small base size.
5. Percentages equal to or greater than 0.5 have been rounded up (e.g. 0.5 per cent = one per cent; 36.5 per cent = 37 per cent).
6. In many tables the proportions of respondents answering "Don't know" or not giving an answer are omitted. This, together with the effects of rounding and weighting, means that percentages will not always add to 100 per cent.
7. The self-completion questionnaire was not completed by all respondents to the main questionnaire (see Appendix I). Percentage responses to the self-completion questionnaire are based on all those who completed it.
8. The bases shown in the tables (the number of respondents who answered the question) are printed in small italics. The bases are unweighted, unless otherwise stated.

Appendix III
The questionnaires

As explained in Appendix I, three different versions of the questionnaire (A, B and C) were administered, each with its own self-completion supplement. The diagram that follows shows the structure of the questionnaires and the topics covered (not all of which are reported on in this volume).

The three interview questionnaires reproduced on the following pages are derived from the Blaise computer program in which they were written. For ease of reference, each item has been allocated a question number. Gaps in the numbering system indicate items that are essential components of the Blaise program but which are not themselves questions, and so have been omitted. In addition, we have removed the keying codes and inserted instead the percentage distribution of answers to each question. We have also included the SPSS variable name, in square brackets, at each question. Above the questions we have included filter instructions. A filter instruction should be considered as staying in force until the next filter instruction. Percentages for the core questions are based on the total weighted sample, while those for questions in versions A, B or C are based on the appropriate weighted sub-samples. The three versions of the self-completion questionnaire follow. We reproduce first version A of the interview questionnaire in full; then those parts of version B and version C that differ.

The percentage distributions do not necessarily add up to 100 because of weighting and rounding, or for one or more of the following reasons:

(i)   Some sub-questions are filtered – that is, they are asked of only a proportion of respondents. In these cases the percentages add up (approximately) to the proportions who were asked them. Where, however, a series of questions is filtered, we have indicated the reduced weighted base (for example, all employees), and have derived percentages from that base.

(ii)   At a few questions, respondents were invited to give more than one answer and so percentages may add to well over 100 per cent. These are clearly marked by interviewer instructions on the questionnaires.

As reported in Appendix I, the 2003 *British Social Attitudes* self-completion questionnaire was not completed by 18 per cent of respondents who were successfully interviewed. The answers in the supplement have been percentaged on the base of those respondents who returned it. This means that the distribution of responses to questions asked in earlier years are comparable with those given in Appendix III of all earlier reports in this series except in *The 1984 Report*, where the percentages for the self-completion questionnaire need to be recalculated if comparisons are to be made.

BRITISH SOCIAL ATTITUDES: 2003 SURVEY

Version A (quarter of sample)	Version B (quarter of sample)	Version C (half sample)

Face-to-face questionnaires

Household grid, newspaper readership and party identification		
—	Public spending and social welfare	
E-society	Giving to charity	E-society
Education	—	Education
Health care		—
Politics & national identity (long)	Politics and national identity (medium)	Politics and national identity (short)
Job details		
—	Employment relations	
Prejudice (short)		Prejudice (long)
Transport	Genomics	
—	Immigration	—
Classification		

Self-completion questionnaires

—	ISSP	—
—	Public spending and social welfare	
E-society	Giving to charity	E-society
Education	—	Education
Health care		—
Politics and national identity		
—	Employment relations	
Transport	Genomics	
Scales		

BRITISH SOCIAL ATTITUDES 2003

FACE-TO-FACE QUESTIONNAIRE

Contents

Introduction

Q1   **ASK ALL**   N=4432
       [SerialNo] **(NOT ON SCREEN)**
       Serial Number

Q17   [GOR2] **(NOT ON SCREEN)**   N=4432
%   Government office region 2003 version
4.5   North East
9.9   North West
8.5   Yorkshire and Humberside
8.7   East Midlands
9.7   West Midlands
8.3   SW
10.0   Eastern
5.2   Inner London
6.3   Outer London
13.4   South East
6.2   Wales
9.3   Scotland

Q27   [ABCVer] **(NOT ON SCREEN)**   N=4432
%   A, B or C?
26.1   A
25.4   B
48.5   C

Household grid

Q37   **ASK ALL**   N=4432
       [Household]
       (You have just been telling me about the adults that
       live in this household. Thinking now of **everyone**
       living in the household, **including children:**)
       Including yourself, how many people live here
       regularly as members of this household?
       CHECK INTERVIEWER MANUAL FOR DEFINITION OF HOUSEHOLD
       IF NECESSARY.
       IF YOU DISCOVER THAT YOU WERE GIVEN THE WRONG
       INFORMATION FOR THE RESPONDENT SELECTION ON THE ARF:
       DO NOT REDO THE ARF SELECTION PRODECURE
       DO ENTER THE CORRECT INFORMATION HERE
       DO USE <CTRL + M> TO MAKE A NOTE OF WHAT HAPPENED.
       Median: 2 people
%
-      (Don't know)
-      (Refusal/Not answered)

       FOR EACH PERSON AT [Household]   N=4432

       [Name] **(NOT ON DATAFILE)**
       FOR RESPONDENT: (Can I just check, what is your first
       name?)
       PLEASE TYPE IN THE FIRST NAME (OR INITIALS) OF
       RESPONDENT
       FOR OTHER HOUSEHOLD MEMBERS: PLEASE TYPE IN THE FIRST
       NAME (OR INITIALS) OF PERSON NUMBER *(number)*

Q39   [RSex] *(Figures refer to respondent)*   N=4432
%   PLEASE CODE SEX OF *(name)*
46.7   Male
53.3   Female
-      (Don't know)
-      (Refusal/Not answered)

[RAge] *(Figures refer to respondent)*   N=4432
FOR RESPONDENT IF ONLY ONE PERSON IN HOUSEHOLD: I would now like to ask you a few details about yourself.
What was your age last birthday?
FOR RESPONDENT IF SEVERAL PERSONS IN HOUSEHOLD: I would like to ask you a few details about each person in your household. Starting with yourself, what was your age last birthday?
FOR OTHER PERSONS IN HOUSEHOLD: What was *(name)*'s age last birthday?
FOR 97+, CODE 97.

	%
Median: 46 years	
(Don't know)	0.0
(Refusal/Not answered)	-

FOR PEOPLE IN THE HOUSEHOLD OTHER THAN RESPONDENT

[P2Rel3] *(Figures refer to second person in household)*   N=4432
PLEASE ENTER RELATIONSHIP OF *(name)* RESPONDENT

	%
Partner/ spouse/ cohabitee	62.5
Son/ daughter (inc step/adopted)	7.6
Grandson/ daughter (inc step/adopted)	0.2
Parent/ parent-in-law	7.5
Grand-parent	0.1
Brother/ sister (inc. in-law)	1.7
Other relative	0.8
Other non-relative	2.4
(Don't know)	-
(Refusal/Not answered)	-

Q133   [MarStat2]   N=4432
ASK ALL
CARD A1
Can I just check, which of these applies to you at present?
CODE FIRST TO APPLY

	%
Married	54.6
Living as married	8.9
Separated (after being married)	2.4
Divorced	6.5
Widowed	7.7
Single (never married)	19.9
(Don't know)	-
(Refusal/Not answered)	-

Q148-   N=4432
Q150
Can I just check which, if any, of these types of relatives do you yourself have alive at the moment. Please include adoptive relatives.
PROBE: Which others?
DO NOT INCLUDE STEP RELATIVES UNLESS LISTED ON THE CARD.
DO NOT INCLUDE FOSTER RELATIVES
CODE ALL THAT APPLY
Multicoded (Maximum of 8 codes)

	%	
Father	44.7	[RelFath]
Mother	56.6	[RelMoth]
Son	52.7	[RelSon2]
Step-son	5.8	[RelStepS]
Daughter	50.4	[RelDaug2]
Step-daughter	4.7	[RelStepD]
Grandchild (daughter's child)	21.1	[RelGrChD]
Grandchild (son's child)	18.4	[RelGrChS]
None of these	5.2	[RelNone2]
(Don't know)	-	
(Refusal/Not answered)	0.0	

Newspaper readership

Q190   **ASK ALL**

[Readpap]   *N=4432*

Do you normally read any daily **morning** newspaper at
least 3 times a
week?

%	
53.0	Yes
47.0	No
0.0	(Don't know)
-	(Refusal/Not answered)

IF 'yes' AT [ReadPap]

Q191   [WhPaper]   *N=4432*

Which one do you normally read?

IF MORE THAN ONE: Which one do you read **most**
frequently?

%	
3.6	(Scottish) Daily Express
9.6	(Scottish) Daily Mail
7.1	Daily Mirror (/Scottish Mirror)
1.4	Daily Star
14.2	The Sun
2.4	Daily Record
4.5	Daily Telegraph
0.4	Financial Times
2.8	The Guardian
0.7	The Independent
2.7	The Times
0.0	Morning Star
3.2	Other Irish/Northern Irish/Scottish regional or local
	daily morning paper (WRITE IN)
0.3	Other (WRITE IN)
0.0	MORE THAN ONE PAPER READ WITH EQUAL FREQUENCY
0.0	(Don't know)
0.1	(Refusal/Not answered)

VERSION A AND B ENGLAND: IF READS A NEWSPAPER

Q196   [NwspSWRg]   *N=1929*

Do you think *(newspaper)* contains ... READ OUT ...
... too much news about *(government office region)*,

%	
0.8	too little,
18.1	or about the right amount?
26.7	(Varies too much to say)
2.1	(Don't know)
1.9	(Refusal/Not answered)
0.1	

Q197   [NwspBrit]   *N=1929*

And do you think *(newspaper)* contains ... READ OUT
...

%	
2.4	... too much news about the rest of Britain,
6.8	too little,
38.0	or about the right amount?
1.1	(Varies too much to say)
1.2	(Don't know)
0.1	(Refusal/Not answered)

Q198   [NwspWrld]   *N=1929*

And do you think *(newspaper)* contains ... READ OUT

%	
2.6	... too much news about the rest of the world,
11.8	too little,
33.4	or about the right amount?
0.9	(Varies too much to say)
0.9	(Don't know)
0.1	(Refusal/Not answered)

Party identification

Q199 **ASK ALL**
[SupParty] N=4432
Generally speaking, do you think of yourself as a supporter of any one political party?

%
34.5 Yes
65.4 No
0.1 (Don't know)
0.0 (Refusal/Not answered)

Q200 **IF 'no' OR DON'T KNOW AT [SupParty]**
[ClosePty] N=4432
Do you think of yourself as a little closer to one political party than to the others?

%
25.6 Yes
39.7 No
0.2 (Don't know)
0.0 (Refusal/Not answered)

Q202 **IF 'yes' AT [SupParty] OR 'yes', 'no' OR DON'T KNOW AT [ClosePty]**
[PartyID] N=4432
IF 'yes' AT [SupParty] OR AT [ClosePty]: Which one?
IF 'no' OR DON'T KNOW AT [ClosePty]: If there were a general election tomorrow, which political party do you think you would be most likely to support?
DO NOT PROMPT

%
25.2 Conservative
37.2 Labour
10.8 Liberal Democrat
1.1 Scottish National Party
0.4 Plaid Cymru
1.0 Other party
1.2 Other answer
16.2 None
1.5 Green Party
3.8 (Don't know)
1.6 (Refusal/Not answered)

Q209 **IF PARTY GIVEN AT [PartyID]**
[Idstrng] N=4432
Would you call yourself very strong (party), fairly strong, or not very strong?

%
6.2 Very strong (party)
23.9 Fairly strong
46.9 Not very strong
0.1 (Don't know)
6.7 (Refusal/Not answered)

Q210 **ASK ALL**
[Politics] N=4432
How much interest do you generally have in what is going on in politics
...READ OUT...

%
8.6 ...a great deal,
21.0 quite a lot,
33.1 some,
24.5 not very much,
12.7 or, none at all?
0.0 (Don't know)
0.0 (Refusal/Not answered)

Q211 **VERSION A: ASK ALL IN ENGLAND**
[DfWnGEE] N=986
CARD A4
Some people say that it makes no difference which party wins in elections, things go on much the same. Using this card, please say how much of a difference you think it makes who wins in general elections to the House of Commons?

%
14.3 A great deal
27.1 Quite a lot
21.1 Some
27.2 Not very much
9.4 None at all
0.9 (Don't know)
0.1 (Refusal/Not answered)

Public spending and social welfare

Q213 ASK ALL
[Spend1]
CARD B1   N=4432
Here are some items of government spending.
Which of them, if any, would be your highest priority
for **extra** spending?
Please read through the whole list before deciding.
ENTER ONE CODE ONLY FOR HIGHEST PRIORITY

IF NOT 'none', DON'T KNOW, REFUSAL AT [Spend1]
Q214 [Spend2]   N=4432
CARD B1 AGAIN
And which next?
ENTER ONE CODE ONLY FOR NEXT HIGHEST

	[Spend1]	[Spend2]
	%	%
Education	27.5	35.9
Defence	1.0	2.2
Health	52.1	27.3
Housing	3.3	6.9
Public transport	4.4	8.4
Roads	2.3	3.6
Police and prisons	4.4	7.5
Social security benefits	2.1	3.5
Help for industry	1.3	2.8
Overseas aid	0.7	0.6
(None of these)	0.6	0.4
(Don't know)	0.3	0.1
(Refusal/Not answered)	–	0.8

Q215 VERSIONS B AND C: ASK ALL
[SocBen1]
CARD B2   N=3276
Thinking now only of the government's spending on
social benefits like those on the card.
Which, if any, of these would be your highest
priority for **extra** spending?
ENTER ONE CODE ONLY FOR HIGHEST PRIORITY

IF NOT 'none', DON'T KNOW, REFUSAL AT [SocBen1]
Q216 [SocBen2]   N=3276
CARD B2 AGAIN
And which next?
ENTER ONE CODE ONLY FOR NEXT HIGHEST

	[SocBen1]	[SocBen2]
	%	%
Retirement pensions	59.4	19.0
Child benefits	14.7	22.7
Benefits for the unemployed	3.5	6.9
Benefits for disabled people	15.8	38.2
Benefits for single parents	5.5	10.4
(None of these)	0.6	1.4
(Don't know)	0.5	0.3
(Refusal/Not answered)	–	–

Q217 VERSIONS B & C: ASK ALL
[FalseClm]   N=3276
I will read two statements. For each one please say
whether you agree or disagree. Firstly....
Large numbers of people these days **falsely** claim
benefits.
IF AGREE OR DISAGREE: Strongly or slightly?

Q218 [FailClm]   N=3276
(And do you agree or disagree that...)
Large numbers of people who are eligible for benefits
these days **fail** to claim them.
IF AGREE OR DISAGREE: Strongly or slightly?

	[FalseClm]	[FailClm]
	%	%
Agree strongly	51.4	42.1
Agree slightly	26.3	37.4
Disagree slightly	10.7	10.3
Disagree strongly	6.2	3.2
(Don't know)	5.3	7.1
(Refusal/Not answered)	–	–

Q219
[Dole]
Opinions differ about the level of benefits for unemployed people.
Which of these two statements comes closest to your own view

...READ OUT...

...benefits for unemployed people are **too low** and cause hardship,

or, benefits for unemployed people are **too high** and discourage them from finding jobs?

(Neither)

EDIT ONLY: Both: Unemployment Benefit causes hardship but can't be higher or there would be no incentive to work

EDIT ONLY: Both: Unemployment Benefit causes hardship to some, while others do well out of it

EDIT ONLY:About right/in between

Other answer (WRITE IN)

(Don't know)

(Refusal/Not answered)

N=3276

%
33.7

40.3

16.9
0.1

0.7

0.4
2.9
4.9
0.0

Q222
[TaxSpend]
CARD B3
Suppose the government had to choose between the three options on this card. Which do you think it should choose?

Reduce taxes and spend **less** on health, education and social benefits

Keep taxes and spending on these services at the **same** level as now

Increase taxes and spend **more** on health, education and social benefits

(None)

(Don't know)

(Refusal/Not answered)

VERSIONS B AND C: ASK ALL
N=3276

%
6.3

38.3

50.9

3.3
1.1
0.0

Q223
[HealResp]
CARD B4
Please say from this card who you think should **mainly** be responsible for paying for the cost of health care when someone is ill?

N=3276

Q224
ASK ALL
[RetResp]
CARD
(Please say from this card/ Still looking at this card,) who you think should **mainly** be responsible for ensuring that people have enough money to live on in retirement?

N=4432

Q225
VERSIONS B AND C: ASK ALL
[SickResp]
CARD B4 AGAIN
And who do you think should **mainly** be responsible for ensuring that people have enough to live on if they become sick for a long time or disabled?

N=3276

Q226
[UnemResp]
CARD B4 AGAIN
And who do you think should **mainly** be responsible for ensuring that people have enough to live on if they become unemployed?

N=3276

	[HealResp]	[RetResp]	[SickResp]
	%	%	%
Mainly the government	83.3	58.3	82.8
Mainly a person's employer	7.1	10.5	8.4
Mainly a person themselves and their family	7.7	29.1	7.2
(Don't know)	1.8	2.1	1.6
(Refusal/Not answered)	0.0	0.0	-

	[UnemResp]
	%
Mainly the government	81.1
Mainly a person's employer	2.9
Mainly a person themselves and their family	13.7
(Don't know)	2.4
(Refusal/Not answered)	

ASK ALL

Q227   [CareResp]   N=4432
CARD
And who do you think should **mainly** be responsible for paying for the care needs of elderly people living in residential and nursing homes?

%
84.3   Mainly the government
12.6   Mainly a person themselves and their family
3.1   (Don't know)
0.0   (Refusal/Not answered)

VERSIONS B AND C: ASK ALL

Q228   [LonPaWk2]   N=3276
Suppose a lone parent on benefits was asked to visit the job centre every year or so to talk about ways in which they might find work. Which of the statements on this card comes closest to what you think should happen to their benefits if they did not go?

%
16.8   Their benefits should not be affected
38.2   Their benefits should be reduced a little
14.2   Their benefits should be reduced a lot
27.3   Their benefits should be stopped
2.1   (Other (PLEASE WRITE IN))
1.4   (Don't know)
0.0   (Refusal/Not answered)

Q231   [SickWk2]   N=3276
Now think about someone on long-term sickness or disability benefits. Which of these statements comes closest to what you think should happen to their benefits if they did not go to the job centre every year or so to talk about ways in which they might find work?

%
40.7   Their benefits should not be affected
32.1   Their benefits should be reduced a little
9.4   Their benefits should be reduced a lot
13.2   Their benefits should be stopped
3.4   (Other (PLEASE WRITE IN))
1.1   (Don't know)
0.1   (Refusal/Not answered)

Q234   [CarerWk2]   N=3276
And suppose a carer on benefits was asked to visit the job centre every year or so to talk about ways in which they might find work. Which of these statements comes closest to what you think should happen to their benefits if they did not go?

%
48.4   Their benefits should not be affected
27.9   Their benefits should be reduced a little
7.2   Their benefits should be reduced a lot
12.7   Their benefits should be stopped
2.0   (Other (PLEASE WRITE IN))
1.8   (Don't know)
-   (Refusal/Not answered)

Q237   [PayHols]   N=3276
Suppose a person wants to go on holiday but hasn't got the money to pay for it. In your view ... **READ OUT** ...

Q238   [PaySofa]   N=3276
Now think about someone else who wants to replace their sofa but hasn't got the money to pay for it. In your view ... **READ OUT** ...

Q239   [PayOven]   N=3276
And now think about someone who wants to replace their broken cooker but hasn't got the money to pay for it. In your view ... **READ OUT** ...

	[PayHols]	[PaySofa]	[PayOven]
	%	%	%
...should they save up the money beforehand, or, should	88.3	74.6	19.5
they borrow the money and pay it back later?	9.1	22.4	78.6
(Don't know)	2.6	3.0	1.8
(Refusal/Not answered)	0.0	0.0	0.0

Q240 [WhenSave] N=3276
Some people regularly put money aside into pensions or savings for their retirement. When do you think a person needs to start doing this in order to be sure of having a decent standard of living when they retire...READ OUT....

%
78.5 ...in their 20s or earlier,
14.2 their 30s,
3.0   40s,
1.1   50s,
0.1   or 60s?
1.9   (Not necessary to do this/Never)
1.2   (Don't know)
0.0   (Refusal/Not answered)

Q241 [MtUnmar1] N=3276
Imagine an unmarried couple who split up. They have a child at primary school who remains with the mother. Do you think that the father should always be made to make maintenance payments to support the child?

Q242 [MtUnmar2] N=3276
If he **does** make the maintenance payments for the child, should the amount depend on his income, or not?

Q243 [MtUnmar3] N=3276
Do you think the amount of maintenance should depend on the **mother's** income, or not?

	[MtUnmar1]	[MtUnmar2]	[MtUnmar3]
	%	%	%
Yes	88.4	88.2	73.7
No	9.9	10.7	24.8
(Don't know)	1.7	1.1	1.5
(Refusal/Not answered)	0.1	0.0	-

Q244 [MtUnmar4] N=3276
Suppose the mother now marries someone else. Should the child's natural father go on paying maintenance for the child, should he stop or should it depend on the step-father's income?

Q245 [MtUnmar5] N=3276
Suppose instead the mother does not marry, but the father has another child with someone else. Should he go on paying maintenance for the first child, should he stop or should it depend on his income?

	[MtUnmar4]	[MtUnmar5]
	%	%
Continue	52.1	70.7
Stop	9.1	1.6
Depends	37.2	26.9
(Don't know)	1.6	0.8
(Refusal/Not answered)	0.0	0.0

Q246 [MuchPov] N=3276
Some people say there is very little **real** poverty in Britain today. Others say there is quite a lot. Which come closest to **your** view .. READ OUT ...

%
41.3 ...that there is very little real poverty in Britain,
54.8 or, that there is quite a lot?
3.9   (Don't know)
-     (Refusal/Not answered)

Q247 [PastPov] N=3276
Over the last ten years, do you think that poverty in Britain has been increasing, decreasing or staying at about the same level?

%
34.9 Increasing
19.3 Decreasing
39.1 Staying at same level
6.7   (Don't know)
-     (Refusal/Not answered)

Q248 [FuturPov] N=3276

And over the **next** ten years, do you think that poverty in Britain will

... READ OUT ...

%
45.9 ... increase,
13.5 decrease,
33.2 or, stay at about the same level?
7.4 (Don't know)
- (Refusal/Not answered)

Q249 [Poverty1] N=3276

Would you say that someone in Britain **was** or **was not** in poverty if...

... they had enough to buy the things they really needed, but not enough to buy the things most people take for granted?

Q250 [Poverty2] N=3276

(Would you say someone in Britain **was** or **was not** in poverty ...)

... if they had enough to eat and live, but not enough to buy other things they needed?

Q251 [Poverty3] N=3276

(Would you say someone in Britain **was** or **was not** in poverty ...)

... if they had not got enough to eat and live without getting into debt?

	[Poverty1]	[Poverty2]	[Poverty3]
	%	%	%
Was in poverty	18.8	47.1	90.2
Was not	78.7	50.2	8.7
(Don't know)	2.5	2.6	1.1
(Refusal/Not answered)	-	-	-

Q252 [WhyNeed] N=3276

CARD B7

Why do you think there are people who live in need? Of the four views on this card, which **one** comes closest to your own?

CODE ONE ONLY

%
13.1 Because they have been unlucky
28.2 Because of laziness or lack of willpower
19.3 Because of injustice in our society
31.8 It's an inevitable part of modern life
4.5 (None of these)
3.0 (Don't know)
0.1 (Refusal/Not answered)

Q253 [PovEver] N=3276

CARD B8

Looking back over your life, how often have there been times in your life when you think you have lived in poverty by the standards of that time? Please choose a phrase from this card.

%
55.5 Never
17.5 Rarely
19.2 Occasionally
5.7 Often
1.9 Most of the time
0.1 (Don't know)
- (Refusal/Not answered)

Q254 [PovChAd] N=3276

IF 'rarely', 'occasionally', 'often' OR 'most of the time' AT [PovEver]

And was this ... READ OUT ...

%
12.6 ... as a child,
21.1 or, as an adult?
10.7 - (Both)
- (Don't know)
0.1 (Refusal/Not answered)

VERSION B: ASK ALL
[IncomGap]   N=1127

Q255   Thinking of income levels generally in Britain today,
       would you say that the **gap** between those with high
       incomes and those with low incomes is

       ...READ OUT...
%
78.1   ... too large,
17.5   ... about right,
1.6   or, too small?
2.8   (Don't know)
-      (Refusal/Not answered)

[SRInc]   N=1127

Q256   Among which group would you place yourself ...READ
%   OUT...
4.1   ... high income,
53.0   middle income,
42.2   or, low income?
0.5   (Don't know)
0.1   (Refusal/Not answered)

ASK ALL
[HIncDiff]   N=4432

Q257   CARD
       Which of the phrases on this card would you say comes
       closest to your
       feelings about your household's income these days?
%
44.3   Living comfortably on present income
42.6   Coping on present income
10.1   Finding it difficult on present income
3.0   Finding it very difficult on present income
0.0   (Other answer (WRITE IN))
0.0   (Don't know)
0.0   (Refusal/Not answered)

Charitable giving

VERSION B: ASK ALL
[CharOft]   N=1127

Q260   CARD C1
       Generally speaking, how often, on average, do you
       give **money** to charity - please do **not** include money
       spent in charity shops or buying lottery or raffle
       tickets?
       Please just tell me a letter from this card.
       IF ASKED: DO NOT INCLUDE MONEY TO BEGGARS OR BUYING
%   THE BIG ISSUE
10.8   A: Never
13.6   B: Occasionally but less often than once a year
21.9   C: Once or twice a year
21.5   D: Once every few months
23.6   E: Once or twice a month
8.6   F: Once a week or more
-      (Don't know)
-      (Refusal/Not answered)

IF NOT 'never', DON'T KNOW, REFUSAL AT [CharOft]
[CharAmt]   N=1127

Q261   CARD C2
       And how much, on average, do you give to charity each
       year?
       Again, please just tell me a letter from this card.
%
14.2   A: Less than £5
20.2   B: £5.00 - £12
25.0   C: £12.01 - £50
16.6   D: £50.01 - £120
8.4   E: £120.01 - £500
3.3   F: More than £500
1.1   (Don't know)
0.4   (Refusal/Not answered)

E-society

ASK ALL

Q264 [Internet]   *N=4432*
Does anyone have access to the Internet or World Wide Web from this address?

Q265 [WWUse]   *N=4432*
Do you yourself ever use the Internet or World Wide Web for any reason *(other than your work)*?

	[Internet]	[WWUse]
	%	%
Yes	51.2	49.8
No	48.7	50.2
(Don't know)	0.0	0.0
(Refusal/Not answered)	-	-

Q266 **VERSIONS A AND C: IF YES AT [WWUse]**   *N=3305*
[WWWHrsWk]
How many **hours** a week on average do you spend using the Internet or World Wide Web *(other than for your work)*?
INTERVIEWER: ROUND UP TO NEAREST HOUR
Median= 2.00 hours
%
0.0 (Don't know)
0.1 (Refusal/Not answered)

Q262 *N=1127*
[CharDD]
Adding up all the money you give to charity each year, do you give the **greatest** amount in the form of ... READ OUT...
%
17.9 ...regular payments from a bank, such as Direct Debits,
66.4 or, as donations to collections when asked?
4.4 (Half and half)
0.3 (Don't know)
0.0 (Refusal/Not answered)

Q267-
Q281   CARD C1   N=3305
For which of the following do you personally use the Internet or World Wide Web (other than for your work)?
PROBE: Which others?
CODE ALL THAT APPLY.
Multicoded (Maximum of 15 codes)

%		
21.1	Shopping	[WWWShop]
2.4	Chat rooms	[WWWChat]
35.3	E-mail	[WWWEmail]
13.6	News and current affairs	[WWWNews]
15.2	Training, education and learning	[WWWEduc]
21.5	Travel and weather information	[WWWTrav]
6.8	Keeping in touch with groups I belong to	[WWWGroup]
23.8	General information	[WWWInfo]
18.3	Banking and bill-paying	[WWWBank2]
8.0	Downloading music	[WWWMusi2]
8.3	Sports information	[WWWSpor2]
5.5	Games	[WWWGame2]
10.7	Job search	[WWWJobs2]
5.5	Accessing local/central government information/services	[WWWGovt]
2.4	Other (PLEASE SPECIFY)	[WWWOth2]
0.2	(None of these)	[WWWNone2]
-	(Don't know)	
0.1	(Refusal/Not answered)	

VERSIONS A AND C: IF IN WORK OR ON GOVERNMENT TRAINING SCHEME   N=3305

Q299   [WWWWork]
And do you yourself ever use the Internet or World Wide Web **for your work?**

%	
25.2	Yes
31.7	No
0.0	(Don't know)
0.0	(Refusal/Not answered)

IF 'yes' AT [WWWWork]

Q300   [WWWHrWk2]   N=3305
How many **hours** a week on average do you spend using the Internet or World Wide Web **for your work?**
INTERVIEWER: ROUND UP TO NEAREST HOUR.
Median: 3.00 hours

%	
0.1	(Don't know)
0.1	(Refusal/Not answered)

VERSIONS A AND C: ASK ALL WHO USE INTERNET (WHETHER FOR WORK OR NOT)

Q301   [WWWLong]   N=1754
CARD C2
Thinking now about **all** the times you use the Internet, either for work or for your own personal use. Can you tell me when you first started using the Internet?

%	
6.1	Within the last 6 months
7.2	Over 6 months, up to 1 year ago
31.9	Over 1 year, up to 3 years ago
29.5	Over 3 years, up to 5 years ago
25.2	More than 5 years ago
-	(Don't know)
0.1	(Refusal/Not answered)

VERSIONS A AND C: ASK ALL WHO DO NOT USE INTERNET (OTHER THAN FOR WORK)

Q332-
Q340

CARD C5   N=1672

Here are some reasons why people might not use the Internet (other than for work).Which of these reasons, if any, apply to you?
PROBE: Which others?
CODE ALL THAT APPLY

%   Multicoded (Maximum of 9 codes)
51.2   Have no interest in using the Internet   [NWWWNInt]
10.5   Don't like using the Internet or computers   [NWWWNLik]
28.4   Don't need to use the Internet   [NWWWNNee]
28.2   Don't know how to use the Internet or computers   [NWWWDKUs]
3.9   Using the Internet takes too long   [NWWWTooL]
24.7   Don't have or can't afford a computer   [NWWWNAFC]
2.2   Have a computer - but it is too old to connect to the Internet   [NWWWCOld]
3.9   Have a computer - but can't afford the cost of Internet access   [NWWWNAFI]
5.1   Other reason (PLEASE SPECIFY)   [NWWWOth]
2.3   (None of these reasons apply)   [NWWWNone]
0.1   (Don't know)
0.1   (Refusal/Not answered)

Q352   [Use1day]   N=1672
        How likely do you think it is, if at all, that you will start using the Internet one day (other than for work)   ...READ OUT...

%   ...very likely,
13.0
23.6   fairly likely,
19.5   not very likely,
43.2   or, not at all likely?
0.7   (Don't know)
0.1   (Refusal/Not answered)

Q302-
Q308

CARD C3   N=1754

On this card are some places where people can use the Internet or send email. In which of these places do **you personally** use the Internet or send email?
PROBE: Which others?
CODE ALL THAT APPLY

%   Multicoded (Maximum of 7 codes)
79.0   At home   [UseWWWHo]
47.6   At work   [UseWWWWo]
10.5   At school / college / university   [UseWWWSc]
14.4   At a friend's or relative's house   [UseWWWFr]
6.7   In a library or community centre   [UseWWWLi]
7.3   At an Internet café   [UseWWWCa]
1.3   Somewhere else (PLEASE SPECIFY)   [UseWWWEl]
-       (Don't know)
0.1   (Refusal/Not answered)

Q318-
Q323

CARD C4   N=1754

And in which of these ways do **you yourself** access the Internet?
PROBE: Which others?
CODE ALL THAT APPLY

%   Multicoded (Maximum of 6 codes)
97.4   Personal or Laptop Computer   [AcWWWPC]
3.4   Television   [AcWWWTV]
7.3   Mobile phone   [AcWWWPh]
1.1   Personal organiser / digital assistant   [AcWWWPO]
0.3   Games console   [AcWWWGa]
0.5   Other (PLEASE SPECIFY)   [AcWWWOt]
0.1   (Don't know)
-       (Refusal/Not answered)

Q353 [WdLkUse]
Regardless of whether you think you ever will, would you **like** to use the Internet *(other than for work)* one day, or not?

N=1672

	%
Yes	46.3
No	52.7
(Don't know)	0.9
(Refusal/Not answered)	0.1

VERSIONS A AND C: ASK ALL

Q354 [MobPhone]
Do you personally have or do you ever use a mobile phone?

N=3305

IF 'yes' AT [MobPhone]

Q355 [TextMes]
Do you ever use your mobile phone to send text messages?

	[MobPhone]	[TextMes]
	%	%
Yes	81.3	51.0
No	18.6	30.4
(Don't know)	0.0	0.0
(Refusal/Not answered)	0.0	0.1

VERSIONS A AND C: ASK ALL

Q356 [NewsPapR]
CARD C6
From what you know or have heard, how reliable a source of information would you say that **newspapers** are about news and current affairs?

N=3305

Q357 [NewsWWWR]
CARD C6 AGAIN
(From what you know or have heard), and how reliable a source of information would you say that **the Internet** is about news and current affairs?

N=3305

Q358 [HeaPapR]
CARD C6 AGAIN
From what you know or have heard, how reliable a source of information would you say that **newspapers** are about what is best for your health?

N=3305

Q359 [HeaWWWR]
CARD C6 AGAIN
(From what you know or have heard), and how reliable a source of information would you say that **the Internet** is about what is best for your health?

N=3305

	[NewsPapR]	[NewsWWWR]	[HeaPapR]
	%	%	%
Very reliable	5.7	9.9	2.5
Fairly reliable	56.8	37.3	36.9
Neither reliable nor unreliable	20.0	16.3	30.7
Fairly unreliable	12.1	3.6	18.9
Very unreliable	4.0	1.5	5.7
(Don't know)	1.3	31.3	5.1
(Refusal/Not answered)	0.0	0.0	0.0

	[HeaWWWR]
	%
Very reliable	6.5
Fairly reliable	28.5
Neither reliable nor unreliable	22.6
Fairly unreliable	5.4
Very unreliable	2.2
(Don't know)	34.8
(Refusal/Not answered)	0.0

Q360 [VoteChoi]
CARD C7   N=3305
There are many different ways of voting in elections.
If you had a choice, which **one** of the ways on this
card would be your **preferred** way
of voting in British elections?

%
12.4 By pressing a button on a computer at a polling station
33.4 By filling in a paper ballot paper at a polling station
16.8 By sending in a ballot paper by post
9.8   By voting over the telephone
15.6 By voting over the Internet
8.7   By sending a text message from a mobile phone
0.4   (None of these)
2.7   (Don't vote at elections)
0.2   (Don't know)
0.0   (Refusal/Not answered)

Q361 [PassPApp]
CARD C8   N=3305
Say you needed to apply for a new passport. Which one
of the ways on
this card would be your **preferred** way of doing this?

%
35.6 In person (e.g. at a post office or passport office)
30.2 By post
18.6 Over the Internet
13.5 Over the telephone
0.2   Another way (PLEASE SPECIFY)
1.8   (Does not apply / wouldn't want a passport)
0.2   (Don't know)
0.0   (Refusal/Not answered)

Q364 [BankBal]
CARD C9   N=3305
And what if you needed to check your bank balance?
Which one of the ways
on this card would be your **preferred** way of doing
this?

%
48.9 In person (e.g. at a cash machine or at a bank branch)
4.5   By post
20.6 Over the Internet
23.8 Over the telephone
0.3   Another way (PLEASE SPECIFY)
1.5   (Does not apply / don't have a bank account)
0.3   (Don't know)
0.1   (Refusal/Not answered)

VERSIONS A AND C: ASK ALL WHO USE INTERNET (WHETHER FOR WORK OR NOT)

Q367 [NetGrpIn]
CARD C10   N=1754
Please tell me how much, if at all, the Internet has
helped you to do each of the following things.
Firstly, how much has the Internet helped you to
become more involved with groups and organisations
you already belong to?

Q368 [NetBelfs]
CARD C10 AGAIN   N=1754
(And how much has the Internet helped you to...)
..find people or groups who share your interests or
beliefs?

Q369 [NetDifAg]
CARD C10 AGAIN   N=1754
(And how much has the Internet helped you to...)
..make contact with people of different ages?

Q370 [NetDifRa]
CARD C10 AGAIN   N=1754
(And how much has the Internet helped you to...)
..make contact with people of different racial or
ethnic backgrounds?

Q371 [NetDifEc]
CARD C10 AGAIN
(And how much has the Internet helped you to...)
..make contact with people of different economic or social backgrounds?
N=1754

Q372 [NetGrpLc]
CARD C10 AGAIN
(And how much has the Internet helped you to...)
..make contact with groups and organisations that are based in your local community?
N=1754

	[NetGrpIn]	[NetBelfs]	[NetDifAg]
	%	%	%
A great deal	6.0	7.0	4.1
Quite a lot	12.7	12.8	7.6
Some	13.4	15.3	10.7
Not very much	21.5	17.5	16.6
Not at all	46.1	47.0	60.5
(Don't know)	0.1	0.1	0.4
(Refusal/Not answered)	0.1	0.1	0.1

	[NetDifRa]	[NetDifEc]	[NetGrpLc]
	%	%	%
A great deal	3.3	2.6	1.6
Quite a lot	5.2	5.0	5.0
Some	9.7	11.3	16.0
Not very much	15.3	16.0	16.5
Not at all	65.6	64.0	60.5
(Don't know)	0.7	1.0	0.3
(Refusal/Not answered)		0.7	

VERSIONS A AND C: ASK ALL

Q373 [NghBrHd]
Can I just check, how long have you lived in your present neighbourhood?
ENTER YEARS. ROUND TO NEAREST YEAR.
PROBE FOR BEST ESTIMATE.
IF LESS THAN ONE YEAR, CODE 0.
N=3305

Median: 15 years

%
0.0 (Don't know)
0.1 (Refusal/Not answered)

VERSIONS A AND C: ASK ALL WHO USE INTERNET (WHETHER FOR WORK OR NOT)

Q374 [MemWWW]
N=1754
Are you a member of, or do you ever join in the activities of, any **Internet based** discussion groups, interest groups or online gaming groups?

%
Yes   9.5
No   90.4
(Don't know)   -
(Refusal/Not answered)   0.1

VERSIONS A AND C: ASK ALL

Q375- CARD C11
Q389
N=3305
Are you currently a member of, or do you regularly join in the activities of, any of the organisations on this card?
IF YES: Which ones? PROBE: Which others?
CODE ALL THAT APPLY
Multicoded (Maximum of 15 codes)

	%	
None of these	43.5	[MemNoGrp]
Political parties or trade unions (inc student unions)	9.5	[MemPtyTU]
An environmental or conservation group	4.7	[MemEnvC]
A pressure group or campaigning organisation	2.3	[MemPress]
Parent-teachers' / school parents Association / Board of Governors etc	6.7	[MemPTA2]
Youth groups (e.g. scouts, guides, youth clubs etc)	4.0	[MemYouth]
Education, arts, drama, reading or music group / evening class	9.1	[MemArtEd]
Religious group or church organisation	12.2	[MemRelg]
A sports or recreation club	19.7	[MemSport]
Tenants' / Residents' group / Neighbourhood watch	9.3	[MemResd2]
Social club / working men's club	2.9	[MemSClub]
Women's group / Women's Institute	2.7	[MemWomen]
Group for older people (e.g. lunch clubs)		[MemOlder]
Local groups which raise money for charity (e.g. The Rotary Club)	4.9	[MemChari]

3.6   Other local community or voluntary group (PLEASE SPECIFY)   [MemOthL]
2.8   Other national or international group (PLEASE SPECIFY)   [MemOthNI]
0.0   (Don't know)
0.1   (Refusal/Not answered)

Q425   [NeigIll]   N=3305
CARD C12
Suppose that you were in bed ill and needed someone to go to the chemist to collect your prescription while they were doing their shopping.
How comfortable would you be asking a neighbour to do this?

Q426   [NeigSink]   N=3305
CARD C12 AGAIN
Now suppose you found your sink was blocked, but you did not have a plunger to unblock it.
How comfortable would you be asking a neighbour to borrow a plunger?

Q427   [NeigMilk]   N=3305
CARD C12 AGAIN
Now suppose the milkman called for payment. The bill was £5 but you had no cash.
How comfortable would you be asking a neighbour if you could borrow £5?

	[NeigIll]	[NeigSink]	[NeigMilk]
	%	%	%
Very comfortable	44.8	53.4	17.5
Fairly comfortable	28.4	29.6	14.7
Fairly uncomfortable	12.9	7.4	16.6
Very uncomfortable	13.2	8.4	50.0
(Don't know)	0.6	1.0	1.1
(Refusal/Not answered)	0.0	0.1	0.1

VERSIONS A AND C: ASK ALL WHO USE INTERNET (WHETHER FOR WORK OR NOT)

Q428   [GovInfoW]   N=1754
CARD C13
How often do you use the Internet to look up information about national or local government or the services they provide, or do you never do this?

Q429   [PolInfoW]   N=1754
CARD C13 AGAIN
And how often do you use the Internet to look up information about political parties, campaigns or events, or do you never do this?

Q430   [NewsWeb]   N=1754
CARD C13 AGAIN
And how often do you use the Internet to visit a news or current affairs web site, including the web sites for any newspapers, radio or television news programmes, or do you never do this?

	[GovInfoW]	[PolInfoW]	[NewsWeb]
	%	%	%
Every day, or nearly every day	2.8	0.8	9.4
2-5 days a week	1.5	0.3	5.8
At least once a week	4.8	1.9	10.7
At least once a fortnight	3.2	0.8	5.4
Less often but at least once a month	11.1	4.3	10.7
Less often than that	17.7	8.2	13.3
Never do this	58.8	83.7	44.6
(Don't know)	-	-	-
(Refusal/Not answered)	0.1	0.1	0.1

VERSIONS A AND C: ASK ALL N=3305
CARD C14

Q431-
Q438

Suppose a law was being considered by parliament which you thought was really unjust and harmful.
Which, if any, of the things on this card do you think you would do?
PROBE: Which others?
CODE ALL THAT APPLY
Multicoded (Maximum of 8 codes)

%		
45.8	Contact my MP or MSP	[DoMP]
16.3	Speak to an influential person	[DoSpk]
12.7	Contact a government department	[DoGov]
16.6	Contact radio, TV or a newspaper	[DoTV]
74.0	Sign a petition	[DoSign]
7.7	Raise the issue in an organisation I already belong to	[DoRais]
18.4	Go on a protest or demonstration	[DoProt]
5.4	Form a group of like-minded people	[DoGrp]
6.5	(None of these)	[DoNone]
0.4	(Don't know)	
0.1	(Refusal/Not answered)	

Q448

VERSION A AND C: IF NOT 'NONE OF THESE' N=3305
[EvDoWWW]
And do you think you would use email or the Internet to help you do (this/any of these things)?
IF WOULD/WOULD NOT: Definitely or probably?

%	
14.7	Definitely would
20.1	Probably would
4.7	Probably would not
9.6	Definitely would not
2.0	(Depends)
0.1	(Don't know)
0.1	(Refusal/Not answered)

VERSIONS A AND C: ASK ALL N=3305
CARD C14 AGAIN

Q449-
Q456

And have you ever done any of the things on this card about a government action which you thought was unjust and harmful?
Which ones? Any others?
CODE ALL THAT APPLY
Multicoded (Maximum of 8 codes)

%		
16.2	Contact my MP or MSP	[DoneMP]
5.0	Speak to an influential person	[DoneSpk]
4.7	Contact a government department	[DoneGov]
5.1	Contact radio, TV or a newspaper	[DoneTV]
41.9	Sign a petition	[DoneSign]
3.3	Raise the issue in an organisation I already belong to	[DoneRais]
10.7	Go on a protest or demonstration	[DoneProt]
1.8	Form a group of like-minded people	[DoneGrp]
45.0	(None of these)	[DoneNone]
0.3	(Don't know)	
0.1	(Refusal/Not answered)	

Q466

VERSIONS A AND C: IF NOT 'NONE OF THESE' N=3305
[EvDonWWW]
And did you use email or the Internet to help you do (this/any of these things)?

%	
6.2	Yes
25.6	No
0.1	(Don't know)
0.1	(Refusal/Not answered)

Q467

VERSIONS A AND C: IFUSE INTERNET (WHETHER FOR WORK OR NOT) N=3305
[WWWProt]
Has anyone ever contacted you by email or via the Internet asking you to join in a protest or campaign about an issue?

%	
9.1	Yes
43.8	No
0.1	(Don't know)
0.1	(Refusal/Not answered)

Education

Q469 **VERSIONS A AND C: FIRST RANDOM HALF OF SAMPLE**
[EdSpend1]   N=1668
CARD D1
Now some questions about education.
Which of the groups on this card, if any, would be your highest priority for **extra** government spending on education?

Q470 **IF ANSWER GIVEN AT [EdSpend1]**
[EdSpend2]   N=1668
CARD D1 AGAIN
And which is your next highest priority?

	[EdSpend1]	[EdSpend2]
	%	%
Nursery or pre-school children	10.1	11.2
Primary school children	20.6	22.8
Secondary school children	26.9	25.2
Less able children with special needs	25.1	21.5
Students at colleges or universities	14.7	15.8
(None of these)	1.1	0.5
(Don't know)	1.4	0.5
(Refusal/Not answered)	0.1	2.6

Q471 **VERSIONS A AND C: SECOND RANDOM HALF OF SAMPLE**
[EdSpnd1b]   N=1637
Card D2
Now some questions about education.
Which of the groups on this card, if any, would be your highest priority for **extra** government spending on education?

Q472 **IF ANSWER GIVEN AT [EdSpnd1b]**
[EdSpnd2b]   N=1637
CARD D2 AGAIN
And which is your next highest priority?

	[EdSpnd1b]	[EdSpnd2b]
	%	%
Nursery or pre-school children	10.1	10.8
Primary school children	19.7	22.1
Secondary school children	27.2	22.3
Children with special educational needs	25.3	23.2
Students at colleges or universities	15.1	18.0
(None of these)	1.5	0.7
(Don't know)	1.0	0.5
(Refusal/Not answered)	-	2.6

Q473 **VERSIONS A AND C: ASK ALL**
[PrimImp1]   N=3305
CARD D3
Here are a number of things that some people think would improve education in our schools. Which do you think would be the **most** useful one for improving the education of children in **primary** schools - aged (5-11/5-12) years? Please look at the whole list before deciding.

	%
More information available about individual schools	1.6
More links between parents and schools	10.2
More resources for buildings, books and equipment	17.0
Better quality teachers	14.1
Smaller class sizes	37.1
More emphasis on exams and tests	0.8
More emphasis on developing the child's skills and interests	14.1
Better leadership within individual schools	2.3
Other (WRITE IN)	1.2
(Don't know)	1.6
(Refusal/Not answered)	0.0

Q482

IF ANSWER GIVEN AT [SecImpl]
[SecImp2]
CARD D4 AGAIN
And which do you think would be the **next** most useful one for children in
secondary schools?

N=3305

%
1.0 More information available about individual schools
7.1 More links between parents and schools
16.0 More resources for buildings, books and equipment
12.1 Better quality teachers
16.4 Smaller class sizes
3.8 More emphasis on exams and tests
16.5 More emphasis on developing the child's skills and interests
19.1 More training and preparation for jobs
4.1 Better leadership within individual schools
1.1 Other (WRITE IN)
0.8 (Don't know)
1.9 (Refusal/Not answered)

Q485

ASK ALL
[SchSelec]
CARD
Which of the following statements comes closest to your views about what
kind of **secondary** school children should go to?

N=4432

%
47.7 Children should go to a different kind of secondary school, according to how well they do at primary school
50.0 All children should go to the same kind of secondary school, no matter how well or badly they do at primary school
2.3 (Don't know)
0.0 (Refusal/Not answered)

Q486

VERSIONS A AND C: ASK ALL
[PrimBet2]
From what you know or have heard, do you think that
primary schools in the area where you live ... READ OUT ...

N=3305

Q476

IF ANSWER GIVEN AT [PrimImpl]
[PrimImp2]
CARD D3 AGAIN
And which do you think would be the **next** most useful one for children in
primary schools?

N=3305

%
1.9 More information available about individual schools
11.6 More links between parents and schools
22.6 More resources for buildings, books and equipment
13.3 Better quality teachers
21.4 Smaller class sizes
1.9 More emphasis on exams and tests
20.1 More emphasis on developing the child's skills and interests
4.2 Better leadership within individual schools
1.0 Other (WRITE IN)
0.3 (Don't know)
1.7 (Refusal/Not answered)

Q479

VERSIONS A AND C: ASK ALL
[SecImpl]
CARD D4
And which do you think would be the **most** useful thing for improving the
education of children in **secondary** schools - aged
(11-18/12-18) years?

N=3305

%
1.2 More information available about individual schools
7.4 More links between parents and schools
15.5 More resources for buildings, books and equipment
16.1 Better quality teachers
24.5 Smaller class sizes
3.6 More emphasis on exams and tests
12.8 More emphasis on developing the child's skills and interests
13.0 More training and preparation for jobs
2.3 Better leadership within individual schools
1.7 Other (WRITE IN)
1.8 (Don't know)
0.0 (Refusal/Not answered)

Q487 [SecBet2]
And from what you know or have heard, do you think that **secondary schools** in the area where you live ... READ OUT ...

N=3305

	[PrimBet2]	[SecBet2]
	%	%
... have got better over the last few years,	33.2	25.1
got worse	11.6	23.6
or, have stayed much the same?	30.2	26.3
(Don't know)	24.9	24.9
(Refusal/Not answered)	0.0	0.0

Q488 [WWWLearn]
N=3305
CARD D6
How important do you think the Internet is for learning new knowledge or skills?

%
42.1 Very important
39.4 Fairly important
9.6 Not very important
2.9 Not at all important
6.0 (Don't know)
0.0 (Refusal/Not answered)

ASK ALL WHO HAVE INTERNET ACCESS IN HOME AND CHILD OF THEIR OWN AGED 5-16 IN HOUSEHOLD

Q489 [WWWenuf]
N=494
Thinking about your (eldest) child, do you think they make enough use of the Internet at home for school work, too much, or not enough?

%
53.4 Enough
8.2 Too much
30.5 Not enough
3.7 (Child no longer at school)
3.5 (Don't know)
0.7 (Refusal/Not answered)

IF 'not enough' AT [WWWenuf]
CARD D7   N=494
What do you think is the main reason your (eldest) child does not make more use of the Internet at home?
CODE ALL THAT APPLY
Multicoded (Maximum of 6 codes)

Q490-Q495

%
4.5 They are not interested [NEnfNInt]
3.6 They do not know enough about computers [NEnfDKCo]
2.7 They have to compete for use of the Internet [NEnfComp]
17.7 They have other interests [NEnfOInt]
3.3 The cost of Internet time [NEnfCost]
3.8 Other reason (WRITE IN) [NEnfOth]
3.5 (Don't know)
0.7 (Refusal/Not answered)

VERSIONS A AND C: ASK ALL
[HEDOpp]
CARD D8   N=3305
Do you feel that opportunities for young people in Britain to go on to **higher education** - to a university or college - should be increased or reduced, or are they at about the right level now?
IF INCREASED OR REDUCED: a lot or a little?

Q504

%
25.2 Increased a lot
24.8 Increased a little
37.2 About right
7.7 Reduced a little
2.2 Reduced a lot
2.8 (Don't know)
0.1 (Refusal/Not answered)

ASK ALL

Q505 [HEFeeNow]
CARD

N=4432

I'm now going to ask you what you think about university or college students paying towards the costs of their tuition - either while they are finished.
Firstly, students and their families paying towards the costs of their tuition **while they are studying**.
Which of the views on this card comes closest to what you think about that?

%
7.7   All students or their families should pay towards their tuition costs while they are studying

62.0   Some students or their families should pay towards their tuition costs while they are studying, depending on their circumstances

29.4   No students or their families should pay towards their tuition costs while they are studying

0.9   (Don't know)
0.1   (Refusal/Not answered)

Q506 [HEFeeAft]
CARD

N=4432

And what about students paying back some of the costs of their tuition **after they have finished studying**?
Which of the views on this card comes closest to what you think about that?

%
14.4   All students should pay back some tuition costs after they have finished studying

53.2   Some students should pay back some tuition costs after they have finished studying, depending on their circumstances

31.2   No students should pay back tuition costs after they have finished studying

1.1   (Don't know)
0.0   (Refusal/Not answered)

VERSIONS A AND C: ASK ALL

Q507 [FeesUni]

N=3305

Which of the following statements comes closest to your own view ...
READ OUT...
%
62.2   ..tuition fees for **all universities and colleges** should be the same,

34.5   or, tuition fees should be different depending on the university or college students go to?

3.2   (Don't know)
0.0   (Refusal/Not answered)

Q508 [FeesSub]

N=3305

And which of these two statements comes closest to your own view ...
READ OUT...
%
53.2   ..tuition fees for **all subjects studied** should be the same,

43.0   or, tuition fees should be different depending on the subject students study at university or college?

3.8   (Don't know)
0.0   (Refusal/Not answered)

Health

Q510

VERSIONS A AND B: ASK ALL
[NHSSat]   N=2284
CARD E1
All in all, how satisfied or dissatisfied would you say you are with the way in which the National Health Service runs nowadays?
Choose a phrase from this card.

Q511

[GPSat]   N=2284
CARD E1 AGAIN
From your own experience, or from what you have heard, please say how satisfied or dissatisfied you are with the way in which each of these parts of the National Health Service runs nowadays:
First, local doctors or GPs?

Q512

[DentSat]   N=2284
CARD E1 AGAIN
(And how satisfied or dissatisfied are you with the NHS as regards...)
... National Health Service dentists?

Q513

[InPatSat]   N=2284
CARD E1 AGAIN
(And how satisfied or dissatisfied are you with the NHS as regards...)
... being in hospital as an **in**-patient?

Q514

[OutPaSat]   N=2284
CARD E1 AGAIN
(And how satisfied or dissatisfied are you with the NHS as regards...)
... attending hospital as an **out**-patient?

Q515

[AESat]   N=2284
CARD E1 AGAIN
(And how satisfied or dissatisfied are you with the NHS as regards...)
... Accident and Emergency departments?

Q516

VERSION A AND B: ASK ALL IN ENGLAND AND WALES
[NDirSat]   N=2072
CARD E1 AGAIN
(And how satisfied or dissatisfied are you with the NHS as regards...)
... NHS Direct, the telephone or internet advice service?

Q517

VERSIONS A AND B: ASK ALL
[MentSat]   N=2284
CARD E1 AGAIN
Now from your own experience, **or from what you have heard**, please say how satisfied or dissatisfied you are with ...
... NHS services for people with mental health problems?

	[NHSSat] %	[GPSat] %	[DentSat] %
Very satisfied	6.0	25.3	14.7
Quite satisfied	37.7	47.0	37.4
Neither satisfied nor dissatisfied	18.4	10.6	15.8
Quite dissatisfied	24.4	11.3	13.4
Very dissatisfied	12.9	5.5	12.1
(Don't know)	0.5	0.4	6.7
(Refusal/not answered)	-	-	-

	[InPatSat] %	[OutPaSat] %	[AESat] %
Very satisfied	13.8	12.3	13.7
Quite satisfied	38.3	41.7	31.1
Neither satisfied nor dissatisfied	17.5	17.0	17.2
Quite dissatisfied	13.5	16.7	18.8
Very dissatisfied	7.6	6.9	12.6
(Don't know)	9.3	5.4	6.6
(Refusal/not answered)	-	-	-

	[NDirSat]	[MenSat]
	%	%
Very satisfied	8.3	3.4
Quite satisfied	18.9	15.2
Neither satisfied nor dissatisfied	28.0	27.6
Quite dissatisfied	4.8	17.4
Very dissatisfied	3.5	9.0
(Don't know)	36.5	27.3
(Refusal/not answered)	-	-

Q518 [InPat1]
CARD E2
N=2284

Now, suppose you had to go into a local NHS hospital for observation and maybe an operation. From what you know or have heard, please say whether you think the hospital doctors would tell you all you feel you need to know?

Q519 [InPat2]
CARD E2 AGAIN
N=2284

(And please say whether you think ...)
...the hospital doctors would take seriously any views you may have on the sorts of treatment available?

Q520 [InPat3]
CARD E2 AGAIN
N=2284

(And please say whether you think ...)
...the operation would take place on the day it was booked for?

Q521 [InPat4]
CARD E2 AGAIN
N=2284

(And please say whether you think ...)
...you would be allowed home only when you were really well enough to leave?

Q522 [InPat5]
CARD E2 AGAIN
N=2284

(And please say whether you think ...)
...the nurses would take seriously any complaints you may have?

Q523 [InPat6]
CARD E2 AGAIN
N=2284

(And please say whether you think ...)
...the hospital doctors would take seriously any complaints you may have

Q524 [InPat7]
CARD E2 AGAIN
N=2284

(And please say whether you think ...)
...there would be a particular nurse responsible for dealing with any problems you may have?

	[InPat1]	[InPat2]	[InPat3]
	%	%	%
Definitely would	20.9	13.2	6.0
Probably would	53.3	53.9	41.2
Probably would not	20.0	25.4	39.7
Definitely would not	4.3	4.3	9.7
(Don't know)	1.4	3.2	3.4
(Refusal/not answered)	-	-	-

	[InPat4]	[InPat5]	[InPat6]
	%	%	%
Definitely would	14.5	20.0	16.7
Probably would	41.7	57.0	58.8
Probably would not	31.9	16.6	17.6
Definitely would not	10.1	3.9	3.9
(Don't know)	1.9	2.5	2.9
(Refusal/not answered)	-	-	-

	[InPat7]
	%
Definitely would	14.5
Probably would	39.5
Probably would not	31.5
Definitely would not	6.8
(Don't know)	7.7
(Refusal/not answered)	-

Q525 [NHSLimit] N=2284
It has been suggested that the National Health Service should be available **only to those with lower incomes**. This would mean that contributions and taxes could be lower and most people would then take out medical insurance or pay for health care.
Do you support or oppose this idea?
IF 'SUPPORT' OR 'OPPOSE': A lot or little?

%	
10.6	Support a lot
16.5	Support a little
14.6	Oppose a little
56.9	Oppose a lot
1.4	(Don't know)
0.0	(Refusal/not answered)

Q526 [SRHealth] N=2284
How is your health in general for someone of your age? Would you say that it is ... READ OUT ...

%	
41.1	... very good,
39.9	fairly good,
13.8	fair,
3.7	bad,
1.4	or, very bad?
0.1	(Don't know)
0.0	(Refusal/not answered)

Q527 [HlthSpnd1] N=2284
CARD E3
Here are some groups of people for whom health services are provided. If the government had some extra money to spend on **one** of these, which, if any, would be your highest priority for extra spending?

Q528 **IF ANSWER GIVEN AT [HlthSpnd1]** N=2284
[HlthSpnd2]
CARD E3 AGAIN
And which next?
ENTER ONE CODE ONLY FOR **SECOND** HIGHEST PRIORITY

	[HlthSpnd1]	[HlthSpnd2]
	%	%
Services for babies and young children	26.5	17.9
Services for the elderly	33.8	26.6
Services for people with mental health problems	12.0	15.6
Services for people with physical disabilities	9.2	18.1
Hospice care for the terminally ill	16.2	18.6
(None of these)	0.9	0.4
(Don't know)	1.4	0.4
(Refusal/not answered)	0.0	2.4

Q529 **VERSIONS A AND B: ASK ALL** N=2284
[PrDepres]
Suppose an employee applied for a promotion. He has had repeated periods off work because of depression but this has been under control for a year or so through medication. Do you think he would be ... READ OUT ...

%	
9.1	... just as likely as anyone else to be promoted,
42.4	slightly less likely to be promoted,
46.4	or, much less likely to be promoted?
2.0	(Don't know)
-	(Refusal/not answered)

Q530 [ShdDep]   N=2284
CARD E4
And what do you think **should** happen? Should his medical history make a difference or not?

%
10.0   Definitely should
28.0   Probably should
28.7   Probably should not
28.9   Definitely should not
2.2   **EDIT ONLY:** Depends on the job/type of work/depends on whether it would affect his/her job
0.7   (Other (PLEASE WRITE IN))
1.4   (Don't know)
0.0   (Refusal/not answered)

Q533 [PrSchiz]   N=2284
And now think about someone who has had repeated periods off work because of schizophrenia but this has been under control for a year or so through medication. Do you think he would be ... READ OUT ...

%
3.6   ... just as likely as anyone else to be promoted,
29.8   slightly less likely to be promoted,
64.2   or, much less likely to be promoted?
2.4   (Don't know)
-   (Refusal/not answered)

Q534 [ShdSchiz]   N=2284
CARD E4 AGAIN
And what do you think **should** happen? Should his medical history make a difference or not?

%
16.7   Definitely should
32.7   Probably should
27.6   Probably should not
18.2   Definitely should not
1.4   **EDIT ONLY:** Depends on the job/type of work/depends on whether it would affect his/her job
0.7   (Other (PLEASE WRITE IN))
2.7   (Don't Know)
-   (Refusal/not answered)

Q537 [PrDiab]
And now think about someone who has had repeated periods off work because of diabetes but this has been under control for a year or so through medication.Do you think he would be ... READ OUT ...

%
50.7   ... just as likely as anyone else to be promoted,
38.0   slightly less likely to be promoted,
9.3   or, much less likely to be promoted?
-   (Other (PLEASE WRITE IN))
2.0   (Don't Know)
-   (Refusal/not answered)

Q538 [ShdDiab]   N=2284
CARD E4 AGAIN
And what do you think **should** happen? Should his medical history make a difference or not?

%
10.2   Definitely should
14.2   Probably should
25.6   Probably should not
47.6   Definitely should not
0.6   **EDIT ONLY:** Depends on the job/type of work/depends on whether it would affect his/her job
0.3   (Other (PLEASE WRITE IN))
1.5   (Don't Know)
-   (Refusal/not answered)

Q541 [MentProb]   N=2284
Have you, a member of your family or a close friend ever sought medical help for a mental health problem?

%
30.4   Yes
69.4   No
0.2   (Don't Know)
-   (Refusal/not answered)

Devolution and constitutional change / Nations and Regions

Proportional representation

VERSIONS A AND B: ASK ALL

Q544 [Monarchy]   *N=2284*

How important or unimportant do you think it is for
Britain to continue
to have a monarchy
... READ OUT ...

%
28.3   ...very important,
30.7   quite important,
21.6   not very important,
8.4   not at all important,
9.9   or, do you think the monarchy should be abolished?
1.2   (Don't know)
-   (Refusal/not answered)

VERSION A: ASK ALL

Q545 [Coalitin]   *N=1157*

Which do you think would generally be better for
Britain nowadays ...
READ OUT ...

%
43.5   ...to have a government at Westminster formed by one
political party on its own,
50.0   or, to have a government at Westminster formed by two
political parties together - in coalition?
6.3   (Don't know)
0.2   (Refusal/not answered)

Q542 [DprHelp]
CARD E5   *N=2284*

Suppose you developed serious depression and wanted
to seek help. Who
would you turn to **first** for help? Please take your
answer from this card

%
59.4   NHS doctor/ GP
3.9   Private counsellor or psychotherapist
32.7   A friend/ someone in my family
1.8   A helpline, such as NHS Direct or the Samaritans
1.3   Someone else
0.1   (This would never happen to me)
0.4   (I would not seek help)
0.3   (Don't know)
0.0   (Refusal/not answered)

Q546   N=1157
[VoteSyst]
Some people say we should change the voting system
for general elections to the UK House of Commons to
allow smaller political parties to get a fairer share
of MPs. Others say that we should keep the voting
system for the House of Commons as it is to
produce effective government. Which view comes **closer**
to your own ... READ OUT ...
IF ASKED: THIS REFERS TO 'PROPORTIONAL
REPRESENTATION'
%
35.6   ... that we should change the voting system for the
        House of Commons,
59.8   or, keep it as it is?
4.4   (Don't know)
0.2   (Refusal/not answered)

Retrospective evaluations

Q548   N=986

VERSION A: ASK ALL IN ENGLAND
[SNHSIESW]
CARD F1
Thinking back over the last four years, would you say
that since then **the standard of the health service** in
England has increased or fallen?
Please choose an answer from this card.
%
3.8   Increased a lot
25.3   Increased a little
23.5   Stayed the same
25.9   Fallen a little
18.9   Fallen a lot
2.5   (Don't know)
0.1   (Refusal/not answered)

Q549   **IF ANSWER GIVEN AT [SNHSIESW]**   N=986
[StNHSWhE]
%   Do you think this has been ... READ OUT ...
64.5   ... mainly the result of the government's policies,
29.0   or, for some other reason?
4.0   (Don't know)
2.6   (Refusal/not answered)

Q550
VERSION A: ASK ALL IN ENGLAND   N=986
[EdstIESW]
CARD F1 AGAIN
And what about the quality of education in England?
Has it increased or fallen (over the last four
years)? (Again, please choose an answer from
the card.)
%
5.0   Increased a lot
28.0   Increased a little
24.0   Stayed the same
23.6   Fallen a little
12.3   Fallen a lot
7.0   (Don't know)
0.1   (Refusal/not answered)

Q551   **IF ANSWER GIVEN AT [EdstIESW]**   N=986
[EdStWhyE]
%   Do you think this has been ... READ OUT ...
63.1   ... mainly the result of the government's policies,
26.2   or, for some other reason?
3.7   (Don't know)
7.1   (Refusal/not answered)

Q552
VERSION A: ASK ALL IN ENGLAND   N=986
[SLivIESW]
CARD F1 AGAIN
And what about the general standard of living in
England? Has it increased or fallen (over the last
four years)? (Again, please choose an
answer from the card).
%
9.2   Increased a lot
33.2   Increased a little
26.7   Stayed the same
18.4   Fallen a little
10.4   Fallen a lot
2.0   (Don't know)
0.1   (Refusal/not answered)

Q553 **IF ANSWER GIVEN AT [SLiVIESW]**
[SLiVWhyE]   N=986
%
Do you think this has been ... READ OUT ...
... mainly the result of the government's policies,
or, for some other reason?
(Don't know)
(Refusal/not answered)

58.9
35.4
3.7
2.1

Political issues

Q554 **VERSION A: ASK ALL IN ENGLAND**
[BPrioF1E]   N=986
CARD F2
Looking at the things on this card, which one do you think should be Britain's highest priority, the most important thing it should do?

Q555 **IF ANSWER GIVEN AT [BPrioF1E]**
[BPrioF2E]   N=986
CARD F2 AGAIN
And which one do you think should be Britain's next highest priority, the second most important thing it should do?

	[BPrioF1E]	[BPrioF2E]
	%	%
Maintain order in the nation	40.8	22.2
Give people more say in government decisions	32.6	27.6
Fight rising prices	12.6	27.0
Protect freedom of speech	12.8	21.7
(Don't know)	1.1	0.3
(Refusal/not answered)	0.1	1.2

Q556 **VERSION A: ASK ALL IN ENGLAND**
[BrWorld]   N=986
CARD F3
How much influence would you say that Britain has in the world nowadays?
(Please take your answer from this card)
%
A great deal
Quite a lot
Some
Not very much
None at all
(Don't know)
(Refusal/not answered)

9.0
34.3
34.2
19.6
2.3
0.5
0.1

Q557 **VERSIONS A AND B: ASK ALL**
[LevelGen]   N=2284
Thinking about things like the health service, schools, the roads, the police and so on, in general do you think it is better that the standards for such services be ...READ OUT...
...the same in every part of Britain,
or, do you think each region should be allowed to set its own standards?
(Don't know)
(Refusal/not answered)
%
65.4
33.8

0.7
-

Q558 [ECPolicy]   N=2284
CARD
Do you think Britain's long-term policy should be... READ OUT ...
... to leave the European Union,
to stay in the EU and try to **reduce** the EU's powers,
to leave things as they are,
to stay in the EU and try to **increase** the EU's powers,
or, to work for the formation of a single European government?
(Don't know)
(Refusal/not answered)
%
15.4
31.8
26.9
11.1

6.3

8.4
0.1

Political trust

VERSIONS A AND C: ASK ALL

Q563　[GovTrust]
CARD
How much do you trust British governments of any party to place the needs of the nation above the interests of their own political party?
Please choose a phrase from this card.

N=3305

Q564　[MpsTrust]
CARD
And how much do you trust politicians of any party in Britain to tell the truth when they are in a tight corner?

N=3305

	[GovTrust]	[MpsTrust]
	%	%
Just about always	1.4	0.7
Most of the time	16.2	5.2
Only some of the time	49.4	38.5
Almost never	31.0	54.2
(Don't know)	2.0	1.3
(Refusal/not answered)	0.0	0.0

ASK ALL

Q565　[GovtWork]
CARD
Which of these statements best describes your opinion on the present system of governing Britain?

N=4432

	%
Works extremely well and could not be improved	1.5
Could be improved in small ways but mainly works well	32.2
Could be improved quite a lot	43.3
Needs a great deal of improvement	21.5
(Don't know)	1.3
(Refusal/not answered)	0.1

Q559　[EuroRef]
If there were a referendum on whether Britain should join the single European currency, the Euro, how do you think you would vote? Would you vote to join the Euro, or not to join the Euro?
IF 'would not vote', PROBE: If you did vote, how would you vote?
IF RESPONDENT INSISTS THEY WOULD NOT VOTE, CODE DON'T KNOW

N=2284

%
29.2	To join the Euro
64.9	Not to join the Euro
5.9	(Don't know)
-	(Refusal/not answered)

Q560　[EurLike]
(Can I just check) how likely do you think that you would be to vote in such a referendum?
Would you be
...READ OUT...

Q561　[EuroLkly]
And how likely do you think it is that Britain **will** join the single European currency in the next ten years
...READ OUT...

	[EurLike]	[EuroLkly]
	%	%
...very likely,	65.5	43.9
fairly likely,	19.8	38.5
not very likely,	7.3	10.7
or, not at all likely?	6.5	3.1
(Don't know)	0.9	3.7
(Refusal/not answered)	-	-

N=2284

N=2284

Q566　[GovNoSay]
CARD　　　　　　　　　　　　　　　　N=4432
Please choose a phrase from this card to say how much you agree or disagree with the following statements. People like me have no say in what the government does.

	[GovNoSay]	[LoseTch]	[VoteIntr]
	%	%	%
Agree strongly	22.7	23.2	25.0
Agree	41.6	51.8	51.1
Neither agree nor disagree	12.1	13.0	10.9
Disagree	21.0	10.2	12.0
Disagree strongly	1.8	0.6	0.3
(Don't know)	0.7	1.1	0.6
(Refusal/not answered)	0.1	0.1	0.1

Q567　[LoseTch]
CARD　　　　　　　　　　　　　　　　N=4432
(Using this card, please say how much you agree or disagree with this statement:)
Generally speaking those we elect as MPs lose touch with people pretty quickly.

Q568　[VoteIntr]
CARD　　　　　　　　　　　　　　　　N=4432
(Using this card, please say how much you agree or disagree with this statement:)
Parties are only interested in people's votes, not in their opinions.

VERSIONS A AND C: ASK ALL

Q569　[VoteOnly]
CARD　　　　　　　　　　　　　　　　N=3305
(Please choose a phrase from this card to say how much you agree or disagree with this statement:)
Voting is the only way people like me can have any say about how the government runs things.

	[VoteOnly]	[GovComp]
	%	%
Agree strongly	15.6	14.7
Agree	48.3	45.3
Neither agree nor disagree	12.0	11.1
Disagree	20.2	24.1
Disagree strongly	2.9	4.0
(Don't know)	0.8	0.6
(Refusal/not answered)		0.6

Q570　[GovComp]
CARD　　　　　　　　　　　　　　　　N=3305
(Please choose a phrase from this card to say how much you agree or disagree with this statement:)
Sometimes politics and government seem so complicated that a person like me cannot really understand what is going on.

Q571　**ASK ALL**
[PtyNMat2]
CARD　　　　　　　　　　　　　　　　N=4432
(Using this card, please say how much you agree or disagree with this statement:)
It doesn't really matter which party is in power, in the end things go on much the same.

	%
Agree strongly	19.8
Agree	49.5
Neither agree nor disagree	7.2
Disagree	20.0
Disagree strongly	2.9
(It depends on the level of government)	0.1
(Don't know)	0.5
(Refusal/not answered)	0.1

Q572 **VERSION A: ASK ALL IN ENGLAND**

[QuizSVoE] *(This is false)*   N=986

Here is a quick quiz. For each thing I say, please tell me whether you think it is true or false. If you don't know, just say so and we'll skip to the next one. Remember - true, false or don't know.

Scottish MPs in the UK House of Commons **cannot** vote on laws that only apply in England.

Q573 [QuizSMPE] *(This is true)*   N=986

It has been decided to cut the number of Scottish MPs in the UK House of Commons.

(True, false or don't know?)

Q574 [QuizBenE] *(This is false)*   N=986

The Scottish parliament **can** increase the level of social security benefits in Scotland.

(True, false or don't know?)

Q575 [QuizLond] *(This is true)*   N=986

London is the only region in England with its own **elected** regional assembly.

(True, false or don't know?)

	[QuizSVoE]	[QuizSMPE]	[QuizBen]	[QuizLond]
	%	%	%	%
True	24.8	18.1	55.5	27.3
False	38.0	34.0	12.8	28.7
(Don't know)	37.2	47.8	31.6	43.9
(Refusal/not answered)	0.1		0.1	0.1

Q576 **VERSIONS A AND B: ASK ALL**

[ImpGSctP]   N=2284

CARD

Do you think that so far **creating the Scottish** Parliament has improved the way Britain as a whole is governed, made it worse, or has it made no difference?

Q577 [ImpGWAs]   N=2284

CARD

(And has this improved the way Britain as a whole is governed, made it worse, or made no difference...)

Creating the Welsh Assembly

Q578 [ImpGNAs]   N=2284

CARD

(And has this improved the way Britain as a whole is governed, made it worse, or made no difference...)

Creating the Northern Ireland Assembly

	[ImpGSctP]	[ImpGWAs]	[ImpGNAs]
	%	%	%
Improved it a lot	1.5	1.1	2.3
Improved it a little	11.2	7.8	16.4
Made no difference	64.1	64.3	54.1
Made it a little worse	4.4	3.8	4.2
Made it a lot worse	2.2	2.2	1.9
(It is too early to tell)	1.5	1.5	1.4
(Don't know)	15.0	19.2	19.7
(Refusal/not answered)	-	-	0.0

Q579 **VERSION A: ASK ALL IN ENGLAND**

[UKInNatE]   N=986

CARD F9

The United Kingdom government at Westminster has responsibility for England, Scotland, Wales and Northern Ireland. How much do you trust the UK government at Westminster to work in the best long-term interest of **England**? Please take your answer from this card.

Just about always	6.5
Most of the time	46.1
Only some of the time	34.6
Almost never	9.0
(Don't know)	3.8
(Refusal/not answered)	0.1

Q580 [RegBias]   N=986
%
17.0   Would you say the government ... READ OUT ...
76.0   ... looks after the interests of all parts of England more or less equally,
       or, would you say that it looks after some parts of England more than others?
3.7   (Neither or both)
3.2   (Don't know)
0.1   (Refusal/not answered)

Q581   IF 'some parts of England more than others'
       [WhBias]   N=986
       CARD F10
       Please look at this card and tell me which parts of England you think the government looks after more than others?
%
30.9   London
36.3   The South of England as a whole
4.2   The rest of England
0.6   Somewhere else (WRITE IN)
1.3   The North
0.9   Urban areas/cities
0.6   The South East
1.3   (Don't know)
3.3   (Refusal/not answered)

Q584   **VERSIONS A AND B: ASK ALL IN ENGLAND**   N=1929
       [ScotPayE]
       CARD
       Taking your answers from this card, please say how much you agree or disagree with this statement:
       Now that Scotland has its own parliament, it should pay for its services out of taxes collected in Scotland.
%
21.8   Agree strongly
52.3   Agree
11.7   Neither agree nor disagree
10.0   Disagree
0.4   Disagree strongly
3.8   (Don't know)
-      (Refusal/not answered)

National identity

Q586   **VERSIONS A AND B: ASK ALL**
       VERSIONS C: ASK ALL IN ENGLAND
       FIGURES REFER TO BRITISH RESPONDENTS ON VERSIONS A&B
       [CloseLoc]   N=2284
       CARD
       I would like you to think about how close you personally feel to different parts of the world, that is, how much you feel a sense of attachment and belonging to them.
       First of all, how closely attached do you feel to **your local area**?
       Please choose a phrase from the card.

Q587   **ASK ALL IN ENGLAND**
       [CloseReg]   N=3742
       CARD
       And how closely attached do you feel to *(government office region)* as a whole?

Q588   **VERSIONS A AND B: ASK ALL**
       VERSIONS C: ASK ALL IN ENGLAND
       FIGURES REFER TO BRITISH RESPONDENTS ON VERSIONS A&B
       [CloseESW]   N=2284
       CARD
       And how closely attached do you feel to *(England/Scotland/Wales)* as a whole?

Q589   **VERSION A AND B: ASK ALL**
       [CloseBr]   N=2284
       CARD
       And how closely attached do you feel to **Britain** as a whole?

Q590 [CloseEur] N=2284
CARD
And how closely attached do you feel to **Europe** as a whole?

	[CloseLoc]	[CloseReg]	[CloseESW]
	%	%	%
Very closely	42.1	27.6	40.6
Fairly closely	43.7	47.5	45.6
Not very closely	11.4	20.2	11.3
Not at all closely	2.4	4.2	2.1
(Don't know)	0.4	0.5	0.4
(Refused/Not answered)	-	-	-

	[CloseBr]	[CloseEur]	[CloseBR]
	%	%	%
Very closely	29.4	5.3	29.4
Fairly closely	50.8	29.6	50.8
Not very closely	16.1	45.2	16.1
Not at all closely	3.3	19.1	3.3
(Don't know)	0.4	0.8	0.4
(Refused/Not answered)	-	-	-

VERSION A: ASK ALL IN ENGLAND N=986

Q591 [SRSocC1E]
Do you ever think of yourself as belonging to any particular class?

%
IF YES: Which class is that?
18.7	Yes, middle class
25.9	Yes, working class
1.9	Yes, other (WRITE IN)
52.7	No
0.7	(Don't know)
0.1	(Refused/Not answered)

Q594 IF 'yes, other', 'no' OR DON'T KNOW AT [SRSocC1E]
[SRSocC2E] N=986
Most people say they belong either to the middle class or the working class. If you **had** to make a choice, would you call yourself ... READ OUT

%
18.2	... middle class
33.3	or, working class
3.6	(Don't know)
0.3	(Refused/Not answered)

VERSIONS A AND B: ASK ALL IN ENGLAND

Q596 [NatID] N=1929
CARD
Some people think of themselves first as British. Others may think of themselves first as English. Which, if any, of the following best describes how you see yourself?

%
16.8	English not British
19.1	More English than British
31.0	Equally English and British
13.3	More British than English
10.4	British not English
6.2	Other description (WRITE IN)
2.9	(None of these)
0.3	(Don't know)
0.1	(Refused/Not answered)

VERSIONS A AND B: ASK ALL

Q599 [GBPride] N=2284
CARD
How proud are you of being British, or do you not see yourself as British at all?

%
40.4	Very proud
37.4	Somewhat proud
9.9	Not very proud
2.9	Not at all proud
8.8	(Not British)
0.5	(Don't know)
-	(Refused/Not answered)

Q600

[NatPride]

VERSIONS A AND B: ASK ALL IN ENGLAND   N=1929

CARD

And how proud are you of being English, or do you not see yourself as English at all?

	%
Very proud	43.3
Somewhat proud	32.9
Not very proud	7.8
Not at all proud	2.2
(Not English)	13.2
(Don't know)	0.7
(Refused/Not answered)	-

Q601

[Ident1Eb]   N=1929

CARD

People differ in how they think of or describe themselves. If you had to pick just one thing from this list to describe yourself - something that is very important to you when you think of yourself - what would it be?

IF ANSWER GIVEN AT [Ident1Eb]

Q604

[Ident2Eb]   N=1929

CARD

And what would the second most important thing be?

IF ANSWER GIVEN AT [Ident2Eb]

Q607

[Ident3Eb]   N=1929

CARD

And what would the third most important thing be?

	[Ident1Eb]	[Ident2Eb]	[Ident3Eb]
	%	%	%
Working class	12.8	5.3	6.0
British	8.0	9.7	9.6
Elderly	2.2	2.5	2.2
A woman / A man	10.7	8.0	7.6
Not religious	0.7	1.6	2.1
A wife / A husband	6.0	14.6	9.3
A Catholic	1.1	1.0	1.4
A country person	2.3	3.3	3.7
A city person	1.0	1.2	2.5
A Protestant	0.1	0.4	0.7
A mother / A father	23.5	14.8	9.4
Middle class	2.2	3.2	2.7
Black	1.1	0.8	0.5
Retired	2.1	3.4	3.3
Religious	1.6	1.7	3.4
A working person	9.2	10.1	10.2
Young	2.9	3.1	5.4
White	1.2	2.6	4.3
English	6.3	6.9	7.5
Asian	1.1	1.0	0.5
Unemployed	0.5	0.5	0.7
Other (WRITE IN)	1.7	1.4	1.6
(None of these/No further answer)	1.3	2.5	4.7
(Don't know)	0.3	0.2	0.2
(Refused/Not answered)	-	0.3	0.5

Q610

VERSION A: ASK ALL IN ENGLAND   N=986

[FlagUJE]

CARD F16

I am going to show you two flags. First of all, here is the Union Jack. When you see the Union Jack, does it make you feel proud, hostile or do you not feel much either way?

IF PROUD/HOSTILE: Is that very proud/hostile or just a bit proud/hostile?

Q611 [FlagNatE]
CARD F17   N=986
And here is the cross of St George. When you see this, does it make you feel proud, hostile or do you not feel much either way?
IF PROUD/HOSTILE: Is that very proud/hostile or just a bit proud/hostile?

	[FlagUE]	[FlagNatE]
	%	%
Very proud	34.2	28.0
A bit proud	27.2	19.3
Does not feel much either way	35.7	48.7
A bit hostile	1.5	2.0
Very hostile	0.8	0.9
(It depends)	0.3	0.7
(Don't know)	0.3	0.4
(Refused/Not answered)	0.1	0.1

VERSIONS A AND B: ASK ALL

Q612 [Passport]
CARD   N=2284
Say you were allowed to choose the nationality that appears on your passport. Which one of the descriptions on this card would you choose?

	%
British	51.2
English	26.8
European	4.8
Irish	1.1
Northern Irish	0.2
Scottish	8.2
Ulster	0.1
Welsh	3.7
Other answer (WRITE IN)	2.6
(None of these)	1.0
(Don't know)	0.2
(Refused/Not answered)	-

VERSIONS A AND B: ASK ALL IN ENGLAND

Q615 [BEngScMo]   N=1929
CARD
I'd like you to think of someone who was born in Scotland but now lives permanently in England and said they were English. Taking your answer from this card ...
... do you think **most people** would consider them to be English?

Q616 [BEngScU]   N=1929
CARD
(Still thinking of someone who was born in Scotland but now lives permanently in England and said they were English...)
And do you think **you** would consider them to be English?

Q617 [NWhScMo]   N=1929
CARD
And now think of a non-white person living in England who spoke with an English accent and said they were English. (Still taking your answer from this card ...)
... do you think **most people** would consider them to be English?

Constitutional issues

Q620　**VERSIONS A AND B: ASK ALL**

[ScotPar2]　　　　　　　　　　　　　　　　　　*N=2284*

CARD

Which of these statements comes closest to your view?

%

7.8	Scotland should become independent, separate from the UK and the European Union
9.8	Scotland should become independent, separate from the UK but part of the European Union
50.5	Scotland should remain part of the UK, with its own elected parliament which has **some** taxation powers
8.2	Scotland should remain part of the UK, with its own elected parliament which has **no** taxation powers
12.8	Scotland should remain part of the UK **without** an elected parliament
10.8	(Don't know)
0.0	(Refused/Not answered)

Q621　[WelshAss]　　　　　　　　　　　　　　　*N=2284*

CARD

Which of these statements comes closest to your view?

%

7.1	Wales should become independent, separate from the UK and the European Union
8.9	Wales should become independent, separate from the UK but part of the European Union
35.9	Wales should remain part of the UK, with its own elected parliament which has law-making **and** taxation powers
18.9	Wales should remain part of the UK, with its own elected assembly which has limited law-making powers **only**
15.3	Wales should remain part of the UK **without** an elected assembly
13.8	(Don't know)
0.0	(Refused/Not answered)

Q618　[NWhScU]

CARD

(Still thinking of a non-white person living in England who spoke with an English accent and said they were English ...)

And do you think **you** would consider them to be English?

N=1929

	[BEngScMo]	[BEngScU]	[NWhScMo]
	%	%	%
Definitely would	5.9	10.0	8.6
Probably would	26.5	24.7	34.2
Probably would not	42.3	34.4	38.6
Definitely would not	22.3	27.7	15.8
(Don't know)	3.1	3.2	2.8
(Refused/Not answered)	0.1	–	–

	[NWhScU]
	%
Definitely would	27.6
Probably would	39.8
Probably would not	19.5
Definitely would not	10.9
(Don't know)	2.1
(Refused/Not answered)	–

Q622 [ESWGoGB]   N=2284
If in the future England, Scotland and Wales were all to become **separate independent countries**, rather than all being part of the United Kingdom together, would you be ... READ OUT ...

%
11.1   ... pleased,
47.8   sorry,
40.1   or, neither pleased nor sorry?
1.0   (Don't know)
0.0   (Refused/Not answered)

VERSIONS A AND B: ASK ALL IN ENGLAND

Q623 [SEBenGBE]   N=1929
On the whole, do you think that England's economy benefits more from having Scotland in the UK, or that Scotland's economy benefits more from being part of the UK, or is it about equal?

%
6.6   England benefits more
39.1   Scotland benefits more
39.6   Equal
2.9   (Neither/both lose)
11.8   (Don't know)
0.1   (Refused/Not answered)

Q624 [UKSpnGBE]   N=1929
CARD
Would you say that compared with other parts of the United Kingdom, Scotland gets **pretty much** its fair share of government spending, **more** than its fair share, or **less** than its fair share of government spending?
Please choose your answer from this card.

%
8.6   Much more than its fair share of government spending
13.2   A little more than its fair share of government spending
44.7   Pretty much its fair share of government spending
7.5   A little less than its fair share of government spending
0.8   Much less than its fair share of government spending
25.1   (Don't know)
0.1   (Refused/Not answered)

VERSIONS A AND B: ASK ALL

Q625 [NIreland]   N=2284
Do you think the long-term policy for Northern Ireland should be for it ... READ OUT ...

%
27.6   ...to remain part of the United Kingdom
54.9   or, to unify with the rest of Ireland?
0.6   Northern Ireland should be an independent state
0.0   Northern Ireland should be split up into two
3.1   It should be up to the Irish to decide
2.2   Other answer (WRITE IN)
11.4   (Don't know)
0.1   (Refused/Not answered)

English regions

ASK ALL IN ENGLAND

Q629 [RegPridE] N=3742
CARD
How much pride do you have in being someone who lives in (government office region) or do you not think of yourself in that way at all?

%
21.5 Very proud
24.5 Somewhat proud
4.1 Not very proud
1.4 Not at all proud
48.1 Don't think of themselves in that way
0.3 (Don't know)
0.0 (Refused/Not answered)

VERSION A: ASK ALL

Q630 [EngParl] N=1157
CARD F24
With all the changes going on in the way the different parts of Great Britain are run, which of the following do you think would be best for England ...READ OUT...

%
55.0 ...for England to be governed as it is now, with laws made by the UK parliament,
22.3 for each region of England to have its own assembly that runs services like health,
17.0 or, for England as a whole to have its own new parliament with law-making powers?
1.3 (None of these)
4.4 (Don't know)
0.0 (Refused/Not answered)

VERSION B: ASK ALL
VERSION C: ASK ALL IN ENGLAND
FIGURES REFER TO BRITISH RESPONDENTS ON VERSION B

Q631 [EngParl2] N=1127
CARD
With all the changes going on in the way the different parts of Great Britain are run, which of the following do you think would be best for England ...READ OUT...

%
55.4 ...for England to be governed as it is now, with laws made by the UK parliament,
21.9 for each region of England to have its own elected assembly that makes decisions about the region's economy, planning and housing,
16.5 or, for England as a whole to have its own new parliament with law-making powers?
1.7 (None of these)
4.4 (Don't know)
0.1 (Refused/Not answered)

ASK ALL IN ENGLAND

Q632 [HearRAss] N=3742
In recent years, the government has set up chambers or assemblies in each of the regions of England. How much have you heard about the work of the (government office region chamber or assembly) ... READ OUT

Q633 [HearRDA] N=3742
The government has also set up regional development agencies in each of the regions of England. How much have you heard about the work of the regional development agency in (government office region) ... READ OUT ...

	[HearRAss]	[HearRDA]
	%	%
...a great deal,	1.9	1.5
quite a lot,	6.1	7.1
not very much,	34.1	36.0
or nothing at all?	56.9	54.3
(Don't know)	0.9	0.9
(Refused/Not answered)	0.1	0.1

Q634 [SayInRE2]   N=3742
From what you have seen or heard so far, do you think
that having (regional chamber or assembly) for
(government office region) is giving ordinary people ... READ OUT ...
%
19.4 ...more of a say in how (government office region) is governed,
4.4   less say,
62.0 or, will it make no difference?
14.1 (Don't know)
0.1   (Refused/Not answered)

Q635 [ERegEcon]   N=3742
And as a result of having (regional chamber or
assembly) for (government office region) will the
region's economy become better, worse or will it
make no difference?
IF BETTER/WORSE: Is that a lot better/worse or a
little better/worse?
%
3.2   A lot better
19.4 A little better
57.8 No difference
2.9   A little worse
1.1   A lot worse
15.5 (Don't know)
0.1   (Refused/Not answered)

Q636 [DoesInfE]   N=3742
CARD
Taking your answers from this card, which of the
following do you think currently has most influence over the way England is
run?
%
1.4   English regional chambers or assemblies
76.2 The UK government at Westminster
7.9   Local councils in England
10.4 The European Union
4.0   (Don't know)
0.1   (Refused/Not answered)

Q637 [OughInfE]   N=3742
CARD
Taking your answers from this card, which do you
think ought to have
most influence over the way England is run?
%
10.6 English regional chambers or assemblies
14.4 A new English parliament
47.6 The UK government at Westminster
21.3 Local councils in England
1.4   The European Union
4.5   (Don't know)
0.1   (Refused/Not answered)

Q638 [ElecRAIn]   N=3742
CARD
What if there were elected regional assemblies in
each of the English regions, which made decisions
about the economy, planning and housing. Which do you
think would have most influence over the way England
is run
then?
%
28.4 Elected regional assemblies
43.0 The UK government at Westminster
18.0 Local councils in England
3.3   The European Union
7.1   (Don't know)
0.1   (Refused/Not answered)

Economic activity

Respondent's job

Q674　**ASK ALL**
[REconAct]　**(percentages refer to highest answer on the list)**
N=4432
Which of these descriptions applied to what you were doing last week, that is the seven days ending last Sunday?
PROBE: Which others? CODE ALL THAT APPLY
Multicoded (Maximum of 11 codes)

%
4.1　In full-time education (not paid for by employer, including on vacation)
0.3　On government training/employment programme
55.8　In paid work (or away temporarily) for at least 10 hours in week
0.4　Waiting to take up paid work already accepted
2.0　Unemployed and registered at a benefit office
1.4　Unemployed, **not** registered, but actively looking for a job (of at least 10 hrs a week)
0.7　Unemployed, wanting a job (of at least 10 hrs per week) but **not** actively looking for a job
4.4　Permanently sick or disabled
19.9　Wholly retired from work
10.5　Looking after the home
0.6　(Doing something else) (WRITE IN)
-　(Don't know)
-　(Refused/Not answered)

Q675　**ASK ALL NOT WORKING OR WAITING TO TAKE UP WORK**
[RLastJob]　N=1943
How long ago did you last have a paid job of at least 10 hours a week?
GOVERNMENT PROGRAMS/SCHEMES DO NOT COUNT AS 'PAID JOBS'.

%
17.9　Within past 12 months
21.2　Over 1, up to 5 years ago
17.3　Over 5, up to 10 years ago
22.0　Over 10, up to 20 years ago
14.7　Over 20 years ago
4.9　Never had a paid job of 10+ hours a week
0.4　(Don't know)
1.6　(Refused/Not answered)

Q676　**ASK ALL WHO HAVE EVER WORKED**
[Title]　**[NOT ON DATAFILE]**　N=4336
Now I want to ask you about your *(present/last/future)* job.
What *(is/was/will)* your job *(be)*?
PROBE IF NECESSARY: What *(is/was)* the name or title of the job?

Q677　[Typewk]　**[NOT ON DATAFILE]**　N=4336
What kind of work *(do/did/will)* you do most of the time?
IF RELEVANT: What materials/machinery *(do/did/will)* you use?

Q678　[Train]　**[NOT ON DATAFILE]**　N=4336
What training or qualifications *(are/were)* needed for that job?

Q679　[REmplyee]　N=4336
In your (main) job *(are/were/will)* you *(be)* ... READ OUT ...

%
88.6　... an employee,
10.5　or self-employed?
0.1　(Don't know)
0.9　(Refused/Not answered)

Q681

ASK ALL WHO HAVE EVER WORKED
[RSuperv]   N=4336
In your job, (do/did/will) you have any formal responsibility for supervising the work of other (employees/people)?
DO NOT INCLUDE PEOPLE WHO ONLY SUPERVISE:
- CHILDREN, E.G. TEACHERS, NANNIES, CHILDMINDERS
- ANIMALS
- SECURITY OR BUILDINGS, E.G. CARETAKERS, SECURITY GUARDS

%	
37.0	Yes
62.0	No
0.1	(Don't know)
0.9	(Refused/Not answered)

Q682

IF 'yes' AT [Supervise]
[RMany]   N=4336
How many?

%	
	Median:6 (Of those supervising any)
0.3	(Don't know)
0.9	(Refused/Not answered)

Q684

ASK ALL EMPLOYEES IN CURRENT/LAST JOB
[RocSect2]   N=3881
CARD G1
Which of the types of organisation on this card (do you work/did you work/will you be working) for?

%	
64.5	PRIVATE SECTOR FIRM OR COMPANY Including, for example, limited companies and PLCs
2.8	NATIONALISED INDUSTRY OR PUBLIC CORPORATION Including, for example, the Post Office and the BBC
27.8	OTHER PUBLIC SECTOR EMPLOYER /Incl eg: - Central govt/ Civil Service/ Govt Agency - Local authority/ Local Educ Auth (INCL 'OPTED OUT' SCHOOLS) - Universities - Health Authority / NHS hospitals / NHS Trusts/ GP surgeries - Police / Armed forces
3.4	CHARITY/ VOLUNTARY SECTOR Including, for example, charitable companies, churches, trade unions
0.3	Other answer (WRITE IN)
0.1	(Don't know)
1.0	(Refused/Not answered)

Q687

ASK ALL WHO HAVE EVER WORKED
[EmpMake]   N=4336
IF EMPLOYEE: What (does/did) your employer make or do at the place where you (will) usually work(ed) from?
IF SELF-EMPLOYED: What (do/did/will) you make or do at the place where you (will) usually work(ed) from?

Open Question (Maximum of 80 characters)

Q689

ASK ALL SELF-EMPLOYED IN CURRENT/LAST JOB
[SEmpNum]   N=469
In your work or business, (do/did/will) you have any employees, or not?
IF YES: How many?
IF 'NO EMPLOYEES', CODE 0.
FOR 500+ EMPLOYEES, CODE 500.
NOTE: FAMILY MEMBERS MAY BE EMPLOYEES ONLY IF THEY RECEIVE A REGULAR WAGE OR SALARY.
Median :0 employees
%
0.1   (Don't know)
3.1   (Refused/Not answered)

Q690

ASK ALL WHO HAVE EVER WORKED (FOR SELF EMPLOYED, DERIVED FROM [SEmpNum])
[REmpWork]   N=4336
Including yourself, how many people (are/were) employed at the place where you usually (work/worked/will work) (from)?
%
7.0   None
17.9   Under 10
13.8   10-24
23.3   25-99
21.4   100-499
14.5   500 or more
1.1   (Don't know)
0.9   (Refused/Not answered)

Q695

ASK ALL IN PAID WORK
[WkJbTim]   N=2472
In your present job, are you working ... READ OUT ...
RESPONDENT'S OWN DEFINITION
%
77.6   ... full-time,
22.3   or, part-time?
0.0   (Don't know)
-      (Refused/Not answered)

Q698

[WkJbHrsI]   N=2472
How many hours do you normally work a week in your main job - I any paid or unpaid overtime?
ROUND TO NEAREST HOUR.
IF RESPONDENT CANNOT ANSWER, ASK ABOUT LAST WEEK.
IF RESPONDENT DOES NOT KNOW EXACTLY, ACCEPT AN ESTIMATE.
FOR 95+ HOURS, CODE 95.
FOR 'VARIES TOO MUCH TO SAY', CODE 96.
Median: 39 hours
%
0.8   (Varies too much to say)
0.2   (Don't know)
-      (Refused/Not answered)

Q699

ASK ALL CURRENT EMPLOYEES
[EJbHrsX]   N=2164
What are your **basic or contractual hours** each week in your main job - **excluding** any paid and unpaid overtime?
ROUND TO NEAREST HOUR.
IF RESPONDENT CANNOT ANSWER, ASK ABOUT LAST WEEK.
IF RESPONDENT DOES NOT KNOW EXACTLY, ACCEPT AN ESTIMATE.
FOR 95+ HOURS, CODE 95.
FOR 'VARIES TOO MUCH TO SAY', CODE 96.
Median: 37 hours
%
2.1   (Varies too much to say)
1.4   (Don't know)
0.1   (Refused/Not answered)

Q700

ASK ALL WHO HAVE EVER WORKED BUT ARE NOT CURRENTLY WORKING
[ExPrtFul]   N=1848
(IS/Was/Will) the job (be) ... READ OUT ...
%
70.8   ... full-time - that is, 30 or more hours per week,
27.0   or, part-time?
0.1   (Don't know)
2.1   (Refused/Not answered)

Employment relations

Q720   **ASK ALL WHO HAVE EVER WORKED**   N=4436
[UnionSA]
(May I just check) are you **now** a member of a trade union or staff association?
CODE FIRST TO APPLY
%
19.2   Yes, trade union
2.6   Yes, staff association
77.1   No
0.2   (Don't know)
0.9   (Refused/Not answered)

Q721   IF 'no' OR DON'T KNOW AT [UnionSA]
[TUSAEver]   N=4436
Have you **ever** been a member of a trade union or staff association?
CODE FIRST TO APPLY
%
26.7   Yes, trade union
2.2   Yes, staff association
48.2   No
0.1   (Don't know)
1.1   (Refused/Not answered)

Q723   **VERSIONS B AND C: ASK ALL CURRENT EMPLOYEES**   N=1555
[EmploydT]
For how long have you been continuously employed by your present employer?
ENTER NUMBER. THEN SPECIFY MONTHS OR YEARS
Median: 48 months
%
0.1   (Don't know)
-      (Refused/Not answered)

Q726   **ASK ALL NOT WORKING**
[NPWork10]   N=1960
In the seven days ending last Sunday, did you have any paid work of less than 10 hours a week?
%
5.6   Yes
92.7   No
0.3   (Don't know)
1.3   (Refused/Not answered)

Q727   **VERSION B: ASK ALL CURRENT EMPLOYEES**   N=527
[WpUnions]
At your place of work are there unions, staff associations, or groups of unions recognised by the management for negotiating pay and conditions of employment?
IF YES, PROBE FOR UNION OR STAFF ASSOCIATION
IF 'BOTH', CODE '1'
%
45.5   Yes : trade union(s)
3.6   Yes : staff association
45.9   No, none
-      (Don't know)
5.1   (Refused/Not answered)

Q728   IF 'yes, trade unions' OR 'yes, staff association' AT [WpUnions]
[WpUnsure]   N=527
Can I just check: does management **recognise** these unions or staff associations for the purposes of negotiating **pay** and **conditions of employment**?
%
45.8   Yes
1.4   No
1.9   (Don't know)
5.1   (Refused/Not answered)

Q729   **VERSION C: ASK ALL CURRENT EMPLOYEES**   N=1030
[WpUnion3]
At your place of work are there any unions or staff associations?
IF ASKED: A union or staff association is any independent organisation that represents the interests of people at work.
IF YES, PROBE FOR UNION OR STAFF ASSOCIATION. CODE FIRST TO APPLY.
%
47.6   Yes : trade union(s)
5.3   Yes : staff association
43.6   No, none
3.4   (Don't know)
0.1   (Refused/Not answered)

Q730

IF 'yes, trade unions' OR 'yes, staff association' AT
[WpUnion3] N=1030
[UnionRec]
Does management recognise these unions or staff
associations for the
purposes of negotiating pay and conditions of
employment?

%
46.8 Yes
4.1 No
2.0 (Don't know)
3.5 (Refused/Not answered)

Q731

IF 'yes, trade unions' OR 'yes, staff association' AT
[WpUnions OR AT [WpUnion3] N=1030
[WpUnioW3]
On the whole, do you think (these unions do
their/this staff association
does its) job well or not?

%
32.0 Yes
14.6 No
6.2 (Don't know)
3.5 (Refused/Not answered)

Q732

[TUElig]
Are people doing your job eligible to join a union or
staff association at your workplace? N=1030
IF ASKED: A union or staff association is any
independent organisation that represents the
interests of people at work.
IF YES, PROBE FOR UNION OR STAFF ASSOCIATION. CODE
FIRST TO APPLY.

%
45.5 Yes : trade union(s)
4.4 Yes : staff association
1.8 No
1.2 (Don't know)
3.5 (Refused/Not answered)

Q733

VERSIONS B AND C: ASK ALL
[TUMstImp]
CARD G2 N=3276
Listed on this card are a number of things that trade
unions or staff associations can do. Which, if any,
do you think should be the **most**
important thing they should try to do?

%
4.7 Reduce pay differences in the workplace
7.4 Promote equality for women or for ethnic and other
minority groups
26.9 Represent individual employees in dealing with their
employer about problems at work
13.2 Protect existing employees' jobs
27.4 Improve working conditions across the workplace
11.9 Improve pay for all employees
2.8 Have an input into the running the business
2.0 (None of these)
3.5 (Don't know)
0.1 (Refused/Not answered)

Q734

VERSIONS B AND C: ASK ALL CURRENT EMPLOYEES
[IndRel] N=1557
In general how would you describe relations between
management and other
employees at your workplace ... READ OUT ...

%
35.1 ... very good,
46.3 quite good,
12.8 not very good,
4.9 or, not at all good?
0.8 (Don't know)
0.2 (Refused/Not answered)

VERSIONS B AND C: ASK ALL EXCEPT THOSE WHOLLY RETIRED OR PERMANENTLY SICK OR DISABLED

[NwEmpErn]   N=2470

IF IN PAID WORK: Now for some more general questions about your work. For some people their job is simply something they do in order to earn a living. For others it means much more than that. On balance, is your present job ... READ OUT ...

IF NOT IN PAID WORK: For some people work is simply something they do in order to earn a living. For others it means much more than that. In general, do you think of work as ... READ OUT ...

...just a means of earning a living,

or, does it mean much more to you than that?

(Don't know)

(Refused/Not answered)

Q735	%
	36.4
	61.9
	0.9
	0.8

VERSIONS B AND C: ASK ALL CURRENT EMPLOYEES

[SayJob]   N=1557

Suppose there was going to be some decision made at your place of work that changed the way you do your job. Do you think that **you personally** would have any say in the decision about the change, or not?

IF 'DEPENDS': Code as 'Don't know'

Yes

No

(Don't know)

(Refused/Not answered)

Q736	%
	57.8
	39.0
	3.0
	0.2

IF 'yes' AT [SayJob]

[MuchSay]   N=1557

How much say or chance to influence the decision do you think you would have ... READ OUT ...

...a great deal,

quite a lot,

or, just a little?

(Don't know)

(Refused/Not answered)

Q737	%
	14.7
	24.7
	18.3
	0.0
	3.2

VERSIONS B AND C: ASK ALL CURRENT EMPLOYEES

[PrefHr2]   N=1557

Thinking about the number of hours you work including regular overtime, would you prefer a job where you worked ... READ OUT ...

...more hours per week,

fewer hours per week,

or, are you happy with the number of hours you work at present?

(Don't know)

(Refused/Not answered)

Q738	%
	4.2
	32.7
	62.9
	0.1
	0.2

IF 'fewer hours per week' AT [PrefHr2]

[EarnHr2]   N=1557

Would you still prefer to work fewer hours, if it meant earning less money as a result?

Yes

No

It depends

(Don't know)

(Refused/Not answered)

Q739	%
	9.1
	21.5
	2.1
	-
	0.3

VERSIONS B AND C: ASK ALL CURRENT EMPLOYEES

[WkWorkHd]   N=1557

CARD G3

Which of these statements best describes your feelings about your job?

I only work as hard as I have to

I work hard, but not so that it interferes with the rest of my life

I make a point of doing the best I can, even if it sometimes does interfere with the rest of my life

(Don't know)

(Refused/Not answered)

Q740	%
	7.8
	46.5
	45.4
	0.1
	0.2

Q741-
Q744

CARD G4
Please tell me which, if any, of the times on this card you have worked in the last month in your main job.
CODE ALL THAT APPLY
Multicoded (Maximum of 4 codes)

N=1557

%		
50.0	Evenings between 6 and 8pm	[AntSocEv]
32.4	Nights after 8pm	[AntSocNi]
47.5	Saturdays	[AntSocSa]
34.4	Sundays	[AntSocSu]
32.5	None of these	[AntSocNo]
0.1	(Don't know)	
0.2	(Refused/Not answered)	

Q745

IF 'evenings' AT [AntiSocH]
[WkEvning]
CARD G5   N=1557
And about how many times did you work evenings between 6 and 8 pm last month, including Saturday or Sunday evenings?

Q746

IF 'nights' AT [AntiSocH]
[WkNights]
CARD G5 AGAIN   N=1557
And about how many times did you work after 8pm last month, including Saturday or Sunday nights?

	[WkEvning]	[WkNights]
	%	%
Once or twice	9.4	6.2
3 or 4 times	9.3	5.7
5-10 times	14.5	9.5
11-20 time	12.5	8.2
More than this	4.2	2.6
(Don't know)	0.0	0.1
(Refused/Not answered)	0.3	0.3

Q747

IF 'Saturdays' AT [AntiSocH]
[WkSatday]
CARD G6   N=1557
And about how many times did you work during the day on Saturday last month?

.3

Q748

IF 'Sundays' AT [AntiSocH]
[WkSunday]
CARD G6 AGAIN   N=1557
And about how many times did you work during the day on Sunday last month?

	[WkSatday]	[WkSunday]
	%	%
None	3.4	3.3
Once or twice	22.5	18.6
3 or 4 times	19.4	11.5
More than this	2.1	1.0
(Don't know)	0.0	0.0
(Refused/Not answered)	0.2	0.2

Q749

VERSIONS B AND C: ASK ALL CURRENT EMPLOYEES
[WorkTrav]
CARD G7   N=1557
On average, how much time do you spend travelling to work each day?
IF ASKED: GIVE TIME FOR JOURNEY TO WORK ONLY, NOT BOTH WAYS

%	
65.0	Less than 30 minutes
23.8	30 minutes - 1 hour
7.1	More than 1 hour - 2 hours
1.3	More than 2 hours
1.1	(I work from home)
1.6	(Varies too much to say)
0.0	(Don't know)
0.2	(Refused/Not answered)

Q750

VERSIONS A AND C: ASK ALL IN FIRST RANDOM HALF OF SAMPLE
[FrstJob1]
CARD   N=1668
Suppose you were advising a young person who was looking for his or her first job. Which one of these would you say is most important?

0.3

Q751

IF ANSWER GIVEN AT [FrstJob1]
[FrstJob2]   N=1668
CARD
(Still supposing you were advising a young person looking for his or her first job.)
And which next?

	[FrstJob1]	[FrstJob2]
	%	%
Good starting pay	6.0	12.5
A secure job for the future	34.9	17.6
Opportunities for promotion	11.7	23.2
Interesting work	38.7	18.6
Good working conditions	8.3	27.7
(Don't know)	0.2	0.1
(Refused/Not answered)	0.1	0.3

VERSIONS A AND C: ASK ALL IN SECOND RANDOM HALF OF SAMPLE

Q752

[FrstJb1c]   N=1637
CARD
Suppose you were advising a young person who was looking for his or her first job. Which **one** of these would you say is **most** important?

IF ANSWER GIVEN AT [FrstJb1c]

Q753

[FrstJb2c]   N=1637
CARD
(Still supposing you were advising a young person looking for his or her first job.)
And which **next**?

	[FrstJb1c]	[FrstJb2c]
	%	%
Good starting pay	12.1	12.1
A secure job for the future	18.5	18.5
Opportunities for promotion	22.0	22.0
Interesting work	22.5	22.5
A good work-life balance	19.8	19.8
A chance to help other people	4.3	4.3
(Don't know)	0.2	0.2
(Refused/Not answered)	0.6	0.6

Q754

VERSIONS A AND C: ASK ALL
[JobBsPy1]   N=3305
CARD
Suppose this young person had the ability to go into any of **these** careers. From what you know or have heard, which one of these careers would offer him or her the **best** **starting pay**?

Q755

IF ANSWER GIVEN AT [JobBsPy1]
[JobBsPy2]   N=3305
CARD
And which would offer him or her the **next best** starting pay?

Q756

VERSIONS A AND C: ASK ALL
[JobMInt1]   N=3305
CARD
Again, from what you know or have heard, which one of these careers would offer him or her the **most** **interesting work**?

Q757

IF ANSWER GIVEN AT [JobMInt1]
[JobMInt2]   N=3305
CARD
And which would offer him or her the **next most** interesting work?

Q758

VERSIONS A AND C: ASK ALL IN SECOND RANDOM HALF OF SAMPLE
[JobWkLif1]   N=1637
CARD
Again, from what you know or have heard, which one of these careers would offer him or her the **best** **work-life balance**?

Q759

IF ANSWER GIVEN AT [JobWkLf1]
[JobWkLf2]
CARD
And which would offer him or her the **next best** work-life balance?   N=1637

	[JobBsPy1]	[JobBsPy2]	[JobMInt1]
	%	%	%
Nurse	1.3	1.9	6.9
Computer engineer	31.8	20.0	6.9
School teacher	1.9	5.1	8.3
Lawyer	33.9	25.8	12.0
Police officer	9.7	10.3	16.8
Journalist	1.6	5.9	30.5
Doctor	15.5	25.6	13.9
(None of these)	0.2	0.1	0.7
(Don't know)	4.1	0.9	3.8
(Refused/Not answered)	0.1	4.2	0.1

	[JobMInt2]	[JobWkLf1]	[JobWkLf2]
	%	%	%
Nurse	9.2	3.0	8.4
Computer engineer	5.8	26.4	20.6
School teacher	11.7	28.6	16.1
Lawyer	16.2	15.7	16.6
Police officer	16.2	6.0	8.4
Journalist	21.0	6.6	12.0
Doctor	14.7	6.0	8.7
(None of these)	0.4	1.8	1.4
(Don't know)	0.8	5.6	2.1
(Refused/Not answered)	3.9	0.1	5.7

Students

Q760

[Digs]
ASK ALL IN FULL-TIME EDUCATION
Do you normally live at the same address during the term-time as during the holidays?   N=180

	%
Same address	77.4
Different addresses	21.7
(Varies too much to say)	0.9
(Don't know)	-
(Refused/Not answered)	-

Q761

[DigsPare]
IF 'different addresses' AT [Digs]   N=180
Can I just check, is **this** address your main term-time address or your main out-of-term address or neither?
INTERVIEWER: 'THIS ADDRESS' = SAMPLE ADDRESS

	%
Main term-time address	4.9
Main out-of-term address	16.5
Neither	0.3
(Don't know)	-
(Refused/Not answered)	-

Q762

[KeepDigs]   N=180
Thinking now of the period from mid June to mid July **this year**, (are/were) you keeping on your main term-time home for all or part of this period?
PROBE FOR CORRECT PRECODE

	%
All	7.3
Part	4.0
No	10.4
(Don't know)	-
(Refused/Not answered)	-

Q763
IF 'all' OR 'part' AT [KeepDigs]
[DigsWks]   N=20
How many weeks (do you plan/did you) spend in your
main term-time home from mid June to mid July this
year?
%   **Median: 2 weeks**
-    (Don't know)
-    (Refused/Not answered)

Q764
[PareWks]   N=20
How many weeks (do you plan/did you) spend in your
main out-of-term home from mid June to mid July this
year?
%   **Median: 2 weeks**
-    (Don't know)
-    (Refused/Not answered)

Prejudice

Racial prejudice

Q766   **ASK ALL**
        [PrejNow]   N=4432
        Do you think there is generally more racial prejudice
        in Britain now
        than there was 5 years ago, less, or about the same
%   amount?
44.7   More now
19.7   Less now
32.3   About the same
0.6   Other (WRITE IN)
2.6   (Don't know)
0.1   (Refused/Not answered)

Q769   [PrejFut]   N=4432
        Do you think there will be more, less, or about the
        same amount of
        racial prejudice in Britain in 5 years time compared
%   with now?
51.7   More in 5 years
17.7   Less
26.3   About the same
0.7   Other (WRITE IN)
3.5   (Don't know)
0.1   (Refused/Not answered)

Q772   [SRPrej]   N=4432
%   How would you describe yourself .... READ OUT ...
2.8   ... as very prejudiced against people of other races,
27.1   a little prejudiced,
68.7   or, not prejudiced at all?
0.9   Other (WRITE IN)
0.2   (Don't know)
0.2   (Refused/Not answered)

Sexual attitudes

Q775
VERSION C: ASK ALL
[PMS]
CARD G11
Now I would like to ask you some questions about sexual relationships. If a man and woman have sexual relations before marriage, what would your general opinion be?
N=2148

Q776
[YoungSex]
CARD G11 AGAIN
What if it was a boy and a girl who were both still **under 16**?
N=2148

Q777
[ExMS]
CARD G11 AGAIN
What about a **married person** having sexual relations with someone other than his or her partner?
N=2148

Q778
[HomoSex]
CARD G11 AGAIN
What about sexual relations between two adults of the same sex?
N=2148

	[PMS]	[YoungSex]	[ExMS]	[HomoSex]
	%	%	%	%
Always wrong	8.1	61.0	56.6	31.4
Mostly wrong	6.1	23.1	26.5	8.7
Sometimes wrong	10.5	9.1	10.6	9.2
Rarely wrong	8.6	2.2	0.9	6.7
Not wrong at all	62.6	2.4	1.7	36.5
(Depends/varies)	2.7	1.4	2.3	5.0
(Don't know)	0.9	0.4	0.8	2.0
(Refused/Not answered)	-	-	-	-

Genomics

Q780
VERSIONS B AND C: ASK ALL
[GenInt]
CARD H1
How much interest, if any, do you have in issues to do with genes and genetics?
N=3276

	%
A great deal	6.8
Quite a lot	16.9
Some	24.6
Not very much	23.7
None at all	27.4
(Don't know)	0.3
(Refused/Not answered)	0.3

Q781
[GenHeard]
CARD H2
Over the past few months, how much, if anything, have you **heard** or **read** about issues to do with genes and genetics?
N=3276

	%
A great deal	5.3
Quite a lot	30.6
A small amount	30.3
Not very much	17.6
Nothing at all	15.5
(Don't know)	0.3
(Refused/Not answered)	0.3

Q782
[GenTalk]
CARD H3
And over the past few months, how much, if at all, have you **talked** about issues to do with genes and genetics?
N=3276

0.5 0.5 0.5

0.5

Q783   [GenThink]
CARD H3 AGAIN   N=3276
Over the past few months, how much, if at all, have you thought about issues to do with genes and genetics?

	[GenTalk]	[GenThink]
	%	%
A great deal	2.1	3.1
Quite a lot	11.8	17.3
A small amount	26.6	25.6
Not very much	24.9	24.1
Not at all	34.0	29.3
(Don't know)	0.3	0.2
(Refused/Not answered)	0.4	0.4

Q784   [GKnowGov]
CARD H4   N=3276
How much do you feel you know about the way the government monitors and controls developments in modern genetic science?

	%
A great deal	1.9
Quite a lot	10.7
A small amount	19.8
Not very much	38.6
Nothing at all	25.3
(Don't know)	3.3
(Refused/Not answered)	0.4

Q785   [GenDSick]
CARD H5   N=3276
Samples of genetic information can be taken from people and the results kept in a database.
Would you be in favour of, or against, setting up such a database if it was....
...used to improve our understanding of illness and disease?

Q786   [GenDCrim]
CARD H5 AGAIN   N=3276
(and would you be in favour of, or against, setting up such a database if it was...)
..used to identify people who have committed serious crimes?

Q787   [GenDOrig]
CARD H5 AGAIN   N=3276
(and would you be in favour of, or against, setting up such a database if it was...)
...used by researchers to find out more about where people's ancestors originally came from?

Q788   [GenDInsu]
CARD H5 AGAIN   N=3276
(and would you be in favour of, or against, setting up such a database if it was...)
...used to judge a person's suitability for getting health and life insurance?

Q789   [GenDJob]
CARD H5 AGAIN   N=3276
(and would you be in favour of, or against, setting up such a database if it was...)
...used to judge a person's suitability for getting a job they've applied for?

Q790

[GenDCrm2]
CARD H5 AGAIN
Some people think everyone in Britain should have to give a sample of their genetic information to a database that would help identify people who have committed serious crimes.
Would you be in favour of, or against, this happening?

N=3276

	[GenDSick]	[GenDCrim]	[GenDOrig]
	%	%	%
Strongly in favour	32.8	43.1	11.7
In favour	52.7	41.7	39.0
Neither in favour or against	6.8	4.9	30.9
Against	3.8	5.4	12.2
Strongly against	1.6	2.5	3.6
(Don't know)	1.9	2.0	2.2
(Refused/Not answered)	0.4	0.4	0.4

	[GenDInsu]	[GenDJob]	[GenDCrm2]
	%	%	%
Strongly in favour	2.7	1.7	21.5
In favour	16.3	11.9	47.4
Neither in favour or against	15.0	11.3	8.2
Against	36.7	39.7	14.7
Strongly against	26.8	32.7	6.0
(Don't know)	2.1	2.3	1.7
(Refused/Not answered)			

Q791

[GenTest]
CARD H6
Genetic tests can be used to tell people whether they are likely to develop a serious genetic condition in the future. If such a test were easily available, would you want to find out your risk of developing such a condition if it could not be treated?

N=3276

	%
Definitely would	16.8
Probably would	21.5
Probably would **not**	28.1
Definitely would **not**	30.7
(Don't know)	2.5
(Refused/Not answered)	0.4

Q792

[GenMental]
CARD H7
Genetic tests can also be carried out on an unborn child. Do you agree or disagree with parents using such tests to help them decide whether or not to have a child that...
...has a serious mental disability and would never be able to live an independent life?

N=3276

Q793

[GnPhyscl]
CARD H7 AGAIN
(Do you agree or disagree with parents using such tests to help them decide whether or not to have a child that...)
...has a serious physical disability and would never be able to live an independent life?

N=3276

0.4

.5

Q794

[GnDieYng]
CARD H7 AGAIN
(Do you agree or disagree with parents using such tests to help them decide whether or not to have a child that...)
...has a condition that means it would live in good health but would then die in its 20s or 30s?

N=3276

Q795   [GnTissue]
CARD H7 AGAIN   N=3276
(Do you agree or disagree with parents using such tests to help them decide whether or not to have a child that...)
...has the same types of body tissues needed to treat a brother or sister who is seriously ill?

Q796   [GnGrlBoy]
CARD H7 AGAIN   N=3276
(Do you agree or disagree with parents using such tests to help them decide whether or not to have a child that...)
...is one sex rather than another?

	[GenMental]	[GnPhyscl]	[GnDieYng]
	%	%	%
Agree strongly	22.6	19.9	9.1
Agree	43.7	44.4	30.4
Neither agree nor disagree	12.5	13.6	21.4
Disagree	11.6	12.8	26.9
Disagree strongly	6.5	6.3	7.7
(Don't know)	2.6	2.6	4.1
(Refused/Not answered)	0.4	0.4	0.4

Q797   [GenCleve]
CARD H8   N=3276
Some things about a person are caused by their **genes**, which they inherit from their parents. Others may be to do with **the way they are brought up**, or **the way they live**. Some may happen just **by chance**.
Using this card, please say what **you** think decides each of the things that I am going to read out. If you don't know, please just say so.
...Firstly, a person's intelligence?

Q798   [GenHeart]
CARD H8 AGAIN   N=3276
And what do you think decides a person's chances ...
... of getting heart disease?
(If you don't know, please just say so).

Q799   [GenViol]
CARD H8 AGAIN   N=3276
(And what do you think decides a person's chances ...
... of being aggressive or violent?
(If you don't know, please just say so).

Q800   [GenGay]
CARD H8 AGAIN   N=3276
(And what do you think decides a person's chances ...
... of being gay or lesbian?
(If you don't know, please just say so).

Q801 [GenCanc]
CARD H8 AGAIN
(And what do you think decides a person's chances ...
... of getting breast cancer?
(If you don't know, please just say so).

N=3276

	[GenClever] %	[GenHeart] %
All to do with genes	8.7	8.9
Mostly to do with genes	21.3	24.3
Mostly to do with upbringing or lifestyle	17.2	15.1
All to do with upbringing or lifestyle	4.9	4.5
An equal mixture of genes and upbringing/lifestyle	35.0	34.6
Just chance	4.6	5.0
(Don't know)	7.9	7.2
(Refused/Not answered)	0.4	0.5

	[GenViol] %	[GenGay] %
All to do with genes	2.6	12.6
Mostly to do with genes	7.8	22.7
Mostly to do with upbringing or lifestyle	34.8	7.4
All to do with upbringing or lifestyle	4.2	15.2
An equal mixture of genes and upbringing/lifestyle	26.0	11.4
Just chance	4.8	19.9
(Don't know)	8.9	21.2
(Refused/Not answered)	0.4	0.6

	[GenCanc] %
All to do with genes	12.1
Mostly to do with genes	42.7
Mostly to do with upbringing or lifestyle	2.7
All to do with upbringing or lifestyle	0.7
An equal mixture of genes and upbringing/lifestyle	16.5
Just chance	11.4
(Don't know)	13.3
(Refused/Not answered)	0.4

Q802 [ChgViol]
CARD H9
Suppose it was discovered that a person's genes **could** be changed.
Taking your answers from this card, do **you** think this should be allowed or **not** allowed to ...
...make a person less aggressive or violent?

N=3276

Q803 [ChgGay]
CARD H9 AGAIN
(Do **you** think this should be allowed or **not** allowed to ...)
... make a person straight, rather than gay or lesbian?

N=3276

Q804 [ChgCanc]
CARD H9 AGAIN
(And should changing a person's genes be allowed or **not** allowed to ...)
... reduce a person's chances of getting breast cancer?

N=3276

Q805 [ChgSex]
CARD H9 AGAIN
(And should changing a person's genes be allowed or **not** allowed to...)
... determine the sex of an unborn baby?

N=3276

Q806 [ChgSick1]
CARD H9 AGAIN   N=3276
I'd like you to think of someone in their 20s who has a life-threatening medical condition. Suppose it were discovered that changing some of their genes by giving them an injection would help treat them. These new genes would not be passed onto any children they might have. Do you think this should be allowed or not allowed?

Q807 [ChgSick2]
CARD H9 AGAIN   N=3276
Now, what if the new genes were passed onto their future children to give them less chance of getting the same medical condition in their 20s? Do you think this should be allowed or not allowed?

	[ChgViol]	[ChgGay]	[ChgCanc]	[ChgSex]
	%	%	%	%
Definitely allowed	15.4	4.8	43.9	2.5
Probably allowed	40.0	13.5	36.8	12.2
Probably not allowed	21.5	25.6	8.2	24.1
Definitely not allowed	16.6	48.3	7.0	57.5
(Don't know)	6.1	7.3	3.7	3.3
(Refused/Not answered)	0.4	0.5	0.4	0.4

	[ChgSick1]	[ChgSick2]
	%	%
Definitely allowed	41.6	36.1
Probably allowed	43.3	42.5
Probably not allowed	5.8	10.0
Definitely not allowed	4.0	5.8
(Don't know)	4.9	5.1
(Refused/Not answered)	0.5	0.5

Q808 [GenTrst1]
CARD H10   N=3276
Please choose a phrase from this card to say how much you agree or disagree with this statement.
Those in charge of new developments in genetic science cannot be trusted to act in society's interests.

Q809 [GenTrst2]
CARD H10 AGAIN   N=3276
(Please choose a phrase from this card to say how much you agree or disagree with this statement.)
Rules set by government will keep us safe from any risks linked to modern genetic science.

Q810 [GenTrst3]
CARD H10 AGAIN   N=3276
(Please choose a phrase from this card to say how much you agree or disagree with this statement.)
Modern genetic science is so complex that public involvement in policy decisions is not realistic.

Q811 [GenTrst4]
CARD H10 AGAIN   N=3276
(Please choose a phrase from this card to say how much you agree or disagree with this statement.)
Genetic scientists only tend to tell us what the people paying their wages want us to hear.

	[GenTrst1]	[GenTrst2]	[GenTrst3]	[GenTrst4]
	%	%	%	%
Agree strongly	7.0	1.5	6.6	13.5
Agree	26.5	21.1	43.2	46.0
Neither agree nor disagree	35.9	26.9	18.0	20.7
Disagree	22.7	37.2	22.9	13.7
Disagree strongly	2.1	7.3	3.8	0.8
(Don't know)	5.2	5.5	5.0	4.8
(Refused/Not answered)	0.5	0.5	0.5	0.6

Q812 [GenQuiz1] *(This is false)*   N=3276
Now for a quick quiz about genetics. For each of the following statements, please tell me whether you think it is true or false. If you don't know, just say so and we'll go on to the next one.
By eating a genetically modified fruit, a person's genes could also become modified.

Q813 [GenQuiz2] (This is true)   N=3276
(Is it true or false that...)
It is possible to transfer animal genes into plants.

Q814 [GenQuiz3] (This is false)   N=3276
(Is it true or false that...)
Ordinary tomatoes do not contain genes, while
genetically modified tomatoes do.

Q815 [GenQuiz4] (This is true)   N=3276
(Is it true or false that...)
It is the father's genes that determine whether a
child is a girl.

	[GenQuiz1]	[GenQuiz2]	[GenQuiz3]	[GenQuiz4]
	%	%	%	%
True	6.8	22.2	11.8	44.2
False	58.3	31.6	42.3	25.4
Don't know	32.3	43.7	43.2	28.4
(Don't know)	2.1	1.9	2.1	1.4
(Refused/Not answered)	0.6	0.6	0.6	0.6

Q817 [GenFamil]   N=3276
Has a **doctor** ever advised you, or any member of your
immediate family, of a serious genetic condition in
your family?
FOR 'NOT SURE', CODE DON'T KNOW.

%
9.3 Yes
89.1 No
1.1 (Don't know)
0.6 (Refused/Not answered)

Immigration

VERSION B: ASK ALL

Q818 [MusKnowB]   N=1127
People from lots of different backgrounds live in
Britain. I would now like to ask you some questions
about one of these groups - Muslims. By Muslims I
mean people who follow the Islamic faith.
Generally speaking, how much would you say you know
about Muslim people in Britain ...READ OUT...

%
2.1 ...a great deal,
13.5 quite a lot,
60.2 not very much,
23.0 or, nothing at all?
0.0 (Don't know)
1.1 (Refused/Not answered)

Q819 [CommitMB]   N=1127
Please look at CARD H11
Some people think that **Muslims living in Britain are
really committed to Britain**, these people would put
themselves in box 1 (INTERVIEWER: POINT TO BOX 1 ON
THE SHOW CARD).
Other people feel that **Muslims in Britain could never
be really committed to Britain** and would put
themselves in box 7 (INTERVIEWER: POINT TO BOX 7).
Other people have views somewhere in between in boxes
2 to 6 (INTERVIEWER: POINT TO BOXES 2-6).
Please can you tell me which number comes closest to
your own views about whether **Muslims in Britain** are really committed
to Britain or not?

%
3.3 1 - are really committed to Britain
8.1 2
16.6 3
22.1 4
16.2 5
9.9 6
16.9 7 - could never be really committed to Britain
5.6 (Don't know)
1.4 (Refused/Not answered)

Q820 [TakeJbMB]   N=1127
Please look at CARD H12
(Some people think that **Muslims who come to live in Britain take jobs, housing and health care** from other people in Britain, these people would put themselves in box 1.
Other people feel that **Muslims in Britain contribute a lot in terms of hard work and much needed skills** and would put themselves in box 7.
Other people have views somewhere in between in boxes 2 to 6.)
Please can you tell me which number comes closest to **your own** views about whether **Muslims who come to live in Britain** take jobs, housing and health care or whether they contribute a lot in terms of hard work and much needed skills?

%	
10.3	1 - take jobs, housing & healthcare
6.8	2
12.6	3
25.6	4
17.3	5
13.2	6
7.5	7 - contribute a lot in terms of hard work & skills
5.5	(Don't know)
1.2	(Refused/Not answered)

Q821 [Terror]   N=1127
CARD H13
How much do you agree or disagree with the following statement:
Muslims living in Britain have done **a great deal** to condemn Islamic terrorism

Q822 [LoyalMuB]   N=1127
CARD H13 AGAIN
(How much do you agree or disagree with the following statement):
British Muslims are more loyal to other Muslims around the world than they are to other people in this country

Q823 [IDLoseM]   N=1127
CARD H13 AGAIN
(How much do you agree or disagree with the following statement:)
(England/Scotland/Wales) would begin to lose its identity if more Muslims came to live in (England/Scotland/Wales).

	[Terror]	[LoyalMuB]	[IDLoseM]
	%	%	%
Agree strongly	3.5	15.5	17.1
Agree	21.4	40.5	31.0
Neither agree nor disagree	30.4	23.4	17.0
Disagree	26.5	10.4	26.1
Disagree strongly	8.7	0.8	4.1
(Don't know)	8.2	8.1	3.4
(Refused/Not answered)	1.2	1.2	1.2

Q824 [MarrMus]   N=1127
CARD H14
How would you feel if a close relative of yours married or formed a long-term relationship with a Muslim?

%	
9.4	Very happy
18.7	Happy
41.8	Neither happy nor unhappy
14.2	Unhappy
10.4	Very unhappy
2.9	(It depends)
1.5	(Don't know)
1.1	(Refused/Not answered)

Q825 [ConMusEn]   N=1127
CARD H15
Thinking now about Muslims and non-Muslims in England. How serious would you say conflict between them is?

Q826   [ConMusWd]   N=1127
CARD H15 AGAIN
And what about Muslims and non-Muslims across the world?
(How serious would you say conflict between them is?)

	[ConMusEn] %	[ConMusWd] %
Very serious conflict	9.7	29.2
Fairly serious conflict	45.6	48.3
Not very serious conflict	32.5	14.0
There is not conflict	3.0	0.7
(Don't know)	7.9	6.7
(Refused/Not answered)	1.2	1.1

Q827   [LivBrit]   N=1127
CARD H16
People have different views about what it takes to be truly British. Some say that as well as living in Britain, to be truly British you have to have been **born in Britain**.
How much do you agree or disagree with this?

Q828   [WhiBrit]   N=1127
CARD H16 AGAIN
And some say that as well as living in Britain, to be truly British you have to be **white** – **rather than Black or Asian**.
How much do you agree or disagree with this?

Q829   [LivNat]   N=1127
CARD H16 AGAIN
And some people have different views about what it takes to be truly (English/Scottish/Welsh). Some say that as well as living in (England/Scotland/Wales), to be truly (English/Scottish/Welsh) you have to have been born in (England/Scotland/Wales).
(How much do you agree or disagree with this?)

Q830   [WhiNat]   N=1127
CARD H16 AGAIN
And some say that as well as living in (England/Scotland/Wales), to be truly (English/Scottish/Welsh) you have to be **white** – **rather than Black or Asian**.
(How much do you agree or disagree with this?)

	[LivBrit] %	[WhiBrit] %	[LivNat] %	[WhiNat] %
Agree strongly	16.9	4.7	14.0	5.3
Agree	35.9	9.7	38.6	12.7
Neither agree nor disagree	12.6	12.4	10.1	13.0
Disagree	44.4	28.3	42.2	26.8
Disagree strongly	5.9	26.4	6.6	24.4
(Don't know)	0.8	1.2	1.3	1.3
(Refused/Not answered)	1.1	1.2	1.1	1.1

Transport

VERSION A: ASK ALL

Q831　[TransCar]　　　　　　　　　　　　　N=1157

(May I just check...) ... do you, or does anyone in your household, own or have the regular use of a car or a van?

%　IF 'YES' PROBE FOR WHETHER RESPONDENT, OR OTHER PERSON(S) ONLY, OR BOTH

28.1　Yes, respondent only
16.7　Yes, other(s) only
36.5　Yes, both
18.5　No
0.1　(Don't know)
0.0　(Refused/Not answered)

IF 'yes, respondent', 'yes, both', DON'T KNOW OR REFUSAL AT [TransCar]

Q832　[GetAbB2]　　　　　　　　　　　　　N=1157
CARD H1

I am going to read out some of the things that might get people to **cut down** on the number of car journeys they take. For each one, please tell me what effect, if any, this might have on how much **you yourself** use the car to get about.

..greatly improving **long distance** rail and coach services?

Q833　[GetAbB3]　　　　　　　　　　　　　N=1157
CARD H1 AGAIN

(What effect, if any, might this have on how much **you yourself** use the car)

..greatly improving the reliability of **local** public transport?

Q834　[GetAbB4]　　　　　　　　　　　　　N=1157
CARD H1 AGAIN

(What effect, if any, might this have on how much **you yourself** use the car)

..charging all motorists around £2 each time they enter or drive through a city or town centre at peak times?

Q835　[GetAbB5]　　　　　　　　　　　　　N=1157
CARD H1 AGAIN

(What effect, if any, might this have on how much **you yourself** use the car)

..charging £1 for every 50 miles motorists travel on motorways?

Q836　[GetAbB11]　　　　　　　　　　　　N=1157
CARD H1 AGAIN

(What effect, if any, might this have on how much **you yourself** use the car)

..increasing parking costs in town and city centres?

Q837　[GetAbB12]　　　　　　　　　　　　N=1157
CARD H1 AGAIN

(What effect, if any, might this have on how much **you yourself** use the car)

..charging all motorists around £5 each time they enter or drive through a city or town centre at peak times?

	[GetAbB2]	[GetAbB3]	[GetAbB4]	[GetAbB5]
	%	%	%	%
Might use car even more	0.9	0.2	0.5	0.7
Might use car a little				
less	18.2	18.8	16.4	14.4
Might use car quite a				
bit less	11.7	15.7	14.4	10.9
Might give up using car	2.3	4.1	3.6	2.6
It would make no difference	31.1	25.6	29.4	35.2
(Don't know)	0.4	0.2	0.4	0.8
(Refused/Not answered)	0.1	0.1	0.1	0.1

	[GetAbB11]	[GetAbB12]
	%	%
Might use car even more	0.3	0.5
Might use car a little less	17.9	14.4
Might use car quite a bit less	10.8	17.6
Might give up using car	4.5	8.3
It would make no difference	30.7	23.4
(Don't know)	0.4	0.3
(Refused/Not answered)	0.1	0.1

Q838 [GetBoth1]
CARD H1b   N=1157
Now suppose that the two things on this card were done **at the same time**. What effect, if any, might this have on how much you yourself use the car?
First, charging motorists £2 for entering town centres at peak times **but at the same time** greatly improving the reliability of local public transport?

%
0.3   Might use car even more
16.8   Might use car a little less
22.3   Might use car quite a bit less
7.0   Might give up using car
17.6   It would make no difference
0.5   (Don't know)
0.1   (Refused/Not answered)

VERSION A: ASK ALL

Q839 [Drive]   N=1157
May I just check, do you yourself drive a car at all these days?

%
68.7   Yes
31.1   No
0.1   (Don't know)
0.1   (Refused/Not answered)

IF 'yes' AT [Drive]

Q840 [Travel1]
CARD H2   N=1157
How often nowadays do you **usually** travel ...by car as a driver?

VERSION A: ASK ALL

Q841 [Travel2]
CARD H2 AGAIN   N=1157
(How often nowadays do you **usually**) ...travel by car as a passenger?

Q842 [Travel3]
CARD H2 AGAIN   N=1157
(How often nowadays do you **usually**) ...travel by local bus?

Q843 [Travel4]
CARD H2 AGAIN   N=1157
(How often nowadays do you **usually**) ...travel by train?

Q844 [Travel6]
CARD H2 AGAIN   N=1157
(How often nowadays do you **usually**) ...travel by bicycle?

Q845 [Travel9]
CARD H2 AGAIN   N=1157
(How often nowadays do you **usually**) ...go somewhere on foot at least 15 minutes' walk away?

	[Travel1]	[Travel2]	[Travel3]
	%	%	%
Every day or nearly every day	49.2	11.9	7.0
2-5 days a week	13.5	23.1	10.0
Once a week	3.4	21.9	7.1
Less often but at least once a month	1.8	15.6	9.3
Less often than that	0.4	12.5	16.2
Never nowadays	0.4	14.6	50.0
(Don't know)	–	0.2	0.1
(Refused/Not answered)	0.2	0.1	0.1

	[Travel4]	[Travel6]	[Travel9]
	%	%	%
Every day or nearly every day	2.8	4.8	31.2
2-5 days a week	2.2	2.9	24.7
Once a week	3.8	5.0	15.8
Less often but at least once a month	13.4	3.4	7.8
Less often than that	32.8	7.9	15.2
Never nowadays	44.8	75.8	5.1
(Don't know)	0.1	0.1	0.1
(Refused/Not answered)	0.1	0.1	0.1

Q846   [TrnNear]
        CARD H3   N=1157
        About how far do you live from your **nearest** railway
        station?
%
23.5   Less than ½ mile (15 mins walk)
20.0   ½ up to 1 mile (15-30 mins walk)
30.7   Over 1 mile, up to 3 miles
19.1   Over 3 miles, up to 10 miles
5.7   Over 10 miles
0.9   (Don't know)
0.1   (Refused/Not answered)

Q847   [AirTrvl]   N=1157
        And how many trips did you make by plane during the
        last 12 months? Please count the outward and return
        flight and any transfers as one trip.
        INTERVIEWER WRITE IN ANSWER
        ACCEPT BEST ESTIMATE IF NECESSARY
        Median: 1 trip
%
0.1   (Don't know)
0.1   (Refused/Not answered)

Classification

Housing and local area

Q848   **ASK ALL**
        [Tenure1]   N=4432
        Does your household own or rent this accommodation?
        PROBE IF NECESSARY
        IF OWNS: Outright or on a mortgage? IF RENTS: From
%   whom?
29.4   Owns outright
42.4   Buying on mortgage
12.6   Rents: local authority
0.1   Rents: New Town Development Corporation
5.8   Rents: Housing Association
1.2   Rents: property company
0.5   Rents: employer
0.8   Rents: other organisation
0.6   Rents: relative
4.6   Rents: other individual
0.3   Rents: Housing Trust
0.2   Rent free, squatting
0.6   Other (WRITE IN)
0.2   (Don't know)
0.6   (Refused/Not answered)

Q852   [ResPres]   N=4432
        Can I just check, would you describe the place where
        you live as ...
        READ OUT ...
%
9.2   ...a big city,
21.8   the suburbs or outskirts of a big city,
50.8   a small city or town,
15.1   a **country** village,
2.1   or, a farm or home in the country?
0.5   (Other answer (WRITE IN))
0.1   (Don't know)
0.5   (Refused/Not answered)

Q855   **VERSION A AND B: ASK ALL**
[RSpBorn]   N=2284
Were (either) you (or your husband/wife/partner) born outside (England/Wales/Scotland)?
IF YES: PROBE FOR CORRECT PRECODE
%
12.3   Yes - respondent (only) born outside (England/Wales/Scotland)
4.9   (Yes - husband/wife/partner only born outside (England/Wales/Scotland))
5.4   (Yes - both respondent **and** husband/wife/partner born outside (England/Wales/Scotland))
76.7   No
0.0   (Don't know)
0.6   (Refused/Not answered)

Q856   [RLivEls2]
N=2284
Have you ever lived anywhere other than (England/Wales/Scotland) for more than a year?
IF YES: Where was that? PROBE TO IDENTIFY CORRECT CODE
ELSEWHERE IN UK = (SCOTLAND/WALES/ENGLAND), N. IRELAND, CHANNEL ISLANDS, ISLE OF MAN
%
71.5   No - have never lived anywhere outside (England/Wales/Scotland) for more than a year
7.7   Yes - elsewhere in UK
15.9   Yes - outside UK
4.2   Yes - elsewhere in UK and outside UK
0.0   (Don't know)
0.6   (Refused/Not answered)

Q857   [ParBorn]
N=2284
And was either or both of your parents born outside (England/Wales/Scotland)?
IF YES: One or both?
%
70.0   Neither parent born outside (England/Wales/Scotland)
11.5   Yes - one parent born outside (England/Wales/Scotland)
17.6   Yes - both parents born outside (England/Wales/Scotland)
0.2   (Don't know)
0.6   (Refused/Not answered)

Q858   [LiveArea]
N=2284
How long have you lived in the (town/city/village) where you live now?
PROBE FOR BEST ESTIMATE
ENTER **TOTAL** NUMBER OF YEARS IN TOWN/CITY/VILLAGE
FOR LESS THAN ONE YEAR, CODE 0
Median : 20
%
0.0   (Don't know)
0.6   (Refused/Not answered)

Religion, national identity and race

Q866   **ASK ALL**
[Religion]
N=4432
Do you regard yourself as belonging to any particular religion?
IF YES: Which?
CODE ONE ONLY - DO NOT PROMPT
%
43.0   No religion
6.6   Christian - no denomination
8.9   Roman Catholic
26.6   Church of England/Anglican
1.0   Baptist
1.7   Methodist
3.4   Presbyterian/Church of Scotland
0.2   Other Christian
1.1   Hindu
0.8   Jewish
2.7   Islam/Muslim
0.7   Sikh
0.3   Buddhist
0.4   Other non-Christian
0.0   Free Presbyterian
0.1   Brethren
0.3   United Reform Church (URC)/Congregational
1.3   Other Protestant
0.4   (Refusal)
0.1   (Don't know)
0.3   (Refusal/Not answered)

Q869 — IF NOT REFUSED AT [Religion]

[FamRelig]   N=4432

In what religion, if any, were you brought up?
PROBE IF NECESSARY: What was your family's religion?
CODE ONE ONLY - DO NOT PROMPT

%
14.4 No religion
7.4   Christian - no denomination
13.2 Roman Catholic
43.8 Church of England/Anglican
1.6   Baptist
4.5   Methodist
6.3   Presbyterian/Church of Scotland
0.3   Other Christian
1.1   Hindu
0.9   Jewish
2.8   Islam/Muslim
0.8   Sikh
0.2   Buddhist
0.1   Other non-Christian
0.1   Free Presbyterian
0.1   Brethren
0.5   United Reform Church (URC)/Congregational
1.1   Other Protestant
0.1   (Don't know)
0.3   (Refusal/Not answered)

Q877 — IF RELIGION GIVEN AT [RelRFW] OR AT [RelFFW]

[ChAttend]   N=4432

Apart from such special occasions as weddings, funerals and baptisms, how often nowadays do you attend services or meetings connected with your religion?
PROBE AS NECESSARY.

%
11.9 Once a week or more
2.1   Less often but at least once in two weeks
5.0   Less often but at least once a month
8.6   Less often but at least twice a year
5.0   Less often but at least once a year
3.7   Less often than once a year
48.6 Never or practically never
0.9   Varies too much to say
0.0   (Don't know)
0.5   (Refusal/Not answered)

Q878-Q885 — ASK ALL

CARD X1   N=4432

Please say which, if any, of the words on this card describes the way you think of yourself. Please choose as many or as few as apply.
PROBE: Any other?
Multicoded (Maximum of 8 codes)

%
67.1 British   [NatBrit]
50.8 English   [NatEng]
12.3 European   [NatEuro]
2.5   Irish   [NatIrish]
0.4   Northern Irish   [NatNI]
10.4 Scottish   [NatScot]
0.3   Ulster   [NatUlst]
5.5   Welsh   [NatWelsh]
3.4   Other answer (WRITE IN)   [NatOth]
1.1   (None of these)   [NatNone]
1.5   EDIT ONLY: Other Asian mentioned   [NatAsia]
1.3   EDIT ONLY: Other African/Caribbean mentioned   [NatAfric]
0.0   (Don't know)
0.5   (Refusal/Not answered)

Q912 — ASK ALL

[RaceOri2]   N=4432
CARD X2

To which of these groups do you consider you belong?

%
1.3   BLACK: of African origin
1.2   BLACK: of Caribbean origin
0.1   BLACK: of other origin (WRITE IN)
2.1   ASIAN: of Indian origin
1.3   ASIAN: of Pakistani origin
0.2   ASIAN: of Bangladeshi origin
0.3   ASIAN: of Chinese origin
0.7   ASIAN: of other origin (WRITE IN)
89.9 WHITE: of any European origin
0.9   WHITE: of other origin (WRITE IN)
1.1   MIXED ORIGIN (WRITE IN)
0.4   OTHER (WRITE IN)
0.1   (Don't know)
0.5   (Refusal/Not answered)

Education

Q923
ASK ALL
[RPrivEd]   N=4432
Have you ever attended a fee-paying, **private** primary or secondary school in the United Kingdom?
'PRIVATE' PRIMARY OR SECONDARY SCHOOLS INCLUDE:
*INDEPENDENT SCHOOLS
*SCHOLARSHIPS AND ASSISTED PLACES AT FEE-PAYING SCHOOLS
THEY EXCLUDE:
*DIRECT GRANT SCHOOLS (UNLESS FEE-PAYING)
*VOLUNTARY-AIDED SCHOOLS
*GRANT-MAINTAINED ('OPTED OUT') SCHOOLS
*NURSERY SCHOOLS

%
10.8 Yes
88.6 No
0.1   (Don't know)
0.5   (Refusal/Not answered)

Q925
IF NO CHILDREN IN HOUSEHOLD (AS GIVEN IN THE HOUSEHOLD GRID)
[OthChld3]   N=4432
Have you ever been responsible for bringing up any children of school age, including stepchildren?

%
31.9 Yes
33.6 No
0.0   (Don't know)
0.3   (Refusal/Not answered)

Q924
IF CHILDREN IN HOUSEHOLD (AS GIVEN IN HOUSEHOLD GRID) OR 'yes' AT [OthChld3]
[ChPrivEd]   N=4432
And (have any of your children/ has your child) ever attended a fee-paying, **private** primary or secondary school in the United Kingdom?
'PRIVATE' PRIMARY OR SECONDARY SCHOOLS INCLUDE:
*INDEPENDENT SCHOOLS
*SCHOLARSHIPS AND ASSISTED PLACES AT FEE-PAYING SCHOOLS
THEY EXCLUDE:
*DIRECT GRANT SCHOOLS (UNLESS FEE-PAYING)
*VOLUNTARY-AIDED SCHOOLS
*GRANT-MAINTAINED ('OPTED OUT') SCHOOLS
*NURSERY SCHOOLS

%
8.0   Yes
57.8 No
0.0   (Don't know)
0.5   (Refusal/Not answered)

Q930
[TEA]   N=4432
How old were you when you completed your continuous full-time education?
PROBE IF NECESSARY
'STILL AT SCHOOL' - CODE 95
'STILL AT COLLEGE OR UNIVERSITY' - CODE 96
'OTHER ANSWER' - CODE 97 AND WRITE IN

%
31.6 15 or under
26.9 16
8.9   17
9.5   18
20.1 19 or over
0.2   Still at school
1.9   Still at college or university
0.2   Other answer (WRITE IN)
0.1   (Don't know)
0.5   (Refusal/Not answered)

Q931   [SchQual]
CARD X3
Have you passed any of the examinations on this card?

%
Yes   64.3
No   35.1
(Don't know)   0.1
(Refusal/Not answered)   0.5

IF 'yes' AT [SchQual]   N=4432
CARD X3 AGAIN Please tell me which sections of the card they are in?
PROBE : Any other sections?
CODE ALL THAT APPLY
Multicoded (Maximum of 4 codes)

Q932-
Q935

%

Section 1:   [Edqual1]
GCSE Grades D-G/Short course GCSE
CSE Grades 2-5
O-level Grades D-E or 7-9
Scottish (SCE) Ordinary Bands D-E
Scottish Standard Grades 4-7
SCOTVEC/SQA National Certificate modules
School leaving certificate (no grade)

30.8

Section 2:   [Edqual2]
GCSE Grades A-C
CSE Grade 1
O-level Grades A-C or 1-6
School Certif/Matriculation
Scottish SCE Ord. Bands A-C or pass
Scottish Standard Grades 1-3 or Pass
Scottish School Leaving Certificate Lower Grade
SUPE Ordinary
N Ireland Junior Certificate

46.6

Section 3:   [Edqual3]
A-level, S-level, A2-level, AS-level
Vocational A-level (AVCE)
Scottish Higher/ Higher-Still Grades
Scottish SCE/SLC/SUPE at Higher Grade
Scot. Higher School Certif
Certif Sixth Year Studies/ Advanced Higher Grades
N Ireland Senior Certificate

23.7

Section 4:   [Edqual4]
Overseas school leaving exam or certificate
(Don't know)
(Refusal/Not answered)

3.3
-
0.6

Q936

ASK ALL
[PschQual]
CARD X4   N=4432
And have you passed any of the exams or got any of
the qualifications on
this card?

	%
Yes	56.5
No	43.0
(Don't know)	0.1
(Refusal/Not answered)	0.5

Q937–
Q961

[PSchQFW]
CARD X4 AGAIN Which ones? PROBE: Which others?   N=4432
PROBE FOR CORRECT LEVEL
Multicoded (Maximum of 25 codes)

%		
1.3	Foundation/advanced **modern** apprenticeship **completed**	[EdQual26]
3.3	Other recognised trade apprenticeship **completed**	[EdQual27]
3.3	OCR/RSA - (Vocational) Certificate	[EdQual28]
2.6	OCR/RSA - (First) Diploma	[EdQual29]
1.3	OCR/RSA - Advanced Diploma	[EdQual30]
0.5	OCR/RSA - Higher Diploma	[EdQual31]
1.8	Other clerical, commercial qualification	[EdQual32]
6.5	City&Guilds Certif - Level 1/ Part I	[EdQual22]
6.0	City&Guilds Certif - Level 2/ Craft/ Intermediate/ Ordinary/ Part II	[EdQual23]
3.8	City&Guilds Certif - Level 3/ Advanced/ Final/ Part III	[EdQual24]
2.0	City&Guilds Certif - Level 4/ Full Technological/ Part IV	[EdQual25]
1.1	Edexcel/BTEC First Certificate	[EdQual33]
1.1	Edexcel/BTEC First/General Diploma	[EdQual34]
4.4	Edexcel/BTEC/BEC/TEC (General/Ordinary) National Certif or Diploma (ONC/OND)	[EdQual10]
4.8	Edexcel/BTEC/BEC/TEC **Higher** National Certif (HNC) or Diploma (HND)	[EdQual11]
3.2	NVQ/SVQ Lev 1/GNVQ/GSVQ Foundation lev	[EdQual17]
5.8	NVQ/SVQ Lev 2/GNVQ/GSVQ Intermediate lev	[EdQual18]
4.4	NVQ/SVQ Lev 3/GNVQ/GSVQ Advanced lev	[EdQual19]
0.6	NVQ/SVQ Lev 4	[EdQual20]
0.2	NVQ/SVQ Lev 5	[EdQual21]
5.5	Teacher training qualification	[EdQual12]
3.0	Nursing qualification	[EdQual13]
5.3	Other technical or business qualification/certificate	
15.9	Univ/CNAA degree/diploma	[EdQual14]
5.7	Other recognised academic or vocational qual (WRITE IN)	[EdQual15]
		[EdQual16]
0.1	(Don't know)	
0.6	(Refusal/Not answered)	

VERSIONS B AND C: ASK ALL   N=2276

Q1019   [BioQual]

Can I just check, have you ever studied for a qualification in biology or genetics, at school, college or anywhere else?

%
19.3   Yes
80.1   No
0.1   (Don't know)
0.6   (Refusal/Not answered)

IF 'yes' A [BioQual]

Q1020- CARD X5   N=3276
Q1025

Which of these qualifications was it? Please tell me which sections of the card they are in. PROBE: Which others? CODE ALL THAT APPLY

Multicoded (Maximum of 6 codes)

%
        O-level/CSE/GCSE
        GNVQ Foundation or Intermediate
        NVQ/SVQ levels 1 or 2
13.5   Edexcel/BTEC First Certificate   [BioQOlev]
        or First/General Diploma
        School Certificate or Matriculation
        Scottish Standard Grades
        SCE/SLC/SUPE ordinary or standard
        Northern Ireland Junior Certificate
        A-level/AS-level/A2-level/ S-level   [BioQAlev]
        GNVQ Advanced
        NVQ/SVQ level 3
        Edexcel/BTEC/BEC/TEC (General/Ordinary) National
        Certif/Diploma (ONC/OND)
5.5   Scottish Higher/ Higher-Still Grades [BioQAlev]
        Scot. Higher School Certif
        SCE/SLC/SUPE at Higher Grade
        Certif. Sixth Year Studies/ Advanced Higher Grades
        Northern Ireland Senior Certificate
        First degree (BA/BSc/BEd)
2.0   Edexcel/BTEC/BEC/TEC **Higher**   [BioQDegr]
        Certificate or Diploma (HNC/HND)
        NVQ/SVQ level 4
0.6   Postgraduate degree (MA/MSc/PhD)   [BioQpstg]
        NVQ/SVQ level 5
0.6   Nursing qualification   [BioQNurs]

                                             [BioQOth]
0.5   Other (WRITE IN)
0.0   (Don't know)
0.6   (Refusal/Not answered)

Vote

ASK ALL

Q1034   [Vote01]   N=4432

May I just check, thinking back to the last **general election** - that is the one in **2001** - do you remember which party you voted for then, or perhaps you didn't vote in that election?
IF 'YES': Which party was that?
IF NECESSARY, SAY: The one where Tony Blair won against William Hague.
IF 'CAN'T REMEMBER', CODE 'DON'T KNOW' (Ctrl + K)
DO NOT PROMPT

%
30.4   Did not vote/Not eligible / Too young to vote
19.7   Yes - Conservative
35.9   Yes - Labour
8.2   Yes - Liberal Democrat
0.9   Yes - Scottish National Party
0.3   Yes - Plaid Cymru
0.6   Yes - Green Party
0.7   Other (WRITE IN)
0.1   Yes - (Socialist Alliance/Scottish Socialist Party)
2.0   Refused to disclose voting
1.2   (Don't know)
-       (Not answered)

Spouse/Partner's job details

ASK ALL WHO ARE MARRIED OR LIVING AS MARRIED (AT [MarStat2]

Q1072 [SEconAct]
CARD X6   N=2814

Which of these descriptions applied to what your (husband/wife/partner) was doing last week, that is the seven days ending last Sunday?
PROBE: Which others? CODE ALL THAT APPLY
Multicoded (Maximum of 11 codes)

%
1.2 In full-time education (not paid for by employer, including on vacation)
0.2 On government training/ employment programme
62.5 In paid work (or away temporarily) for at least 10 hours in week
0.1 Waiting to take up paid work already accepted
0.7 Unemployed and registered at a JobCentre or JobCentre Plus
0.7 Unemployed, **not** registered, but actively looking for a job (of at least 10 hrs a week)
0.4 Unemployed, wanting a job (of at least 10 hrs a week) but **not** actively looking for a job
3.4 Permanently sick or disabled
17.0 Wholly retired from work
12.6 Looking after the home
0.7 (Doing something else) (WRITE IN)
- (Don't know)
0.6 (Refusal/Not answered)

ASK ALL WHO ARE MARRIED OR LIVING AS MARRIED AND WHOSE SPOUSE/PARTNER IS NOT WORKING OR WAITING TO TAKE UP WORK

Q1073 [SLastJob]   N=1051

How long ago did (he/she) last have a paid job of at least 10 hours a week?
GOVERNMENT PROGRAMS/SCHEMES DO NOT COUNT AS 'PAID JOBS'.

%
11.3 Within past 12 months
20.8 Over 1, up to 5 years ago
20.9 Over 5, up to 10 years ago
23.9 Over 10, up to 20 years ago
14.3 Over 20 years ago
6.9 Never had a paid job of 10+ hours a week
0.3 (Don't know)
1.6 (Refusal/Not answered)

ASK ALL WHERE SPOUSE/PARTNER'S JOB DETAILS ARE BEING COLLECTED Spouse/partner's job details are collected if respondent is not working or waiting to take up work, but partner is working or waiting to take up work.

Q1074   [Title] **[NOT ON DATAFILE]**   N=406
Now I want to ask you about your
(husband's/wife's/partner's) (present/future) job.
What (is his/her job/ will that job be)?
PROBE IF NECESSARY: What is the name or title of that job?
Open Question (Maximum of 80 characters)

Q1075   [Typewk] **[NOT ON DATAFILE]**   N=406
What kind of work (do/will) (he/she) do most of the time?
IF RELEVANT: What materials/machinery (do/will) (he/she) use?
Open Question (Maximum of 80 characters)

Q1076   [Train] **[NOT ON DATAFILE]**   N=406
What training or qualifications are needed for that job?
Open Question (Maximum of 80 characters)

Q1077   [PEmploye]   N=406
In your (husband's/wife's/partner's) (main) job
(is/will) (he/she) (be)
... READ OUT ...

%
79.4   ... an employee,
17.6   or self-employed?
–   (Don't know)
3.0   (Refusal/Not answered)

Q1079   [PSuperv]   N=406
In your job, (does/will) (he/she) have any formal responsibility for supervising the work of other (employees/people)?
DO NOT INCLUDE PEOPLE WHO ONLY SUPERVISE:
- CHILDREN, E.G. TEACHERS, NANNIES, CHILDMINDERS
- ANIMALS
- SECURITY OR BUILDINGS, E.G. CARETAKERS, SECURITY GUARDS

%
40.9   Yes
55.8   No
0.3   (Don't know)
3.0   (Refusal/Not answered)

IF 'yes' AT [Supervise]

Q1080   [PMany]   N=406
How many?
Median: 8 (of those supervising any)

%
4.9   (Don't know)
3.3   (Refusal/Not answered)

ASK ALL WHERE SPOUSE/PARTNER'S JOB DETAILS ARE BEING COLLECTED AND SPOUSE/PARTNER IS/WILL BE EMPLOYEE

Q1082 [POcSect2] N=335
CARD X7
Which of the types of organisation on this card (does/will) (he/she) (work/be working) for?

%
69.9 PRIVATE SECTOR FIRM OR COMPANY Including, for example, limited companies and PLCs
2.0 NATIONALISED INDUSTRY OR PUBLIC CORPORATION Including, for example, the Post Office and the BBC
22.4 OTHER PUBLIC SECTOR EMPLOYER
Incl eg: - Central govt/ Civil Service/ Govt Agency
- Local authority/ Local Educ Auth (INCL 'OPTED OUT' SCHOOLS)
- Universities
- Health Authority / NHS hospitals / NHS Trusts/ GP surgeries
- Police / Armed forces
2.1 CHARITY/ VOLUNTARY SECTOR Including, for example, charitable companies, churches, trade unions
- Other answer (WRITE IN)
- (Don't know)
3.6 (Refusal/Not answered)

ASK ALL WHERE SPOUSE/PARTNER'S JOB DETAILS ARE BEING COLLECTED [NOT ON DATAFILE]

Q1085 [EmpMake] N=406
IF EMPLOYEE: What (his/her) employer make or do at the place where (he/she) (usually works/ will usually work (from)?
IF SELF-EMPLOYED: What (does/will) (he/she) make or do at the place where (he/she) (works/ will work) (from)?
Open Question (Maximum of 80 characters)

Q1090 [PEmpWrk2]
IF EMPLOYEE: Including (himself/herself), how many people are employed at the place where (he/she) usually works from? N=406
IF SELF-EMPLOYED: (Does/Will) (he/she) have any employees?
IF YES: PROBE FOR CORRECT PRECODE.

%
16.1 Under 10
10.2 10-24
11.2 25-49
8.0 50-99
9.6 100-199
8.5 200-499
14.2 500+
7.3 (Don't know)
3.0 (Refusal/Not answered)

ASK ALL WHO ARE MARRIED OR LIVING AS MARRIED AND WHOSE SPOUSE PARTNER IS WORKING, WAITING TO TAKE UP WORK OR HAS EVER WORKED

Q1120 [SPartFU2] N=1779
(Is/Was) the job ... READ OUT ...
%
79.1 ... full-time - that is, 30 or more hours per week,
19.8 or, part-time?
- (Don't know)
1.1 (Refusal/Not answered)

ASK ALL

Q1122 [AnyBN3] N=4432
CARD X8
Do you (or your husband/wife/partner) receive any of the **state** benefits or tax credits on this card at present?
%
59.5 Yes
39.8 No
0.0 (Don't know)
0.6 (Refusal/Not answered)

Income

IF 'yes' AT [AnyBN3]
CARD X8 AGAIN   N=4432
Which ones?
PROBE: Which others?
Multicoded (Maximum of 17 codes)

Q1123-
Q1139

%

%		Code
22.3	State retirement pension (National Insurance)	[BenefOAP]
0.5	War Pension (War Disablement Pension or War Widows Pension)	[BenefWar]
0.8	Bereavement Allowance/ Widow's Pension/ Widowed Parent's Allowance	[BenefWid]
2.2	Jobseeker's Allowance	[BenefUB]
6.8	Income Support/ Minimum Income Guarantee for pensioners	[BenefIS]
27.0	Child Benefit (formerly Family Allowance)	[BenefCB]
11.5	Child Tax Credit	[BenefCTC]
6.2	Working Tax Credit/ Childcare Tax Credit	[BenefFC]
7.1	Housing Benefit (Rent Rebate/ Rent Allowance)	[BenefHB]
8.8	Council Tax Benefit (or Rebate)	[BenefCT]
4.6	Incapacity Benefit / Sickness Benefit / Invalidity Benefit	[BenefInc]
5.2	Disability Living Allowance (for people under 65)	[BenefDLA]
2.3	Attendance Allowance (for people aged 65+)	[BenefAtA]
0.9	Severe Disablement Allowance	[BenefSev]
1.4	Invalid Care Allowance	[BenefICA]
0.6	Industrial Injuries Disablement Benefit	[BenefInd]
0.4	Other state benefit (WRITE IN)	[BenefOth]
0.0	(Don't know)	
0.7	(Refusal/Not answered)	

[MainInc3]   N=4432
CARD X9
Which of these is the **main** source of income for you and your (husband/wife/partner) at present?

Q1177

%

%	
63.8	Earnings from employment (own or spouse / partner's)
8.0	Occupational pension(s) - from previous employer(s)
2.0	Private pension(s)
11.2	State retirement or widow's pension(s)
1.7	Jobseeker's Allowance/ Unemployment benefit
4.4	Income Support/ Minimum Income Guarantee (for pensioners)
3.0	Invalidity, sickness or disabled pension or benefit(s)
0.7	Other state benefit or tax credit (WRITE IN)
1.1	Interest from savings or investments
1.1	Student grant, bursary or loans
1.3	Dependent on parents/other relatives
0.7	Other main source (WRITE IN)
0.1	(Don't know)
0.8	(Refusal/Not answered)

VERSIONS B AND C: ASK ALL WHO ARE NOT WHOLLY RETIRED AND MALE AGED 65 OR UNDER OR WOMAN AGED 60 OR UNDER   N=2465
[PenXpct1]
CARD X10
When you have retired and have stopped doing paid work, where do you think **most** of your income will come from?
INTERVIEWER: IF RESPONDENT SAYS 'SPOUSE/ PARTNER'S COMPANY/OCCUPATIONAL PENSION', CODE AS 'A COMPANY/OCCUPATIONAL PENSION'.
SIMILARLY FOR STATE AND PERSONAL/STAKEHOLDER PENSIONS.

Q1182

%

%	
27.0	State retirement pension
35.8	A company or occupational pension
17.1	A personal or stakeholder pension
14.5	Other savings or investments
1.1	From somewhere else (WRITE IN)
0.5	**EDIT ONLY:** Earnings from job/still working
3.5	(Don't know)
0.4	(Refusal/Not answered)

Q1185

IF 'company or occupational pension' OR 'personal or stakeholder pension' AT [Penxpct1] AND RESPONDENT IS MARRIED, LIVING AS MARRIED, SEPARATED, WIDOWED OR DIVORCED
[PenOwn1]   N=2465
And would that be your own pension or your (husband's/wife's/partner's/ex-husband's/ex-wife's/late husband's/late wife's) pension?

	%
Own pension	21.3
Spouse/partner's pension	8.2
(Both)	11.5
(Don't know)	-
(Refusal/Not answered)	3.9

Q1186

VERSIONS B AND C: ASK ALL WHO ARE NOT WHOLLY RETIRED AND (MALE AGED 65 OR UNDER OR WOMAN AGED 60 OR UNDER)
[PenXpct2]   N=2465
CARD X10
And which do you think will be your second most important source of income?
INTERVIEWER: IF RESPONDENT SAYS 'SPOUSE/ PARTNER'S COMPANY/OCCUPATIONAL PENSION', CODE AS 'A COMPANY/OCCUPATIONAL PENSION'. SIMILARLY FOR STATE AND PERSONAL/STAKEHOLDER PENSIONS.

	%
State retirement pension	28.4
A company or occupational pension	16.0
A personal or stakeholder pension	10.5
Other savings or investments	28.2
From somewhere else (WRITE IN)	1.8
(None)	9.3
Earnings from job/still working	1.0
(Don't know)	4.3
(Refusal/Not answered)	0.4

Q1189

IF 'company or occupational pension' OR 'personal or stakeholder pension' AT [PenXpct2] AND RESPONDENT IS MARRIED, LIVING AS MARRIED, SEPARATED, WIDOWED OR DIVORCED
[PenOwn2]   N=2465
And would that be your own pension or your (husband's/wife's/ex-husband's/ex-wife's/late husband's/late wife's)pension?

	%
Own pension	11.1
Spouse/partner's pension	5.7
(Both)	3.3
(Don't know)	-
(Refusal/Not answered)	4.8

Q1190

VERSIONS B AND C: ASK ALL WHO ARE NOT WHOLLY RETIRED AND (MALE AGED 65 OR UNDER OR WOMAN AGED 60 OR UNDER)
[SellHome]   N=2465
CARD X11
And how likely do you think it is that you will sell a home to help fund your retirement?
IF ASKED: 'Home' is the building but not the contents

	%
Very likely	10.9
Fairly likely	18.6
Not very likely	33.8
Not at all likely	30.4
(Don't know)	6.1
(Refusal/Not answered)	0.4

Q1191

ASK ALL
[HHIncome]   N=4432
CARD
Which of the letters on this card represents the total income of your household from all sources before tax?
Please just tell me the letter.
NOTE: INCLUDES INCOME FROM BENEFITS, SAVINGS, ETC.

ASK ALL IN PAID WORK

Q1192   [REarn]   N=2472

CARD

Which of the letters on this card represents your **own** gross or total **earnings**, before deduction of income tax and national insurance?

	[HHIncome]	[REarn]
	%	%
Less than £3,999	1.8	3.9
£4,000 - £5,999	5.2	5.0
£6,000-£7,999	5.8	5.2
£8,000-£9,999	4.7	5.6
£10,000-£11,999	4.5	7.9
£12,000-£14,999	6.0	10.7
£15,000-£17,999	5.0	8.3
£18,000-£19,999	3.7	6.5
£20,000-£22,999	5.0	7.9
£23,000-£25,999	5.4	7.6
£26,000-£28,999	4.4	4.8
£29,000-£31,999	4.6	4.3
£32,000-£37,999	6.5	5.0
£38,000-£43,999	5.3	3.1
£44,000-£49,999	4.3	2.0
£50,000-£55,999	3.4	1.2
£56,000 or more	8.4	3.9
(Don't know)	8.4	5.8
Refusal/Not answered	7.4	1.4

VERSION B: ASK ALL

Q1193   [Ownshar2]   N=1127

Do you (or your husband/wife/partner) own any shares quoted on the Stock Exchange, including unit trusts and PEPs and stocks and shares ISAs?

DO NOT INCLUDE CASH OR INSURANCE ISAs.

(PEP = PERSONAL EQUITY PLAN)

	%
Yes	34.9
No	62.6
(Don't know)	0.4
(Refusal/Not answered)	2.1

VERSIONS B AND C: ASK ALL (FOR VERSION A; COMPUTED FROM [TransCar])   N=4432

Q1194   [CarOwn]

Do you, or does anyone else in your household, own or have the regular use of a car or van?

	%
Yes	79.8
No	19.7
(Don't know)	0.1
(Refusal/Not answered)	0.4

Administration

ASK ALL

Q1199 [PhoneX] *N=4432*
Is there a telephone in (your part of) this accommodation?

%
94.8 Yes
4.2 No
0.0 (Don't know)
1.0 (Refusal/Not answered)

IF 'yes' AT [PhoneX]

Q1200 [PhoneBck] *N=4432*
A few interviews on any survey are checked by a supervisor to make sure that people are satisfied with the way the interview was carried out. In case my supervisor needs to contact you, it would be helpful if we could have your telephone number. ADD IF NECESSARY: Your 'phone number will **not** be passed to anyone outside the National Centre without your consent.
IF NUMBER GIVEN, WRITE ON THE ARF

%
88.7 Number given
5.9 Number refused
0.1 (Don't know)
1.1 (Refusal/Not answered)

ASK ALL

Q1201 [ComeBac3] *N=4432*
From time to time we do follow-up studies and may wish to contact you again. Would this be all right?

%
81.8 Yes
16.4 No
0.5 (Don't know)
1.3 (Refusal/Not answered)

IF 'yes' AT [ComeBac3]

Q1202 [Stable] *N=4432*
Could you give us the address and phone number of someone who knows you well, just in case have difficulty in getting in touch with you.
IF NECESSARY, PROMPT: Perhaps a relative or friend who is unlikely to move?
WRITE DETAILS ON THE BACK PAGE OF THE ARF.

%
31.9 INFORMATION GIVEN
49.8 INFORMATION NOT GIVEN
0.0 (Don't know)
1.9 (Refusal/Not answered)

NatCen

National Centre for Social Research

A company limited by guarantee
Registered in England No. 4392418
Charity No. 1091768

Head Office
35 Northampton Square
London EC1V 0AX
Telephone 020 7250 1866
Fax 020 7250 1524

Operations Department
100 Kings Road, Brentwood
Essex CM14 4LX
Telephone 01277 200 600
Fax 01277 263 978

A

P.2265   Green team

BRITISH SOCIAL ATTITUDES 2003

SELF-COMPLETION QUESTIONNAIRE

Summer 2003

INTERVIEWER TO ENTER

2001-6 1 5	Serial number
2009-11	Sampling point
2012-15	Interviewer number

OFFICE USE ONLY

2007-8 2 0	Card number
2016-20	Batch Number
2021 1	Version
SPARE 2022-34	

To the selected respondent:

Thank you very much for agreeing to take part in this important study - the nineteenth in this annual series. The study consists of this self-completion questionnaire, and the interview you have already completed. The results of the survey are published in a book each autumn; some of the questions are also being asked in nearly forty other countries, as part of an international survey.

Completing the questionnaire:

The questions inside cover a wide range of subjects, but most can be answered simply by placing a tick (✓) in one or more of the boxes. No special knowledge is required: we are confident that everyone will be able to take part, not just those with strong views or particular viewpoints. The questionnaire should not take very long to complete, and we hope you will find it interesting and enjoyable. **Only you should fill it in, and not anyone else at your address.** The answers you give will be treated as confidential and anonymous in accordance with the Data Protection Act.

Returning the questionnaire:

Your interviewer will arrange with you the most convenient way of returning the questionnaire. If the interviewer has arranged to call back for it, please fill it in and keep it safely until then. If not, please complete it and post it back in the pre-paid, addressed envelope, AS SOON AS YOU POSSIBLY CAN.

THANK YOU AGAIN FOR YOUR HELP.

The National Centre for Social Research is an independent social research institute and a company limited by guarantee, registered as a charity. Its projects are funded by government departments, local authorities, universities and foundations to provide information on social issues in Britain. The British Social Attitudes survey series is funded through contributions from various grant-giving bodies and government departments. Please contact us if you would like further information.

1. Please tick one box to show how much you agree or disagree with each of these statements.

N=2753

PLEASE TICK ONE BOX ON EACH LINE		Agree strongly	Agree	Neither agree nor disagree	Disagree	Disagree strongly	Can't choose	(Not answered)
[NETTALK] a. Using the Internet a lot makes people less likely to go out and talk to other people	%	8.5	38.6	21.8	20.6	2.1	6.9	1.6
[NETCOST] b. Using the Internet is too expensive	%	4.7	25.7	26.5	27.8	2.2	11.1	2.0
[NETINFFD] c. Most of the information available on the Internet cannot easily be found elsewhere	%	4.1	39.9	22.2	20.6	1.9	9.1	2.3
[NETSHOP] d. It is much safer to use a credit card in a shop than it is to use one over the Internet	%	10.1	34.8	22.3	19.6	2.2	9.1	1.8
[NET2COMP] e. The Internet is too complicated for someone like me to use fully	%	6.2	20.0	13.2	32.5	19.9	6.2	2.0
[NETDNGER] f. Many people exaggerate the dangers children can come across when they use the Internet	%	5.2	12.6	13.0	40.4	20.9	6.1	1.9
[NETMISSO] g. People miss out on important things by not using the Internet and email	%	3.7	24.4	27.2	30.6	3.7	8.6	1.8

[FRIELIV]
2a. Where would you say that most of your close friends live?
PLEASE TICK ONE BOX ONLY

N=2753

	%
...here in your local neighbourhood or area,	35.4
...somewhere else, further away from here,	14.9
or, is it a mixture of both?	45.6
Don't have any close friends	2.2
Can't choose	0.5
Not answered	1.4

[FAMLIV]
2b. Where would you say that most of your relatives and family members live?
PLEASE TICK ONE BOX ONLY

N=2753

	%
...here in your local neighbourhood or area,	27.0
...somewhere else, further away from here,	37.0
or, is it a mixture of both?	34.2
Don't have any relatives or family members	0.8
Can't choose	0.4
Not answered	0.6

3. The following questions are about how much time you spend with various people – other than those you live with.

N=2753

PLEASE TICK ONE BOX ON EACH LINE		Weekly, or nearly every week	Once or twice a month	A few times a year	Very rarely or never	Does not apply	Can't choose	(Not answered)
[TIMEFAM] a. Firstly, how often do you spend time with members of your family or other relatives?	%	63.1	16.3	15.7	2.8	1.1	0.6	0.4
[TIMEFRIE] b. How often do you spend time with friends?	%	64.0	22.0	8.2	3.3	0.8	0.8	1.0
[TIMECOLL] c. How often do you spend time socialising with people you know from work?	%	9.7	16.1	24.5	18.8	25.4	3.1	2.4
[TIMEORGS] d. How often do you spend time socialising with people you know through groups or organisations you belong to?	%	17.2	14.1	16.6	21.8	26.7	2.4	1.2

[COMPADV]
4. How much do you agree or disagree with this statement?

"Children with a computer at home have an unfair advantage in their schoolwork over those without a computer."

PLEASE TICK ONE BOX ONLY

N=2753

	%
Strongly agree	12.6
Agree	41.9
Neither agree nor disagree	22.5
Disagree	14.6
Strongly disagree	2.2
Can't choose	5.6
Not answered	0.6

5. How important do you think it is for parents with a computer at home to encourage their children to use this to...

PLEASE TICK ONE BOX ON EACH LINE

N=2753

		Very important	Fairly important	Not very important	Not at all important	Can't choose	(Not answered)
[COMPHWK1] a.	...complete their homework? %	25.0	46.2	16.3	3.1	7.9	1.4
[COMPHWK2] b.	...contact teachers at their school about work or other problems? %	14.3	30.9	27.5	12.4	9.6	5.4
[COMPHWK3] c.	...look at their school's website? %	12.2	36.2	28.6	8.1	9.5	5.5

6. From what you know or have heard, please tick one box on each line to show how well you think state secondary schools nowadays...

PLEASE TICK ONE BOX ON EACH LINE

N=2753

		Very well	Quite well	Not very well	Not at all well	(Not answered)
[STATSEC1] a.	...prepare young people for work? %	5.7	45.0	41.5	4.9	2.9
[STATSEC2] b.	...teach young people basic skills such as reading, writing and maths? %	16.8	58.5	18.8	2.9	3.0
[STATSEC3] c.	...bring out young people's natural abilities? %	7.9	45.2	37.5	6.2	3.2

7. Please tick one box on each line to show how important you think each of these are...

PLEASE TICK ONE BOX ON EACH LINE

N=2753

		Very important	Fairly important	Not very important	Not at all important	Can't choose	(Not answered)
[UNISPEC] a.	...that parents encourage children to go to university? %	29.6	49.8	14.7	1.3	3.4	1.3
[UNISTEC] b.	...that teachers encourage more children to go to university? %	28.9	49.3	14.4	1.8	3.6	1.8
[UNISWEC] c.	...that more people from working class backgrounds go to university? %	35.5	41.7	14.5	2.3	4.0	1.9

[UNIBCKGR]
8. Suppose two young people with the same A/A2-level (or Scottish Higher) grades apply to go to university. One is from a well-off background and the other is from a less well-off background. Which one do you think would be more likely to be offered a place ...

PLEASE TICK ONE BOX ONLY

N=2753

	%
...the young person from the well-off background,	43.2
the young person from the less well-off background,	4.0
or would they both be equally likely to be offered a place?	42.3
Can't choose	9.7
Not answered	0.8

9. And again, suppose two young people with the same A/A2-level (or Scottish Higher) grades apply to go to university. This time one is from a comprehensive school and the other is from a private school.

[UNICOMPW]
a. Which one do you think **would** be more likely to be offered a place ...

PLEASE TICK ONE BOX ONLY

N=2753

	%
...the young person from the comprehensive school,	4.2
the young person from the private school,	53.0
or would they both be equally likely to be offered a place?	32.3
Can't choose	9.6
Not answered	0.9

[UNICOMPS]
b. And which one do you think **should** be offered a place at university ...

PLEASE TICK ONE BOX ONLY

	%
...the young person from the comprehensive school,	5.0
the young person from the private school,	3.7
or should they both be equally likely to be offered a place?	85.7
Can't choose	4.4
Not answered	1.2

10. Please tick one box to show how much you agree or disagree with each of these statements.

N=2753

PLEASE TICK ONE BOX ON EACH LINE	Agree strongly	Agree	Neither agree nor disagree	Disagree	Disagree strongly	Can't choose	(Not answered)
[RELSCH1] b. The government should fund single religion schools if parents want them	% 4.6	21.4	21.6	30.6	13.2	6.5	2.1
[RELSCH2] b. If the government funds separate Christian faith schools, it should also fund separate schools for other faiths	% 6.8	35.6	19.3	19.7	8.8	7.6	2.2
[RELSCH3] b. Single religion schools have a better quality of education than other schools	% 3.2	16.6	31.7	27.4	7.8	11.0	2.5
[RELSCH4] b. Single religion schools give children a better sense of right and wrong than other schools	% 4.7	19.6	26.7	28.5	9.1	9.3	2.1

11. From what you know or have heard, please tick a box for each of the items below to show whether you think the National Health Service in your area is, on the whole, satisfactory or in need of improvement.

N=1848

PLEASE TICK ONE BOX ON EACH LINE	In need of a lot of improvement	In need of some improvement	Satisfactory	Very good	(Not answered)
[HSAREA3] a. Being able to choose which GP to see	% 17.4	26.1	43.3	11.7	1.5
[HSAREA4] b. Quality of medical treatment by GPs	% 8.1	26.0	45.5	18.7	1.8
[HSAREA9] c. Staffing level of nurses in hospitals	% 30.8	40.7	21.3	4.4	2.8
[HSAREA10] d. Staffing level of doctors in hospitals	% 31.2	42.4	19.9	3.9	2.6
[HSAREA11] e. Quality of medical treatment in hospitals	% 18.3	35.5	33.8	9.8	2.6
[HSAREA12] f. Quality of nursing care in hospitals	% 15.8	32.6	35.6	13.9	2.1

12. In the last twelve months, have you or a close family member ...

N=1848

PLEASE TICK ONE BOX ON EACH LINE	Yes, just me	Yes, not me but close family member	Yes, both	No, neither	(Not answered)
[GPUSESC] a. ... visited an NHS GP?	% 22.2	15.7	54.6	5.7	1.8
[OUTPUSSC] b. ... been an out-patient in an NHS hospital?	% 21.5	25.6	15.3	33.6	4.2
[INPUSSC] c. ... been an in-patient in an NHS hospital?	% 11.3	21.2	4.2	58.2	5.0
[VISTUSSC] e. ... visited a patient in an NHS hospital?	% 17.3	12.2	26.4	40.0	4.1
[PRIVUSSC] e. ... had any medical treatment as a private patient?	% 5.5	5.7	2.2	83.6	2.9

13. Please tick one box for each statement to show how much you agree or disagree with it.

N=1848

PLEASE TICK ONE BOX ON EACH LINE	Agree strongly	Agree	Neither agree nor disagree	Disagree	Disagree strongly	Can't choose	(Not answered)
[MENTHOUS] e. I would worry if housing were provided near my home for people with mental health problems leaving hospital	% 12.8	31.0	29.8	16.8	4.6	3.6	1.4
[MENTFAM] f. Serious mental health problems are just as likely to affect my family as anyone else's	% 18.9	56.8	15.3	3.8	0.7	3.0	1.5

14. Please tick one box to show how much you agree or disagree with each of these statements.

PLEASE TICK ONE BOX ON EACH LINE	Agree strongly	Agree	Neither agree nor disagree	Disagree	Disagree strongly	Can't choose	(Not answered)
[WESTLOTH] N=1848 a. Now that Scotland has its own parliament, Scottish MPs should no longer be allowed to vote in the House of Commons on laws that only affect England	% 20.5	38.8	18.2	9.5	1.6	10.1	1.3
[ENGRGDEV] N=3634 b. Now that Scotland has its own Parliament and Wales its own Assembly, every English region should have its own elected assembly too	% 6.3	23.4	25.1	26.0	7.3	10.8	1.0
[PROPREP] N=967 c. Britain should introduce proportional representation, so that the number of MPs in the House of Commons each party gets matches more closely the number of votes each party gets	% 12.6	31.9	23.9	11.7	3.7	14.5	1.7

15a. Which of these statements comes closest to your views?

PLEASE TICK *ONE BOX ONLY*
[ELECTSY1]

N=967

	%
It is more important that elections should produce a clear winner so that it is voters who decide who forms the government	46.8
OR	
It is more important that elections should produce a fair result, even if this it means it is not clear who should form the government	31.2
Can't choose	20.3
Not answered	1.7

b. And which of these statements comes closest to your views?

PLEASE TICK *ONE BOX ONLY*
[ELECTSY2]

N=967

	%
It is better to have just one party in government so that it is very clear who should be blamed if things go wrong	37.3
OR	
It is better to have two or more parties in the government so that more people's views are represented	47.8
Can't choose	13.3
Not answered	1.6

16. Now some questions about Britain's railways. By railways we mean train services, and not metro or underground services. If you don't use trains regularly please answer according to what you know or have heard from other people.

Please tick one box on *each* line to show how much you agree or disagree with the following statements.

N=967

PLEASE TICK *ONE BOX ON EACH LINE*		Agree strongly	Agree	Neither agree nor disagree	Disagree	Disagree strongly	Can't choose	(Not answered)
[TRAINS1] a. It is easy to find out what time trains run	%	7.0	52.1	12.9	16.9	3.3	6.3	1.5
[TRAINS2] b. Trains generally run often enough	%	2.3	37.7	19.0	28.4	3.9	6.7	2.0
[TRAINS3] c. Trains generally run on time	%	1.2	19.7	16.9	43.7	10.8	6.1	1.7
[TRAINS4] d. Train fares are fairly reasonable	%	1.1	15.4	16.0	38.9	20.7	6.1	1.8
[TRAINS5] e. Trains are a fast way to travel	%	5.3	52.0	17.7	14.7	3.8	4.6	1.9
[TRAINS6] f. It is difficult to find out the cheapest train fares	%	9.5	42.0	18.5	16.4	3.0	8.5	2.0
[TRAINS7] g. Trains have a good safety record	%	3.5	32.7	26.6	24.6	6.5	4.3	1.8

17. Please tick one box for each statement to show how much you agree or disagree.

N=967

PLEASE TICK *ONE BOX ON EACH LINE*		Agree strongly	Agree	Neither agree nor disagree	Disagree	Disagree strongly	Can't choose	(Not answered)
[CARTAXHI] a. For the sake of the environment, car users should pay higher taxes	%	3.8	10.8	11.4	49.7	20.8	1.8	1.7
[MOTORWAY] b. The government should build more motorways to reduce traffic congestion	%	6.9	39.5	19.5	23.8	5.6	2.5	2.2
[CARCONV] c. Driving one's own car is too convenient to give up for the sake of the environment	%	5.3	38.8	23.4	21.6	3.9	4.8	2.2
[BUILDTRA] d. Building more roads just encourages more traffic	%	8.0	38.1	17.3	28.9	2.7	2.6	2.4
[CARALLOW] e. People should be allowed to use their cars as much as they like, even if it causes damage to the environment	%	3.3	18.3	31.1	32.4	8.5	4.3	2.1

[CUTCARS]
18a. How important do you think it is to cut down the number of cars on Britain's roads?

PLEASE TICK *ONE BOX ONLY*

N=967

	%
Very important	26.4
Fairly important	43.9
Not very important	17.6
Not at all important	4.3
Can't choose	6.7
Not answered	1.0

[PTIMPRIM]
b. And how important is it to improve public transport in Britain?

PLEASE TICK *ONE BOX ONLY*

	%
Very important	77.9
Fairly important	17.7
Not very important	1.8
Not at all important	0.4
Can't choose	1.1
Not answered	1.0

19. Many people feel that public transport should be improved. Here are some ways of finding the money to do it. How much would you support or oppose each one, as a way of raising money to improve public transport?

PLEASE TICK ONE BOX ON EACH LINE

N=967

	Strongly support	Support	Neither support nor oppose	Oppose	Strongly oppose	Can't choose	(Not answered)
[PTIMPR2B] a. Charging all motorists around £5 each time they enter or drive through a city or town centre at peak times %	6.0	19.6	15.4	32.1	21.2	3.6	1.9
[PTIMPR3] b. Cutting in half spending on new roads %	3.9	16.1	21.3	33.7	16.0	5.9	3.2
[PTIMPR4] c. Cutting in half spending on maintenance of the roads we already have %	1.7	5.9	12.8	44.0	28.0	4.7	3.0
[PTIMPR5] d. Charging £1 for every 50 miles motorists travel on the motorways %	5.2	23.0	14.9	28.7	21.8	4.2	2.2

20. Now some questions about air travel. Please tick one box for each statement to show how much you agree or disagree.

PLEASE TICK ONE BOX ON EACH LINE

N=967

	Agree strongly	Agree	Neither agree nor disagree	Disagree	Disagree strongly	Can't choose	(Not answered)
[PLNALLOW] a. People should be able to travel by plane as much as they like %	19.3	59.2	11.9	4.0	0.5	3.5	1.5
[PLNTERM] b. People should be able to travel by plane as much as they like, even if new terminals or runways are needed to meet the demand. %	10.2	41.7	24.3	15.6	2.3	3.9	2.1
[PLNENVT] c. People should be able to travel by plane as much as they like, even if this harms the environment %	3.4	15.8	29.5	37.6	7.2	4.2	2.3

[FLYLMRES]
21a. Which of these statements comes closest to your own views?
PLEASE TICK ONE BOX ONLY

N=967

In order to improve quality of life for local residents, we should limit growth in the number of flights to and from British airports % 24.5
OR
Limiting growth in flights to and from British airports wouldn't be fair on business travellers and people going on holiday 47.3
Can't choose 26.6
Not answered 1.6

[FLYLMENV]
b. And which of these statements comes closest to your views?
PLEASE TICK ONE BOX ONLY

In order to protect the environment, we should limit growth in the number of flights to and from British airports % 22.6
OR
Limiting growth in flights to and from British airports would be too damaging to Britain's business and tourist economy 51.8
Can't choose 24.0
Not answered 1.6

22. Please tick one box for each statement below to show how much you agree or disagree with it.

PLEASE TICK ONE BOX ON EACH LINE

N=3634

	Agree strongly	Agree	Neither agree nor disagree	Disagree	Disagree strongly	(Not answered)
[REDISTRB] a. Government should redistribute income from the better-off to those who are less well off %	10.3	31.7	23.7	26.0	5.9	2.3
[BIGBUSNN] b. Big business benefits owners at the expense of workers %	12.3	44.9	24.1	14.3	1.7	2.7
[WEALTH] c. Ordinary working people do not get their fair share of the nation's wealth %	13.6	47.3	23.4	12.0	1.3	2.4
[RICHLAW] d. There is one law for the rich and one for the poor %	19.5	38.1	22.0	15.3	2.9	2.2
[INDUST4] e. Management will always try to get the better of employees if it gets the chance %	16.7	40.9	23.9	14.2	2.0	2.3

23. Please tick one box for each statement below to show how much you agree or disagree with it.

PLEASE TICK ONE BOX ON EACH LINE

N=3634

	Agree strongly	Agree	Neither agree nor disagree	Disagree	Disagree strongly	(Not answered)
[TRADVALS] a. Young people today don't have enough respect for traditional British values %	19.4	48.6	21.2	8.2	0.9	1.7
[STIFSENT] b. People who break the law should be given stiffer sentences %	32.6	46.4	13.4	5.4	0.5	1.7
[DEATHAPP] c. For some crimes, the death penalty is the most appropriate sentence %	29.8	28.4	13.2	16.4	10.3	1.8
[OBEY] d. Schools should teach children to obey authority %	28.9	54.0	9.7	4.9	0.6	1.9
[WRONGLAW] e. The law should always be obeyed, even if a particular law is wrong %	7.7	31.8	30.9	24.5	2.8	2.3
[CENSOR] f. Censorship of films and magazines is necessary to uphold moral standards %	19.1	45.4	18.1	11.7	3.9	1.8

[FEMP2]
24. When you were 14, did your father work as an employee, was he self-employed, or was he not working then?

PLEASE TICK ONE BOX

%

He was an employee	74.7	PLEASE ANSWER QUESTION 25 →
He was self-employed	12.9	PLEASE ANSWER QUESTION 26 →
He was not working	4.2	
My father had died or I don't know what he was doing when I was 14	6.7	QUESTION 28 ON PAGE 12
Working – don't know whether employed or unemployed	0.2	
Not answered	1.3	

N=1848

PLEASE ANSWER IF YOUR FATHER WAS AN EMPLOYEE WHEN YOU WERE 14

[FNEMPE]
25a. How many people worked for his employer at the place where he worked?
IF YOU DON'T KNOW, PLEASE GIVE YOUR BEST ESTIMATE
PLEASE TICK ONE BOX ONLY

%

1 to 24	19.3
25 or more	54.3
Don't know	15.1
Not answered	11.4

N=1531

[FSUPERV]
b. Did he have any responsibility for supervising the work of other employees?
PLEASE TICK ONE BOX ONLY

%

Yes	40.2	
No	33.9	PLEASE GO TO QUESTION 27 ON PAGE 12
Don't know	14.2	
Not answered	11.8	

N=1531

[FNEMPS]
PLEASE ANSWER IF YOUR FATHER WAS SELF-EMPLOYED WHEN YOU WERE 14
26. How many employees did he have?
IF YOU DON'T KNOW, PLEASE GIVE YOUR BEST ESTIMATE
PLEASE TICK ONE BOX ONLY

%

No employees	28.4	
1 to 24	47.7	PLEASE GO TO QUESTION 27
25 or more	5.0	
Don't know	6.8	
Not answered	12.0	

N=265

[FTYPEJB2]
PLEASE ANSWER THIS QUESTION
IF YOUR FATHER WAS WORKING WHEN YOU WERE 14
27. Which of these descriptions on this card best describes the sort of work your father did when you were 14?

PLEASE TICK ONE BOX

%

Modern professional occupations
such as: teacher – nurse – physiotherapist – social worker – welfare officer – artist – musician – police officer (sergeant or above) – software designer   5.9

Clerical and intermediate occupations
such as: secretary – personal assistant – clerical worker – office clerk – call centre agent – nursing auxiliary – nursery nurse   3.2

Senior manager or administrators
such as: finance manager – chief executive   5.7

Technical and craft occupations
such as: motor mechanic – fitter – inspector – plumber – printer – tool maker – electrician – gardener – train driver   26.7

Semi-routine manual and service occupations
such as: postal worker – machine operative – security guard – caretaker – farm worker – catering assistant – receptionist – sales assistant   14.7

Routine manual and service occupations
such as: HGV driver – van driver – cleaner – porter – packer – sewing machinist – messenger – labourer – waiter/waitress – bar staff   16.1

Middle or junior managers
such as: office manager – retail manager – bank manager – restaurant manager – warehouse manager – publican   6.6

Traditional professional occupations
such as: accountant – solicitor – medical practitioner – scientist – civil/mechanical engineer   6.4

| Don't know | 4.0 |
| Not answered | 10.5 |

N=1770

EVERYONE PLEASE ANSWER
28a. To help us plan better in future, please tell us about how long it took you to complete this questionnaire.

PLEASE TICK ONE BOX ONLY

%

Less than 15 minutes	35.4
Between 15 and 20 minutes	38.7
Between 21 and 30 minutes	16.4
Between 31 and 45 minutes	6.4
Between 46 and 60 minutes	1.6
Over one hour	0.5
Not answered	1.1

b. And on what date did you fill in the questionnaire?

PLEASE WRITE IN:

DATE ☐☐   MONTH ☐☐   2003

29. And lastly just a few details about yourself.

a. Are you ....

(✓)

Male ☐

Female ☐

b. What was your age last birthday?

PLEASE WRITE IN: ☐☐ YEARS

Thank you very much for your help

Please keep the completed questionnaire for the interviewer if he or she has arranged to call for it. Otherwise, please post it as soon as possible in the pre-paid envelope provided.

NatCen
National Centre for Social Research

A company limited by guarantee
Registered in England No. 4392418
Charity No 1091768

35 Northampton Square
London EC1V 0AX
Telephone 020 7250 1866
Fax 020 7250 1524

100 Kings Road, Brentwood
Essex CM14 4LX
Telephone 01277 200 600
Fax 01277 263 578

B

P.2265   Green team

BRITISH SOCIAL ATTITUDES 2003

Summer 2003

SELF-COMPLETION QUESTIONNAIRE

INTERVIEWER TO ENTER

2001-6	1 5	Serial number
2009-11		Sampling point
2012-15		Interviewer number

OFFICE USE ONLY

2007-8	2 0	Card number
2016-20		Batch Number
2021	2	Version
SPARE 2022-34		

To the selected respondent:

Thank you very much for agreeing to take part in this important study - the nineteenth in this annual series. The study consists of this self-completion questionnaire, and the interview you have already completed. The results of the survey are published in a book each autumn; some of the questions are also being asked in nearly forty other countries, as part of an international survey.

Completing the questionnaire:

The questions inside cover a wide range of subjects, but most can be answered simply by placing a tick (✓) in one or more of the boxes. No special knowledge is required: we are confident that everyone will be able to take part, not just those with strong views or particular viewpoints. The questionnaire should not take very long to complete, and we hope you will find it interesting and enjoyable. **Only you should fill it in, and not anyone else at your address.** The answers you give will be treated as confidential and anonymous in accordance with the Data Protection Act.

Returning the questionnaire:

Your interviewer will arrange with you the most convenient way of returning the questionnaire. If the interviewer has arranged to call back for it, please fill it in and keep it safely until then. If not, please complete it and post it back in the pre-paid, addressed envelope. AS SOON AS YOU POSSIBLY CAN.

THANK YOU AGAIN FOR YOUR HELP.

The National Centre for Social Research is an independent social research institute and a company limited by guarantee, registered as a charity. Its projects are funded by government departments, local authorities, universities and foundations to provide information on social issues in Britain. The British Social Attitudes survey series is funded through contributions from various grant-giving bodies and government departments. Please contact us if you would like further information.

1. We are all part of different groups. Some are more important to us than others when we think of ourselves. In general, which in the following list is most important to you in describing who you are? Please tick one box in the first column. And which is the second most important? And the third most important?

N=881

PLEASE TICK ONE BOX IN EACH COLUMN

	[GPIDENT1] Most important %	[GPIDENT2] Second most important %	[GPIDENT3] Third most important %
Your current or previous occupation (or being a homemaker)	9.1	17.5	12.8
Your race or ethnic background	1.7	1.2	2.7
Your gender (that is, being a man or a woman)	7.0	10.9	8.6
Your age group (that is, young, middle aged, or old)	3.0	6.8	8.4
Your religion (or being agnostic or an atheist)	2.2	3.3	3.9
Your preferred political party, group or movement	0.2	0.7	3.0
Your nationality	6.7	10.5	12.4
Your family or marital status (that is, being a son/daugher, mother/father grandfather/grandmother, husband/wife, widower/widowed, not married etc).	40.6	12.1	4.2
Your social class (that is, upper, middle, lower, working, or similar)	1.4	4.6	7.1
The part of Britain that you live in	1.3	6.4	10.1
Not answered	26.6	25.9	26.9

2. How close do you feel to …

N=881

PLEASE TICK ONE BOX ON EACH LINE

	Very close	Fairly close	Not very close	Not at all close	Can't choose	(Not answered)
[CLOSTOW2] a. … your town or city? %	30.3	47.6	13.7	5.1	0.7	2.6
[CLOSCNT2] b. … your county? %	25.5	45.5	18.5	5.7	0.9	3.8
[CLOSBRT2] c. … Britain? %	31.7	45.3	15.2	4.0	0.7	3.1
[CLOSEUR2] d. … Europe? %	4.2	21.1	38.4	29.4	1.9	5.1

3. Some people say the following things are important for being truly British. Others say they are not important. How important do you think each of the following is?

N=881

PLEASE TICK ONE BOX ON EACH LINE

	Very important	Fairly important	Not very important	Not at all important	Can't choose	(Not answered)
[PATRIOT1] a. To have been born in Britain %	44.2	25.5	19.2	8.1	1.2	1.8
[PATRIOT2] b. To have British citizenship %	47.0	35.9	9.5	2.6	1.5	3.5
[PATRIOT3] c. To have lived in Britain for most of one's life %	32.4	37.0	21.4	4.9	1.0	3.4
[PATRIOT4] d. To be able to speak English %	60.9	25.6	5.5	3.3	0.5	4.2
[PATRIOT5] e. To be a Christian %	15.1	15.7	23.7	39.0	3.1	3.4
[PATRIOT6] f. To respect Britain's political institutions and laws %	47.3	34.6	9.1	4.4	1.5	3.2
[PATRIOT7] g. To feel British %	40.7	33.6	13.1	7.1	1.4	4.2
[PATRIOT8] h. To have British ancestry %	26.2	20.1	28.2	20.1	1.7	3.7

4. Please tick one box to show how much you agree or disagree with each of these statements.

N=881

PLEASE TICK ONE BOX ON EACH LINE

	Agree strongly	Agree	Neither agree nor disagree	Disagree	Disagree strongly	Can't choose	(Not answered)
[NATCITZN] a. I would rather be a citizen of Britain than of any other country in the world %	38.7	31.0	20.6	6.6	0.8	1.1	1.2
[NATASHMD] b. There are some things about Britain today that make me feel ashamed of Britain %	17.8	55.6	16.0	6.1	1.6	1.0	2.1
[NATLIKE] c. The world would be a better place if people from other countries were more like the British %	8.7	20.8	36.7	23.3	5.9	2.7	1.9
[NATBEST] d. Generally speaking, Britain is a better country than most other countries %	11.8	34.6	33.4	15.1	2.1	1.4	1.6
[NATSUPP] e. People should always support their country, even if the country is in the wrong %	5.4	13.8	18.6	48.7	10.0	1.5	2.1
[NATSPORT] f. When my country does well in international sports, it makes me feel proud to be British %	27.3	42.4	21.6	4.7	0.9	1.0	2.1
[NATPRDBR] g. I am often less proud of Britain than I would like to be %	6.8	42.3	26.6	18.4	1.7	2.4	1.7

5. How proud are you of Britain in each of the following?

N=881

PLEASE TICK ONE BOX ON EACH LINE	Very proud	Somewhat proud	Not very proud	Not proud at all	Can't choose	(Not answered)
[NATPRID1] a. The way democracy works	% 14.7	47.5	23.7	4.2	7.9	2.0
[NATPRID2B] b. Its political influence in the world	% 8.9	45.0	28.9	7.7	7.4	2.1
[NATPRID3] c. Britain's economic achievements	% 12.6	49.6	24.4	3.2	7.2	3.0
[NATPRID4] d. Its social security system	% 10.0	37.3	32.9	10.9	6.4	2.5
[NATPRID5] e. Its scientific and technological achievements	% 26.0	51.4	10.2	2.4	7.2	2.8
[NATPRID8] f. Its achievements in sports	% 15.8	48.8	23.6	6.1	5.6	2.2
[NATPRID7] g. Its achievements in the arts and literature	% 20.7	46.6	14.1	3.5	11.4	3.6
[NATPRID8] h. Britain's armed forces	% 49.0	35.2	6.8	2.7	4.8	1.4
[NATPRID9] i. Its history	% 46.7	35.3	9.5	2.1	4.3	2.1
[NATPRID10] j. Its fair and equal treatment of all groups in society	% 13.6	39.8	26.8	9.1	8.9	1.9

6. Now we would like to ask a few questions about relations between Britain and other countries. How much do you agree or disagree with these statements?

N=881

PLEASE TICK ONE BOX ON EACH LINE	Agree strongly	Agree	Neither agree nor disagree	Disagree	Disagree strongly	Can't choose	(Not answered)
[FORGREL1] a. Britain should limit the import of foreign products in order to protect its national economy	% 17.1	38.8	24.0	14.6	1.6	2.7	1.1
[FORGREL2] b. For certain problems, like environmental pollution, international bodies should have the right to enforce solutions	% 20.3	43.4	17.1	11.5	0.8	4.7	2.2
[FORGREL4] c. Britain should follow its own interests even if this leads to conflicts with other nations	% 13.5	32.4	20.0	26.3	3.6	2.9	1.4
[FORGREL5] d. Foreigners should not be allowed to buy land in Britain	% 11.1	16.6	26.7	30.9	9.7	3.8	1.2
[FORGREL6] e. Britain's television should give preference to British films and programmes	% 9.8	18.9	31.4	29.7	7.2	1.7	1.3

7. Please tick one box to show how much you agree or disagree with each of these statements.

N=881

PLEASE TICK ONE BOX ON EACH LINE	Agree strongly	Agree	Neither agree nor disagree	Disagree	Disagree strongly	Can't choose	(Not answered)
[MNNTDNMG] a. Large international companies are doing more and more damage to local businesses in Britain	% 17.6	44.9	23.5	7.4	0.7	4.2	1.7
[FREETRDE] b. Free trade leads to better products becoming available in Britain	% 8.5	48.6	28.7	7.5	0.2	5.2	1.3
[GBFOLLOW] c. In general, Britain should follow the decisions of international organisations to which it belongs, even if the government does not agree with them	% 1.6	22.2	32.0	31.9	2.9	7.4	1.8
[MNNTPOWR] d. International organisations are taking away too much power from the British government	% 14.4	37.3	27.4	13.1	0.4	5.9	1.6
[GBCULTRE] e. Increased exposure to foreign films, music and books is damaging our national and local cultures	% 6.9	17.4	22.7	36.7	11.1	3.6	1.7
[INTERADV] f. A benefit of the internet is that it makes information available to more and more people worldwide	% 33.9	47.5	10.3	1.6	0.3	4.7	1.7

8. Now a few questions about minority groups in Britain. Please tick one box to show how much you agree or disagree with each of these statements.

N=881

PLEASE TICK ONE BOX ON EACH LINE	Agree strongly	Agree	Neither agree nor disagree	Disagree	Disagree strongly	Can't choose	(Not answered)
[SHARTRAD] a. It is impossible for people who do not share Britain's customs and traditions to become fully British	% 15.6	36.0	16.9	24.2	3.9	2.4	1.0
[ETHNCAID] b. Ethnic minorities should be given government assistance to preserve their customs and traditions	% 1.9	15.0	27.3	38.0	13.4	3.5	0.9

[ETHNCVW]
9. Some people say that it is better for a country if different racial and ethnic groups maintain their distinct customs and traditions. Others say that it is better if these groups adapt and blend into the larger society. Which of these views comes closer to your own?

PLEASE TICK ONE BOX ONLY

%

It is better for society if groups maintain their distinct customs and traditions	19.6
It is better if groups adapt and blend into the larger society	53.8
Can't choose	24.4
Not answered	2.3

10. There are different opinions about immigrants from other countries living in Britain. (By 'immigrants' we mean people who come to settle in Britain). Please tick one box to show how much you agree or disagree with each of these statements.

N=881

PLEASE TICK ONE BOX ON EACH LINE

	Agree strongly	Agree	Neither agree nor disagree	Disagree	Disagree strongly	Can't choose	(Not answered)
[IMMIGRT1] a. Immigrants increase crime rates	% 12.5	25.0	31.4	23.8	3.0	2.7	1.6
[IMMIGRT2] b. Immigrants are generally good for Britain's economy	% 1.1	19.9	34.7	31.4	8.2	2.6	2.1
[IMMIGRT3] c. Immigrants take jobs away from people who were born in Britain	% 11.8	31.2	24.5	24.1	4.5	2.1	1.7
[IMMIGRT4] d. Immigrants improve British society by bringing in new ideas and cultures	% 4.1	28.8	35.2	22.0	6.1	2.7	1.2
[IMMIGRT5] e. Government spends too much money assisting immigrants	% 30.0	33.1	20.4	10.3	2.4	2.7	1.0

[IMMNUMB]
11. Do you think the number of immigrants to Britain nowadays should be.
PLEASE TICK ONE BOX ONLY

N=881

	%
Increased a lot	1.9
Increased a little	3.8
Remain the same as it is	15.7
Reduced a little	22.8
Reduced a lot	48.6
Can't choose	6.8
Not answered	0.4

[CITIZEN]
12. Are you a citizen of Britain?

N=881

	%
Yes	96.3
No	3.0
Not answered	0.7

[CITZPAR]
13. At the time of your birth, were both, one or neither of your parents citizens of Britain?
PLEASE TICK ONE BOX ONLY

N=881

	%
Both were British citizens	91.1
Only father was a British citizen	0.9
Only mother was a British citizen	1.6
Neither parent was a British citizen	5.7
Not answered	0.7

14. Please tick one box to show how much you agree or disagree with each of these statements.

N=881

PLEASE TICK ONE BOX ON EACH LINE

	Agree strongly	Agree	Neither agree nor disagree	Disagree	Disagree strongly	Can't choose	(Not answered)
[CITZSHP1] a. Children born in Britain of parents who are not citizens should have the right to become British citizens	% 12.2	49.2	15.9	15.5	2.4	2.7	2.1
[CITZSHP2] b. Children born abroad should have the right to become British citizens if at least one of their parents is a British citizen	% 9.9	56.2	19.6	8.7	1.3	2.4	1.7
[CITZSHP3] c. Legal immigrants to Britain who are not citizens should have the same rights as British citizens	% 5.9	34.5	19.1	28.0	7.9	2.6	1.9
[CITZSHP4] d. Britain should take stronger measures to exclude illegal immigrants	% 51.7	28.2	11.1	2.3	3.3	2.1	1.3

[GBPRIDSC]
15. How proud are you of being British?
PLEASE TICK ONE BOX ONLY

N=881

	%
Very proud	43.1
Somewhat proud	39.1
Not very proud	10.0
Not proud at all	2.0
I am not British	2.2
Can't choose	2.1
Not answered	1.4

[MONEYGO]
16. Which one of these two statements comes closest to your own view?
PLEASE TICK ONE BOX ONLY

N=2667

	%
If the money is there, I find it just goes	21.0
OR	
I always try to keep some money in hand for emergencies	75.9
Can't choose	2.5
Not answered	0.6

[NEVBORRO]
17. And which of these two statements comes closest to your own view?
PLEASE TICK ONE BOX ONLY

N=2667

	%
People should never borrow money	9.9
OR	
There is nothing wrong with borrowing money as long as you can manage the repayments	87.3
Can't choose	2.2
Not answered	0.5

[MONEYRET]
18. And which of these two statements comes closest to your own view?

N=2667

PLEASE TICK ONE BOX ONLY

%

Young people should spend their money while they are young and worry about saving for retirement when they are older 15.5

OR

Young people should start saving for their retirement as soon as they can even if they have to cut back on other things 72.8

Can't choose 11.2

Not answered 0.6

19. Please tick one box for each statement to show how much you agree or disagree with it.

N=2667

PLEASE TICK ONE BOX ON EACH LINE	Agree strongly	Agree	Neither agree nor disagree	Disagree	Disagree strongly	Can't choose	(Not answered)
[CREDPLAN] a. Credit makes it easier for people to plan their finances %	3.0	34.3	23.1	27.8	6.1	2.2	3.5
[BOROHARD] b. It should be made much harder to borrow money even if this means that more people can't get credit %	9.6	41.2	21.9	19.8	2.0	2.4	3.2
[CREDSPND] c. Credit encourages people to spend more money than they can really afford to %	36.2	49.8	7.6	3.6	0.4	1.0	1.5

20. How much do you agree or disagree with each of these statements?

N=2667

PLEASE TICK ONE BOX ON EACH LINE	Agree strongly	Agree	Neither agree nor disagree	Disagree	Disagree strongly	Can't choose	(Not answered)
[RETSTAND] a. I worry a lot about the standard of living I will have when I reach retirement age %	18.0	37.2	19.0	13.3	2.1	4.7	5.7
[RTFAROFF] b. My retirement is so far off, it is not worth worrying about what I will live on %	2.1	6.9	12.1	40.9	16.1	7.1	14.7

21. And how much do you agree or disagree with each of these statements?

N=2667

PLEASE TICK ONE BOX ON EACH LINE	Agree strongly	Agree	Neither agree nor disagree	Disagree	Disagree strongly	Can't choose	(Not answered)
[FALSCONF] a. A lot of false benefit claims are a result of confusion rather than dishonesty %	3.2	19.5	18.8	41.3	11.3	3.8	2.1
[CHEATPOR] b. The reason that some people on benefit cheat the system is that they don't get enough to live on %	4.6	27.4	16.6	36.1	9.7	2.9	2.6

[GOVBEN]
22. Which is it more important for the government to do?

N=2667

PLEASE TICK ONE BOX ONLY

%

To get people to claim benefits to which they are entitled 35.0

OR

To stop people claiming benefits to which they are not entitled 53.9

Can't choose 10.3

Not answered 0.7

[INFORMBN]
23. How much do you agree or disagree with this statement? "People who know someone is cheating the benefit system should always report this."

N=2667

PLEASE TICK ONE BOX ONLY

%

Strongly agree 23.4

Agree 39.8

Neither agree nor disagree 24.3

Disagree 6.3

Strongly disagree 0.9

Can't choose 4.8

Not answered 0.5

[TOPUPCHN]
24. Some working couples with children find it hard to make ends meet on low wages. In these circumstances, do you think ...

N=2667

PLEASE TICK ONE BOX ONLY

%

... the government should top-up their wages. 59.4

or ... is it up to the couple to look after themselves and their children as best they can? 28.6

Can't choose 11.5

Not answered 0.5

[TOPUPNCH]
25. And what about working couples without children?
If they find it hard to make ends meet on low wages, do you think ...
PLEASE TICK ONE BOX ONLY

N=2667

	%
... the government should top-up their wages,	28.4
or, is it up to the couple to look after themselves as best they can?	62.6
Can't choose	10.4
Not answered	0.6

[TOPUPLPA]
26. And what about working lone parents?
If they find it hard to make ends meet on low wages, do you think ....
PLEASE TICK ONE BOX ONLY

N=2667

	%
... the government should top-up their wages,	66.3
or, is it up to the parents to look after themselves and their children as best they can?	21.6
Can't choose	11.6
Not answered	0.6

[CHARBUSN]
27. How much do you agree or disagree with this statement?
"Large businesses should give some of their profits each year to charities, even if this means that shareholders lose out."

N=881

PLEASE TICK ONE BOX ONLY	%
Strongly agree	19.9
Agree	33.1
Neither agree nor disagree	21.1
Disagree	17.5
Strongly disagree	3.4
Can't choose	4.4
Not answered	0.6

28. Here are some things on which money is spent. For each one, please tick one box to show where you think the money should come from:

N=881

PLEASE TICK ONE BOX ON EACH LINE	Entirely from government	Mainly from government	Shared equally	Mainly from charities	Entirely from charities	Can't choose	(Not answered)
[ANIMALGB] a. Helping to prevent cruelty to animals in Britain %	3.6	8.9	39.7	31.9	10.8	3.3	1.6
[HOUSESGB] b. Housing for homeless people in Britain %	21.8	49.9	22.8	1.8	0.3	1.5	1.9
[AIDSWW] c. Helping AIDS sufferers worldwide %	6.8	19.9	43.0	16.9	4.7	6.2	2.6
[KIDSGB] d. Helping British children in need %	27.1	40.7	26.0	2.8	0.4	0.7	2.2
[FOODWW] e. Giving food aid to starving people in poor countries %	7.6	15.6	42.4	20.2	9.1	3.0	2.1
[KIDSWW] f. Helping children in need throughout the world %	6.5	13.2	45.7	21.5	8.5	2.7	1.9

Note: Questions 29-32 on Version B are the same as Questions 11-14 on Version A

[PDJOBSC]
33. Are you currently in paid work for at least 10 hours a week?
PLEASE TICK ONE BOX ONLY

N=2667

	%	
Yes	56.5	→ PLEASE ANSWER QUESTION 34
No	42.4	→ PLEASE GO TO QUESTION 42 ON PAGE 16
Not answered	1.2	

[EMPLOYSC]
PLEASE ANSWER IF YOU ARE CURRENTLY IN PAID WORK FOR AT LEAST 10 HOURS A WEEK
34. Are you an employee or self-employed?
(If you have several jobs, please answer about your main job.)
PLEASE TICK ONE BOX ONLY

N=1537

	%	
Employee	85.6	→ PLEASE ANSWER QUESTION 35
Self-employed	11.7	→ PLEASE GO TO QUESTION 42 ON PAGE 16
Working – don't know whether employed or self employed	0.5	
Not answered	2.2	

PLEASE ANSWER IF YOU ARE AN EMPLOYEE
35. Do you agree, or disagree, with the following statements about working at your present workplace?
PLEASE TICK ONE BOX ON EACH LINE

N=1356

	Agree strongly	Agree	Neither agree nor disagree	Disagree	Disagree strongly	Can't choose	(Not answered)
[SAFEJOB] a. I feel there will be a job for me where I work now for as long as I want it %	16.5	40.0	16.5	18.0	4.2	1.2	3.6
[WELLINF] b. People at my workplace usually feel well-informed about what is happening there %	7.4	42.1	16.1	24.7	4.8	1.2	3.7
[PROUDJB] c. I am proud to tell people which organisation I work for %	15.9	45.1	25.8	7.0	1.5	1.0	3.8
[LOGGERH] d. At my workplace, management and employees are always at loggerheads %	3.6	12.4	22.0	46.2	10.5	1.4	3.9
[MANPROM] e. Managers at my workplace usually keep their promises to the employees %	6.0	41.4	25.9	16.4	4.6	2.2	3.5
[LOOKBJOB] f. I'm always on the look-out for a job that is better than mine %	6.4	20.7	20.3	36.2	10.9	1.9	3.7
[SHAREVAL] g. I share many of the values of my organisation %	8.5	40.9	28.5	12.0	2.0	4.1	3.9
[LOYALORG] h. I feel loyal to my organisation %	14.2	46.6	22.7	8.8	1.9	2.1	3.8

36. Thinking now about your current employer.
In the last 5 years, are you aware of your employer treating an employee unfairly because of their sex?

N=1356

	%
[DISXNONE] NO: — None of the following	87.5
YES: PLEASE TICK ALL THAT APPLY	
[DISXJOB] — Getting a job	2.5
[DISXPROM] — Promotion	4.7
[DISXTRAI] — Getting training	2.4
[DISXDISC] — Discipline or grievance procedures	3.0
[DISXFLEX] — Access to flexible working arrangements	3.3
[DISXRED] — Redundancies	0.6
[DISXBULL] — Bullying or harassment	4.2
[DISXOTH] — In any other way (PLEASE WRITE IN)	0.6
Not answered	1.1

37. In the last 5 years, are you aware of your employer treating an employee unfairly because of their race or ethnic origin?

N=1356

	%
[DIRCNONE] NO: — None of the following	91.4
YES: PLEASE TICK ALL THAT APPLY	
[DIRCJOB] — Getting a job	2.2
[DIRCPROM] — Promotion	3.3
[DIRCTRAI] — Getting training	0.9
[DIRCDISC] — Discipline or grievance procedures	1.3
[DIRCFLEX] — Access to flexible working arrangements	1.0
[DIRCRED] — Redundancies	0.2
[DIRCBULL] — Bullying or harassment	2.0
[DIRCOTH] — In any other way (PLEASE WRITE IN)	0.1
Not answered	0.9

38. In the last 5 years, are you aware of your employer treating an employee unfairly because of their age?

N=1356

	%
[DIAGNONE] NO: — None of the following	88.3
YES: PLEASE TICK ALL THAT APPLY	
[DIAGJOB] — Getting a job	3.3
[DIAGPROM] — Promotion	4.1
[DIAGTRAI] — Getting training	2.1
[DIAGDISC] — Discipline or grievance procedures	0.7
[DIAGFLEX] — Access to flexible working arrangements	1.1
[DIAGRED] — Redundancies	1.4
[DIAGBULL] — Bullying or harassment	1.5
[DIAGOTH] — In any other way (PLEASE WRITE IN)	0.5
Not answered	1.2

39. In the last 5 years, are you aware of your employer treating an employee unfairly because of their sexual orientation (e.g. being gay, lesbian or straight)?

N=1356

	%
[DISONONE] NO: — None of the following	94.9
YES: PLEASE TICK ALL THAT APPLY	
[DISOJOB] — Getting a job	0.7
[DISOPROM] — Promotion	0.6
[DISOTRAI] — Getting training	0.2
[DISODISC] — Discipline or grievance procedures	0.6
[DISOFLEX] — Access to flexible working arrangements	0.2
[DISORED] — Redundancies	0.2
[DISOBULL] — Bullying or harassment	0.8
[DISOOTH] — In any other way (PLEASE WRITE IN)	-
Not answered	1.0

N=1356

40. In the last 5 years, are you aware of your employer treating an employee unfairly because of <u>their religion or beliefs</u>?

%

[DIRLNONE]
NO: 95.0
YES: — None of the following
PLEASE TICK ALL THAT APPLY

[DIRLJOB]
— Getting a job. 0.4

[DIRLPROM]
— Promotion. 0.4

[DIRLTRAI]
— Getting training. 0.0

[DIRLDISC]
— Discipline or grievance procedures 0.4

[DIRLFLEX]
— Access to flexible working arrangements 0.7

[DIRLRED]
— Redundancies 0.0

[DIRLBULL]
— Bullying or harassment. 0.7

[DIRLOTH]
— In any other way *(PLEASE WRITE IN)* 0.2

Not answered. 1.1

N=1356

41. In the last 5 years, are you aware of your employer treating an employee unfairly because of <u>a disability</u>?

%

[DIDINONE]
NO: 93.5
YES: — None of the following
PLEASE TICK ALL THAT APPLY

[DIDIJOB]
— Getting a job. 1.4

[DIDIPROM]
— Promotion. 0.9

[DIDITRAI]
— Getting training. 0.6

[DIDIDISC]
— Discipline or grievance procedures 0.4

[DIDIFLEX]
— Access to flexible working arrangements 1.0

[DIDIRED]
— Redundancies 0.0

[DIDIBULL]
— Bullying or harassment. 0.3

[DIDIOTH]
— In any other way *(PLEASE WRITE IN)* 0.3

Not answered. 0.8

N=2667

EVERYONE PLEASE ANSWER

42. Please tick one box for each statement to show how much you agree or disagree with it.

PLEASE TICK ONE BOX ON EACH LINE

	Agree strongly	Agree	Neither agree nor disagree	Disagree	Disagree strongly	Can't choose	(Not answered)
[GENHARM] a. Research into human genes will do more harm than good.	% 4.6	12.1	27.0	39.4	7.7	7.0	2.2
[GENEXAGG] b. Many of the claims about the benefits of modern genetic science are greatly exaggerated.	% 3.5	22.9	35.9	23.0	2.5	9.1	3.0
[GENOTKNW] c. Nobody really knows what impact modern genetic science will have on society.	% 16.5	53.5	16.6	4.5	0.6	5.9	2.4

43. How likely or unlikely do you think it is <u>within the next 25 years</u> that genetic information will be used to judge a person's suitability for getting ...

PLEASE TICK ONE BOX ON EACH LINE

	Very likely	Quite likely	Not very likely	Not at all likely	Can't choose	(Not answered)
[DNAINSUR] a. ...health or life insurance?	% 23.4	46.2	15.0	3.7	10.3	1.5
[DNAJOB] b. ...a job they've applied for?	% 14.0	37.6	28.2	6.5	10.5	3.1

N=2667

44. You may have heard of genetically modified or 'GM' foods. These are made from plants from plants which have had their genes altered. Some people say that growing these plants may damage other plants and wildlife and that food made from them may not be safe to eat. Other people say that growing these plants may mean lower food prices and less use of pesticides and weedkillers. Please say how much you agree or disagree with each of these statements about genetically modified (GM) foods.

PLEASE TICK ONE BOX ON EACH LINE

	Agree strongly	Agree	Neither agree nor disagree	Disagree	Disagree strongly	Can't choose	(Not answered)
[GMGROW] a. In order to compete with the rest of the world, Britain should grow genetically modified (GM) foods	% 1.3	13.4	29.7	34.4	10.6	9.6	1.2
[GMBAN] b. Genetically modified (GM) foods should be banned, even if food prices suffer as a result	% 8.2	21.1	32.7	22.9	3.0	10.5	1.6
[GMDANGER] c. On balance, the advantages of genetically modified (GM) foods outweigh any dangers	% 1.2	12.5	37.7	24.9	8.3	13.7	1.7
[GMCHECK] d. It is important for me to check whether or not foods contain genetically modified ingredients.	% 10.9	32.1	28.7	15.4	2.1	9.2	1.7

[GMWILDLF]
45. In general, do you think that growing genetically modified (GM) foods poses a danger to other plants and wildlife?
PLEASE TICK *ONE BOX ONLY*

	%
Definitely	18.5
Probably	36.9
Probably not	21.6
Definitely not	1.5
Can't choose	20.5
Not answered	1.0

[GMSAFE]
46. Do you think that all genetically modified (GM) foods already available in the shops are safe to eat?
PLEASE TICK *ONE BOX ONLY*

	%
Definitely	4.0
Probably	43.0
Probably not	24.2
Definitely not	5.7
Can't choose	22.2
Not answered	1.0

47. You might have heard of something called human cloning. One type of cloning would be if a person's genes were copied exactly and used to make an embryo. Cells from the embryo could be used to supply the person with tissues or organs that would be a perfect match for them, meaning their body would not reject them. Do you think this should be allowed or not allowed if a person....

PLEASE TICK *ONE BOX* ON EACH LINE		Definitely allowed	Probably allowed	Probably not allowed	Definitely not allowed	Don't know	(Not answered)
[CLONEORG] a. ...needs an organ transplant?	%	24.2	39.6	11.2	12.7	10.7	1.6
[CLONEPAR] b. ...needs treatment for Parkinson's disease?	%	24.7	39.2	11.7	11.3	10.8	2.3
[CLONELIV] c. ...is generally in good health and wants to live longer?	%	5.0	9.9	27.2	45.5	10.3	2.1

[CLONCHLD]
48. Another type of human cloning might be used to treat a young couple who are infertile and cannot have a child. Suppose that the genes from one of them were copied exactly and used to make an embryo with exactly the same genetic make up as that parent. Do you think this should be allowed or not allowed for a young couple who are infertile and cannot have a child?

PLEASE TICK *ONE BOX ONLY*

	%
Definitely allowed	10.2
Probably allowed	27.4
Probably not allowed	21.2
Definitely not allowed	26.4
Can't choose	13.3
Not answered	1.5

[NATCONTR]
49. Each question shows two opposing views about science and nature. For each, please tick one of the boxes to show whether you agree with the opinion at the top, with the opinion at the bottom, or whether your views are somewhere in between the two.
PLEASE TICK *ONE BOX ONLY*

Human intelligence and creativity means that we will eventually be able to control nature.

	%
	2.6
	5.6
	7.1
	13.7
	12.7
	16.1
	26.6
Can't choose	13.7
Not answered	2.0

Despite our intelligence and creativity, we will never be able to control nature.

[NATFRAGL]
50. Do you agree with the opinion at the top, the opinion at the bottom, or are your views somewhere in between?
PLEASE TICK *ONE BOX ONLY*

The balance of nature is fragile and can be permanently damaged by human actions.

	%
	30.4
	20.8
	13.7
	11.5
	5.1
	3.0
	4.0
Can't choose	9.3
Not answered	2.1

Nature is strong enough to cope with the effects of human actions.

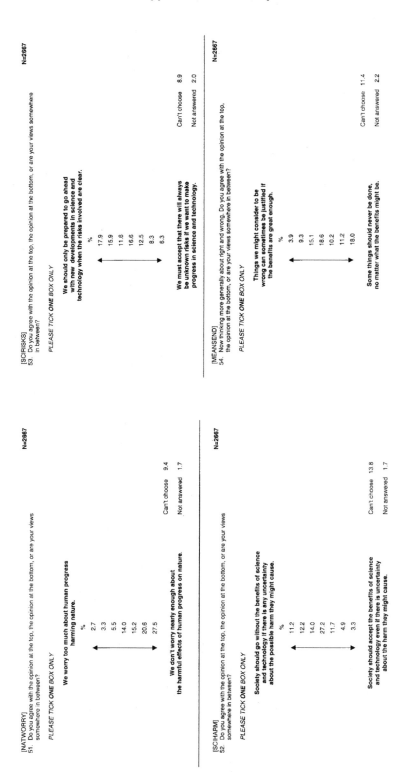

[NATWORRY]
51. Do you agree with the opinion at the top, the opinion at the bottom, or are your views somewhere in between?

PLEASE TICK ONE BOX ONLY

N=2667

We worry too much about human progress harming nature.

%
2.7
3.3
5.5
14.0
15.2
20.6
27.5

We don't worry nearly enough about the harmful effects of human progress on nature.

Can't choose 9.4
Not answered 1.7

[SCIHARM]
52. Do you agree with the opinion at the top, the opinion at the bottom, or are your views somewhere in between?

PLEASE TICK ONE BOX ONLY

N=2667

Society should go without the benefits of science and technology if there is any uncertainty about the possible harm they might cause.

%
11.2
12.2
14.0
27.2
11.7
4.9
3.3

Society should accept the benefits of science and technology even if there is uncertainty about the harm they might cause.

Can't choose 13.8
Not answered 1.7

[SCIRISKS]
53. Do you agree with the opinion at the top, the opinion at the bottom, or are your views somewhere in between?

PLEASE TICK ONE BOX ONLY

N=2667

We should only be prepared to go ahead with new developments in science and technology when the risks involved are clear.

%
17.9
15.9
11.6
16.6
12.5
8.3
6.3

We must accept that there will always be unknown risks if we want to make progress in science and technology.

Can't choose 8.9
Not answered 2.0

[MEANSEND]
54. Now thinking more generally about right and wrong. Do you agree with the opinion at the bottom, or are your views somewhere in between?

PLEASE TICK ONE BOX ONLY

N=2667

Things we might consider to be wrong can sometimes be justified if the benefits are great enough.

%
3.9
9.3
15.1
18.6
10.2
11.2
18.0

Some things should never be done, no matter what the benefits might be.

Can't choose 11.4
Not answered 2.2

55. Please tick one box for each statement to show how much you agree or disagree with it.

N=881

PLEASE TICK ONE BOX ON EACH LINE		Agree strongly	Agree	Neither agree nor disagree	Disagree	Disagree strongly	(Not ans-wered)
[WELFHELP] a. The welfare state encourages people to stop helping each other	%	5.6	29.0	34.2	27.4	2.2	1.7
[MOREWELF] b. The government should spend more money on welfare benefits for the poor, even if it leads to higher taxes	%	6.4	36.9	28.8	23.7	2.1	2.2
[UNEMPJOB] c. Around here, most unemployed people could find a job if they really wanted one	%	17.4	48.9	17.1	13.7	0.8	2.1
[SOCHELP] d. Many people who get social security don't really deserve any help	%	8.5	30.0	29.6	26.1	3.4	2.4
[DOLEFIDL] e. Most people on the dole are fiddling in one way or another	%	9.9	29.1	30.9	23.9	4.2	2.0
[WELFFEET] f. If welfare benefits weren't so generous, people would learn to stand on their own two feet	%	11.4	30.2	27.3	25.3	3.2	2.6
[DAMLIVES] g. Cutting welfare benefits would damage too many people's lives	%	8.5	45.9	26.7	15.8	1.1	1.9
[PROUDWLF] h. The creation of the welfare state is one of Britain's proudest achievements	%	17.3	41.4	28.9	8.4	1.8	2.2

Note: Questions 56-61 on Version B are the same as Questions 22-27 on Version A

N=881

EVERYONE PLEASE ANSWER
62. To help us plan better in future, please tell us about how long it took you to complete this questionnaire.

%

PLEASE TICK ONE BOX ONLY	
Less than 15 minutes	12.6
Between 15 and 20 minutes	27.1
Between 21 and 30 minutes	29.8
Between 31 and 45 minutes	19.7
Between 46 and 60 minutes	6.0
Over one hour	3.6
Not answered	1.2

Note: Question 62b-63 on Version B are the same as Questions 28b-29 on Version A

NatCen
National Centre for Social Research

A company limited by guarantee.
Registered in England No. 4392418
Charity No. 1097768

Head Office
35 Northampton Square
London EC1V 0AX
Telephone 020 7250 1866
Fax 020 7250 1524

Operations Department
100 Kings Road, Brentwood
Essex CM14 4LX
Telephone 01277 200 600
Fax 01277 263 578

C

P.2265   Green team

BRITISH SOCIAL ATTITUDES 2003

Summer 2003

SELF-COMPLETION QUESTIONNAIRE

INTERVIEWER TO ENTER

2001-6 1 5 □□□□	Serial number
2009-11 □□□	Sampling point
2012-15 □□□□	Interviewer number

OFFICE USE ONLY

2007-8 2 0	Card number
2016-20	Batch Number
2021 3	Version
SPARE 2022-34	

To the selected respondent:

Thank you very much for agreeing to take part in this important study - the nineteenth in this annual series. The study consists of this self-completion questionnaire, and the interview you have already completed. The results of the survey are published in a book each autumn; some of the questions are also being asked in nearly forty other countries, as part of an international survey.

Completing the questionnaire:

The questions inside cover a wide range of subjects, but most can be answered simply by placing a tick (✓) in one or more of the boxes. No special knowledge is required: we are confident that everyone will be able to take part, not just those with strong views or particular viewpoints. The questionnaire should not take very long to complete, and we hope you will find it interesting and enjoyable. **Only you should fill it in, and not anyone else at your address.** The answers you give will be treated as confidential and anonymous in accordance with the Data Protection Act.

Returning the questionnaire:

Your interviewer will arrange with you the most convenient way of returning the questionnaire. If the interviewer has arranged to call back for it, please fill it in and keep it safely until then. If not, please complete it and post it back in the pre-paid, addressed envelope, AS SOON AS YOU POSSIBLY CAN.

THANK YOU AGAIN FOR YOUR HELP.

The National Centre for Social Research is an independent social research institute and a company limited by guarantee, registered as a charity. Its projects are funded by government departments, local authorities, universities and foundations to provide information on social issues in Britain. The British Social Attitudes survey series is funded through contributions from various grant-giving bodies and government departments. Please contact us if you would like further information.

Note: Questions 1-11 on Version C are the same as Questions 16-26 on Version B.

Note: Question 12-21 on Version C is the same as Questions 1-10 on Version A.

Note: Questions 22-4b on Version C are the same as Questions 32-51 on Version B.

N=1786

47a. To help us plan better in future, please tell us about
how long it took you to complete this questionnaire.

%

PLEASE TICK ONE BOX ONLY

	%
Less than 15 minutes	26.7
Between 15 and 20 minutes	40.3
Between 21 and 30 minutes	20.3
Between 31 and 45 minutes	7.0
Between 46 and 60 minutes	1.9
Over one hour	1.8
Not answered	2.0

Note: Questions 47b-48 on Version C are the same as Questions 28b-29 on Version A.

Subject index